# ADVANCES IN GRID COMPUTING

Edited by **Zoran Constantinescu**

**Advances in Grid Computing**
Edited by Zoran Constantinescu

**Published by InTech**
Janeza Trdine 9, 51000 Rijeka, Croatia



**Publishing Process Manager** Katarina Lovrecic

**Technical Editor** Teodora Smiljanic

**Cover Designer** InTech Design Team

Additional hard copies can be obtained from orders@intechopen.com

Advances in Grid Computing, Edited by Zoran Constantinescu
p. cm.
ISBN 978-953-307-301-9

For EU product safety concerns:
IN TECH d.o.o., Prolaz Marije Krucifikse Kozulić 3, 51000 Rijeka, Croatia,
info@intechopen.com or visit our website at intechopen.com.

# Meet the editor

Zoran Constantinescu got his MSc (1997) at the Department of Computer Science from the Politehnica University of Bucharest, Romania. He has been working since, both in the Software Engineering industry and in Higher Education. He got his doctoral degree in Computer Science (2008) from The Norwegian University of Science and Technology, Trondheim, Norway, with a thesis on a desktop grid computing approach to scientific computing and visualization. In fact, he has developed from scratch a new open source desktop grid computing system, named QADPZ, and has proved its viability by testing it on some scientific computing and visualization experiments. Since QADPZ became openly available in 2003, thousands of users around the world have been using it for their computationally intensive tasks and contributed with their feedback to the system's improvement. Broadly, his research interests include parallel and distributed computing, desktop grid computing, GPS systems, and embedded systems, and he has published 25 research papers dealing with these topics. He is very committed to the open source world and actively participates in this endeavor.

# Contents

# Preface

During the last decades we have been experiencing the historic evolution of Information and Communication Technology's integration into our society to the point that many times people use it transparently. As we become able to do more and more with our advanced technologies, and as we hide them and their complexities completely from their users, we will have accomplished the envisioned "magic" desideratum that any advanced technology must fulfill in Arthur Clarke's vision. Internet has enabled a major breakthrough, not so long ago, when its standards and technologies provided for near-universal connectivity, broad access to content, and, consequently, for a new model for science, engineering, education, business, and life itself. That development has been extraordinary in many respects, and, the Grid is expected to continue this momentous evolution toward fulfilling of Licklider's vision of man-computer symbiosis and intergalactic network that enable people and computers to *cooperate in making decisions and controlling complex situations without inflexible dependence on predetermined programs.*

Grid Computing is a model of distributed computing that uses geographically and administratively distinct resources that can be reached over the network: processing power, storage capacity, specific data, input and output devices, etc. Foster's canonical definition of Grid states that *it is a system that coordinates distributed resources using standard, open, general-purpose protocols and interfaces to deliver nontrivial qualities of service.* In grid computing, individual users can access computers and data transparently, without having to consider location, operating system, account administration, and other details, which are abstracted from the users. Grid computing aims to achieve a secured, controlled and flexible sharing of virtualized resources among various dynamically created virtual organizations. However, the construction of an application that may benefit from advantages of grid computing, i.e. faster execution speed, connecting of geographically separated resources, interoperation of software, and so on, typically requires the installation of complex supporting software, and, moreover, an in-depth knowledge of how this software works.

This book approaches grid computing from the perspective of the latest achievements in the field, providing an insight into the current research trends and advances, and presents a large range of innovative research in this field. The topics covered in this book include resource and data management, grid architectures and development, and grid-enabled applications. The book consists of 13 chapters, which are grouped into three sections as follows. First section, entitled *Resource and Data Management*, consists of chapters 1 to 6, and discusses two main aspects of grid computing: the availability of resources for jobs (*resource management*), and the availability of data to the jobs (*data management*). New ideas employing heuristic methods from swarm intelligence or genetic algorithm, and quantum encryption are introduced. For instance, Chapter 1 focuses on applying discrete particle swarm optimization algorithm, a swarm intelligence inspired technique, to solve the task scheduling problem in grid computing. Chapter 2 discusses the use of application specific Quality of Service (QoS) parameters for resource management, and proposes a framework for task scheduling using a multi objective genetic algorithm. Chapter 3 proposes a new QoS guided scheduling algorithm. Chapter 4 introduces an autonomic network-aware metascheduling architecture, evaluating the benefits of taking the network into account when performing metascheduling, along with the need to react autonomically to changes in the system. Chapter 5 presents an attempt to use quantum encryption for data transmission in the grid. Chapter 6 proposes a number of data consolidation and information aggregation techniques, and evaluates by simulation the improvements in the reduction of congestion and information exchanged.

The second section, named *Grid Architectures and Development*, includes chapters 7 to 9, and addresses some aspects of grid computing that regard architecture and development. Chapter 7 describes the development of a virtual laboratory for environmental applications, based on grid computing, cloud computing and GPU computing components. Chapter 8 presents the architecture of an open source, heterogeneous, desktop grid computing system, together with some examples of using it in the fields of scientific computing and visualization. Chapter 9 defines a systematic development process for grid systems that supports the participation of mobile nodes, and it incorporates security aspects from the earliest stages of development.

*Grid Enabled Applications*, the last section of this book, includes chapters 10 to 13, and provides a diverse range of applications for grid computing, including a possible human grid computing system, a simulation of the fusion reaction, ubiquitous healthcare service provisioning and complex water systems. Chapter 10 introduces the idea of using grid computing in artificial intelligence, namely for thinking routines for the next move problems in the game of *shogi* (Japanese chess), and presents the possibility of the human Grid computing, which assists the position evaluation function with human intuition. Chapter 11 presents the application of grid computing in fusion research, the problems involved in porting fusion applications to the grid towards the final quest of a numerical fusion reactor. Chapter 12 describes the effort to design and evaluate a grid enabled framework for ubiquitous healthcare service provisioning, by integrating different emerging technologies like telemedicine, wireless body area network and wireless utility grid computing technologies, to address the challenges of conventional healthcare system. Chapter 13 presents grid computing as a promising approach for scaled-up simulation analysis of complex water system with high uncertainty on hydrological series.

In summary, this book covers significant aspects related to resource and data management, grid architectures and development, and grid-enabled applications, and it constitutes an invaluable asset for people interested in Grid Computing, from researchers and scholars/scientists to students and experts in the field.

Hopefully, this book will contribute to the thoroughly integrated infrastructure of the future, in which systems, businesses, organizations, people etc., everything required for a smoothly working whole, will be in close, transparent and dynamic communication. As this infrastructure will become more and more autonomous, the quality of services will significantly improve, enabling people to make technology choices based on their needs rather than on anything else. Thus, the grid-enabled computational and data management infrastructure will evolve constantly toward a global phenomenon that will become a key enabler for science, in particular, and for society, in general.

I would like to acknowledge the contribution of the authors, of the reviewers, and of the INTECH editors to this book, each of them having his or her merit to the quality of the final outcome.

**Zoran Constantinescu**
Department of Research and Development
ZealSoft Ltd.
Bucharest, Romania

# Part 1

## Resource and Data Management

# 1

# Application of Discrete Particle Swarm Optimization for Grid Task Scheduling Problem

Ruey-Maw Chen
*National Chin-Yi University of Technology, Taichung, 411, Taiwan, R. O. C.*

## 1. Introduction

Many applications involve the concepts of scheduling, such as communications, packet routing, production planning [Zhai et al., 2006], classroom arrangement [Mathaisel & Comm, 1991], aircrew scheduling [Chang, 2002], nurse scheduling [Ohki et al., 2006], food industrial [Simeonov & Simeonovova, 2002], control system [Fleming & Fonseca, 1993], resource-constrained scheduling problem [Chen, 2007] and grid computing. There are many different types of scheduling problems such as real-time, job-shop, permutation flow-shop, project scheduling and other scheduling problems have been studied intensively. However, in this work, the studied grid task scheduling problem is much more complex than above stated classic task scheduling problems. Restated, a grid application is regarded as a task scheduling problem involving tasks with inter-communication and distributed homogeneous or heterogeneous resources, and can be represented by a task interaction graph (TIG).

Grid is a service for sharing computing power and data storage capacity over the Internet. The grid systems outperform simple communication between computers and aims ultimately to turn the global network of computers into one vast computational resource. Grid computing can be adopted in many applications, such as high-performance applications, large-output applications, data-intensive applications and community-centric applications. These applications major concern to efficiently schedule tasks over the available multi-processor environment provided by the grid. A grid is a collaborative environment in which one or more tasks can be submitted without knowing where the resources are or even who owns the resources [Foster et al., 2001]. The efficiency and effectiveness of grid resource management greatly depend on the scheduling algorithm [Lee et al., 2007]. Generally, in the grid environment, these resources are different over time, and such changes will affect the performance of the tasks running on the grid. In grid computing, tasks are assigned among grid system [Salman, 2002]. The purpose of task scheduling in grid is to find optimal task-processor assignment and hence minimize application completion time (total cost). Most scheduling problems in these applications are categorized into the class of *NP-complete* problems. This implies that it would take amount of computation time to obtain an optimal solution, especially for a large-scale scheduling problem. A variety of approaches have been applied to solve scheduling problems, such as simulated annealing (SA) [Kirkpatrick, 1983], neural network [Chen, 2007], genetic algorithm (GA) [Holland, 1987], tabu search (TS) [Glover, 1989; Glover, 1990], ant colony optimization (ACO) [Dorigo & Gambardella, 1997] and particle swarm optimization [Kennedy & Eberhart, 1995]. Among above stated schemes, many PSO-based approaches were suggested for solving different scheduling application problems including production scheduling [Watts & Strogatz, 1998], project scheduling [Chen, 2010], call center scheduling [chiu et al., 2009], and others [Behnamian et al., 2010; Hei et al., 2009].

In light of different algorithms studied, PSO is a promising and well-applied meta-heuristic approach in finding the optimal solutions of diverse scheduling problems and other applications. The particle swarm optimization (PSO) is a swarm intelligent inspired scheme which was first proposed by Kennedy and Eberhart [Kennedy & Eberhart, 1995]. In PSO, a swarm of particles spread in the solution search space and the position of a particle denotes a solution of studied problem. Each particle would move to a new position (new solution) determined by both of the individual experience (particle individual) and the global experience (particle swarm) heading toward the global optimum. However, many PSO derivatives have been studied, and one of them was named "discrete" particle swarm optimization (DPSO) algorithm proposed by Kennedy et al. [Kennedy & Eberhart, 1997] representing how DPSO can be used to solve problems. Hence, this study focuses on applying discrete particle swarm optimization algorithm to solve the task scheduling problem in grid computing.

To enhance the performance of the applied DPSO, additional heuristic was introduced to solve the investigated scheduling problem in grid. Restated, simulated annealing (SA) algorithm was incorporated into DPSO to solve task assignment problem in grid environment. Moreover, the resulting change in position is defined by roulette wheel selection rule rather than the used rule in [Kennedy & Eberhart, 1997]. Furthermore, the dynamic situations are not considered; the distributed homogeneous resources in grid environment are considered in this investigation.

## 2. The task scheduling problem in grid computing

There are different grid task scheduling problems exist including homogeneous and heterogeneous architectures. This section gives a class of task scheduling problem in homogeneous grid. Definition, limitation and objective of a grid computing system are presented. The introduced grid task scheduling problem can be represented as a task interaction graph (TIG) proposed by Salman *et.al.* [Salman, 2002], as displayed in Fig. 1. Figure 1 presents available memory in homogeneous grid, task processing time, memory requirement of each task, data exchange between tasks, and communication cost between grids. Meanwhile, two possible solutions are displayed in Fig. 2.

| Grid # | 1 | 2 | 3 | 4 |
|---|---|---|---|---|
| Memory available | 25 | 40 | 30 | 25 |

| Task # | 1 | 2 | 3 | 4 | *5* |
|---|---|---|---|---|---|
| Process time | 15 | 10 | 20 | 30 | *15* |
| Memory requirement | 20 | 30 | 25 | 20 | *10* |

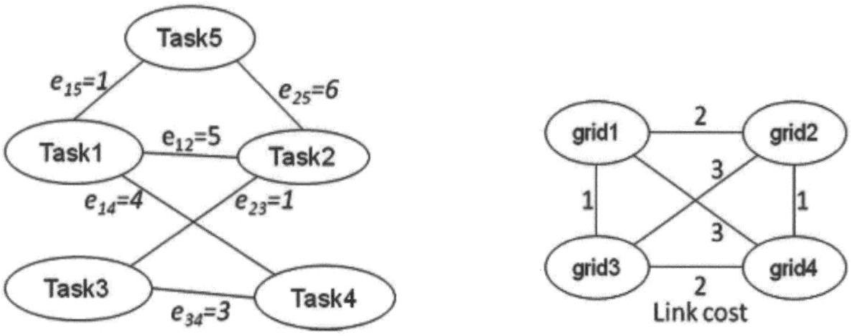


Fig. 1. Grid task scheduling problem representation [Salman et al., 2002]

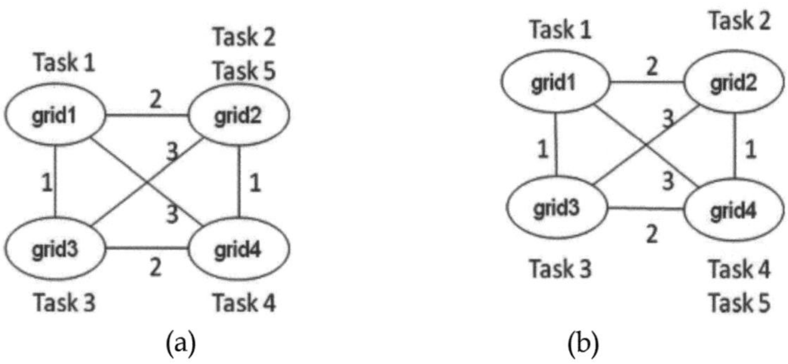


Fig. 2. Possible solutions

A meta-heuristic algorithm that is based on the principles of discrete particle swarm optimization (PSO) is proposed for solving the grid scheduling problem. The traditional assignment problems are only concerned to minimize the total processing cost, and there is no communication cost between these tasks and grids.

In homogeneous system, a grid environment can be represented as task interaction graph (TIG), $G$ ($V$, $E$), where $V \in \{1, 2, \ldots, M\}$ is the set of the tasks and $E$ are the interactions between these tasks as in Fig. 1. The $M$ and $N$ are the total number of tasks and the total number of grids (resources), respectively. The total amount of transmission data weight $e_{ij}$ denotes the information exchange (interactive) data between tasks $i$ and $j$. The $p_i$ is the processing time (cost) corresponding to the work load to be performed by task $i$ on grid. In the example of TIG problem shown in Figure 1, the tasks 2 and 5 are processed on the grid 2. Restated, no communication cost exists between these two tasks (task 2 and 5). Additionally, each task $i$ has memory requirement $m_i$ to be processed on one grid, and each grid requires enough memory to run their tasks.

For example, the processing time of task 1 is 15 and scheduled on grid 1. The task 1 has to exchange data with the tasks 2, 4 and 5. However, the tasks 2, 4 and 5 are on different grids, this means that there are communication costs with task 1. Furthermore, tasks 4 and 5 are on the same grid and there is no communication cost required between them. Therefore, the total cost for grid 1 of possible solution case (a) is $(15) + (5 \times 2 + 1 \times 2 + 4 \times 3) = 39$. Moreover, task 1 satisfies the memory constraint; that is, the memory requirement is 20 for task 1, which is less than the memory available of 25 for grid 1. The communication cost is computed by the communication cost (link cost) multiplies the edge weight (exchange data). The total cost for grids of different possible solutions as demonstrated in Fig. 2 are determined as follows.

| Grids | Total cost - case (a) | Total cost - case (b) |
|---|---|---|
| Grid 1 | (15)+(5×2+1×2+4×3)=39 | (15)+(5×2+4×3+1×3)=40 |
| Grid 2 | (10+15)+(5×2+1×3)+(1×2)=40 | (10)+(5×2+1×3+6×1)=29 |
| Grid 3 | (20)+ (1×3+3×2)=29 | (20)+ (1×3+3×2)=29 |
| Grid 4 | (30)+ (4×3+3×2)=48 | (30+15)+(4×3+3×2)+(1×3+6×1)=72 |

A grid application completion time is defined as the latest time that grid finishes all scheduled tasks processing and communication. According to above total cost calculation, different task assignment in grid would obtain different application completion time. For example, case (b) solution of Fig. 2 yields application completion time 72; case (a) solution of Fig. 2 has less application completion time 48. Restated, the resulting schedule of case (a) is better than that of case (b).

The grid system can be represented as a grid environment graph (GEG) $G(P, C)$, where $P = \{1, 2, \ldots, N\}$ is the set of grids in the distributed system. The $C$ represents the set of communication cost between these grids. The $d_{ij}$ between grids $i$ and $j$ represents the link cost between the grids. The problem of this study is to assign these tasks in $V$ to the set of grids $P$. The objective function is to minimize the maximum total execution time required by each grid and the communication cost among all the interactive tasks that satisfies the memory constraint on different grids. The problem can be defined as:

$$\text{Minimize } \{\max (C_{exe}(k)+C_{com}(k))\},\ k\in\{1, 2, \ldots, N\} \tag{1}$$

Where

$$C_{exe}(k) = \sum_{i\in A_k} p_i \quad, A_k \text{ is the set of tasks assigned to grid } k \tag{2}$$

$$C_{mem}(k) = \sum_{i\in A_k} m_i \quad, A_k \text{ is the set of tasks assigned to grid } k \tag{3}$$

$$C_{com}(k) = \sum_{i\in A_k} \sum_{j\notin A_k} d_{kp}\cdot e_{ij} \quad, \text{for all grids } p\neq k,\ p=1 \text{ to } N;\ i,j=1 \text{ to } M \tag{4}$$

Subject to

$$C_{mem}(k) \le MemAvail(k) \tag{5}$$

Where $C_{exe}(k)$ is the total execution time of all tasks assigned to grid $k$ and $C_{com}(k)$ is the total communication cost between tasks assigned to grid $k$. Those relative tasks are assigned to other grids in an assignment. The $C_{mem}(k)$ is the total memory requirement of all tasks assigned to grid $k$, for which the value of $C_{mem}(k)$ have to less than or equal than the total available memory of grid $k$; *MemAvail(k)* as listed in Eq. (5). The objective of the task assignment problem is to find an assignment schedule that the cost is minimized of one grid for a given TIG on a given GEG. In this study, the penalty function is adopted in the proposed algorithms.

$$\text{Penalty}(k) = C_{mem}(k) - \text{MemAvail}(k) \tag{6}$$

In Eq. (6), the *penalty(k)* is set to zero if the constraint of Eq. (5) is satisfied.

## 3. Particle swarm optimization

The particles swarm optimization (PSO) was first proposed by Kennedy and Eberhart in 1995. The original PSO is applied in real variable number space. There are a lot of task-resource assignment related works have been introduced in recent years [Kuo et al. 2009; Sha & Hsu, 2006; Bokhari, 1987; Chaudhary & Aggarwal, 1993; Norman & Thanisch, 1993]. These works indicated that the problems are set in a space featuring of continuous. However, the combinatorial problems are most of discrete or quantitative variables [Liao et al., 2007].PSO schematic diagram is displayed as in Fig. 3. The introduced grid task scheduling problem as in Fig. 1 can be regarded as a task-grid assignment problem in a graph as in Fig. 2.

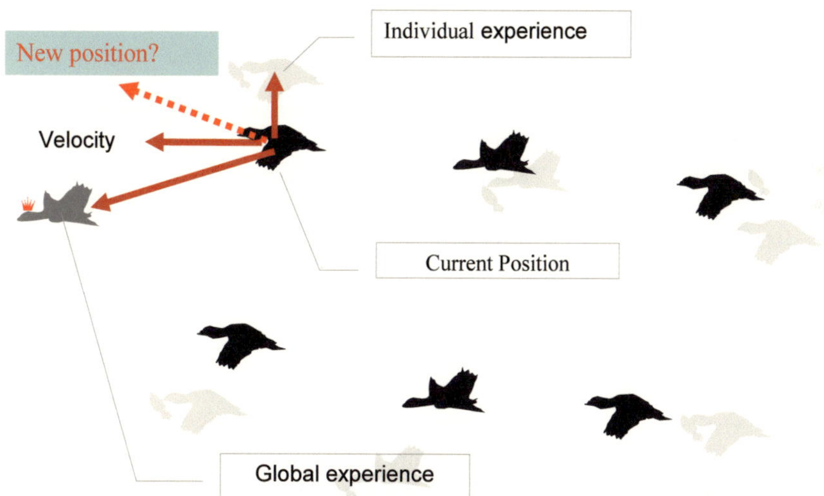


Fig. 3. PSO schematic diagram

The particle swarm optimization is a multi-agent general meta-heuristic method, and can be applied extensively in solving many NP-complete or combinatorial problems. The PSO consists of a swarm of particles in the search space; the position of a particle is indicated by a vector which presents a potential solution of the problem. PSO is initialized with a population of particles (randomly assigned or generated by heuristic) and searches for the best position (solution or schedule) with the best fitness. In every generation or iteration, the local bests and global best are determined through evaluating the performances, i.e., the fitness values of current population of particles. A particle moves to a new position obtaining a new solution guided by the velocity (a vector). Hence, the velocity plays an important role in affecting the characters of creating new solution. There are two experience positions are used in the PSO; one is the global experience position of all particles, which memorizes the global best solution obtained from all positions (solutions) of all particles; the other is the individual experience position of each particle, which memorizes the local best solution acquired from the positions (solutions) of the corresponding particle has been at. These two experience positions and the inertia weight of the previous velocities used to determine the impact on the current velocity. The velocity retains part of prior velocity (the inertia) and driving particle toward the direction based on the global experience position and the individual experience position. Thus, the particles can derive new positions (solutions) by their own inertia and experience positions.

In traditional PSO, the search space (solution space) is $D$ dimension space (the number of dimension is corresponding to the parameters of solutions) and the population consists of $N_p$ particles. For the $i$th particle ($i = 1, \ldots, N_p$), the position consists of $M$ components $X_i = \{X_{i1}, \ldots, X_{iM}\}$, $X_{ij}$ is the $j^{th}$ component of the $i^{th}$ position. The velocity $V_i = \{V_{i1}, \ldots, V_{iM}\}$, where $V_{ij}$ is the velocity component corresponding to the component of $X_{ij}$, and the individual experience is a position $L_i = \{L_{i1}, \ldots, L_{iM}\}$ which is the local best solution for the $i^{th}$ particle. Additionally, $G = \{G_1, \ldots, G_M\}$ represents the global best experience shared among all particles achieved so far. The mentioned parameters above are used to calculate the updating of the $j^{th}$ component of the position and velocity for the $i^{th}$ particle, as shown in Eq. (7).

$$\begin{cases} V_{ij}^{new} = wV_{ij} + c_1 r_1 (L_{ij} - X_{ij}) + c_2 r_2 (G_j - X_{ij}) \\ X_{ij}^{new} = X_{ij} + V_{ij}^{new} \end{cases} \tag{7}$$

Where $w$ is an inertia weight used to determine the influence of the previous velocity to the new velocity. The $c_1$ and $c_2$ are learning factors used to derive how the $i^{th}$ particle approaching the position either closes to the individual experience position or global experience position respectively. Furthermore, the $r_1$ and $r_2$ are the random numbers uniformly distributed in [0, 1], influencing the tradeoff between the global exploitation (based on swarm's best experience) and local exploration (based on particle's best experience) abilities during search.

## 4. Simulated annealing algorithm

Other meta-heuristics are usually combined into PSO to increase the problem solving performance. SA is one of the popular algorithms to be combined with other meta-heuristic schemes. Simulated annealing (SA) was first introduced by Metropolis in 1953 [Metropolis et al., 1953]. Meanwhile, SA is a stochastic method for combinatorial problem optimization. Furthermore, SA is one of the efficient methods applied to solve widely complex problems [Kirkpatrick, 1983]. The original SA procedure is listed as shown in Fig. 4.

```
Initial solution S, compute corresponding energy E
Set the initial temperature (T), cooling rate (r)
While E <> 0
        S' = Generate the new solution
        Compute new energy E'corresponding to S' and calculate ΔE = E'- E
        If ΔE<0 then accept S = S', E = E'
        Else Compute the δ = e^(-(ΔE/T))
            Accept the new solution when random number < δ
    Decrease the temperature T = T × r
```

Fig. 4. Simulated annealing algorithm

In Fig.4, the energy $E$ is corresponding to solution $S$, and energy $E'$ is correlated to solution $S'$. However, energy definition is determined by the studied problem. Hence, $E$ is defined as $\{\max(C_{exe}(k)+C_{com}(k))\}+Penalty(k)$, $k \in \{1, 2, \ldots, N\}$ in this investigation. The temperature, $T$, is the magnitude of fluctuation; it is a key parameter in controlling the search direction as well as the step size toward the global minimum. The applied cooling schedule is controlled by

$T=T\times r$. The acceptance criterion of worse solution is based on the probabilistic process which is dependent on the temperature and energy difference between two states. Restated, the probability is determined by $\delta=exp(-\Delta E/T)$.

## 5. Discrete particle swarm optimization method

Kennedy and Eberhart developed a discrete version of PSO in 1997 [Kennedy & Eberhard, 1997]. The discrete PSO essentially differs from the original PSO in two characteristics. Firstly, the particle is composed of the binary variable. Secondly, the velocity represents the probability of the binary variable taking the value of one, i.e., the probability of task $i$ is assigned to grid $k$ in this study ($i\in$ {1, 2, . . . , $M$}; $k\in${1, 2, . . . , $N$}). The discrete PSO is adopted by generating solutions for updating the particle's position and velocity vectors to solve the task scheduling problem in parallel machines [Kashan & Karimi, 2009; Kashan et al., 2008; Lee et al., 2006]. Another similar to the discrete PSO optimization technique developed by Laskari et al. [Laskari et al., 2002], which is based on the truncation of the real values to their nearest integer. In this study, employed discrete PSO equations were introduced by Kennedy and Eberhard for solving the task assignment problem. The discrete PSO was also applied to solve the flowshop scheduling problem, and performed well in the computation result. This study conducts the discrete PSO method introduced by [Liao et al., 2007] and combines the SA algorithm for solving the task assignment problems in grid. The task-grid assignment problem will be then introduced.

Assumes there are $N_p$ particles, and each particle searches for $D = M\times N$ dimension space (the number of tasks and grids). For the $h^{th}$ particle ($h$ =1, . . . , $N_p$), the position consists of $M\times N$ components $X_h = \{X_{h11}, \ldots, X_{hMN}\}$, $X_{hij} \in\{0,1\}$is the $i^{th}$ task assigned to grid $j$ for particle $h$ ( $i$ =1, . . . , $M$; $j$ =1, . . . , $N$ ). The velocity $V_h = \{V_{h11}, \ldots, V_{hMN}\}$, where $V_{hij}$ is the velocity associated with component $X_{hij}$, and the individual experience for particle $h$ is $L_h = \{L_{h11}, \ldots, L_{hMN}\}$, the local best solution for the $h^{th}$ particle. Additionally, $G = \{G_{11},\ldots, G_{MP}\}$ represents the global best experience obtained and shared among all the population of particles. Above stated parameters are then used to update all components of the $V_h$. The velocity components updating for the $h^{th}$ particle is shown as in Eq. (8).

$$V_{hij}^{new} = wV_{hij} + c_1r_1(L_{hij} - X_{hij}) + c_2r_2(G_{ij} - X_{hij}) \quad (8)$$

According to Eq. (8), each particle moves to new position according to its new velocity. However, the new position generation is not the same as in original PSO, Eq. (7). Kennedy and Eberhart claim that the higher velocity component value is more likely to choose 1 for the corresponding position component, while lower velocity component value favors the position component value of 0. Hence, a probability function is used as shown in Eq. (9).

$$s(V_{hij}) = \frac{1}{1+\exp(-V_{hij})} \quad (9)$$

Equation (9) is the sigmoid function as displayed in Fig. 5, where $s(V_{hij})$ is defined as representing the probability of $X_{hij}$ to be set to 0 or 1. To avoid the value of $s(V_{hij})$ approaching 0 or 1, a constant $V_{max}$ is used to limit the range of $V_{hij}$. In practice, $V_{max}$ is often set at 4, i.e., $V_{hij} \in [-V_{max}, +V_{max}]$. After transformation via Eq. (9), $s(V_{hij})$ is mapped to a value between 0 and 1, i.e., $s(V_{hij}) \in (0, 1)$. For example, if $V_{max}$ =4 then probabilities will be

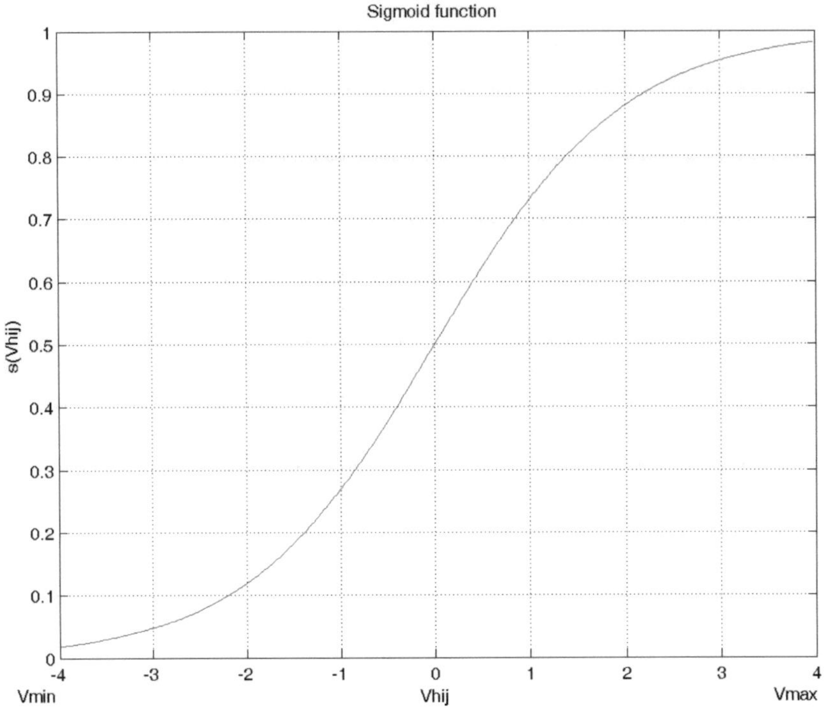


Fig. 5. Sigmoid function

limited to $s(V_{hij})$, between 0.9820 and 0.018. In [Kennedy & Eberhart, 1997], the resulting change in position is defined by the following rule (Eq. (10)).

$$\begin{cases} X_{hij} = 1, & \text{if } rand(\ ) < s(V_{hij}) \\ X_{hij} = 0, & else \end{cases} \tag{10}$$

Where the *rand( )* is a quasi-random number selected from a uniform distribution in [0.0, 1.0]. For task-grid assignment problem, each task can only be assigned to one grid. Therefore, in the proposed algorithm, each particle $h$ places the unscheduled task $i$ to grid $j$ according to the following normalized probability [Liao et al., 2007]:

$$q_h(i,j) = \frac{s(V_{hij})}{\sum_{j \in U} s(V_{hij})}, \ U \text{ is the set of grids} \tag{11}$$

Restated, the determination of which grid to be assigned to an unscheduled task in the study is based on the roulette wheel selection rule which is well applied in genetic algorithm. Hence, according to roulette wheel selection rile, grid $j$ is randomly selected from $U$ for task $i$ based on the probability distribution given by Eq. (11) and a generated random number. Based on the pseudo code of discrete PSO given by Kennedy et al. [Kennedy & Eberhard, 1997], the proposed algorithm is modified and showed in Fig. 6. The computation steps of the proposed algorithm in the simulation system can be summarized as:

1. Initialize the parameters and input the problem data.

2. Generate the initial particle solution, including velocity matrix ($V_{N_pMN}$), and then transform the velocity to a matrix of $s(V_{hij})$, and use Eq. (11) to generate the matrix ($X_{N_pMN}$), and update the local best and global best solution.
3. Use Eq. (8) to generate new velocity of particles for the next generation until a specified stopping criterion is reached.

---

```
Initialize and generate each particle solution of Xh matrix and velocity Vh
Set Lh =Xh, h=1,..., Np, G = X1
Loop
//find the global best solution
For h= 1 to Np
        If Z(Xh)<Z(G) then        // Z( ) objective function
                 g = h  //g is the index of the global best G
End if
Next h
    For h= 1 to Np
         Update the velocity matrix Vh based on Eq. (8)
               subject to Vhij∈ [−Vmax,+Vmax]
               map Vhij to s(Vhij) based on Eq. (9)
               calculate normalized probability qh(i, j) using Eq. (11)
               select grid j for task i (Xhij) by roulette wheel selection rule
          Update the assignment matrix Xh based on Simulated annealing
        ΔE = Z(Xh)-Z(Lh)
        if ΔE<0 then
              Lh = Xh
else
              Compute the δ = e^(-(ΔE/T))
              Lh = Xh  when a generated random number Pa<δ
 End if
Next h
// find the local best solution
    For h = 1 to Np
             If Z(Xh)<Z(Lh) then           // Z( ) objective function
                  Lh = Xh  // Lh is the best so far for particle h
End if
Next h
     decrease the temperature T
Until the end of criterion is reached
```

---

Fig. 6. The proposed discrete PSO combined with SA

### 5.1 DPSO encoding representation

Encoding the task assignment problem in grid into the position vector of particle is necessary. Hence, encoding is illustrated by an example as follows. For example, there are 5 tasks to be distributed to 3 grids; the initial velocity for particle h ($V_{hij}$) is

| Task \ Grid | 1 | 2 | 3 |
|---|---|---|---|
| 1 | -1.2 | -3.9 | 3.1 |
| 2 | 1.1 | -2 | -2.8 |
| 3 | 1.2 | -2.6 | 3.2 |
| 4 | -0.2 | -1.9 | -2 |
| 5 | 3.8 | -0.4 | 0.4 |

According to Eq. (8), the updated velocity ($V_{hij}$) becomes

| Task \ Grid | 1 | 2 | 3 |
|---|---|---|---|
| 1 | -1.1 | -3.5 | 2.8 |
| 2 | 1 | -1.8 | -2.5 |
| 3 | 1.1 | -2.3 | 2.9 |
| 4 | -0.2 | -1.7 | -1.8 |
| 5 | 3.4 | -0.4 | 0.4 |

Then, the corresponding probability $s(V_{hij})$ is determined by Eq. (9) as follows.

| Task \ Grid | 1 | 2 | 3 |
|---|---|---|---|
| 1 | 0.25 | 0.03 | 0.94 |
| 2 | 0.73 | 0.14 | 0.08 |
| 3 | 0.75 | 0.09 | 0.95 |
| 4 | 0.45 | 0.15 | 0.14 |
| 5 | 0.97 | 0.4 | 0.6 |

Hence, the normalized probability $q_h(i, j)$ (based on Eq. (11)) for applying roulette wheel selection rule is

| Task \ Grid | 1 | 2 | 3 |
|---|---|---|---|
| 1 | 0.20 | 0.02 | 0.77 |
| 2 | 0.77 | 0.15 | 0.08 |
| 3 | 0.42 | 0.05 | 0.53 |
| 4 | 0.61 | 0.20 | 0.19 |
| 5 | 0.49 | 0.20 | 0.30 |

Where, $q_h(1, 1)=0.25/(0.25+0.03+0.94)\fallingdotseq 0.20$; $q_h(2, 1)=0.73/(0.73+0.14+0.08)\fallingdotseq 0.77$ and so forth. Finally, task-grid assignment based on roulette wheel selection rule will be

| Task \ Grid | 1 | 2 | 3 |
|---|---|---|---|
| 1 | 0 | 0 | 1 |
| 2 | 1 | 0 | 0 |
| 3 | 0 | 0 | 1 |
| 4 | 0 | 1 | 0 |
| 5 | 0 | 0 | 1 |

Restated, grid 1 would execute task 2; grid 2 services task 4; grid 3 is responsible for executing tasks 1, 3, and 5.

## 6. Experimental results

To verify the performance of the presented algorithm (SA + discrete PSO), some simulation cases will be tested. Simulations use the cases of 5 and 10 tasks in 4 grids and 5 grids respectively to verify the performance of the proposed algorithm. According to Fig. 1, the 5-task case only uses 4 grids and suffers the heavy loading from the computation effort in which the processing time is much more than the communication cost. For the 10-task case, the setting of processing time is in the range of [5, 10], and it needs more communications than the processing cost. Tables 1-4 demonstrate simulation data for 5-task case. Simulation data for 10-task case are listed in Tables 5-8. The other parameters used in this study are set as following: The temperature $T$ was set to 100 and cooling scheduling was set to 0.99 ($r$=0.99), i.e., $T = T \times 0.99$, $w = 0.7$, $c_1 = c_2 = 1$ and $V_{max} = 4$. There are 10 particles involved in simulation tests. The interactive matrix is symmetrical matrix as the grid distance matrix.

| Task # | 1 | 2 | 3 | 4 | 5 |
|---|---|---|---|---|---|
| Process time | 15 | 10 | 20 | 30 | 15 |
| Memory requirement | 20 | 30 | 25 | 20 | 10 |

Table 1. Simulation data with 5 tasks

| Grid # | 1 | 2 | 3 | 4 |
|---|---|---|---|---|
| Memory available | 25 | 40 | 30 | 25 |

Table 2. Memory available for 4 grids

| Task # | 1 | 2 | 3 | 4 | 5 |
|---|---|---|---|---|---|
| 1 | 0 | 5 | 0 | 4 | 1 |
| 2 | 5 | 0 | 1 | 0 | 6 |
| 3 | 0 | 1 | 0 | 3 | 0 |
| 4 | 4 | 0 | 3 | 0 | 0 |
| 5 | 1 | 6 | 0 | 0 | 0 |

Table 3. Interaction cost matrix for 5 tasks

| Task # | 1 | 2 | 3 | 4 |
|---|---|---|---|---|
| 1 | 0 | 2 | 3 | 1 |
| 2 | 2 | 0 | 1 | 3 |
| 3 | 3 | 1 | 0 | 2 |
| 4 | 1 | 3 | 2 | 0 |

Table 4. Distance cost matrix for 4 grids

| Task # | 1 | 2 | 3 | 4 | 5 | 6 | 7 | 8 | 9 | 10 |
|---|---|---|---|---|---|---|---|---|---|---|
| Process time | 10 | 9 | 8 | 7 | 6 | 5 | 5 | 9 | 8 | 10 |
| Memory requirement | 10 | 15 | 10 | 20 | 10 | 10 | 20 | 15 | 20 | 10 |

Table 5. Simulation data with 10 tasks

| Grid # | 1 | 2 | 3 | 4 | 5 |
|---|---|---|---|---|---|
| Memory available | 100 | 90 | 130 | 90 | 100 |

Table 6. Memory available for 5 grids

| Task # | 1 | 2 | 3 | 4 | 5 | 6 | 7 | 8 | 9 | 10 |
|---|---|---|---|---|---|---|---|---|---|---|
| 1 | 0 | 1 | 2 | 3 | 4 | 5 | 5 | 4 | 3 | 4 |
| 2 | 1 | 0 | 5 | 1 | 2 | 3 | 4 | 3 | 5 | 4 |
| 3 | 2 | 5 | 0 | 3 | 2 | 1 | 0 | 1 | 2 | 3 |
| 4 | 3 | 1 | 3 | 0 | 4 | 5 | 4 | 3 | 2 | 1 |
| 5 | 4 | 2 | 2 | 4 | 0 | 1 | 2 | 3 | 4 | 5 |
| 6 | 5 | 3 | 1 | 5 | 1 | 0 | 4 | 3 | 2 | 1 |
| 7 | 5 | 4 | 0 | 4 | 2 | 4 | 0 | 2 | 3 | 1 |
| 8 | 4 | 3 | 1 | 3 | 3 | 3 | 2 | 0 | 5 | 1 |
| 9 | 3 | 5 | 2 | 2 | 4 | 2 | 3 | 5 | 0 | 2 |
| 10 | 4 | 4 | 3 | 1 | 5 | 1 | 4 | 1 | 2 | 0 |

Table 7. Interaction cost matrix for 10 tasks

| Grid # | 1 | 2 | 3 | 4 | 5 |
|---|---|---|---|---|---|
| 1 | 0 | 2 | 3 | 1 | 5 |
| 2 | 2 | 0 | 1 | 3 | 3 |
| 3 | 3 | 1 | 0 | 2 | 4 |
| 4 | 1 | 3 | 2 | 0 | 6 |
| 5 | 5 | 3 | 4 | 6 | 0 |

Table 8. Distance cost matrix for 5 grids

In the example of 5-task in 4 grids environment, the best solution can be found in Table 9. Table 9 indicates that task 4 is assigned to grid 4; task 1 is assigned to grid 1, and so on. The total processing cost for task 4 on grid 4 is 30. Based on Tables 3 and 4, task 4 has interaction with tasks 1 and 3, and the communication cost to tasks 1 and 3 is $1\times4 + 2\times3 = 10$. Thus, the total cost for grid 4 is 48. Similarly, the obtained best solution of 10-task case is displayed in Table 10.

| Task # | Grid # | | | |
|---|---|---|---|---|
| | 1 | 2 | 3 | 4 |
| 1 | 1 | 0 | 0 | 0 |
| 2 | 0 | 1 | 0 | 0 |
| 3 | 0 | 0 | 1 | 0 |
| 4 | 0 | 0 | 0 | 1 |
| 5 | 0 | 1 | 0 | 0 |

Table 9. The assignment results for 5 tasks in 4 grids with cost of 40

| Task # | Grid # | | | | |
|---|---|---|---|---|---|
| | 1 | 2 | 3 | 4 | 5 |
| 1 | 0 | 1 | 0 | 0 | 0 |
| 2 | 0 | 0 | 1 | 0 | 0 |
| 3 | 0 | 0 | 1 | 0 | 0 |
| 4 | 0 | 1 | 0 | 0 | 0 |
| 5 | 0 | 1 | 0 | 0 | 0 |
| 6 | 0 | 0 | 1 | 0 | 0 |
| 7 | 0 | 0 | 1 | 0 | 0 |
| 8 | 0 | 0 | 1 | 0 | 0 |
| 9 | 0 | 1 | 0 | 0 | 0 |
| 10 | 0 | 0 | 1 | 0 | 0 |

Table 10. The assignment results for 10 tasks in 5 grids with cost of 138

Table 10 shows the result of 10-task case that more grids may not decrease the total cost due to the communication cost. Furthermore, extra tests were simulated; the total numbers of tasks were set 20 to 50, the processing times of tasks are uniform distribution in [5, 10] and the memory requirement is also uniform distribution in [50, 100]. The numbers of grids are from 6 to 15, the total available memory is uniform distribution in [200, 400]. The interactive data between of tasks are varying from 1 to 10, and the communications between grids are varied by uniform distribution from 1 to 10. Simulation results demonstrate that more iterations or number of particles obtain the better solution since more solutions were generated as displayed in Table 11.

| (Task, Grid) | Number of particles | | | | |
|---|---|---|---|---|---|
| | 10 | | 20 | | |
| | # of iterations | | # of iterations | | |
| | 100 | 300 | 100 | 300 | 500 |
| 20,6 | 1967 | 1888 | 1946 | 1872 | 1818 |
| 20,8 | 1619 | 1611 | 1611 | 1608 | 1569 |
| 20,12 | 1308 | 1249 | 1263 | 1241 | 1163 |
| 30,8 | 3347 | 3325 | 3329 | 3325 | 3315 |
| 30,12 | 2514 | 2359 | 2470 | 2359 | 2359 |
| 30,15 | 1998 | 1998 | 1998 | 1957 | 1957 |
| 40,12 | 4276 | 4276 | 4276 | 4276 | 4276 |
| 40,15 | 4008 | 3808 | 3808 | 3562 | 3562 |
| 50,15 | 5157 | 5157 | 5741 | 5157 | 5156 |

Table 11. Simulation results

## 7. Summary

This study introduces the discrete PSO algorithm for solving task-grid assignment problem in a distributed grid environment. Experiment results indicate that the discrete version of PSO combining simulated annealing is effective for solving task-grid assignment problems. However, more complicated cases can be considered in-depth, such as more realistic examples and more tasks involved. For example, a grid system consists of heterogeneous grids (with different process capabilities) is given. Restated, more complicated scheduling problem can be further solved using discrete PSO. Moreover, to further improve the discrete PSO performance, some other heuristics are suggested to be included, for example, insertion, 2-opt or others. Further research encourages that the extension of the discrete PSO by incorporating other meta-heuristics for solving different scheduling problems is recommended.

## 8. References

Behnamian, J.; Zandieh, M. & Ghomi, S. M. T. F. (2010). Due windows group scheduling using an effective hybrid optimization approach. *International Journal of Advanced Manufacturing Technology*, Vol. 46, No. 5-8 (2010), pp. 721-735, ISSN (printed): 0268-3768.

Bokhari, S. H. (1987). *Assignment Problems in Parallel and Distributed Computing*, Kluwer Academic Publishers, ISBN: 0-89838-240-8, Boston (1987).

Chang, S.C. (2002). A new aircrew-scheduling model for short-haul routes. *Journal of Air Transport Management*, Vol. 8, No. 4 (July 2002), pp. 249-260, ISSN: 0969-6997.

Chaudhary, V. & Aggarwal, J. K. (1993). A generalized scheme for mapping parallel algorithms. *IEEE Transactions on Parallel and Distributed Systems*, Vol. 4, No. 3 (March 1993), pp. 328-346, ISSN: 1045-9219.

Chen, R. M.; Lo, S. T. & Huang, Y. M. (2007). Combining competitive scheme with slack neurons to solve real-time job scheduling problem. *Expert Systems with Applications*, Vol. 33, No. 1 (July 2007), pp. 75–85, ISSN: 0957-4174.

Chen, R. M.; Wu, C. L.; Wang, C. M. & Lo, S. T. (2010). Using novel particle swarm optimization scheme to solve resource-constrained scheduling problem in PSPLIB. *Expert systems with applications*, Vol. 37, No. 3 (March 2010), pp. 1899-1910, ISSN: 0957-4174.

Dorigo, M. & Gambardella, L. M. (1997). Ant colony system: A cooperative learning approach to the traveling salesman problem. *IEEE Transactions on Evolutionary Computation*, Vol. 1, No. 1 (April 1997), pp. 53-66, ISSN: 1089-778X.

Fleming, P. J. & Fonseca, C. M. (1993). Genetic algorithms in control systems engineering: a brief introduction. *Proceedings of IEE Colloquium on Genetic Algorithms for Control Systems Engineering*, London UK, 28 May 1993, pp. 1/1 - 1/5.

Foster, I.; Kesselman, C. & Tuecke, S. (2001). The Anatomy of the Grid: Enabling Scalable Virtual Organizations. *Int'l J. of High Performance Computing Applications*, Vol. 15, No. 3 (Fall 2001), pp. 200-222, ISSN (printed): 1094-3420.

Glover, F. (1989). Tabu Search – Part I, *ORSA Journal on Computing*, Vol. 1, No. 3 (Summer 1989), pp. 190–206, ISSN: 0899-1499.

Glover, F. (1990). Tabu Search – Part II, *ORSA Journal on Computing*, Vio. 2, No. 1 (Winter 1990), pp. 4–32, ISSN: 0899-1499.

Hei, Y. Q.; Li, X. H.; Yi, K. C. & Yang, H. (2009). Novel scheduling strategy for downlink multiuser MIMO system: Particle swarm optimization. *Science in China - Series F: information Sciences,* Vol. 52, No. 12 (2009), pp. 2279-2289, ISSN (printed): 1009-2757.

Holland, J. H. (1987). Genetic algorithms and classifier systems: foundations and future directions. *Proceedings of 2nd international conference on genetic algorithms and their application,* pp. 82-89, ISBN:0-8058-0158-8, Cambridge, Massachusetts, United States, 1987, L. Erlbaum Associates Inc., Hillsdale, NJ, USA.

Kashan, A. H. & Karimi, B. (2009). A discrete particle swarm optimization algorithm for scheduling parallel machines. *Computers & Industrial Engineering,* Vol. 56, No. 1 (February 2009), pp. 216-223, ISSN: 0360-8352.

Kashan, A. H.; Karimi, B. & Jenabi, M. (2008). A hybrid genetic heuristic for scheduling parallel batch processing machines with arbitrary job sizes. *Computers and Operations Research,* Vol. 35, No. 4 (April 2008), pp. 1084-1098, ISSN: 0305-0548.

Kennedy, J. & Eberhart, R. C. (1995). Particle swarm optimization. *Proceedings of IEEE Int'l. Conf. on Neural Networks,* pp. 1942-1948, ISBN: 0-7803-2768-3, Perth, WA , Australia, Nov/Dec 1995.

Kennedy, J., Eberhard, R.C. (1997). A discrete binary version of the particle swarm algorithm. *Proceedings of IEEE Conference on Systems, Man, and Cybernetics,* pp. 4104--4109, ISBN: 0-7803-4053-1, Orlando, FL , USA, Oct. 1997, Piscataway, NJ.

Kirkpatrick, S.; Gelatt, C. D. & Vecchi, M. P. (1983). Optimization by Simulated Annealing. *Science,* Vol. 220, No. 4598 (May 1983), pp. 671 - 680, ISSN: 0036-8075.

Kuo, I. H.; Horng, S. J.; Kao, T. W.; Lin, T. L.; Lee, C. L.; Terano, T. & Pan, Y. (2009). An efficient flow-shop scheduling algorithm based on a hybrid particle swarm optimization model. Expert systems with applications, Vol. 36, No. 3 (April 2009), pp. 7027-7032, ISSN: 0957-4174.

Laskari, E. C.; Parsopoulos, K. E. & Vrahatis, M. N. (2002). Particle swarm optimization for integer programming. *Proceedings of the IEEE Congress on Evolutionary Computation,* pp. 1582-1587, ISBN: 0-7803-7282-4, Honolulu, HI , USA, May 2002.

Lee, L. T.; Tao, D. F. & Tsao, C. (2007). An adaptive scheme for predicting the usage of grid resources. *Computers & Electrical Engineering,* Vol. 33, No. 1 (Jan. 2007), pp. 1-11, ISSN:0045-7906.

Lee, W. C.; Wu, C. C. & Chen, P. (2006). A simulated annealing approach to makespan minimization on identical parallel machines. *International Journal of Advanced Manufacturing Technology,* Vol. 31, No. 3-4 (2006), pp. 328-334, ISSN (printed): 0268-3768.

Liao, C. J.; Tseng, C. T. & Luarn, P. (2007). A discrete version of particle swarm optimization for flowshop scheduling problems. *Computers and Operations Research,* Vol. 34, No. 10 (October 2007), pp. 3099-3111, ISSN: 0305-0548.

Mathaisel, D. & Comm, C. (1991). Course and classroom scheduling: an interactive computer graphics approach. *Journal of Systems and Software,* Vol. 15 (May 1991), pp. 149-157, ISSN: 0164-1212.

Metropolis, N.; Rosenbluth, A. W.; Rosenbluth, M. N.; Teller, A. H. & Teller, E. (1953). Equation of State Calculations by Fast Computing Machines. *The Journal of Chemical Physics,* Vol. 21, No. 6 (June 1953), pp. 1087-1092, ISSN (printed): 0021-9606.

Norman, M. G. & Thanisch, P. (1993). Models of machines and computation for mapping in multicomputers. *ACM Computing Surveys*, Vol. 25, No. 3 (September 1993), pp. 263-302, ISSN: 0360-0300.

Ohki, M.; Morimoto, A. & Miyake, K. (2006). Nurse Scheduling by Using Cooperative GA with Efficient Mutation and Mountain-Climbing Operators. *Proceedings of 2006 3rd International IEEE Conference on Intelligent System*, pp. 164–169, London, Sept. 2006.

Salman, A.; Ahmad, I. & Al-Madani, S. (2002). Particle swarm optimization for task assignment problem. *Microprocessors and Microsystems*, Vol. 26, No. 8 (November 2002), pp. 363-371, ISSN: 0141-9331.

Sha, D. Y. & Hsu, C. Y. (2006). A hybrid particle swarm optimization for job shop scheduling problem. *Computers and Industrial Engineering*, Vol. 51, No. 4 (December 2006), pp. 791-808, ISSN:0360-8352.

Simeonov, S. & Simeonovova, J. (2002). Simulation Scheduling in Food Industry Application, Mathematical and statistical methods. *Food processing and preservation*, Vol. 20, No. 1 (Jan. 2002), pp. 31-37, ISSN: 1212-1800.

Watts, D. J. & Strogatz, S. H. (1998). Collective dynamics of 'small-world' networks. Nature, Vol. 393, No. 6684 (June 1998), pp. 440–442, ISSN (printed): 0028-0836.

Zhai, X.; Tiong, R.L.K.; Bjornsson, H.C. & Chua, D.K.H. (2006). A Simulation-Ga Based Model for Production Planning in Precast Plant, *Proceedings of Winter Simulation Conference*, pp. 1796 - 1803, ISBN: 1-4244-0500-9, Monterey, CA, Dec. 2006.

2

# A Framework for Problem-Specific QoS Based Scheduling in Grids

Mohamed Wahib[1], Asim Munawar[2], Masaharu Munetomo[3] and Kiyoshi Akama[4]
[1,2]*Gradute School of Information Science and Technology, Hokkaido University, Sapporo*
[3,4]*Information Initiative Center, Hokkaido University, Sapporo*
*Japan*

## 1. Introduction

Grid computing is generally viewed as task assignment to distributed resources. While in practice many factors do complicate this scheduling process (e.g. resource monitoring and discovery, resource failures, resources ownership and policies ... etc), the process is still viewed as resource scheduling according to some criteria. The criteria are referred to as Quality of Service (QoS) attributes in grid computing context. QoS in general are non-functional characters describing a process. QoS attributes are divided into two main groups, namely objective QoS and subjective QoS. Objective QoS attributes are used to specify performance parameters including timeliness, precision, accuracy, security requirements and availability. Subjective QoS attributes, on the other hand, capture application specific policies that govern how an application is treated by the resource manager. In this chapter, objective QoS attributes are referred to as basic QoS attributes, while subjective QoS attributes are referred to as application-specific QoS attributes. In comparison to application-specific QoS attributes, a huge legacy of scheduling with the basic QoS attributes exists. This chapter proposes adopting application-specific QoS attributes to define new criteria other than the basic ones to enhance the preference of which resources to choose in the task assignment process as the QoS attributes are application-specific (e.g. a Grid application involving service tasks that retrieve images from a service resource could have the color depth and resolution as QoS attributes).
For grid computing to go beyond the basic QoS attributes the following challenges need to be addressed: a) A method to formally define new application-specific QoS attributes. b) A method to measure the QoS attribute fidelity of a specific resource. c) Scheduling the tasks over the resources taking into consideration the defined application-specific QoS attributes. This chapter addresses these challenges and proposes a framework that starts from defining new application-specific QoS attributes until the tasks are executed over the resources. As for the first challenge, a system for defining QoS using a formal language is inspired from Canfora et al. (2006) which proposes service composition binding driven by application-specific QoS. The domain of Canfora et al. (2006) is different from the work in this chapter. This is because the authors are concerned with the composition of services that are initially defined as an abstract workflow, where for each service in the workflow a set of service providers are defined. Then the scheduler/binder makes a concrete workflow at which each service in the abstract workflow is bind to a service provider. Canfora et al. addressed how application

specific QoS attributes can be defined and aggregated to be used for scheduling. The basic idea is implementing a QoS aggregation function definition interface and a QoS definition language, so the administrator through a simple QoS aggregation function editor could define new QoS(s). The QoS definition in this framework here builds on and extends the work done by Canfora though it is defined for a different discipline (i.e. SOA). It is of no-awkwardness to use a mechanism that was originally defined in SOA (Service Oriented Architecture) service workflows to be used in grid computing. As grid computing and SOA have many tangency points. And this point in particular could be considered a convergence point between grid computing and SOA.
At the first glance, scheduling tasks in such an environment seem to add more complexity to the traditional problems of task assignment. However, the definition of task associated QoS attributes is utilized to enrich the task assignment process. The Chapter illustrates the framework, describes the design and implementation of the framework and finally demonstrates a use case to emphasize on the functional efficiency of the framework. The rest of this paper is organized as follows; the next section is a brief review on subjective QoS representation in service environments. Section 3.discusses the proposed framework. Section 4. discusses the experiments that were conducted using the proposed framework. Finally section 5.concludes and adds insight to future work.

## 2. Subjective QoS representation in service environments

Quality of Service is an overarching term covering different parts of end-to-end service quality. The general definition of QoS provided by the International Telecommunication Union (ITU)Recommendation (1994) is that QoS is Ştthe collective effect of service performance, which determines the degree of satisfaction of a user of the serviceŤ. Different people and communities nevertheless interpret QoS differently, and at least the following viewpoints of QoS can be distinguished: QoS requirements of a user, QoS perceived by the user, QoS offered or planned by a provider, and QoS delivered or achieved by the provider. We are discussing QoS in the userŠs point of view. There are two main aspects of QoS: subjective and objective. Subjective QoS essentially is the userŠs overall perception of service quality, that is, it is the userŠs opinion whether a service is working satisfactorily or not. Subjective QoS is often difficult to be specified with objective measures, at least in a way meaningful for users, and thus user-perceived quality is often expressed also non-technicallyBouch et al. (2000). Objective QoS then refers to the technical aspects of QoS, and can be specified with quantitative measures. Grid Application QoS parameters are not necessarily applicable to express subjective QoS, since a user has a high-level perspective over application performance, rather than an in-depth conception of details of the underlying implementation and operation of the service. Therefore, application quality and its variation need to be expressed in terms that describe user-perceivable effects, instead of their causes in the end-to-end functionality. It should be noted also that subjective application quality deterioration is not solely caused by operational QoS fluctuations, but is attributable to numerous other factors, including characteristics of the ongoing task (e.g. urgency), applicationŠs incompatibility with the service provided, application or protocol malfunction, disturbing factors in usage environment (e.g. faulty equipment), and so forth.
Two principal approaches for subjective application quality assessment exist: user study methods and objective measurements. The user study methods include, e.g. Mean Opinion Scores (MOS), continuous assessment, Task Performance Measures (TPMs), and qualitative methodsBouch et al. (2001). Objective measurements, on the other hand, rely on measurement

of some application quality metric(s) (e.g. Peak-Signal-to-Noise-Ratio (PSNR) for video)Wang et al. (2003). Generally, MOS are used on a wide scale to collect the subjectsŠ opinions of the experienced service quality. In short, MOS enables performing controlled assessment of subjective QoS with untrained subjects and controlled levels of qualityBouch et al. (2001). The method employs a 5-point scale, according to which subjects judge the experienced quality after conducting a task. The given ratings are then averaged across the subjects to get the final MOS.
This paper proposes a problem-specific QoS based scheduling in grids. To determine the optimal choice of services/applications, the approach needs to estimate the subjective QoS. This can be done using some aggregation formulae. The formulae define aggregation functions for defined QoS attributes. While this approach is far from being general (i.e. needs to be customized for each application as the QoS aggregator can operate differently). Yet, we argue that the proposed approach gives a methodology for quantifying subjective QoS and thus is more reliable compared to the user study methods.

## 3. The proposed framework

### 3.1 Defining and evaluating subjective QoS attributes

In order for the framework to define and evaluate subjective QoS attributes we developed a language that permits to specify a new QoS attribute. As mentioned in the introduction, the language proposed here extends the work by Canfora et al. (2006) which defined QoS aggregation formulae for each pair QoS attribute–workflow construct. In most cases, the aforementioned aggregation formulae are cabled in the optimization algorithm the binder is using. Therefore, it is necessary to provide a language and a tool to specify aggregation formulae, and to allow the schedular to interpret such formulae for estimating the QoS of the grid services. The method by which the framework defines and evaluates subjective QoS attributes is as follows:
***QoS definition language***: For a language to permit specifying new QoS attributes, two things are required; type and scale. The type can be only primitive types (integer, real and Boolean) as in WSLA+ languageNepal et al. (2008), or include collection types (i.e. a set constituted of sets of atomic values) as Canfora did. The scale limits the set of admissible operations. The language developed by Canfora includes the scales required for our framework, so no change is required in this part. The point of difference here is the set of operators and functions inherited form the Object Constraint Language (OCL) Warmer & Kleppe (2003) that is used by Canfora. This is due to using those operators and functions in computing overall workflow QoS, while in the proposed framework accepts both inter-dependent task (i.e. workflows) and individual tasks. In the case of workflow tasks, the operators and functions defined by Canfora are sufficient, while in the case of individual tasks the operators are not used due to tasks independency. The next step is to show how the QoS formula specification is supported by a guided editor and type-checker.
***QoS aggregation***: The QoS aggregator introduced by Canfora et al. (2006) was implemented in Java using the Java Compiler (JavaCC) parser generator, while for the GUI, JSP was used. The aggregator was adopted here by including the aggregator in a Vine portlet and adding it to the gridsphere portal. Modifications were done to drop operators for individual tasks as mentioned earlier, associate the newly defined Qos attribute to any of the task types registered by the administrator and finally adapting the original JSP to work with the Adobe Flex GUI used in gridsphere 3.1. The aggregator include three basic modules; *QoS aggregation function editor* a portlet that the administrator can use to define new QoS attributes and their aggregation formula (see figure1), *Type checker* used at design time for verifying

integrity of the aggregation formula, *QoS formula interpreter* that at run time evaluates QoS for a possible workflow/individual task assignment.
An important point to note, the model for determining the expected QoS from each resource is executed as agents hosted on the resources. Note that these agents are also used for resource monitoring and discovery. As for the scheduling process, several projects in the literature attempted multiple QoS job scheduling. Generally speaking, these projects addressed mainly the basic QoS attributes in their work; cost, time, availability and fidelity. Those basic QoS attributes are agreed upon in literature to be the metrics for job scheduling in grids. Application specific QoS attributes were not considered in any of them as no service level presentation of resources provided features into which application-specific QoS attributes could be mapped. Li & Li (2007); Li et al. (2007) defined the 4 basic QoS attributes as utilities and identified an Integrated Utility Function (IUF) to be used for scheduling. A slight difference between them is that Li & Li (2007) used an iterative scheduling technique by separating the task agents and resources agents. Doğan & özgüner (2006) proposed a static scheduling algorithm that uses utility functions for scheduling meta-task with QoS requirements in heterogeneous computing systems. The main aim of this project was to provide resource transparency and not include application-specific QoS attributes. Kim et al. (2006) did not define a scheduling method, yet it defined for the basic QoS attributes a flexible multi-dimensional QoS performance measure that could be later aggregated to be used for scheduling. A notable point is that the authors defined a method that is theoretically applicable to model any new QoS attribute by representing the QoS attribute by a feature vector. This approach is generic but if used will shift the entire load to the application developer.

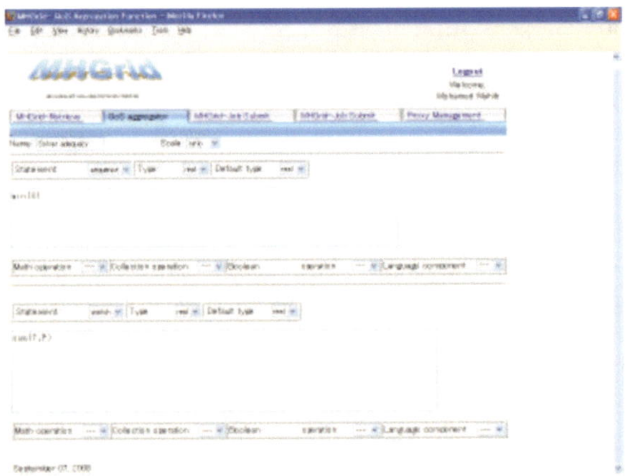

Fig. 1. QoS aggregation function definition interface

### 3.2 Problem formulation

Suppose that there are $n$ independent users and user $i$ is associated with task $T_i$, let $T = \{T_1, T_2, ..., T_n\}$ denote the set of $n$ independent tasks where task $T_i$ is assigned to resource $R_j$ and $R = \{R1, R_2, ..., R_m\}$. Further, $R_j$ can be composed of $v$ resources, where $1 \le v \le m$. The process of QoS-constrained task scheduling could be summarized in three steps. Step one is Resource Discovery, which is finding available resources complied by QoS constraints and generate a list of resources. Step two is Resource Planning, which involves selecting the optimized resources from the available resources list according to the scheduling strategy satisfying user's QoS constrains. The $\Gamma : T \rightarrow R$ denoting the matching function is a NP complete problemChristensen (2007). The third step is Task Execution. The tasks are scheduled or mapped onto selected resources to be executed.

In the proposed framework, QoS attributes are described as utility functions. So the integrated utility function is the accumulation of all QoS attributes utility functions. The integrated utility is considered as the objective function of the scheduling algorithm to drive the scheduling of resources and optimizing the task execution with maximum utility. A very important point here is that utility functions have long been used in QoS constrained scheduling, but for this case a new factor requires special handling. The new factor is having different QoS attributes defined according to underlying application. Thus, the integrated utility function includes a set of mutually exclusive utility functions corresponding to the QoS attributes. The next step, after defining the integrated utility function, is to compute the value of the utility $u_k$, $1 \leq k \leq d$ where $d$ is the total number of QoS constraints defined by the administrator, what we will call the *dimension of QoS*. The method used for computing the utility functions uses switch constructs as in Anselmi et al. (2007) to iteratively update the selection probabilities of the selected resources. For each task $T_i$ a *decision matrix* $Q = \left(q_{ij}\right)_{m \times d}$ is created, among it, m represents the number of resources that can host $T_i$, $d$ represents the dimension of QoS attributes considered by the this type of task. $Q$ matrix is not used directly, $Q$ is normalized to make the *normalized matrix* $P = \left(p_{ij}\right)_{m \times d}$, $j = 1, ..., m, k = 1, ..., d$, where normalizing is done as follows:

$$p_{jk} = \begin{cases} min_j \left(q_{jk}\right) / q_{jk} \text{ if } u_k \text{ is optimally minimized} \\ \\ q_{jk} / max_j \left(q_{jk}\right) \text{ if } u_k \text{ is optimally maximized} \end{cases}$$

Supposing $\omega = (\omega_1, \omega_2, ..., \omega_d)$ is attribute weighting vector, Then the integrated utility function for the evaluation of the selected resources can be defined as:

$$U_{ij}\left(\omega\right) = \sum_{t=1}^{S} \left( C_t \sum_{l=x}^{y} p_{jl} \omega_l \right)$$

where $S$ is the number of subjective QoS attributes defined by the administrator to be used in the system, $C_t$ is a Boolean constant having value 1 only for the QoS attributes subset of the task scheduled (i.e. QoS divided to subsets having a mutually exclusive relation.). $x$ and $y$ denote the start and end of the QoS attributes subset from the set of all QoS attributes defined. By sorting and computing $U_i\left(\omega\right)$, the best resource can be selected. Weights for utility functions in the mentioned related work are calculated by maximizing the deviations in utiliy values. In our case the QoS attributes are defined by the administrator according to the application. Therefore, the default weights are defined by the administrator according to the system used. The end user could calibrate the weights according to his interest in which QoS attributes significant for the job he is about to submit.

### 3.3 Scheduling using quantified subjective QoS attributes

The scheduling process is basically viewed as a combinatorial optimization problem for the integrated utility function. Several approaches are used in the literature to solve this optimization problem, most approaches depend on a heuristic algorithms. Generally, GA (Genetic Algorithms)Jong (1992) based heuristic algorithms do not impose constraints on the linearity of the QoS composition operators, so they are considered the best option. However, the prime focus in this work is to represent and utilize subjective QoS attributes. Thus, a simple rank-based algorithm is used to determine the focus on the aforementioned process As shown in the previous section, QoS attributes are described as utility functions, The integrated utility function aggregating all utility functions is regarded as an objective function of the scheduling algorithm to drive dynamic scheduling to the resources and optimizing the task execution with maximum utility by accumulating all QoS attributes utility functions. Figure2 shows the algorithm used for scheduling. One important point to note here, the algorithm is designed in a central way, which leads to weak scalability. Yet, the design of centralized scheduling algorithms is an important step towards developing more complex decentralized scheduling algorithms.

1- For all $T_i$ if $T_i$ is a workflow or nested tasks, then $T_i = (T_{i1}, T_{i2}, \ldots, T_{im})$,

$m \geq 2$. For each $T_{i2}$ go to step 1.

2- Use $T_i$ category to create available resources list that can host $T_i$.

3- For all $k \in m$, evaluate QoS attributes of all services in service list.

4- Create decision matrix $Q_i$.

5- Compute the integrate utility function of multiple QoS attributes $U_i(\omega)$.

6- Sort resources according to $U_i(\omega)$.

7- Execute $T_i$ on the selected resource.

Fig. 2. Algorithm used for scheduling

## 4. Use case and results

| Task type | QoS attributes | Individual | | Nested | | Workflow | | |
|---|---|---|---|---|---|---|---|---|
| Opimization algorithms as services (Service tasks) | * Solver to problem adequacy<br>* Parallel pattern<br>* Fidelity | Small | 50 | Small | 50 | Random size, 20 tasks | | |
| | | HPC | 20 | HPC | 20 | | | |
| | | HTC | 10 | HTC | 10 | | | |
| Optimization algorithms as computational tasks | * Latency tolerance<br>* Data accuracy | Small | 50 | Small | 50 | | | Random size, 20 tasks |
| | | HPC | 20 | HPC | 20 | | | |
| | | HTC | 10 | HTC | 10 | | | |
| Data tasks | * Priority | Small size staging | 50 | N/A | N/A | | Random size, 20 tasks | |
| | | Large size staging | 20 | N/A | N/A | | | |
| | | Large size flow | 10 | N/A | N/A | | | |

Table 1. Test bed configuration

This section presents the approach at work over Meta Heuristics Grid (MHGrid): a service oriented grid application offering meta heuristics based solvers for global optimization problems. MHGrid is designed to offer optimizing algorithms as grid services. The experiments were designed to cover possible task types in the framework. For the service tasks, individual and nested tasks of different sizes were introduced. The size is controlled by the problem length that the algorithms should solve. Three specific QoS attributes were defined; Solver to problem adequacy, the parallel pattern used and the fidelity or quality of output. These attributes are explained in details in Munawar et al. (2008). The same applies for computational tasks but with two different QoS attributes. Long timeouts were added in the solvers to test the latency tolerance with the solvers running in parallel mode. The other QoS

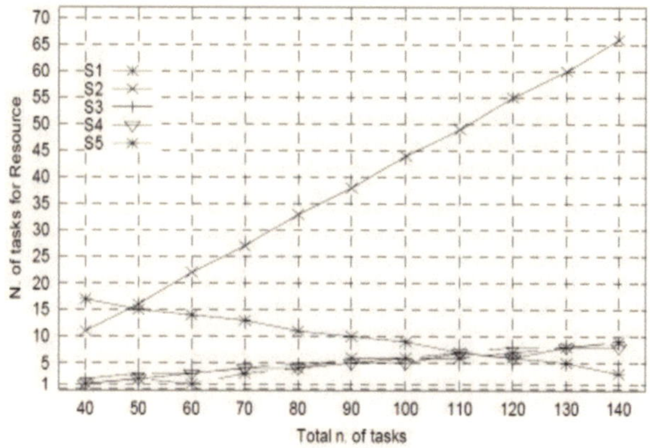


Fig. 3. Tasks assigned to each service varying the total amount of tasks

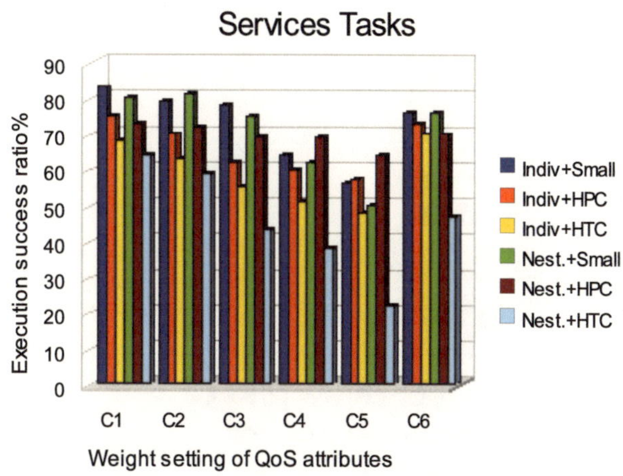


Fig. 4. The effect of services tasks weight vector on execution success ratio

attribute is data accuracy which is measured by round off errors resulting from float-point operations intentionally introduced to the solvers. As for the data tasks, dummy files where used to be transferred via GridFTPFoster (2006). The file sizes varied from 100MB to 20TB to represent different task sizes. One QoS attribute (i.e. priority) was defined for the data tasks where each task was assigned priority rank for the scheduler to attempt to meet the priority requirement of those tasks. In addition to that, workflow tasks for different task types where also created by the workflow portlet to be tested. Finally two basic QoS attributes (make span time and cost) were used for all tasks along with the specific QoS attributes defined for each task type. Table 1 shows the configuration used in the experiments. Note that tasks were introduced randomly with 20 tasks a time. Figure 3 shows the distribution different task sets over the resources. Each task was assigned to one of the five services (S1,S2,S3,S4,S5) overlaying the computational and data requirements.

The experiments were executed on a grid having a dedicated 64 core mini-cluster with 2 x AMD Opteron 2.6 GHz Dual Core 64 bit processors and 2GB RAM for each node, the grid also has 2 dedicated servers each having a 2 x Xeon 2.8 GHz Dual Core with 2GB RAM. Execution

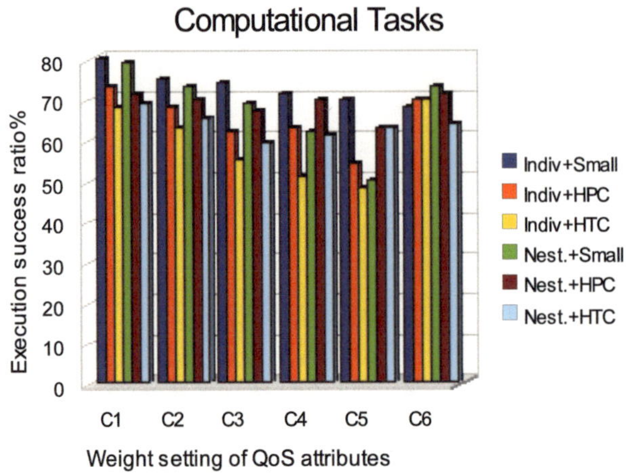


Fig. 5. The effect of computational tasks weight vector on execution success ratio

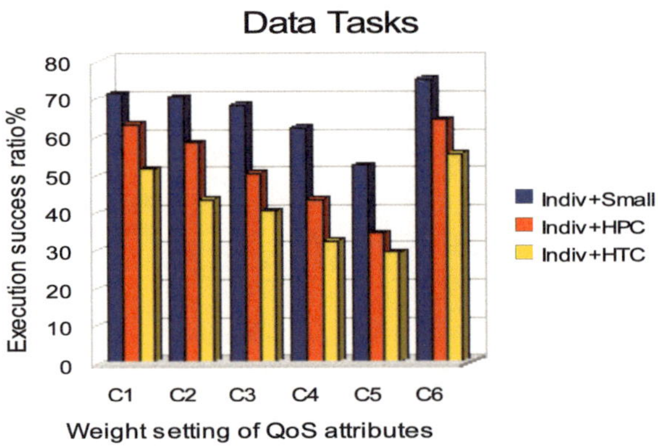


Fig. 6. The effect of data tasks weight vector on execution success ratio

success ratio is the metric used in the experiments to measure the framework's ability to host and schedule variant task triplets. Other metrics such as resource utilization and task waiting time are important as well, but due to space limitation, results in terms of execution success ratio only are illustrated to evidate that a system can function whilst benefiting from subjective QoS attributes. Figures 4, 5 and 6 show the execution success ratio for the individual and nested tasks on different task types/sizes. The x axis in all three figures is a configuration state for the QoS attributes considered. The last state (i.e. C6) is the plain state where all weights for task specific QoS attributes are set to zero and only the basic time and cost QoS attributes with weight = 0.5 are considered. For the other states (i.e. C1 to C5) the weights are having values with an increasing mean from C1 to C5 and also an increasing standard deviation to represent variant weight vector settings. Note that upon moving from C1 to C5 the success rate tends to decrease which is normal as the more the mean of the weight vector increases the more the scheduling process relay on QoS other than the time and cost. This consequently minimizes the set of resource candidates for each task and causes less success rate. Another point to note is that for figure6, C6 gives much better performance than other weight settings.

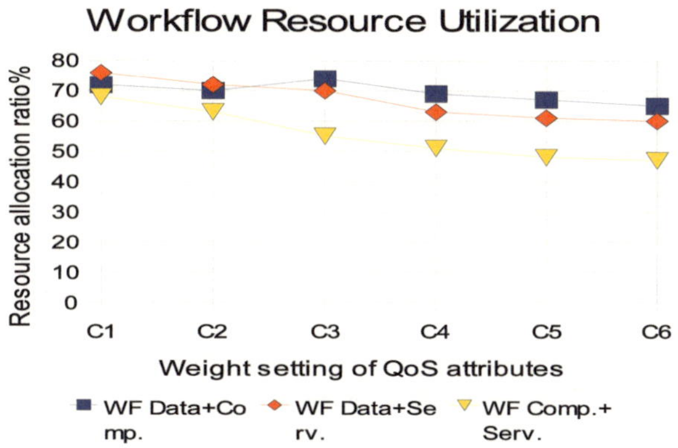


Fig. 7. Resource utilization for workflows with variant tasks weight values

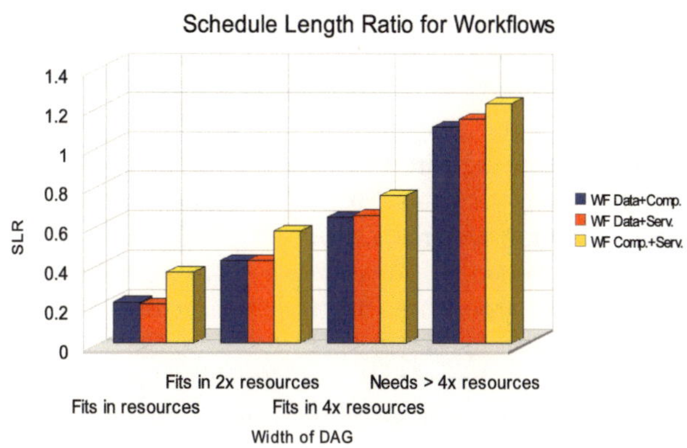


Fig. 8. SLR for the workflows with different DAG width

This is because the *priority* QoS defined for data tasks highly effects the scheduling process making it mostly depending on what the user wants. Figure7 shows the resource utilization for workflow tasks. Again the change in weight value does not have a significant effect on the resource utilization and this is because the workflows enforce an order for task execution on the system. Figure8 shows another aspect of the workflows. The figure shows the Schedule Length Ratio (SLR) for the workflows that were created with different DAG widths.

## 5. Conclusion and future work

This chapter introduced a system for quantifying subjective QoS attributes and using them for assigning tasks in a grid application. First a close-up was given to the representation of subjective QoS attributes in service-based environments. The framework was inspired by a system of application-specific QoS attributes in service composition. While the domain is apparently different, the flexibility offered by the service composition in defining subjective QoS attributes is of great relevance to the requirements of establishing an enviroment that is not only relying on conventional QoS attributes in job assignment. The framework allows the administrator to define subjective QoS attributes through a QoS aggregation function editor enclosed in a portlet. After the administrator registers the categorized resources, the end user can start submitting tasks to the system. With the user unaware, the system schedules the tasks on behalf of the user, and assures the use of the subjective QoS attributes to assign the tasks to the most appropriate resources. Experiments were conducted to assure that the framework is functioning as designed. Many points are promising to be considered as future work. Making the best use of subjetuve QoS attributes by incorporating a SLA mechanism is pivot point. Expanding the function aggregation editor to make the framework generic is as well a challenging task.

## 6. References

Anselmi, J., Ardagna, D. & Cremonesi, P. (2007). A qos-based selection approach of autonomic grid services, *SOCP '07: Proceedings of the 2007 workshop on Service-oriented computing performance: aspects, issues, and approaches*, ACM, pp. 1–8.

Bouch, A., Kuchinsky, A. & Bhatti, N. (2000). Quality is in the eye of the beholder: meeting users' requirements for internet quality of service, *CHI '00: Proceedings of the SIGCHI conference on Human factors in computing systems*, pp. 297–304.

Bouch, A., Sasse, M. A., Demeer, H. & Bt, W. (2001). Of packets and people: A user-centered approach to quality of service.

Canfora, G., Penta, M. D., Esposito, R., Perfetto, F. & Villani, M. L. (2006). Service composition (re)binding driven by application-specific qos, *ICSOC*, pp. 141–152.

Christensen, T. V. (2007). Heuristic algorithms for NP-complete problems.

Doğan, A. & özgüner, F. (2006). Scheduling of a meta-task with qos requirements in heterogeneous computing systems, *J. Parallel Distrib. Comput.* 66(2): 181–196.

Foster, I. (2006). Globus toolkit version 4: Software for service-oriented systems, pp. 2–13.

Jong, K. A. D. (1992). Are genetic algorithms function optimizers?, *PPSN*, pp. 3–14.

Kim, J.-K., Hensgen, D. A., Kidd, T., Siegel, H. J., John, D. S., Irvine, C., Levin, T., Porter, N. W., Prasanna, V. K. & Freund, R. F. (2006). A flexible multi-dimensional qos performance measure framework for distributed heterogeneous systems, *Cluster Computing* 9(3): 281–296.

Li, C. & Li, L. (2007). Utility-based qos optimisation strategy for multi-criteria scheduling on the grid, *J. Parallel Distrib. Comput.* 67(2): 142–153.

Li, Y., Zhao, D. & Li, J. (2007). Scheduling algorithm based on integrated utility of multiple qos attributes on service grid, *GCC '07: Proceedings of the Sixth International Conference on Grid and Cooperative Computing*, IEEE Computer Society, Washington, DC, USA, pp. 288–295.

Munawar, A., Wahib, M., Munetomo, M. & Akama, K. (2008). *Linkage in Evolutionary Computation*, Springer Berlin / Heidelberg, chapter Parallel GEAs with Linkage Analysis over Grid, pp. 159–187.

Nepal, S., Zic, J. & Chen, S. (2008). Wsla+: Web service level agreement language for collaborations, *scc* 2: 485–488.

Recommendation, I.-T. (1994). Terms and definitions related to quality of service and network performance including dependability, *Technical Report E.800*.

Wang, Z., Banerjee, S. & Jamin, S. (2003). Studying streaming video quality: from an application point of view, *MULTIMEDIA '03: Proceedings of the eleventh ACM international conference on Multimedia*, ACM.

Warmer, J. & Kleppe, A. (2003). *The Object Constraint Language: Getting Your Models Ready for MDA*, Addison-Wesley.

# 3

# Grid-JQA: A QoS Guided Scheduling Algorithm for Grid Computing

Leyli Mohammad Khanli[1], Assistance Professor
and Saeed Kargar[2], M.S. student
[1]*C.S. Dept., University of Tabriz*
[2]*Islamic Azad University, Tabriz Branch*
*Iran*

## 1. Introduction

The development of grid computing technologies (Foster & Kesselman, 2004) over the past several years has provided us a means of using and sharing heterogeneous resources over local/wide area networks, and geographically dispersed locations. This has resulted in the ability to form loosely coupled, high-performance computational environment comprising numerous scalable, fault tolerant, and platform-independent services across the entire Internet. The grid infrastructure provides a way to execute applications over autonomous, distributed and heterogeneous nodes by secure resource sharing among individuals and institutions. Typically, a user can submit jobs to a grid without necessarily knowing (or even caring) where it will be executed. It is the responsibility of the grid resource management system to distribute such jobs among a heterogeneous pool of servers, trying to optimize the resource usage and provide the best possible quality of service.

Thus, the resource matching problem is an important task in the Grid environment which involves assigning resources to tasks in order to satisfy task requirements and resource policies. This contribution presents algorithms, methods, and software for a Grid resource manager, responsible for resource brokering and scheduling in Grids. The broker selects computing resources based on actual job requirements and a number of criteria identifying the available resources, with the aim to minimize the turnaround time for the individual application.

In this chapter, we proposed Grid-JQA (Khanli & Analoui, 2006a,b) that explains in next sections. The Grid Java based Quality of service management by Active database (Grid-JQA) is a framework that aims to address the above mentioned requirements. Grid-JQA provides management for quality of service on different types of resources, including networks, CPUs, and disks. It also encourages Grid customers to specify their quality of service needs based on their actual requirements. The main goal of this system is to provide seamless access to users for submitting jobs to a pool of heterogeneous resources, and at the same time, dynamically scheduling in multi policy mode and monitoring the resource requirements for execution of applications. We proposed an optimal solution but not practical for comparing with other practical solution.

Also, we propose an aggregation formula for the QoS parameters. The formula is a unit less combination of the parameters together with weighting factors. It is shown that the formula needs to put into a threshold consideration. A discussion on the threshold and its level is also provided. In this chapter we introduce an optimum but not practical solution for matching. The optimum method is considered for comparing other practical solutions. Main features of the resource manager include resource selection based on active database rules (Khanli & Analoui, 2008) and environmental conditions and a basic adaptation facility. The chapter is finalized by the results obtained from simulation and a comparison study.

The reminder of this chapter is organized as follows: In section 2 we present an overview of related work, in section 3 we introduce three methods for matching in the grid environment. We discuss a proof-of-concept implementation of a prototype and the preliminary performance results by simulation in Section 4, whereas Section 5 concludes with a summary of our work.

## 2. A brief history of the resource management in grid

Due to the grid computing is a dynamic and uncertainly environment, the grid system needs a resource management mechanism which provides a set of available appropriate resources for requesters. There are many resource management approaches that proposed in different grid projects and researches, but a few of them guarantee QoS. This section provides a brief description of these systems and compares some of them with our project.

Foster et al. (Foster et al. 1999) propose a framework for QoS in Grid computing, called the Globus Architecture for Reservation and Allocation (GARA), which enables programmers and users to specify and manage end-to end QoS for Grid-based applications. It also provides a uniform mechanism for making QoS reservations for different types of Grid resources, such as processors, networks and storage devices. The main drawback of GARA is its inability to support subtask management, which is one of Grid's main goals. There are two more drawbacks in GARA: the topology of domain should be known in advance and also the resources can not publish themselves. Grid-JQA is going to address the subtask management while the topology information and resource publishing are handled management, formulating the matching problem as an object placement problem dynamically (Khanli & Analoui, 2006a,b).

Y. Han et al. (Han & Youn, 2009) proposed a new architecture that called Resource-Aware Policy Administrator (RAPA) with Service Level Agreement (SLA) to find appropriate resources. SLA operates as a contract agreed between users and resource providers in order to achieve requested QoS (Han & Youn, 2009; Document for Web Services Agreement Specification).

Chauhan & Joshi (2010a) proposed a QoS Guided Weighted Mean Time Min-Min Max-Min selective heuristic for QoS based task scheduling. In fact this work adds QoS parameters to weighted Mean Time Min-Min Max-Min Selective (WMTS) heuristic (Chauhan & Joshi, 2010b). In this method, first the meta tasks divided into high and low QoS groups, that the high QoS group contains the tasks with high requirement QoS and the other one includes the tasks with low QoS requirements. In mentioned work after mapping all tasks with high Qos requirements, the tasks with low QoS group are mapped (Chauhan & Joshi, 2010a).

Selvi Somasundaram et al. (2010) proposed a metascheduling structure that called CARE Resource Broker (CRB). For resource management they are proposed Virtual Resource Management Protocol (VRMP). In this method scheduler is responsible for choose a suitable resource between available matching resources, and Virtual resource manager is responsible for formation of virtual cluster and virtual machine (Somasundaram et al., 2010).

Darby III & Tzeng (2010) proposed a Checkpointing arrangement in Mobile Grid Computing that provide QoS through Mobile hosts. In other words current work focus on the Mobile hosts Checkpointing arrangement method that QoS is a user's application responsibility.

Rodero et al. (2010) proposed Grid broker selection strategies to resolve the broker selection problem in multiple grid scenarios (Rodero et al., 2010). They also proposed two different resource aggregation algorithms (SIMPLE and CATEGORIZED aggregation algorithms) that used for broker selection.

Javelin (Neary et al., 2000) is a Java based infrastructure for internet-wide parallel computing. The three key components of Javelin system are the clients or applications, hosts, and brokers. A client is a process seeking computing resources, a host is a process offering computing resources, and a broker is a process that coordinates the allocation of computing resources. The Javelin system can be considered a computational Grid for high-throughput computing. It has a hierarchical machine organization where each broker manages a tree of hosts. Resources are simple fixed objects with a tree namespace organization. The resources are simply the hosts that are attached to a broker. Any host that wants to be part of Javelin contacts JavelinBNS system, a Javelin information backbone that maintains the list of available brokers. The host then communicates with brokers, chooses a suitable broker, and then becomes part of the broker-managed resources. Thus the information store is a network directory implemented by JavelinBNS. Hosts and brokers update each other as a result of scheduling work. Thus, Javelin uses demand resource dissemination. The broker manages the host-tree or resource information through a heap-like data structure. Resource discovery uses the decentralized query based approach since queries are handled by the distributed set of brokers. In Javelin the burden of the subtask management and monitoring is layered on the client side. The client should also look for a broker that matches its requirements. Thus the clients are thick. Grid-JQA tries to keep the clients as thin as possible and refers the subtask management and monitoring, and the matching to the broker of the system (Khanli & Analoui, 2006a,b).

Legion (Chapin et al., 1999) takes an object-oriented approach to resource (Chapin et al., 1999). The identification of a candidate resource is performed by an object mapper, whose recommendation is then implemented by a different object. The Legion system defines a notation (Chapin et al., 1999) that is similar to classAds, although it uses an object oriented type system with inheritance to define resources, as contrasted with the simple attribute-oriented Boolean logic of classAds. Legion supports autonomy with a jurisdiction magistrate (JM), which may reject requests if the offered requests do not match the policy of the site being managed by the JM. While the JM gives a resource veto power, there is no way for a resource to describe those requests that it would rather serve (Khanli & Analoui, 2006a,b).

UDDI (Uddi.com) and eSpeak (Hewlett Packard) are two specifications being defined to enable automation of business-to-business interactions. Both systems use XML as a specification language to describe services, and define a rich framework for service discovery. Like most other systems, neither UDDI nor eSpeak exports a symmetric interface to servers and customers. Furthermore, since the emphasis in these frameworks is on service discovery and not resource allocation, the matchmaker provides a list of candidate servers to the customer, who then chooses one or more servers based on subjective criteria.

Recently, to solving the grid resource management problem, many of technologies proposed that based on matchmaking or bidding (Fig. 1). In the matchmaking (Khanli & Analoui, 2008; Litzkow et al., 1988; Liu et al., 2002; Ludwig & Reyhani, 2006; Raman et al., 1998;

Raman et al., 2003; Tangmunarunkit et al., 2003; Yu et al., 2005), there are a resource matchmaker that responsible for recording resource status. When a resource matchmaker gives job requests, executes matching algorithms to find a set of appropriate resources for request.

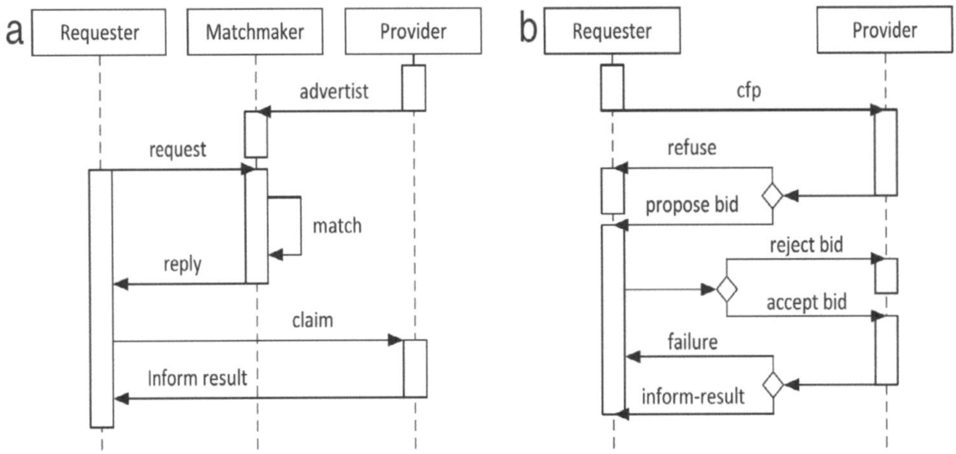


Fig. 1. (a) The abstract process of the matchmaking model. (b) The abstract process of the bidding model (Wang et al., 2010).

Another model for resource management is bidding-based model (Bubendorfer, 2006; Buyya et al., 1980; Das & Grosu, 2005; Goswami & Gupta, 2008; Kakarontzas & Savvas, 2006; Kolano, 2004; Leal et al., 2009; Smith, 1980; Wang et al., 2010; Xiao et al., 2008). In this model there is no centralized matchmaker/broker. However, the bidding model has some advantages over the matchmaking one, but in this model the critical problem for resource selection is that there is no universal information to find suitable match, and requests only have deficient information (Wang et al., 2010).

The Condor (Raman et al., 2003) equivalent of an information system such as UDDI is a matchmaker that maintains a pool of ClassAds representing candidate resources and then matches each incoming request ClassAd with all candidates, returning a highest-ranked matching candidate. Redline (Liu & Foster, 2004) formulates the matching problem as a constraint satisfaction problem. These latter systems allow expression of resource groups, but they do not offer a concise method to express network topologies. Set-matching extends the ClassAds language to provide a multilateral matchmaking mechanism where the number of resources is not known a priory (Liu et al., 2002). However, the set matching mechanism is not capable of marshaling a heterogeneous mix of resources.

Our work is similar to Condor. That is the resources advertise themselves to the broker and the users send their requests to the broker. Then the broker matches the resources and the tasks by using some policies. The differences between our work and Condor are after this time. Because, after matching the broker does not interfere in Condor. And the user works with resources directly. But in our work, the broker manages the activities till the results return to the user. The disadvantage of managing broker till the end is that the broker becomes too busy. For correcting this disadvantage, we use hierarchical broker, in a way that when the broker becomes too busy, one new broker is introduced in the low level and busy broker can send new application for execution to lower level broker. So the problem is solved by hierarchical broker.

## 3. Model description

Looking on the matching problem, we bring about the following solutions:
First, resources introduce themselves to all clients and each client decides where to send its request, thus matching is accomplished by the client.
Second, the clients send their request to all resources and each resource decides which request to reply, therefore matching is done in the resources.
Third, the resources introduce themselves to a broker and each client sends its request to the broker, then the broker decides how to match the requests with the resources. Here there are two possible methods, (a) after the broker finds the best matched resource; the resource and the client negotiate with each other directly. (b) The broker interferes in the process until end of job, in order to guarantee the quality of service and perform subtask management.
In this work, we implement the third mentioned solution (b). The advantages of the broker management till end are:

1. For guarantying the QoS parameters, the broker should monitor till the results return to the user.
2. May be all requested resources are not free, so application can not start execution, but in our work as soon as one resource is free, the execution of user's task can be started. Gradually, the remained tasks can be executed when the other resources are released.
3. Adaptation is possible only in this method that the broker monitors till the end, as duplicate execution of strong tasks which are being executed in weak resources.
4. By using the broker, the user can be thin client that is the users can execute their application by PDA or Mobile handset considering the user want the power of processing like supercomputer. Because the broker manages for matching, monitoring, sending task, receiving results, and managing failed tasks, the user only sends the request and waits until it receives the results.
5. Managing failed tasks is simpler than the other methods. Because the broker can assign more priority to failed tasks and matches them as soon as possible.
6. Fault tolerance is possible. The broker can execute the tasks with more priority in duplicate mode.

## 4. Matching

Efficient resource selection in every resource management approach is one of the major challenges. There is one problem about matching in grid environment. Following model explains the problem:

1. The problem input
   1.1. A set of resources with their capabilities
   1.2. A set of tasks with their requirements
2. The problem output: Matching the best resource for each task
3. The problem purpose: Minimizing turnaround time

There are two managing models:

- *Local*
- *Global*

In Local model, the manager finds the best resource for each task locally regardless of other tasks. Whereas in Global model, the manager finds the proper resource for each task in relation with other tasks and the strong resource is assigned to strong task (The task is strong / weak if its requirement is high / low). Whereas in local model the manager may assign the strongest resource to first task that may be the weakest one. Therefore for the next task which may happen to be a strong task, the strong resource doesn't exist anymore. So it is better to apply the matching management in a global model.
We propose three methods for matching. They are compared using simulation in the next section. Three methods are:

1. *Optimum*
2. *Grid-JQA*
3. *Dup Grid-JQA*

That we can consider:

- n: the task number
- m: the resource number
- k: the number of QoS parameters

As it was explained, the resources should introduce themselves to the broker. Each introduction includes resource specifications as CPU, Memory, etc. Using schedulers, such as (Xen Scheduler Howto, 2005), a resource can assign a percentage of CPU to a given machine effectively regulating the CPU usage of the group of processes encapsulated in it. And also it includes some parameters such as the bandwidth and the delay were calculated or estimated by the broker. Finally the broker inserts the record of QoS parameters for each resource into the database. We define the vector $q^{res}$ which gives the capabilities of a resource as follows.

$$q^{res} = \left\langle q_1^{res}, q_2^{res}, \ldots, q_k^{res} \right\rangle \tag{1}$$

Generally it can be said that the client sends its request accompanied by vector of QoS parameters and the weights for the parameters as it appears in equations 2 and 3.

$$q^{task} = \left\langle q_1^{task}, q_2^{task}, \ldots, q_k^{task} \right\rangle \tag{2}$$

$$W = <w_1, w_2, \ldots, w_k> \quad 0 \le w_i \le 1 \quad \sum_{i=1}^{k} w_i = 1 \tag{3}$$

Each weight is used to show the importance of each parameter. For example, if CPU is important for one task, the client will set 1 for the CPU weight and zero for the others.
Note that, $q_i^{res}$ and $q_i^{task}$ have the same unit, and the broker compares $q_i^{res}$ with $q_i^{task}$ for each i from 1 to k. If the resource provides the requirements needed for the task, it can be chosen as the best matched resource. We introduce *satisfy operator* ₪. $R_i$ ₪ $T_j$ means that the resource Ri can satisfy the task Tj and guarantees QoS parameters.

$$R_i \text{ ₪ } T_j = \left(\left(\sum_{l=1}^{k} \frac{q_l^{Res_i}}{q_l^{task_j}} \times w_l\right) \ge 1\right) \quad (k = \text{the number of QoS parameters}) \tag{4}$$

The solution proposed here is that, we normalize the resource specification by the client requirement ($q_i^{res}$ / $q_i^{task}$) and therefore the summation will be possible whereas the units of each parameter are different such as byte, bps, Mflops. When the resource capability exceeds the task demand, ($q_i^{res}$ / $q_i^{task}$) is more than one.

Also, the client introduces a weight for each parameter to show the importance of the parameter. The weights range from 0 to 1 and the sum of all the weights is equal to one. We multiply the weight into ($q_i^{res}$ / $q_i^{task}$) as mentioned in (4). Finally the best match resource will be the one that can provide the maximum of summation in (4).

Note that matching is done by aggregating QoS parameters which simplifies the matching method. You may say that using aggregated QoS parameters, some requirements may be neglected. This argument can be addressed by the introduction of the proper weights. If user assigns a higher weight for a QoS parameter, the requirement surely will be met.

The proposed aggregation in (4) has one more advantage, whereas the overheads and matching time is concerned. It is obvious that the matching time for aggregated QoS is a fraction of time when we do not aggregate the k parameters.

The three methods for matching are proposed by using summation in (4).

### 4.1 Optimum

Assigning m resources to n tasks is the NP complete problem. The Optimum method has time complexity $O(n^3)$ to find the best matched resource for each task globally. Practically the Optimum method cannot be used because it has high overhead. We take into consideration the Optimum solution just for the sake of the comparison.

The problem is assigning m resources to n tasks with k QoS parameters. There are three matrices, one is $T_{n*k}$ matrix given by (5) for task requirements, another is $W_{n*k}$ matrix given by (6) for weight of requirements, and the other is $R_{k*m}$ matrix given by (7) for resource capabilities. These matrices are shown in below.

$$T_{n*k} = \begin{bmatrix} q_1^{task_1} & q_2^{task_1} & \cdots & q_k^{task_1} \\ q_1^{task_2} & q_2^{task_2} & \cdots & q_k^{task_2} \\ \vdots & \vdots & \ddots & \vdots \\ q_1^{task_n} & q_2^{task_n} & \cdots & q_k^{task_n} \end{bmatrix} \quad (5)$$

$$W_{n*k} = \begin{bmatrix} w_1^{task_1} & w_2^{task_1} & \cdots & w_k^{task_1} \\ w_1^{task_2} & w_2^{task_2} & \cdots & w_k^{task_2} \\ \vdots & \vdots & \ddots & \vdots \\ w_1^{task_n} & w_2^{task_n} & \cdots & w_k^{task_n} \end{bmatrix} \quad (6)$$

$$R_{k*m} = \begin{bmatrix} q_1^{res_1} & q_1^{res_2} & \cdots & q_1^{res_m} \\ q_2^{res_1} & q_2^{res_2} & \cdots & q_2^{res_m} \\ \vdots & \vdots & \ddots & \vdots \\ q_k^{res_1} & q_k^{res_2} & \cdots & q_k^{res_m} \end{bmatrix} \quad (7)$$

We define $WdT_{n*k}$ matrix as below.

$$WdT_{n*k} = \begin{bmatrix} w_1^{task_1}/q_1^{task_1} & w_2^{task_1}/q_2^{task_1} & \cdots & w_k^{task_1}/q_k^{task_1} \\ w_1^{task_2}/q_1^{task_2} & w_2^{task_2}/q_2^{task_2} & \cdots & w_k^{task_2}/q_k^{task_2} \\ \vdots & \vdots & \ddots & \vdots \\ w_1^{task_n}/q_1^{task_n} & w_2^{task_n}/q_2^{task_n} & \cdots & w_k^{task_n}/q_k^{task_n} \end{bmatrix} \quad (8)$$

So, equation (4) is based on multiplying $WdT_{n*k}$ matrix to $R_{k*m}$ matrix and the result is $V_{n*m}$ matrix given by (9) and (10).

$$V_{n*m} = WdT_{n*k} * R_{k*m} \quad (9)$$

$$V_{n*m} = \begin{bmatrix} \sum_{i=1}^{k}\left(\frac{w_i^{task_1}}{q_i^{task_1}} * q_i^{res_1}\right) & \sum_{i=1}^{k}\left(\frac{w_i^{task_1}}{q_i^{task_1}} * q_i^{res_2}\right) & \cdots & \sum_{i=1}^{k}\left(\frac{w_i^{task_1}}{q_i^{task_1}} * q_i^{res_m}\right) \\ \sum_{i=1}^{k}\left(\frac{w_i^{task_2}}{q_i^{task_2}} * q_i^{res_1}\right) & \sum_{i=1}^{k}\left(\frac{w_i^{task_2}}{q_i^{task_2}} * q_i^{res_2}\right) & \cdots & \sum_{i=1}^{k}\left(\frac{w_i^{task_2}}{q_i^{task_2}} * q_i^{res_m}\right) \\ \vdots & \vdots & \ddots & \vdots \\ \sum_{i=1}^{k}\left(\frac{w_i^{task_n}}{q_i^{task_n}} * q_i^{res_1}\right) & \sum_{i=1}^{k}\left(\frac{w_i^{task_n}}{q_i^{task_n}} * q_i^{res_2}\right) & \cdots & \sum_{i=1}^{k}\left(\frac{w_i^{task_n}}{q_i^{task_n}} * q_i^{res_m}\right) \end{bmatrix} \quad (10)$$

$V_{i,j}$ shows the value of (4) for assigning resource $j$ to task $i$. If $V_{i,j} = 1$, the resource $j$ exactly will provide the task $i$ requirements. If $V_{i,j} < 1$, the resource $j$ will be weaker than task $i$ requirements. If $V_{i,j} > 1$, the resource $j$ will be stronger than task $i$ requirements.
We define MAX unary operator that it gets one n*m matrix and produces n*3 matrix. In the following, the operator semantic is explained.

$$B_{n*3} = MAX\ A_{n*m} \quad (11)$$

$$B_{n*3} = \begin{bmatrix} \underset{j=1}{\overset{m}{Max}}\left(A_{1,j}\right) & \underset{j=1}{\overset{m}{IMax}}\left(A_{1,j}\right) & \begin{cases} True & if B_{1,1} = 0 \\ False & else \end{cases} \\ \underset{j=1}{\overset{m}{Max}}\left(A_{2,j}\right) & \underset{j=1}{\overset{m}{IMax}}\left(A_{2,j}\right) & \begin{cases} True & if B_{2,1} = 0 \\ False & else \end{cases} \\ \vdots & \vdots & \vdots \\ \underset{j=1}{\overset{m}{Max}}\left(A_{n,j}\right) & \underset{j=1}{\overset{m}{IMax}}\left(A_{n,j}\right) & \begin{cases} True & if B_{n,1} = 0 \\ False & else \end{cases} \end{bmatrix} \quad (12)$$

*Max* returns the maximum value for each row of operand and *IMax* returns the index of maximum value in each row of operand. Third column of matrix B shows that if the first column of matrix B is zero, it will be True (i.e. this row's task is tested for matching) otherwise it will be False (i.e. this row's task is not matched yet). So we define matrix $M_{n*3}$ as below:

$$M_{n*3} = MAX\ V_{n*m} \tag{13}$$

Fig. 2 shows the Optimum algorithm that matches the best resource for each task globally. The algorithm finds the values of the assignment of each resource to n tasks at first. The purpose is assigning the maximum value resource for each task. Next, the algorithm finds the maximum value at each row which belongs to a task. It is possible that the resource with maximum value in one row may be also is maximum in other rows. Because of that, the algorithm chooses the row (task) which has minimum value (this task has maximum requirements). If the number of matching becomes equal to number of tasks (n) (that is the all of third column of matrix M is True), then the algorithm will finish.

```
matched = 0;
V_{N*M} = WdT_{N*k} * R_{k*M} ;
while ( matched != N ) {
  M N*3 = MAX V N*M
  matched = FindMatch ( )
}

int FindMatch ( ) {
  int matched = 0;
  for ( i = 1; i <= N; i++) {
    if (M[i,3] == false ) {
      M[i,3] = true; Min = M[i,1]; Ind = M[i,2];
      for (j = i + 1; j < N ; j++) {
        if ( M[j,2] = M[i,2]) { // resource M[j,2] is max for both task i and task j
          M[j,3] = true;
          if (M[j,1] < Min ) { //select minimum value for matching with resource M[j,2]
            Min = M[j,1];
            Ind = M[j,2];
          }
        }
      } // end of finding minimum
      V[i,*] = 0; V[*,Ind} = 0; // matched task i with resource Ind
    }
    else matched ++;
  }
  return (matched);
}
```

Fig. 2. Optimum Algorithm

### 4.2 Grid-JQA

Grid-JQA has time complexity O($n$) instead of O($n^3$) for Optimum method and (as shown in next section by simulation), the difference between Grid-JQA and Optimum is acceptable. Grid-JQA uses threshold in (4) instead of finding maximum and minimum for each assignment (Fig. 2).

$$\text{Ri ฅ Tj} = \left(\left(\sum_{l=1}^{k} \frac{q_l^{Res_i}}{q_l^{task_j}} \times w_l\right) \geq \mathit{Threshold}\right) \text{ (k = the number of QoS parameters)} \quad (14)$$

The proposed solution is that instead of using maximum, we use a threshold (*Threshold* in (14)). If summation is more than the *Threshold*, the broker will choose it as the best matched resource.
The broker starts calculating (14) for record $R_1$. It keeps calculation till finds $R_i$ that satisfies the task. So the broker assigns $R_i$ to the task. For next task to be matched, the broker starts from $R_{i+1}$ in a round robin fashion, so that all resources can be covered.
Now, the problem is "what can be the amount of the threshold? ". For solving this problem, tacking into consideration that the active database is used, we introduce a rule in active database for calculating threshold in relation to environmental changes.
Suppose $q_k^R$ equals $q_k^T$ for all k from 1 to n to n (i.e. the requirements of task equal the capabilities of resource), then:

$$\sum_{k=1}^{n} \frac{q_k^{Ri}}{q_k^{Tj}} \times w_k = \sum_{k=1}^{n} 1 \times w_k = 1 \quad (15)$$

So the minimum of threshold is 1.
If $q_k^R$ equals $P^*( q_k^T )$ for all k from 1 to n, then:

$$\sum_{k=1}^{n} \frac{q_k^{Ri}}{q_k^{Tj}} \times w_k = \sum_{k=1}^{n} P \times w_k = P \quad (16)$$

Therefore if we assign P to the threshold, it means that the selected resource should provide P times capability more than the requirements by the task.
Therefore when there are a lot of strong and free resources it is better that the broker assigns the strong resource to weak task. So the *Threshold* should be greater than one and the broker should select a resource precisely. In this method Grid-JQA acts like an Optimum method. But when there are a few strong resources it is better that to set the threshold equal one. So the broker should select a resource as soon as it finds a free resource and the broker does not wait for strong resources.
The value of threshold is changed by a rule of active database related to the number of times that equation 14 returns true or false. In this way if the number of true is more than false, the rule should be increased threshold for finding strong resource and otherwise should be decreased threshold for assigning resource to task as soon as possible.
Next section shows that Grid-JQA is similar to Optimum using simulation. But Grid-JQA has time complexity O(n) instead of time complexity $O(n^3)$ for Optimum.

**4.3 Dup Grid-JQA**

After assigning m resources to n tasks, definitely some tasks are executed in weak resources which results is increasing the turnaround time of entire application. Dup Grid-JQA assigns free strong resources to tasks executed in weak resources in duplicate mode. Reference (Kondo, 2005) shows that for the application with 100 tasks, 90% of the tasks are completed in about 39 minutes, but the application does not finish until 79 minutes have passed, which is almost identical to the turnaround time for a much larger application with 400 tasks.

There are two main causes of this plateau. The first cause is task failures that occur near the completion of the application. When a task fails, it must be restarted from scratch, and when this occurs near the end of the application execution, it will delay the application completion. The second cause is tasks assigned to slow resources. Once a task is assigned to a slow host, a FCFS scheduler without task preemption or replication capabilities will be forced to wait until the slow resource produces the result.
Dup Grid-JQA is a solution for the second cause. As when the 60% of execution time of application completes Dup Grid-JQA schedules remaining tasks in duplicate mode. In duplicate mode, the broker will send that results which is obtained first. Next section shows that duplicate method decreases the turnaround time significantly.
As the number of tasks gets large in comparison with the number of resources in the platform, the plateau becomes less significant, thus justifies the use of a FCFS strategy. However, for applications with a relatively small number of tasks, resource selection could improve the performance of application significantly.

## 5. Simulation

There are three subsections: 1) Application Definition 2) Resource definition 3) Matching methods and comparisons.

### 5.1 Application definition

We use XML as input language. Fig. 3 shows one example of application definition in simulation.
The random function is used to provide random number between Min and Max for each field in simulation so that the environment gets more similar to grid environment that rapidly changes.


```
<Applications>
 <Application>
  <Name>a</Name>
  <CpuRequestMin>1000</CpuRequestMin>
  <CpuRequestMax>6000</CpuRequestMax>
  <CpuScoreMin>.9</CpuScoreMin>
  <CpuScoreMax>.9</CpuScoreMax>
  <MemoryNeedMin>300</MemoryNeedMin>
  <MemoryNeedMax>300</MemoryNeedMax>
  <BandwidthRequestMin>70</BandwidthRequestMin>
  <BandwidthRequestMax>70</BandwidthRequestMax>
  <CountMin>20</CountMin>
  <CountMax>20</CountMax>
  <CpuCycleMin>800000000</CpuCycleMin>
  <CpuCycleMax>800000000</CpuCycleMax>
 </Application>
</Applications>
```


Fig. 3. Application Definition

### 5.2 Resource definition

Fig. 4 shows one example of resource definition by XML language. The requirement of memory must be completely satisfied by the resource, but the assignment of the memory more than requirements can not improve performance. Thus the requirement of memory is not used in aggregated QoS parameters in equation 14. Therefore the weight of bandwidth is the weight of CPU subtracted from one. The CPU power and bandwidth have a main role in improving turnaround time and if the broker assigns stronger CPU or more bandwidth, this assignment will cause the reduction of turnaround time. The application definition consists of the following fields:

1. Min/Max of CPU power requirement in cycle/sec (CpuRequestMin/Max)
2. Min/Max of CPU requirement's weight (CpuScoreMin/Max)
3. Min/Max of memory requirement (MemoryNeedMin/Max)
4. Min/Max of bandwidth requirement (BandwidthRequestMin/Max)
5. Min/Max of the number of tasks in application (CountMin/Max)
6. Min/Max of size of tasks in cycle/sec (CpuCycleMin/Max)

```
<Resources>
 <Resource>
  <Name>r1</Name>
        <CpuPowerMin>1000</CpuPowerMin>
        <CpuPowerMax>6000</CpuPowerMax>
  <MemoryMin>400</MemoryMin>
  <MemoryMax>400</MemoryMax>
  <BandwidthMin>100</BandwidthMin>
  <BandwidthMax>100</BandwidthMax>
  <StopQueueTimeMin>100000</StopQueueTimeMin>
  <StopQueueTimeMax>100000000</StopQueueTimeMax>
 </Resource>
</Resources>
```

Fig. 4. Resource Definition

The resource definition consists of the following fields:

1. Min/Max of CPU cycle capabilities in cycle/sec (CpuPowerMin/Max)
2. Min/Max of memory in KB (MemoryMin/Max)
3. Min/Max of available bandwidth from the resource to the broker (BandwidthMin/Max)
4. Min/Max of availability duration for the resource (StopQueueTimeMin/Max)

As the application definition, the random function generates the random number between Min and Max for each above fields.

**5.3 Matching methods and comparisons**

In simulation we use following five methods for matching:

1. The General method that matches resources with tasks in FIFO mode (first task to first free resource) regardless of QoS parameters.
2. The Optimum method, as described in section 4.1, selects the best resources for tasks but it has time complexity $O(n^3)$.
3. The Grid-JQA, our proposed solution, does matching almost like Optimum method but it has much less time complexity (O(n)) than Optimum matching.
4. Dup Grid-JQA, out proposed solution, that adds new feature to Grid-JQA. This feature is duplicate execution of delayed tasks (i.e. executed in weak resources).
5. The Wait method. In all other methods, if the broker does not find the proper resource, it will assign the best available resource to task. So the task will not wait for the proper resource. But in the Wait method tasks wait until the proper resource is found.

In this simulation, we assume that the CPU cycle is from 1000 to 6000, and all resources have same amount of memory and bandwidth. The number of tasks in application is 20 and the CPU weight is 0.9. All tasks require same amount of memory and bandwidth.

We choose the CPU cycle requirement of application in range 1000 to 6000 which is similar to the range chosen for resource's CPU cycle power. We do simulation 6 times and each time we consider the amount of CPU cycle requirement 1000, 2000, 3000, 4000, 5000 and 6000. For each CPU cycle requirement, the simulation is repeated 100 times and finally we use the average turnaround time.

Fig. 5 shows the result of simulation for 6000 CPU cycle requirement with resource number from 10 (half of the task number) to 60 (three time more than the task number). After this, in all figures, horizontal axis indicates the number of the resources, and the vertical axis indicates the turnaround time in msec.

The simulation results show that:

1. Executing in weak resource in comparison with waiting to proper resource produces less turnaround time.
2. For strong requirement Grid-JQA is like Optimum method. Because, if Grid-JQA does not find the proper resource, it will assign the best resource as like Optimum.
3. General method does not change after 20 free resources, because it uses the 20 first free resources.
4. Dup Grid-JQA has minimum turnaround time when the number of free resource is from 10 (half of the task number) to 30 (1.5 times more than the task number). Because there are some tasks executed in weak resources (e.g. 1000-2000 CPU cycle/sec), they can find chance of executing in strong resources (e.g. 5000-6000 CPU cycle/sec). So the turnaround time is decreased.
5. When the number of free resources is less than the number of tasks, the Optimum method and Grid-JQA do not have better performance than the General method. They improve the results when the number of free resources gets more than the number of tasks. This situation is more likely because we suppose the environment has a lot of free resources (e.g. Internet).
6. Also, when the number of free resources is more than two times of the task number, the results are not improving.

Comparing below figures, we can find following results:

1. Most of the time, Grid-JQA has less turnaround time than Wait method (figures 5, 6, and 10). Only when the CPU cycle request is low (e.g. 2000 and 3000) and the number of free resource is from 10 ( half of the task number ) to 30 (1.5 times ore than the task

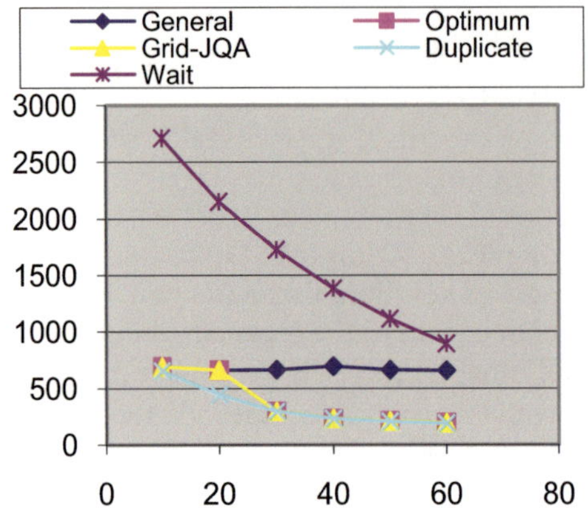


Fig. 5. 6000 CPU cycle request

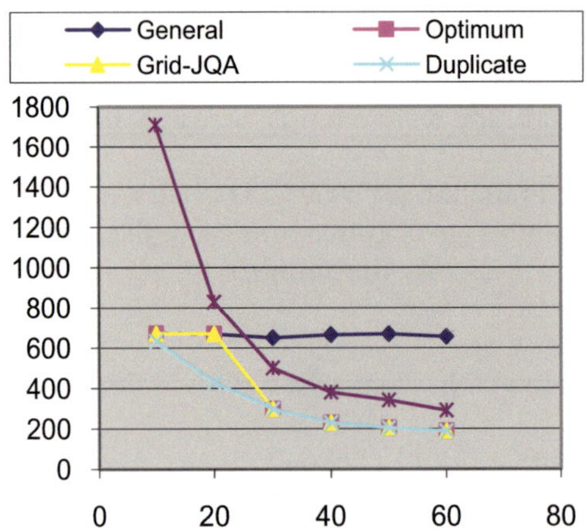


Fig. 6. 5000 CPU cycle request

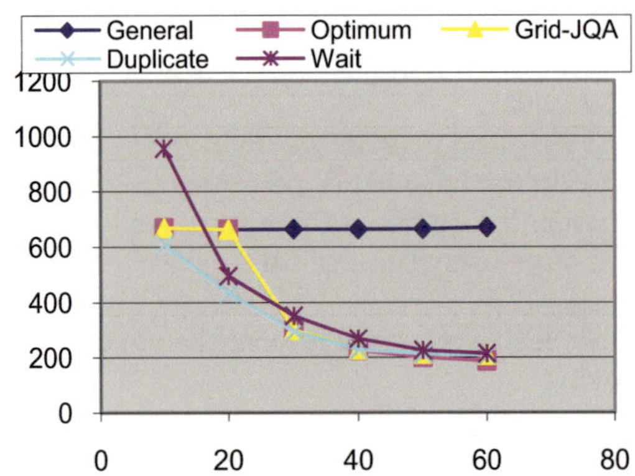


Fig. 7. 4000 CPU cycle request

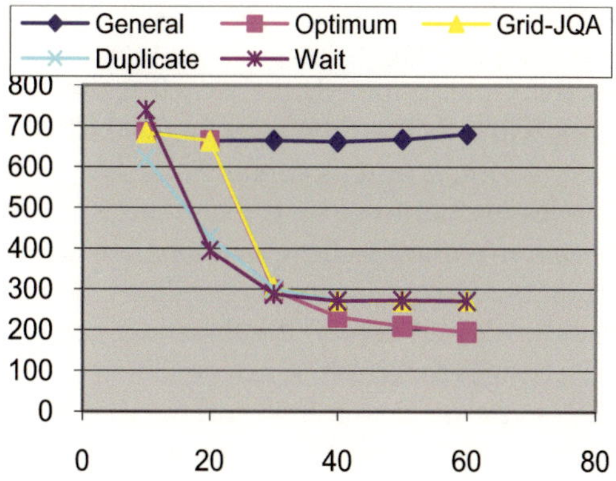


Fig. 8. 3000 CPU cycle request

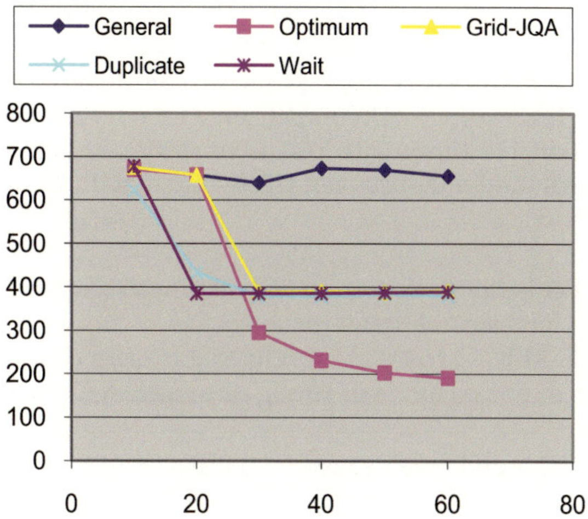


Fig. 9. 2000 CPU cycle request

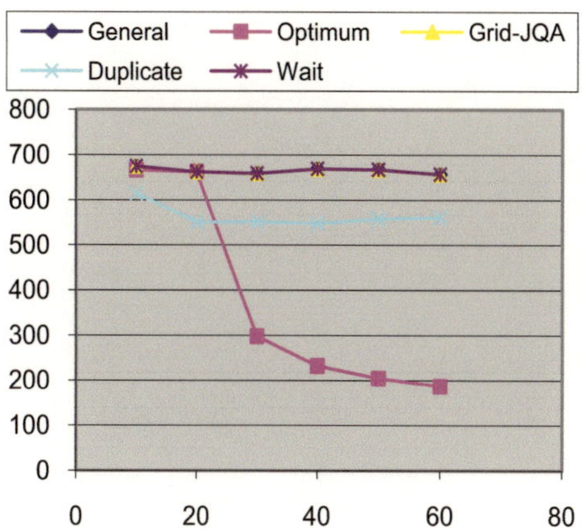


Fig. 10. 1000 CPU cycle request

number), the Wait method has less turnaround time (Figures 8 and 9). So executing in weak resource is better than waiting for proper resource.

2. Comparing Grid-JQA and Optimum method shows that they are same for strong request (e.g. 4000-6000) in fig. 5, 6 and 7. The difference for 3000 CPU cycle request is ignorable. The difference between Grid-JQA and Optimum is for low requests (e.g. 1000-2000) that Optimum method has less turnaround time than Grid-JQA. But two points should be noted: First the user has low request so the execution time is longer and if the user wants less execution time, it should require more capabilities. Second, in this simulation the threshold is one, but as explained before, the threshold can be changed dynamically in related to environment changes so Grid-JQA can be similar to Optimum method.
   For example if the CPU cycle request is 1000 and the threshold is 2, as shown in fig. 11 the difference between Grid-JQA and Optimum will be decreased. By increasing the threshold, the difference decreases. So with changing the threshold, Grid-JQA approaches to Optimum method.
3. Grid-JQA, our proposed solution, can provide the results close to the Optimum method and has the advantage of time complexity O(n) instead of $O(n^3)$.
4. Most of the time Dup Grid-JQA has less turnaround time in comparison with other methods. And also it has less cost in comparison with retrying and check pointing.

Finally, we do simulation 100 times with resources randomly between (1000 - 6000) and application with requests randomly between (1000 - 6000) with 20 tasks. Fig. 12 shows the results of this simulation.

Final results are:

1. Wait method has not better performance and starting execution in available resource is better than waiting for a suitable resource.
2. Adaptation (Dup Grid-JQA) has good results that is tasks executed in weak resources, can be executed in duplicate mode in strong resources. And the broker uses the results produced sooner.

So Dup Grid-JQA is suitable and reliable method for matching in grid environment.

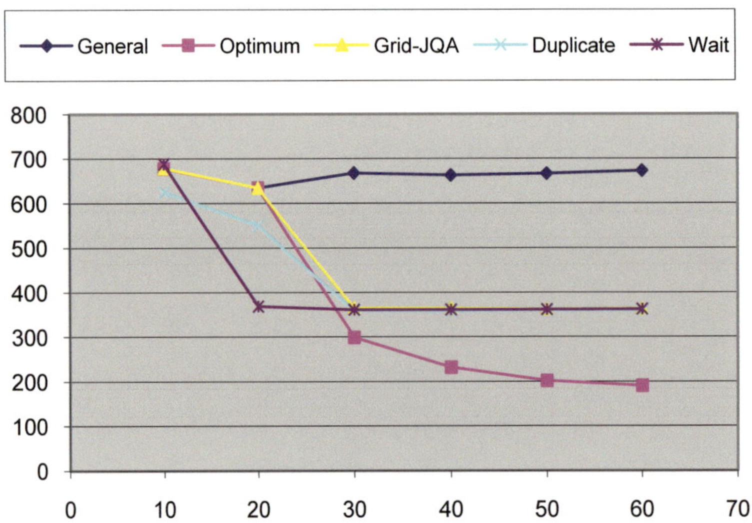


Fig. 11. 1000 cpu cycle request with threshold is 2

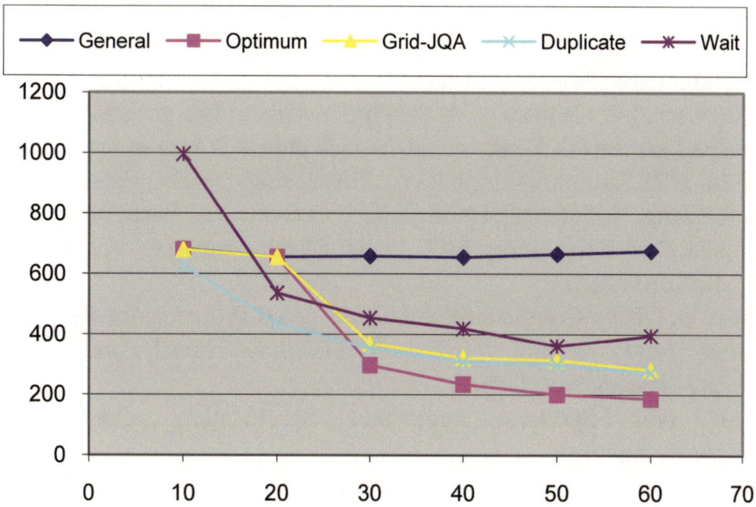


Fig. 12. Simulation for random request (1000-6000) and random capabilities (1000-6000)

## 6. Conclusions

This chapter discusses the matching methods in grid environment when QoS parameters are concerned. The Optimum method for matching n tasks with m resources is proposed by using matrices formalism. Grid-JQA and Dup Grid-JQA are proposed and compared with Optimum method.

Three heuristic approaches have been designed and compared via simulations to match tasks which take into account the QoS requested by the tasks, and at the same time, to minimize the tasks makespan as much as possible.

The Optimum method has time complexity $O(n^3)$ that is decreased to O(n) by using Grid-JQA with ignorable differences. The Dup Grid-JQA resource selection selects resources based on threshold scheduling and fault tolerance by duplicating the execution of failed tasks or delayed tasks. The simulation shows that Dup Grid-JQA performs best.

Meanwhile, the Wait method is evaluated and the simulation results show that executing in available resource has better performance than waiting for proper resource. Finally, Dup Grid-JQA has minimum turnaround time and it is the best solution for matching in grid environment.

In future, we plan to implement our resource manager as a part of the Globus Toolkit and to do various experiments to measure the efficiency of the resource manager and job duplication. Also, we will investigate ways to select the best value of the threshold.

## 7. References

Bubendorfer, K. (2006). Fine grained resource reservation in open Grid economies, *in: Proceedings of the 2nd IEEE International Conference on e-Science and Grid Computing*, e-Science '06.

Buyya, R.; Abramson, D.; Giddy, J. & Stockinger, H. (1980). Economic models for resource management and scheduling in Grid computing, *Concurrency and Computation: Practice and Experience* 14, 1104_1113.

Chapin, S.; Karpovich, J. & Grimshaw, A. (1999). The Legion Resource Management System, *Proceedings oh the 5th Workshop on Job Scheduling Strategies for Parallel Processing,* April 16, 1999, San Juan, Puerto Rico, USA, Springer Verlag Press, Germany.

Darby III, P.J. & Tzeng, N.-F. (2010). Decentralized QoS-Aware Checkpointing Arrangement in Mobile Grid Computing. IEEE Trans. *Mobile computing,* vol. 9, no. 8,pp. 1173-1186, AUGUST. 2010.

Das, A. & Grosu, D. (2005). Combinatorial Auction-Based Protocols for Resource Allocation in Grids, *in: Proceedings of the 19th IEEE International Parallel and Distributed Processing Symposium,* IPDPS'05.

Document for Web Services Agreement Specification, Open Grid Forum. http://www.ogf.org.

Foster, I.; Kesselman, C.; et al. (1999). A Distributed resource management architecture that supports advance reservation and co-allocation. *In proceedings of the international workshop on Quality of Service,* page 27-36

Foster, I. & Kesselman, C. (2004). *"The GRID: Blueprint for a New Computing Infrastructure",* 2nd Edition.Morgan-Kaufmann, San Mateo, CA.

Goswami, K. & Gupta, A. (2008). Resource selection in Grids using contract net, *in: Proceedings of 16th Euromicro Conference on Parallel,* Distributed and Network-Based Processing.

Han, Y. & Youn, C.-H. (2009). A new grid resource management mechanism with resource-aware policy administrator for SLA-constrained applications, *Future Generation Computer Systems* 25,768_778.

Hewlett Packard Inc. espeak: The Universal Language of E-Services. http://www.e-speak.net/.

Kakarontzas, G. & Savvas, I.K. (2006). Agent-based resource discovery and selection for dynamic Grids, *in: Proceedings of 15th IEEE International Workshops on Enabling Technologies: Infrastructure for Collaborative Enterprises,* WETICE '06.

Khanli, L. M. & Analoui, M. (2006a). "Grid-JQA - a new architecture for QoS-guaranteed grid computing system", *Proc. of the 14th Euromicro Conference on Parallel, Distributed and Network-based processing,* France, PDP2006, Feb 15-17.

Khanli, L. M. & Analoui, M. (2006b). "Grid-JQA - grid java based quality of service management by active database", *Proc. of the 4th Australian Symposium on Grid Computing and e-Research,* AusGrid06, Jan.

Khanli, L. M. & Analoui, M. (2008). An approach to Grid resource selection and fault management based on ECA rules, *Future Generation Computer Systems* 24 (4).

Kolano, P.Z. (2004). Surfer: An extensible pull-based framework for resource selection and ranking, *in: Proceedings of the 4th IEEE International Symposium on Cluster Computing and the Grid.*

Kondo, D. (2005). "Scheduling task parallel applications for rapid turnaround on desktop grids", Ph.D. thesis, university of California, San Diego

Leal, K.; Huedo, E. & Llorente, I.M. (2009). A decentralized model for scheduling independent tasks in federated Grid, *Future Generation Computer Systems* 25 (8) 840_852.

Litzkow, M.J.; Livny, M. & Mutka, M.W. (1988). Condor: A Hunter of Idle Workstations, *in: Proceedings of the 8th International Conference on Distributed Computing Systems.*

Liu, C.; Yang, L.; Foster, I. & Angulo, D. (2002). Design and Evaluation of a Resource Selection Framework for Grid Applications, *in: Proceedings of the 11th IEEE International Symposium on High Performance Distributed Computing.*

Liu, C. & Foster, I. (2004). "A constraint language approach to matchmaking". *In International workshop on Research Issues on Data Engineering* (RIDE 2004).

Ludwig, S.A. & Reyhani, S.M.S. (2006). Semantic approach to service discovery in a Grid environment, *Future Generation Computer Systems* 4 (1)1_13.

Neary, M.; Phipps, A.; Richman, S. & Cappello, P. (2000). Javelin 2.0: Java-Based Parallel Computing on the Internet, *Proceedings of European Parallel Computing Conference (Euro-Par 2000)*, Germany.

Raman, R.; Livny, M. & Solomon, M. (1998). Matchmaking: Distributed resource management for high throughput computing, *in: Proceedings of the 7th IEEE International Symposium on High Performance.*

Raman, R.; Livny, M. & Solomon, M. (2003). Policy driven heterogeneous resource coallocation with gangmatching, *in: Proceedinsg of 12th IEEE International Symposium on High Performance Distributed Computing*. In HPDC-12.

Rodero, I.; Guim, F.; Corbalan, J.; Fong, L. & Sadjadi, S. M. (2010). Grid broker selection strategies using aggregated resource information, *Future Generation Computer Systems* 26 (2010) 72_86.

Sameer Singh Chauhan & R. C. Joshi, "A Heuristic for QoS Based Independent Task Scheduling in Grid Environment", *5th International Conference on Industrial and Information Systems* (ICIIS'10), Jul 29 - Aug 01, 2010a, India pp. 102-106.

Sameer Singh Chauhan & R. C. Joshi, "A Weighted Mean Time Min- Min Max-Min Selective Scheduling Strategy for Independent Tasks on Grid", *In proceedings of 2nd IEEE Advance Computing Conference,* pp 4-9, February, 2010b.

Selvi Somasundaram, T.; Amarnath, B.R.; Kumar, R.; Balakrishnan, P.; Rajendar, K.; Rajiv, R.; Kannan, G.; Rajesh Britto, G.; Mahendran, E & Madusudhanan, B. (2010). CARE Resource Broker: A framework for scheduling and supporting virtual, *Future Generation Computer Systems* 26 (2010) 337_347

Smith, R.G. (1980). The contract net protocol: High level communication and control in a distributed problem solver, *IEEE Transactions on Computers* 29 (12).

Tangmunarunkit, H.; Decker, S. & Kesselman, C. (2003). Ontology-based Resource Matching in the Grid, *in: Proceedings of workshop on Semantics in Peer-to- Peer and Grid Computing,* SemPGRID'03.

Uddi.com. UDDI: Technical White Paper.http://www.uddi.com/pubs/Iru UDDI Technical White Paper.pdf.

Wang, C.-M.; Chen, H.-M.; Hsu, C.-C. & Lee J. (2010). Dynamic resource selection heuristics for a non-reserved bidding-based Grid environment, *Future Generation Computer Systems* 26, 183_197.

Xen Scheduler Howto. 2005: http://xen.terrabox.com/index.php/Sched-HOWTO.

Xiao, L.; Zhu, Y.; Ni, L.M. & Xu, Z. (2008). Incentive-based scheduling for market-like computational Grids, *IEEE Transactions on Parallel and Distributed Systems* 19 (7).

Yu, H.; Bai, X. & Marinescu, D.C. (2005). Workflow management and resource discovery for an intelligent Grid, *Future Generation Computer Systems* 31 (7) 797_811.

# 4

# Autonomic Network-Aware Metascheduling for Grids: A Comprehensive Evaluation

Agustín C. Caminero[1], Omer Rana[2],
Blanca Caminero[3] and Carmen Carrión[4]
[1]*The National University of Distance Education*
[2]*Cardiff School of Computer Science*
[3,4]*The University of Castilla La Mancha*
[1,3,4]*Spain*
[2]*UK*

## 1. Introduction

Grid technologies allow the aggregation of dispersed heterogeneous resources for supporting large-scale parallel applications in science, engineering and commerce (Foster & Kesselman (2003)). Current Grid systems are highly variable environments, made of a series of independent organizations sharing their resources, creating what is known as *Virtual Organizations* (VOs) (Foster & Kesselman (2003)). This variability makes Quality of Service (*QoS*) highly desirable, though often very difficult to achieve in practice. One reason for this limitation is the lack of control over the network that connects various components of a Grid system. Achieving an *end-to-end* QoS is often difficult, as without resource reservation any guarantees on QoS are often hard to satisfy. However, for applications that need a timely response (i.e., collaborative visualization (Marchese & Brajkovska (2007))), the Grid must provide users with some kind of assurance about the use of resources – a non-trivial subject when viewed in the context of network QoS (Roy (2001)). In a VO, entities communicate with each other using an interconnection network – resulting in the network playing an essential role in Grid systems (Roy (2001)).

In (Caminero et al. (2009a)), authors proposed an autonomic network-aware Grid scheduling architecture as a possible solution, which can make scheduling decisions based on the current status of the system (with particular focus on network capability). This architecture focuses on the interchange of I/O files between users and computing resources, and the impact these interchanges have on the performance received by users. This work presented a performance evaluation in which the proposal was compared with one existing non network-aware meta-scheduler. Besides, authors have also presented an evaluation in which the proposal is compared with an existing network-aware meta-scheduler (Caminero et al. (2009b)).

The main contribution of this work is a comprehensive evaluation in which our proposal is compared with existing commercial meta-schedulers and heuristics found in literature, both network-aware and non-network-aware. These proposals are the GridWay meta-scheduler (Huedo et al. (2007)), the Gridbus Broker (Venugopal et al. (2008)), Min-min (Freund et al. (1998)), Max-min (Freund et al. (1998)), and XSufferage (Casanova et al. (2000)). Thus, the benefits of taking the network into account when performing meta-scheduling tasks is evaluated, along with the need to react autonomically to changes in the system.

The structure of the paper is as follows: Section 2 reviews the two existing meta-schedulers against which our proposal is evaluated along with other heuristics found in literature. Section 3 shows a sample scenario in which an autonomic scheduler can be used and harnessed. Section 4 shows the solution we propose – consisting of a network-aware autonomic meta-scheduling architecture capable of adapting its behavior depending on the status of the system. In this section the main functionalities of the architecture are presented, including models for predicting latencies in a network and in computing resources. Section 5 presents a performance evaluation of our approach. Section 6 draws conclusions and provides suggestions for future work.

## 2. Meta-scheduling in Grids

Since the purpose of this work is the provision of QoS in Grids by means of an efficient meta-scheduling of jobs to computing resources, existing proposals aimed at this point are reviewed in this Section. Imamagic et al. (2005) provide a survey of Grid meta-scheduling strategies, some of them are reviewed below. Also, an in-depth study of meta-schedulers in the context of TeraGrid is presented in (Metascheduling Requirements Analysis Team (2006)), where key capabilities of meta-schedulers are identified, and meta-schedulers are classified based on them.

In this section two widely used meta-schedulers are reviewed, along with other proposals found in literature. These will be used to compare our proposal. The meta-schedulers reviewed are GridWay and Gridbus, and the heuristics are Min-min, Max-min, and XSufferage.

### 2.1 GridWay meta-scheduler

The *GridWay* meta-scheduler (Huedo et al. (2007)) enables large-scale, reliable and efficient sharing of computing resources (clusters, computing farms, servers, supercomputers...), managed by different *Local Resource Management* (*LRM*) systems, (such as PBS (Mateescu (2000)), SGE (Gentzsch (2001)), or Condor (Litzkow et al. (1988))) within a single organization (enterprise Grid) or scattered across several administrative domains (partner or supply-chain Grid). GridWay is a Globus project (Globus Projects (2010)), adhering to Globus philosophy and guidelines for collaborative development. Besides, GridWay comes with the Globus releases from version GT4.0.5 onwards. GridWay has been used for a variety of research works, among others (Vázquez et al. (2010)); (Bobroff et al. (2008)); (Tomás et al. (2010)). Thus, it can be concluded that GridWay is a widely used tool, and that is the reason why it has been chosen to compare our proposal with.

GridWay works as follows. Users willing to submit jobs to the Grid infrastructure managed by GridWay need to generate a *job template*. This template includes the information needed for job execution, such as the names of input, output and executable files, as well as some control parameters related to meta-scheduling, performance, fault tolerance or resource selection, among others.

The way how GridWay performs the meta-scheduling is explained the following. There are two parameters related to this issue within the job template, namely `REQUIREMENTS` and

RANK. They together allow users to specify the criteria used to select the most appropriate computing resource to run their jobs, in a two-step process.
The REQUIREMENTS tag is processed first. Within this tag, the user can specify the *minimal requirements* needed to run the job. Thus, it acts as a filter on all the resources known to GridWay. As a result, only the resources that fulfill the REQUIREMENTS condition are considered in the next step. Then, with the RANK tag, the characteristics taken into account when ordering resources are specified. This means that all the resources that fulfill the REQUIREMENTS specifications are ordered following the criteria specified with the RANK tag (i.e., the set of resources is ordered with regard to their amount of free RAM). For both tags, several characteristics as type of CPU, operating system, CPU speed, amount of free memory, etc. can be specified. Network status is not one of them at present. Many of these values are gathered through the Globus GIS module (Czajkowski et al. (2001)), while others (specifically the dynamic ones, such as amount of free RAM) are monitored through Ganglia (Massie et al. (2004)).

### 2.2 The gridbus broker

The *Gridbus Broker* (Venugopal et al. (2008)) is a network-aware meta-scheduler that mediates access to distributed resources by (a) discovering suitable data sources for a given analysis scenario, (b) discovering suitable computing resources, (c) optimally mapping analysis jobs to computing resources, (d) deploying and monitoring job execution on selected resources, (e) accessing data from local or remote data source during job execution and (f) collecting and presenting results. The broker supports a declarative and dynamic parametric programming model for creating Grid applications (Venugopal et al. (2006)).
The Gridbus Broker has been designed to operate with different Grid middleware frameworks and toolkits such as Globus 2.4 (Foster & Kesselman (1997)), that primarily runs on Unix-class machines, and Alchemi (Luther et al. (2005)), which is a .NET based Grid computing platform for Microsoft Windows-enabled computers. Hence, it is possible to create a cross-platform Grid implementation using the Gridbus Broker (Venugopal et al. (2006)).
The meta-scheduling of jobs is performed as follows. The broker tries to choose the best resource from the users' point of view, this is, the resource that can have jobs executed the fastest. Thus, Gridbus works by trying to minimize the amount of data transfer involved for executing a job by dispatching jobs to compute servers which are close to the source of data. The meta-scheduler uses the *average job completion ratio* (the ratio of the number of jobs completed to the number of jobs allocated) to evaluate the performance of the computing resources. The job completion ratio of a resource is calculated as follows:

$$r_S = \frac{J_C}{J_Q} \quad (1)$$

where $r_s$ is the job completion ratio for a particular resource, $J_C$ is the number of jobs that were completed on that particular resource in the previous polling interval, and $J_Q$ is the number of jobs that were queued on that resource in the previous allocation. Then, the meta-scheduler calculates the average job completion ratio, $R_S$, at the $N^{th}$ polling interval as:

$$R_S = R_S^{'} * (1 - 1/N) + r_S/N \quad (2)$$

where $R_S^{'}$ is the average job completion ratio for the $N - 1^{th}$ polling interval. The averaging of the ratio provides a measure of the resource performance from the beginning of the

**Algorithm 1** Min-min scheduling algorithm.

1: Let $T$ = bag of independent tasks<br>
2: Let $t_i$ = a task<br>
3: Let $R$ = set of computing resources<br>
4: Let $r_j$ = a computing resource<br>
5: Let $C_i^j$ = expected completion time of task $t_i$ in the computing resource $r_j$<br>
6: **repeat**<br>
7:     **for all** $t_i$ in $T$ **do**<br>
8:         **for all** $r_j$ in $R$ **do**<br>
9:             calculate $C_i^j$<br>
10:         **end for**<br>
11:     **end for**<br>
12:     find the task $t_i$ with the *minimum* expected completion time<br>
13:     find the resource $r_j$ that obtains the *minimum* expected completion time for task $t_i$<br>
14:     map task $t_i$ to resource $r_j$<br>
15:     remove $t_i$ from $T$<br>
16: **until** $T$ is empty

meta-scheduling process and can be considered as an approximate indicator of the future performance of that resource.

Each resource is assigned a *job limit*, the maximum number of jobs that can be allocated among those jobs waiting for execution, which considers its average job completion ratio and the resource share available for Grid users. The meta-scheduler then iterates through the list of unassigned jobs one at a time. For each job, it first selects the data host that contains the file required for the job and then, selects a compute resource that has the highest available bandwidth to that data host. If this allocation plus previously allocated jobs and current running jobs on the resource exceeds the job limit for that resource, then the meta-scheduler looks for the next available nearest compute resource.

Thus, it is necessary to keep the bandwidth between each data host and each compute resource, which makes this approach unfeasible for a real-sized Grid, because of the huge amount of bandwidth data to keep. An example of such a real-sized Grid is LHC Computing Grid (LCG (LHC Computing Grid) Project (2010)), which has around 200 sites and tens of thousands of CPU (for a map showing real time information, see (GridPP, Real Time Monitor (2010))).

### 2.3 Heuristics for meta-scheduling

Three heuristics are reviewed in this section, namely Min-min, Max-min, and XSufferage.

*Min-min* (Freund et al. (1998)) is presented in Algorithm 1, which works as follows. First, an estimation on the completion time of each task in each computing resource is calculated (line 9). Then, the task with the minimum completion time is chosen (line 12), and mapped to the computing resource providing that completion time (line 14). After that, the task is removed from the bag of tasks (line 15), and estimated completion times are updated for all the remaining tasks (line 9).

*Max-min* (Freund et al. (1998)) is similar to *Min-min*, the only difference is that instead of getting the minimum expected completion time (line 13), the *maximum* expected completion time is chosen. Max-min is likely to do better than the Min-min heuristic in cases where

**Algorithm 2** XSufferage scheduling algorithm.

1: Let $T$ = bag of independent tasks
2: Let $t_i$ = a task
3: Let $R$ = set of computing resources
4: Let $r_j$ = a computing resource
5: Let $C_i^j$ = expected completion time of task $t_i$ in the computing resource $r_j$
6: Let $m_i$ = minimum completion time for task $t_i$
7: Let $m_i^2$ = second minimum completion time for task $t_i$
8: Let $S_i$ = sufferage value of task $t_i$
9: **repeat**
10:     **for all** $t_i$ in $T$ **do**
11:         **for all** $r_j$ in $R$ **do**
12:             calculate $C_i^j$
13:         **end for**
14:     **end for**
15:     **for all** $t_i$ in $T$ **do**
16:         calculate $m_i$ and $m_i^2$
17:         find the computing resource $r_j$ that gives $m_i$
18:         $S_i = m_i^2 - m_i$
19:     **end for**
20:     find the task $t_i$ with the *maximum* $S_i$
21:     map task $t_i$ to resource $r_j$
22:     remove $t_i$ from $T$
23: **until** $T$ is empty

there are many more shorter tasks than long tasks. For example, if there is only one long task, Max-min will execute many short tasks concurrently with the long task. The resulting makespan might just be determined by the execution time of the long task in theses cases. Min-min, however, first finishes the shorter tasks and then executes the long task, increasing the makespan.

*XSufferage* (Casanova et al. (2000)) calculates the priority of a task based on its sufferage value. The sufferage of a task is calculated as the difference between the least and the second least expected completion time for that task. Algorithm 2 presents this approach. First of all, and in the same way as the algorithms presented before, the expected completion time of each task in each computing resource is calculated (line 12). Then, the sufferage value for each task is calculated as explained above (line 18). The next step is finding the task with the highest sufferage value, this is, the task that would suffer the most if it were not mapped to the resource with the lowest estimated completion time. Then, this task is mapped to the resource providing the lowest estimated completion time for it (line 21), and it is removed from the bag of tasks (line 22).

## 3. Sample scenario

A sample scenario in which an autonomic scheduler could be used to improve the QoS perceived by users is depicted in Figure 1. In this scenario, a user has a number of jobs, $m$, and requires computing resource(s) to run his jobs. The user will have some Quality of Service

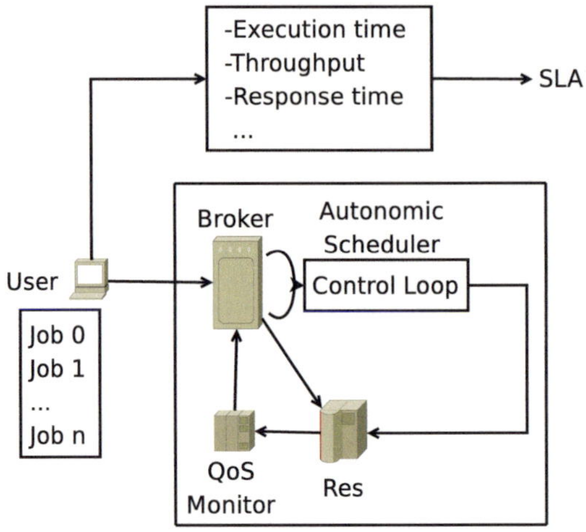


Fig. 1. Scenario.

(*QoS*) requirements, such as execution time, throughput, response time, etc. Each such QoS requirement could be represented as $(a_1, a_2, ..., a_n)$, where each $a_i$ is a constraint associated with an attribute (e.g. $a_1$ : *throughput* $> 5$). Hence, a user's job $m_i$ could be expressed as a set of constraints $\{a_j\}$ over one or more resources – expressed by the set $R = \{r_1, ..., r_k\}$. Let us consider that the QoS requirement of the user is that all his jobs must be finished within one hour. This deadline includes the transmission of jobs and input data to the resources, and the delivery of results. In order to have his jobs executed within the deadline, the user will contact a broker, and will tell it his QoS requirements. The role of the broker is to discover resource properties that fulfill the QoS constraints identified in the job. The constraint matching is undertaken by the broker – by contacting a set of known registry services. Once suitable resources have been discovered, the next step involves establishing Service Level Agreements (*SLAs*) to provide some degree of assurance that the requested QoS requirements are likely to be met by the resources.

When the user has already submitted his jobs to the computing resource, the broker will monitor the resource, to check whether the QoS requirements of the user are being met or not. The broker must decide when corrective action should be taken if particular QoS constraints are not being met. For instance, in our example, the user requirement is a one hour deadline; hence, the broker may consider that after 30 minutes half of the jobs should be finished (assuming that all the jobs require only one CPU). If this is not true, and less jobs have been finished, then the broker may decide to allocate more resources to run those jobs. This way, the broker modifies the initial set of resources allocated to run this user's jobs so that the deadline can be met. A key requirement in this scenario is for the broker to develop a *predictive* model identifying the *likely* completion times of the jobs that have been submitted by the user, and identifying whether the QoS constraints are *likely* to be violated.

Consider the scenario where the deadline for a job cannot be met. In this case, the broker can attempt to migrate this job to another resource, but depending on the type of job (for instance, if this job cannot be checkpointed) we have lost the time up to this moment (if after 30 minutes we discover that the job will not meet the deadline and decide to move it, we have only 30 minutes left to have the job executed in the new resource within the 1 hour deadline). Therefore, when choosing resources, it is necessary to take into account the

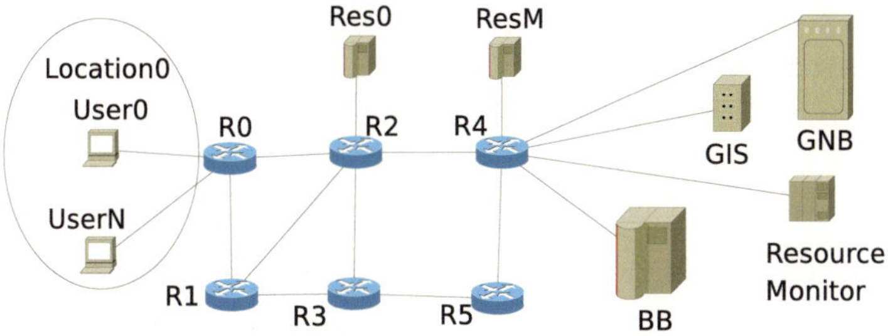


Fig. 2. Topology.

characteristics of each resource and each job during the resource allocation process. Therefore, we propose the following alternative resource selection strategy. When the user submits his resource request to the broker, including his QoS requirements, the broker will perform a resource selection taking into account the features of the resources available at this moment. Also, features of the jobs and their QoS requirements should also be taken into account. When the jobs have been allocated to a resource, the broker performs the monitoring. If the broker infers that the requirement will not be met (for instance, after 30 minutes it may deduce that the 60 minute deadline will not be met) it will proceed with a new resource allocation. Again, this resource allocation must be done taking into account the features of resources, jobs and QoS requirements. This scenario is focused on *high throughput computing*, where there are no dependencies among jobs.

## 4. Network-aware scheduling

Our initial approach, whose structure was presented in (Caminero et al. (2007)), provides an efficient selection of resources in a single administrative domain, taking into account the features of the jobs and resources, including the status of the network. However, only data associated with Grid jobs was considered – which is unlikely to be the case in practice. We improve upon this by considering a more realistic way of checking the status of the network. Also, we extend our previous proposal by means of considering autonomic computing (Caminero et al. (2009a;b)). This means that our model will use feedback from resources and network elements in order to improve system performance. Our scheduler will therefore adapt its behavior according to the status of the system, paying special attention to the status of the network.

Our scenario is depicted in Figure 2 and has the following entities (Caminero et al. (2009a;b)):

- **users**, each one has a number of jobs to run;
- **computing resources**, e.g. may consist of a single machine or clusters of machines;
- **routers**;
- **GNB** (*Grid Network Broker*), an autonomic network-aware scheduler;
- **GIS** (*Grid Information Service*), such as (Fitzgerald et al. (1997)), which keeps a list of available resources;
- **resource monitor** (for example, Ganglia (Massie et al. (2004))), which provides detailed information on the status of the resources;

- **BB** (*Bandwidth Broker*) such as (Sohail et al. (2003)), which is in charge of the administrative domain, and has direct access to routers. BB can be used to support reservation of network links, and can keep track of the interconnection topology between two end points within a network.

The interaction between components within the architecture is as follows:

- Users ask the GNB for a resource to run their jobs. Users provide jobs and deadlines.
- The GNB performs two operations for each job. First, it performs scheduling of that job to a computing resource, and second, performs connection admission control (CAC). The GNB uses link latencies to carry out the scheduling, and effective bandwidth of the network to perform the CAC. The information on the network status is collected by means of SNMP queries that the GNB sends to the computing resources, as Section 4.3 explains. This way, the GNB gets real information on the current status of the network. Once the GNB has decided the computing resource where a job will be executed, it carries on with the next scheduling request.
- The GNB makes use of the GIS in order to get the list of available resources, and then it gets their current load from the resource monitor.
- The GNB makes use of the BB in order to carry out operations requiring the network. We assume the independence and autonomy of each administrative domain.
- Once the GNB has chosen a computing resource to run a job, it submits the job to that resource. On the completion of a job, the GNB will get the output sent back from the resource, and will forward it to the user. Also, the GNB will update information about the accuracy of its decisions, considering CPU and transmission delays.

The monitoring of the network and resources is carried out with a given frequency, called *monitoring interval*. In order to perform scheduling more efficiently, each monitoring interval is divided into a number of *subintervals*, each with an associated effective bandwidth. When the monitoring takes place, all the subintervals are updated with the effective bandwidth obtained from monitoring. As the GNB performs scheduling of jobs to computing resources, the effective bandwidth of each subinterval is updated independently, so that it reflects the jobs that are being submitted to resources. This way, GNB tries to infer the effect of the jobs being transmitted over the network. This process is depicted in Figure 3. In this figure, subintervals are numbered from 0 to 9, from left to right. We can see that when the monitoring took place, the effective bandwidth of all the subintervals was set to 100 Mbps. Then, *job* 0 (requiring 35 Mbps) is scheduled to be submitted to a resource in subinterval 1. Thus, the effective bandwidth of that subinterval is updated to 65 Mbps. Similarly, jobs 1, 2 and 3 are scheduled and submitted to a resource in different subintervals. As a result of that, subintervals 2, 3, 4, and 5 have their effective bandwidths updated, and set to 0 Mbps. The number of subintervals a job occupies is calculated based on the bandwidth required by the job, by subtracting the bandwidth of the job from the effective bandwidth of the subinterval where it is being submitted. If the new effective bandwidth of the subinterval is $< 0.0$, then it is set to 0.0 and the next subinterval is updated with the remaining of the bandwidth of the job. Thus, we update consecutive subintervals until the whole job is submitted to the resource.

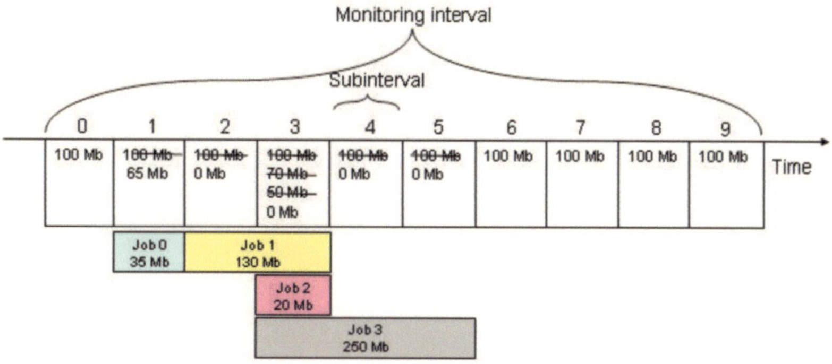


Fig. 3. Monitoring intervals and subintervals.

**Algorithm 3** Scheduler algorithm.

1: Let u = a user (job owner)
2: Let R = set of computing resources
3: **for all** $r_i$ in R **do**
4: $latency_{job}(u, r_i) =$
$latency_{cpu(r_i)} * TOLERANCE_{cpu}^{r_i} + latency_{network(u,r_i)} * TOLERANCE_{net}^{r_i}$
5: increment(i)
6: **end for**
7: Rmin = Ordered set {min($latency_{job}(u, r_i)$)}, $\forall(i)$

#### 4.1 Scheduler

The GNB performs scheduling for each job request on arrival. Algorithm 3 explains how the GNB performs the scheduling. It needs to predict the latency for a job in each computing resource (line 4). For this, it is necessary to consider the network latency between the GNB and the resource, as well as the CPU latency of the resource. The former is described in Section 4.3 and is based on the effective bandwidth of the network, whilst the estimation of the CPU latency is explained in Section 4.4. The resources are then sorted based on the expected latency of the job, from the resource with the smallest latency to the biggest one (line 7). The result is an sorted list of computing resources, from the best to the worst one.

The terms $TOLERANCE_x^{r_i}$, $x = \{net, cpu\}$, represent the accuracy of the previous predictions carried out by the GNB for the resource $r_i$. For $TOLERANCE_{net}^{r_i}$, for instance, we consider the last measurement for network latency, collected from the last job that came back to the GNB after being executed at resource $r_i$, and the network latency estimation for that job. Equations 3 and 4 show the actual formulas used, where $MB$ represents the size of the job in mega-bytes, and $MI$ represents the length of the job in millions of instructions.

$$TOLERANCE_{net}^{r'_i} = \frac{t_{net}^{real} - t_{net}^{estimated}}{MB} \tag{3}$$

$$TOLERANCE_{cpu}^{r'_i} = \frac{t_{cpu}^{real} - t_{cpu}^{estimated}}{MI} \tag{4}$$

This is, however, the current $TOLERANCE$ (the accuracy of the predictions for the last job that was executed). Therefore, we must use a predictive model to determine the future values for

**Algorithm 4** CAC algorithm.

1: Let $j$ be a job
2: Let $j_{bw}$ be the bandwidth required for the job $j$
3: **repeat**
4:     **for all** $r_i \in Rmin$ **do**
5:         **if** $(resEffectiveBandwidth(r_i, j)! = OK)$ **then**
6:             discard($r_i$)
7:         **else**
8:             choose($r_i$)
9:         **end if**
10:     **end for**
11: **until** (choose($r_i$)) or ($i$ == sizeOf(Rmin))

these terms. A predictive model can be similar to the one used by Transport Control Protocol (TCP) for computing the retransmissions time-outs (Stevens (1994)), for instance. Hence, we can consider:

$$diff = TOLERANCE_x^{r'_i} - TOLERANCE_x^{r_i} \tag{5}$$

$$TOLERANCE_x^{r_i} = TOLERANCE_x^{r_i} + diff * \delta \tag{6}$$

where $\delta$ reflects the importance of the last sample in the calculation of the next $TOLERANCE$. GNB keeps a $TOLERANCE$ for each computing resource, for network and for CPU. Using one $TOLERANCE$ for pair $< user, computing\ resource >$ has also been considered, and discarded, since GNB would not "learn" from scheduling decisions already made for other users. By modifying $TOLERANCEs$, the GNB reacts to changes in the status of the system. Thus, the autonomic features of GNB lie on the $TOLERANCEs$.

### 4.2 Connection admission control (CAC)

Once the scheduler has sorted the available resources, the connection admission control (CAC) algorithm is activated. The overall algorithm is shown in Algorithm 4. It is necessary to estimate the effective bandwidth between two end points in the network – these being the GNB and the computing resource from which an estimate is desired. Thus, for each resource, we check the effective bandwidth of the path between the GNB and the resource (line 5). If the test returns $OK$, the resource is accepted for its execution (line 8). Otherwise, we check the next resource (line 6).

The effective bandwidth test is carried our according to Algorithm 5. First, we calculate the monitoring subinterval when scheduling is performed. Recall that GNB monitors computing resources every *monitoring interval*. This interval is divided into a number of subintervals, and each subinterval has an associated effective bandwidth. When the GNB performs the monitoring, the effective bandwidth of all subintervals is updated with the value obtained. As GNB schedules jobs to computing resources, the effective bandwidth of subintervals is updated separately.

If the effective bandwidth of the subinterval in which the job is to be scheduled is higher or equal to the bandwidth required by the job, then the effective bandwidth of the subinterval is updated (the job's bandwidth is subtracted from it) (line 12). If the effective bandwidth of the subinterval is lower than the bandwidth required by the job, then this subinterval's effective

**Algorithm 5** Resources' Effective Bandwidth Test.

Let $r$ be a computing resource
Let $j$ be a job
Let $j_{bw}$ be the bandwidth required for the job $j$
Let $s_i$ be the subinterval of the moment when the job is to be scheduled
Let $m$ be the monitoring interval
Let $n$ be the number of subintervals $m$ is divided in
**while** $(j_{bw} > 0) \& (i < n)$ **do**
    **if** $(effectiveBandwidth(s_i, r) >= j_{bw})$ **then**
        $effectiveBandwidth(s_i, r) = effectiveBandwidth(s_i, r) - j_{bw}$
        $j_{bw} = 0$
    **else**
        $effectiveBandwidth(s_i, r) = 0$
        $j_{bw} = j_{bw} - effectiveBandwidth(s_i, r)$
        $i = i + 1$
    **end if**
**end while**
**if** $j_{bw} = 0$ **then**
    return OK
**else**
    return NO_OK
**end if**

bandwidth is set to 0.0, and the next subintervals are also updated. This is undertaken because the job cannot be transmitted in one subinterval. We consider all the subintervals till the end of this monitoring interval, and in this moment the effective bandwidth is updated with the new data collected from the system.

### 4.3 Calculating the performance of the network.

A useful way to estimate the latency of a link would be sending ping messages with real data payloads (the size of the I/O files of the jobs, for instance), but this approach is not acceptable, because these ping messages would congest the network. An alternative approach would be for the GNB to send a query to all the computing resources it knows. This query asks for the number of transmitted bytes, for each interface that the query goes through (the *OutOctets* parameter of SNMP (McCloghrie & Rose (1991))). Using two consecutive measurements ($m1$ and $m_2$, $m_1$ shows $X$ bytes, and $m_2$ shows $Y$ bytes), considering the time of measurement ($m_1$ collected at time $t_1$ seconds and $m_2$ at $t_2$ seconds), and the capacity of the link $C$, we can calculate the effective bandwidth of a link $l$ as follows:

$$eff\_bw(l) = C - \frac{Y - X}{t_2 - t_1} \tag{7}$$

Then, the effective bandwidth of a network path is calculated as the effective bandwidth of the bottleneck link. This procedure can be graphically seen in Figure 4. In this figure, `GNB` wants to know the effective bandwidth of the resource `Res`, so it sends a query to the resource. This query goes through routers `R0` and `R1`. Each router fills the query message with the number of *OutOctets* forwarded through that interface. For the first query (depicted as *monitoring round 1*), the interface `GNB-R0` has forwarded 134 *bytes* up to now, the interface `R0-R1` 1234 *bytes*,

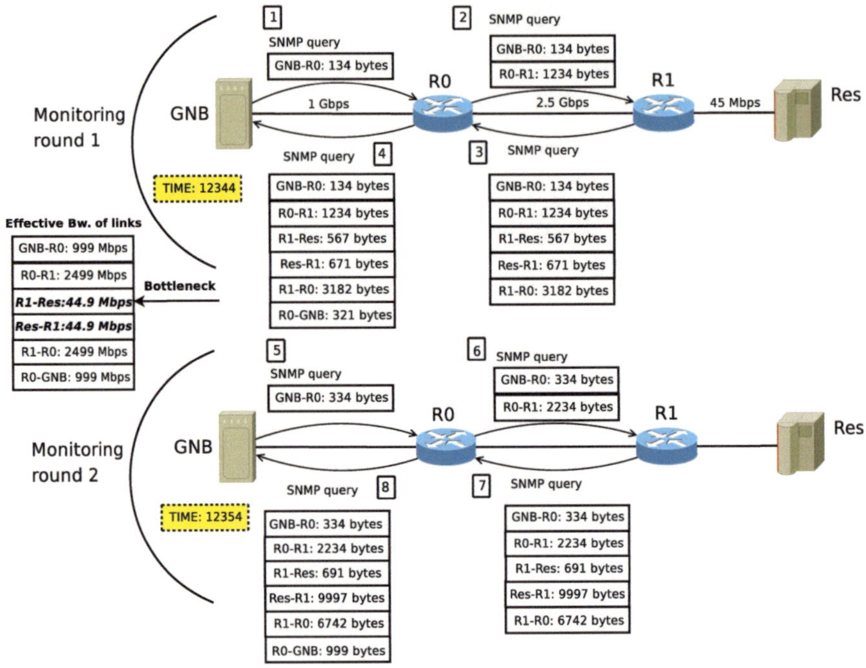


Fig. 4. Calculation of the effective bandwidth of a network path.

and so on. Once we have two measurements (which we have after *monitoring round* 2), GNB can calculate the effective bandwidth for each link in the path to the resource. Then, the effective bandwidth of the path to the resource is computed as the effective bandwidth of the bottleneck.

Since the GNB is a part of the infrastructure of an administrative domain, it is allowed to get such information using SNMP. Another possibility is that BB, which is in charge of the administrative domain and has direct access to routers, gets such information and presents it to the GNB. This way, independence and autonomy of the administrative domain is kept.

Once we have the effective bandwidth of a network path, we can calculate the latency of a job over a network path just by dividing the job's I/O file size in MB (mega bytes) by the effective bandwidth. These data (I/O file sizes) are known since I/O files are stored in the user's computer.

### 4.4 Calculating CPU latency

The CPU latency of a job is estimated as follows:

$$CPU\_lat \, \alpha \left( \frac{jobs\_already\_submitted + 1}{cpu\_speed} \right) * current\_load \tag{8}$$

meaning that the CPU latency of a job in a computing resource is proportional to the jobs already assigned to the resource, the CPU speed and current load of the resource. $Jobs\_already\_submitted + 1$ is the number of jobs already submitted to that resource by the architecture in the current monitoring round (assuming all the jobs require only one CPU) plus the current job which is being checked, and *cpu_speed* and *current_load* are metrics obtained from a resource monitor. *Jobs_already_submitted* refers to job submissions in the current

| Location | Res. Name | # Nodes | CPU Rating | Policy | # Users |
|---|---|---|---|---|---|
| Loc_0 | Res_0 | 41 | 49,000 | Space-shared | 35 |
| Loc_1 | Res_1 | 17 | 20,000 | Space-shared | 10 |
| Loc_2 | Res_2 | 2 | 3,000 | Time-shared | 5 |
| Loc_3 | Res_3 | 5 | 6,000 | Space-shared | 10 |
| Loc_4 | Res_4 | 67 | 80,000 | Space-shared | 35 |
| Loc_5 | Res_5 | 59 | 70,000 | Space-shared | 70 |
| Loc_6 | Res_6 | 12 | 14,000 | Space-shared | 40 |

Table 1. Resource specifications.

monitoring interval – the monitoring information available at the GNB does not contain them. Thus, these jobs must be considered for the scheduling of jobs in the next interval.
*Current_load* is an average load, for example *load_fifteen*, *load_five* or *load_one* metrics measured by Ganglia. It is normalized to lie in the range $[0, 1]$, meaning 0 totally idle, 1 totally busy. Also, a prediction on the next *current_load* can be calculated in a similar way to *TOLERANCE*s and effective bandwidth.

## 5. Experiments and results

The main contribution of this work is an comprohensive evaluation in which our proposal is compared with existing commercial meta-schedulers and heuristics found in literature, both network-aware and non-network-aware. This evaluation is presented in the current section.
A simulated model using GridSim Toolkit (Sulistio et al. (2008)) has been developed. This has been decided because simulations allow the creation of repeatable and controlled experiments. The experiments carried out have been divided in two groups. First, the autonomic network-aware meta-scheduling strategy (ANM) has been compared with existing Grid meta-scheduling strategies, which are neither network-aware nor autonomic. One of them is similar to the way how meta-scheduling is performed in the GridWay meta-scheduler – which, given a job submission, selects a computing resource at any given time based on the number of currently available CPUs. This has been chosen because it is a commercial meta-scheduler, which is released along with the Globus Toolkit from version GT4.0.5 onwards. The way how GridWay performs the meta-scheduling is presented in Section 2.1, and GridWay is labeled as `GW` in figures. The other heuristics are Max-Min, Min-min and XSufferage algorithms, explained in Section 2.3.
Second, ANM has been compared with the Gridbus strategy (presented in Section 2.2), which is network-aware. Thus, the way how ANM checks the status of the network and computing resources is compared with Gridbus.
For ANM, several details must be mentioned. As both the meta-scheduling algorithm and the CAC use the effective bandwidth of the network, a combined version of these has been utilized in the implementation. Hence, when calculating the estimated latency of a job in a computing resource, it is considered the effective bandwidth of the path from the broker to the resource. If the path does not have enough bandwidth, the estimated completion time will be infinity – thus the resource will not be chosen to run the job. Results focus on network and CPU latencies, makespan, and load balancing over resources, and illustrate that ANM outperforms the other meta-scheduling strategies.

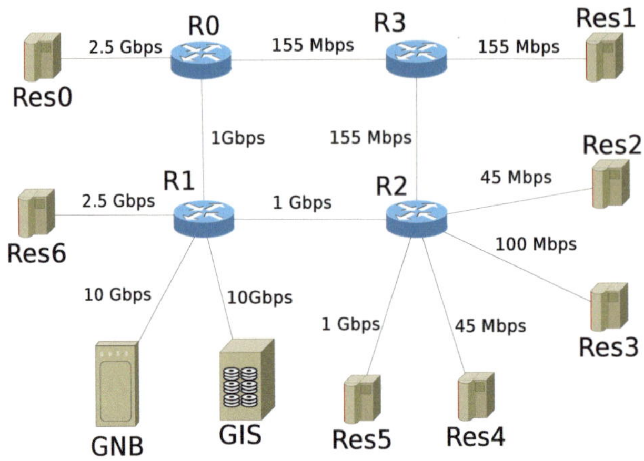


Fig. 5. Topology simulated.

| Location Name | # Users |
|---|---|
| Loc_0 | 16 |
| Loc_1 | 10 |
| Loc_2 | 2 |
| Loc_3 | 5 |
| Loc_4 | 16 |
| Loc_5 | 35 |
| Loc_6 | 16 |

Table 2. Users' locations.

Figure 5 shows the topology used in experiments. In order to reduce the amount of memory and the length of our simulations, the bandwidth of the links appearing in the figure was scaled down by 0.1 %.

Table 1 summarizes the characteristics of the simulated resources, which were obtained from a real LCG testbed (LCG Computing Fabric Area (2010)). The parameters regarding to a CPU rating are defined in the form of *MIPS* (*Million Instructions Per Second*) as per *SPEC* (*Standard Performance Evaluation Corporation*) benchmark. Moreover, the number of nodes for each resource are scaled down by 10, for the same reasons mentioned before. Finally, each resource node has four CPUs.

Each computing resource also has local (non-Grid) computing load. Variable load follows the default local load provided by GridSim. This load is based on traces obtained from common observation of relative local usage behavior of resource per hour in a day (Buyya & Murshed (2002)). The local load is not the same for all the resources. Resources `Res_0`, `Res_5` and `Res_6` have a full local load that covers around 95 % of the computing power of the resources. That is, only around 5 % of the computing power of each CPU at those resources is available for Grid users. For the other resources, the local load is nearly 0 %. This has been decided in order to simulate a real Grid scenario, in which resources may have local load, that may differ between resources.

For these experiments, 100 users were created and distributed among the locations, as shown in Table 2. Each user executes three *bags-of-tasks* (Cirne et al. (2003)), with four jobs each one.

| Job type | Power | Network |
|---|---|---|
| 0 | low (1,200,000 MI) | low (24 MB) |
| 1 | low (1,200,000 MI) | high (48 MB) |
| 2 | high (2,400,000 MI) | low (24 MB) |
| 3 | high (2,400,000 MI) | high (48 MB) |

Table 3. Job types.

Users want to submit all the jobs in a bag at the same time, and the time difference between bags submission is 80,000 sec (approximately 1 day).

Each job in each bag has different characteristics. The characteristics are *heavy* and *low* processing requirements. Jobs with *heavy* processing requirements have 2,400,000 MI, which means that each job takes about 4 seconds if it is run on the `Loc_5` resource. On the other hand, jobs with *low* processing requirements have 1,400,000 MI, which means that each job takes about 2 seconds if it is run on the `Loc_5` resource. For the size of IO files, there are also *heavy* and *low* requirements. Jobs with *heavy* I/O requirements have I/O files whose sizes are 48 MB, and for jobs with *low* I/O requirements, I/O file sizes are 24 MB. Thus, there are four different job types, which are depicted in Table 3. Since these jobs do not require more than a few seconds of processing in the `Loc_5` resource, they are not CPU intensive, but I/O intensive. Features of jobs have been decided keeping in mind those from the ATLAS online monitoring and calibration system (ATLAS online monitoring and calibration system (2010)).

The GNB performs the monitoring of the network and computing resources with a 600 seconds (10 minutes) interval. This way, every 600 seconds the GNB gets information on the real status of the system, giving the load on the computing resources and the effective bandwidth of network paths. The GNB performs the meta-scheduling of jobs to computing resources as jobs arrive. At first, it was considered that the GNB would perform the meta-scheduling after a particular interval, i.e. jobs would be queued at the GNB, and from time to time, it would schedule the jobs received. However, this approach was considered to be inaccurate as it would synchronize jobs – i.e. jobs would be submitted to the corresponding computing resources at the same time, thus overloading the network. Another way of avoiding the synchronization would be submitting jobs to resources with a given delay, so that jobs scheduled at the same meta-scheduling round would not be submitted to the computing resource at the same time.

For the Max-Min, Min-min, XSufferage and Gridbus algorithms, the meta-scheduling interval is the same as the monitoring interval (600 seconds). Thus, at each monitoring interval they also perform the meta-scheduling of those jobs received during last 600 seconds.

### 5.1 Network-awareness vs. Network-awareless

Figure 6 shows the average and standard deviation for the CPU latencies for all the jobs, for all the meta-scheduling policies studied. It can be seen that Min-min, Max-min and XSufferage outperform the other strategies, including ANM, in terms of average CPU latency (see Figure 6 (a)). This is because they only consider CPU when deciding to which computing resource a job should be submitted, and ANM performs the worst of all of them, followed by GridWay. With regard to the standard deviation (see Figure 6 (b)), ANM strategy shows bigger results than the other strategies. As before, Min-min, Max-min and XSufferage present the smallest standard deviation. This means that for ANM, CPU latencies are less stable – meaning that there is more difference between values. On the contrary, the CPU latencies of

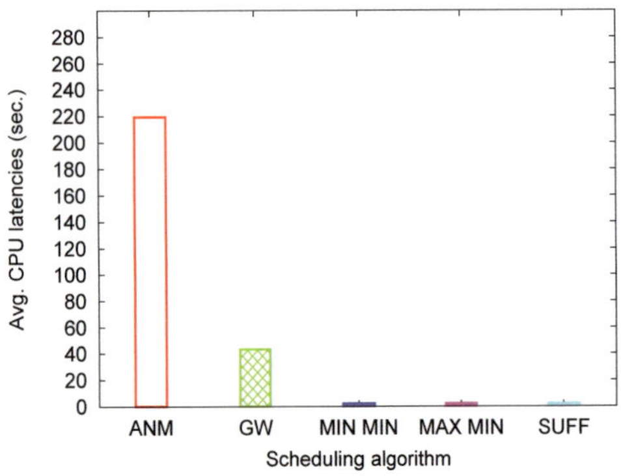


(a) Average

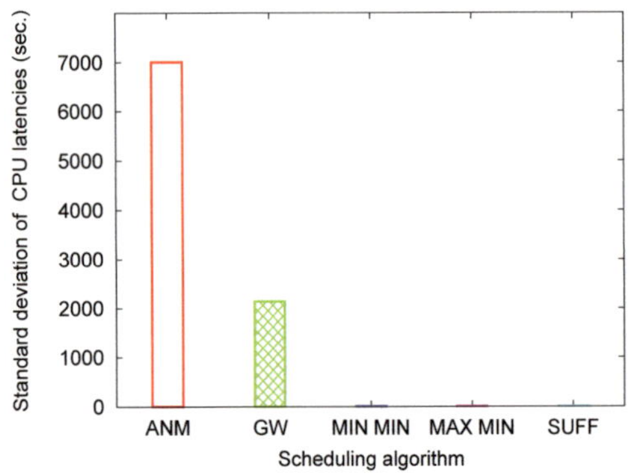


(b) Standard deviation

Fig. 6. Statistics on CPU latencies

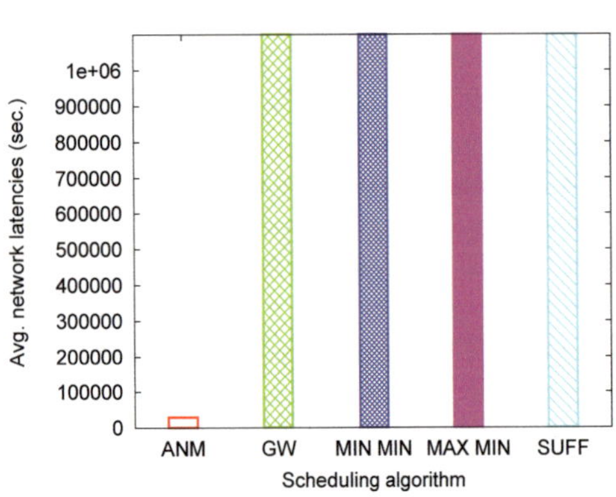


(a) Average

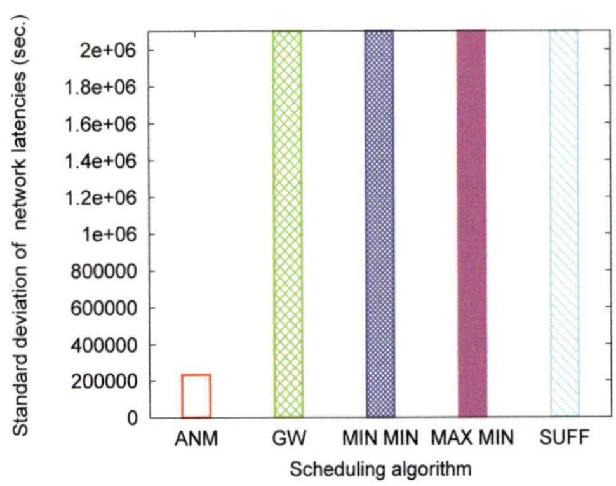


(b) Standard deviation

Fig. 7. Statistics on network latencies.

jobs for Max-min (also for Min-min and XSufferage) are very similar, being less difference between them.

Figure 7 presents the average and standard deviation of network latencies. Here it can be seen that ANM clearly outperforms the others (since it presents lower average and standard deviation than the other strategies), because jobs are I/O intensive and the performance of the network is significant – which is not considered by the other strategies. So, not only average network latencies are smaller for ANM than for the other strategies studied, but also network latencies are more stable, since the standard deviation is also smaller. Total latencies (Figure 8) show similar tendencies.

Figure 9 presents the average and standard deviation of the makespan of users, i.e. the time users take to get all their jobs executed. As before, since the network is a key requirement for jobs, ANM outperforms the others. Regarding the average makespan (see Figure 9 (a)), GridWay, Min-min, Max-min, and XSufferage present results which are more than 10 times worse than ANM. Since ANM can have jobs executed with a lower latency (as explained above), jobs from different bags scarcely overlap each other in the network (i.e. when jobs from one bag are submitted, jobs from the previous bags have finished). On the contrary, when the others strategies are running, jobs overlap other jobs from the previous bags, thus

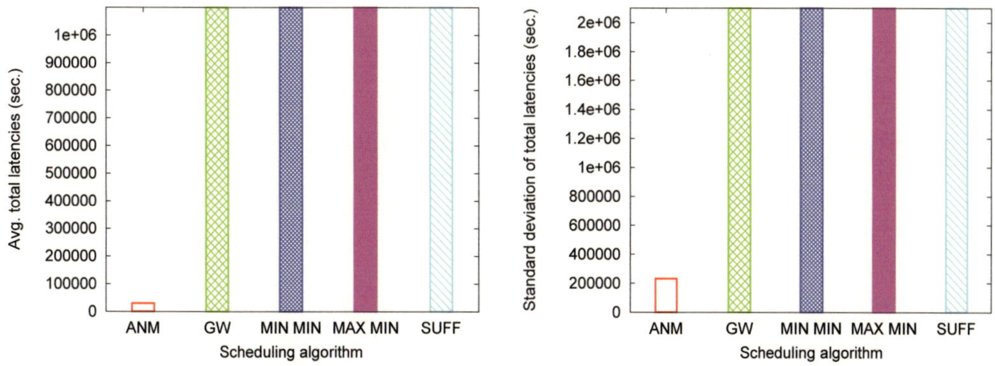


(a) Average (b) Standard deviation

Fig. 8. Statistics on total latencies (CPU + Network).

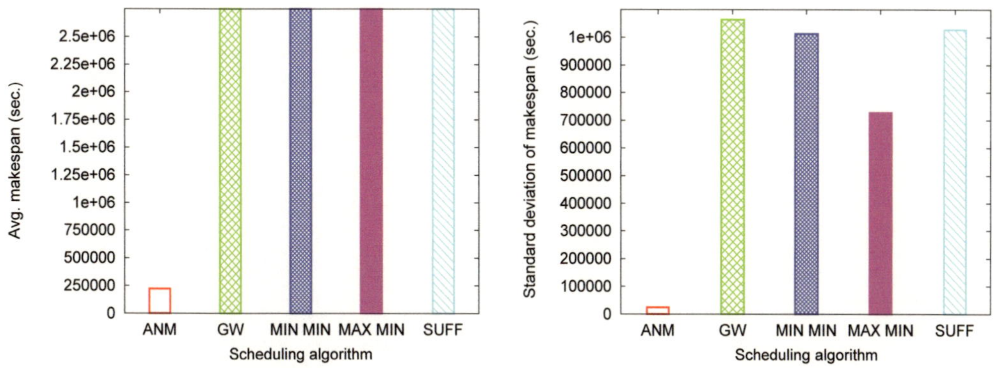


(a) Average (b) Standard deviation

Fig. 9. Statistics on users' makespan.

interfering each other and making the overall makespan of users higher. Also, ANM presents the smallest standard deviation, with a noticeable difference with the other strategies (see Figure 9 (b)). This means that ANM can perform more efficient meta-scheduling, as there are less variability among its results.

Figure 10 illustrates the number of jobs that have been submitted to each computing resource. Since GridWay only considers the number of idle CPUs when performing the meta-scheduling of jobs to computing resources, jobs are scheduled to the resource having more CPUs. Thus, resources `Res_0`, `Res_1`, `Res_2`, `Res_3`, and `Res_6` scarcely receive any job for execution. Only the computing resources which have more idle CPUs (namely, `Res_4` and `Res_5`) receive a noticeable amount of jobs.

When Min-min, Max-min and XSufferage strategies are running, since they do not take the network into account when performing the meta-scheduling, they always choose the most powerful computing resource to run jobs (namely, `Res_4`). This leads to a bad overall performance, since this computing resource does not have a good network connection.

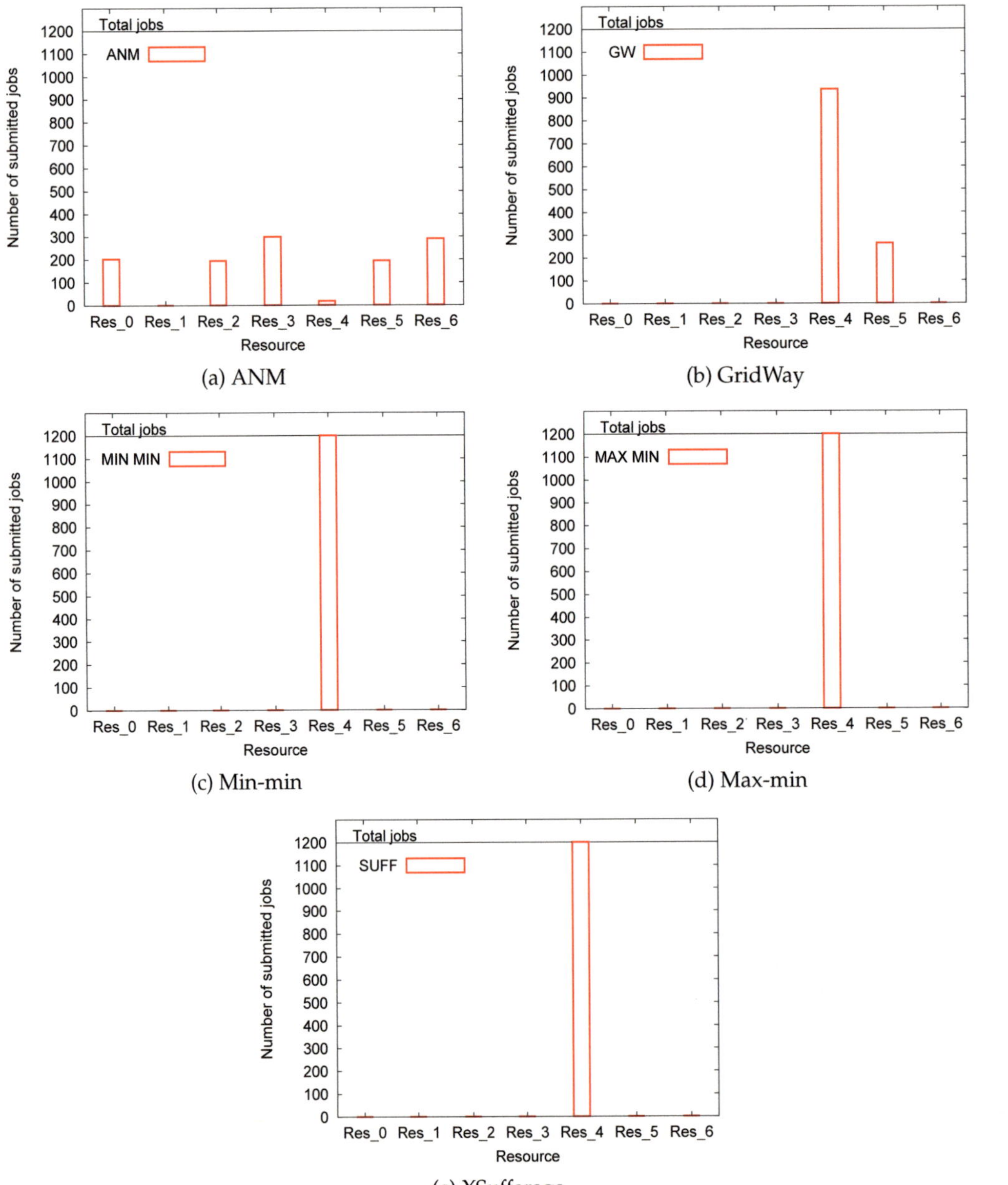


(a) ANM

(b) GridWay

(c) Min-min

(d) Max-min

(e) XSufferage

Fig. 10. Computing resource selected by the meta-scheduling algorithm.

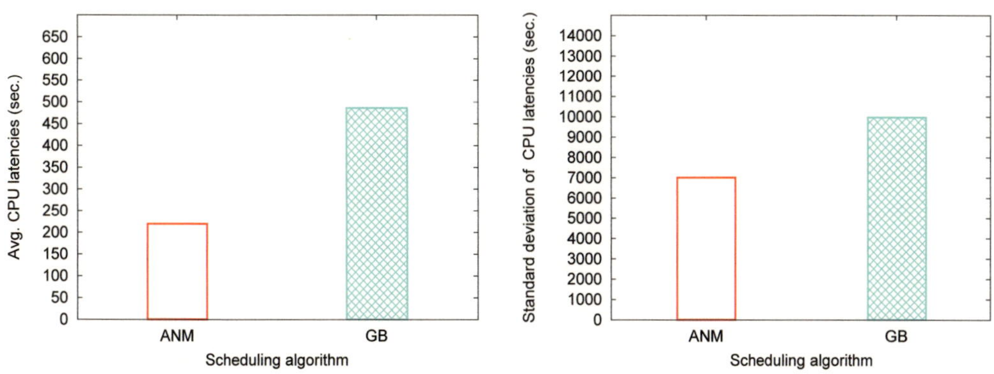


(a) Average (b) Standard deviation

Fig. 11. Statistics on CPU latencies.

But when ANM is used, network connections are considered to perform the meta-scheduling. Thus, jobs are submitted to several resources, and all the resources receive a noticeable number of jobs. This way, network connections do not become overloaded, which heavily influences the performance received by jobs. Since jobs used in experiments are not CPU-intensive (they are I/O-intensive) this results in a better choice of resources. This leads to the better overall execution performance as previous figures shown. Besides, load is better balanced over the resources.

### 5.2 ANM vs. Gridbus

Now, an evaluation comparing ANM with another network-aware proposal for meta-scheduling in Grids is presented. The network-aware proposal chosen is Gridbus (Venugopal et al. (2008)), which was explained in Section 2.2. Results using Gridbus are labeled as `GB` in figures. The parameters of experiments presented are the same as the previous evaluation. Thus, results using ANM are the same.

As before, the first results to be presented are regarding average and standard deviation of latencies of jobs. CPU, network and total latencies are presented. Figure 11 presents the average and the standard deviation of CPU latencies of jobs, for ANM and Gridbus. It can be seen that ANM outperforms Gridbus both in average and standard deviation. Thus, ANM makes better decisions with regard to CPU, since average latencies are lower, and CPU latencies are more stable (lower standard deviation).

Figure 12 presents average and standard deviation of network latencies. In this case, ANM also outperforms Gridbus since both average and standard deviation are lower. Similar tendencies also observed in the total latencies (shown in Figure 13) and makespan (shown in Figure 14). The reason for this better behavior of ANM compared with Gridbus lies on the computing resource chosen to execute each job, and this can be seen in Figure 15. Both ANM and Gridbus choose the computing resource to execute a job considering the network bandwidth, thus the resources that run more jobs are those whose bandwidth is the highest, namely `Res_6`, `Res_0`, `Res_5`, and `Res_3`. But the key difference between ANM and Gridbus is related to `Res_4`. This resource is the most powerful, since it has the most powerful CPUs, and it has more CPUs than the others. But the effective bandwidth between the GNB and it is the worst of all the computing resources.

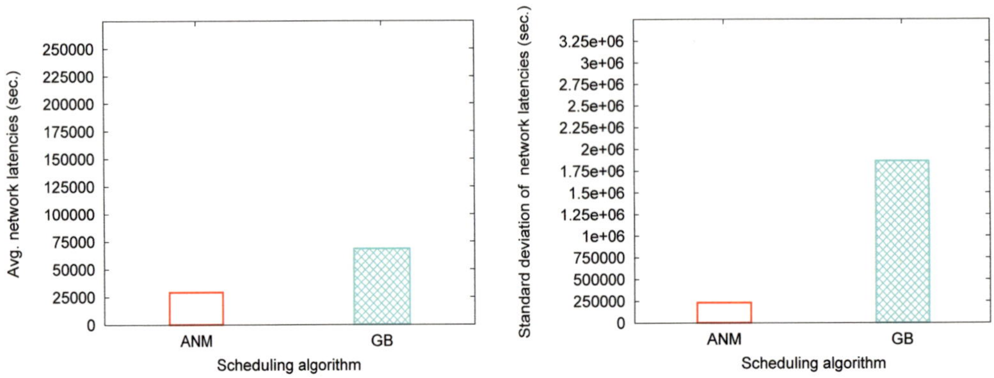


(a) Average (b) Standard deviation

Fig. 12. Statistics on network latencies.

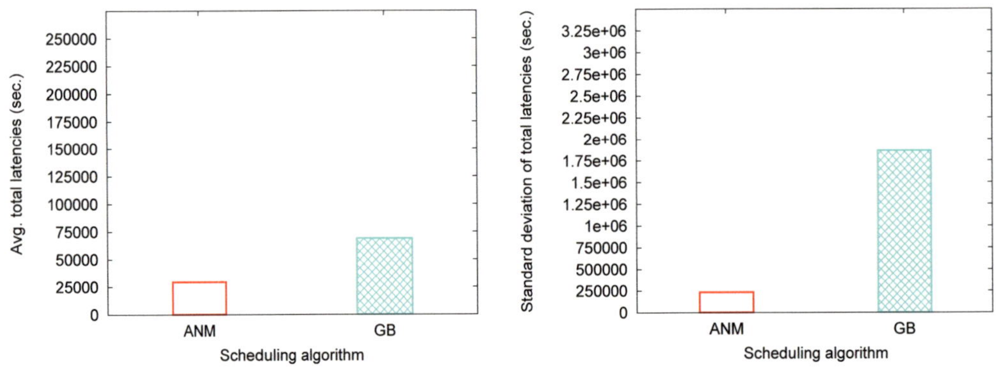


(a) Average (b) Standard deviation

Fig. 13. Statistics on total latencies (CPU + Network).

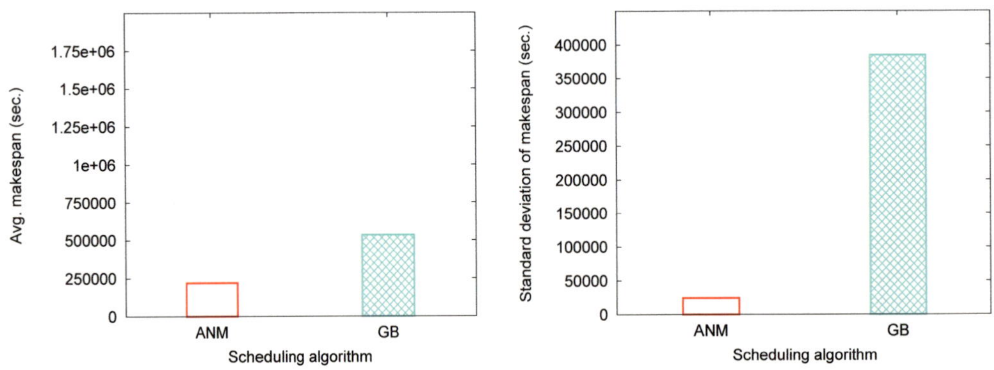


(a) Average (b) Standard deviation

Fig. 14. Statistics on users' makespan.

Recall that for resources `Res_0`, `Res_5`, and `Res_6`, only 5 % of the computing power is available for Grid users, since they have local load covering 95 % of their computing power.

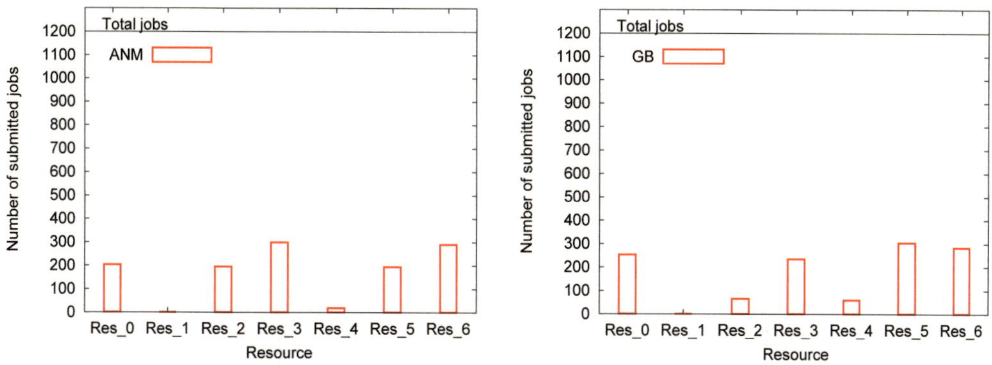


(a) ANM

(b) Gridbus

Fig. 15. Computing resource selected by the meta-scheduling algorithm.

On the other hand, `Res_1`, `Res_2`, `Res_3`, and `Res_4` have almost no local load, so 100 % of computing power is available for Grid users. As explained before, when performing the meta-scheduling of a job, Gridbus starts checking the resource with the highest available bandwidth. If the job limit for it has not been reached, the resource is chosen to execute the job. Thus, the job limit for Gridbus is key. It is calculated by considering the resource share available for Grid users. Thus, since some computing resources have a heavy local load, this greatly influences the job limit for those resources. But, since jobs are not CPU intensive, the CPU load is not an important restriction for a computing resource. Because of this, loaded resources may reach their job limit, and jobs may be submitted to computing resources with lower available bandwidth.

As opposed to it, ANM can predict the performance of jobs at each resource more accurately. Thus, less jobs are submitted to resource `Res_4` (which is the most powerful, with no local load, but also has the worst network connection). Thus, jobs are submitted to other resources such as `Res_2` and `Res_3`, which provide a better performance to jobs.

## 6. Conclusions

The network, as the communication media for Grid applications, is a critical resource to be considered by the Grid management architecture. In this chapter, algorithms aimed at performing connection admission control (CAC) and meta-scheduling of jobs to computing resources within one single administrative domain (*intra-domain* meta-scheduling) have been presented.

This paper presents a comprehensive performance evaluation of an *autonomic network-aware meta-scheduler* (*ANM*), that combines concepts from Grid meta-scheduling with autonomic computing, in order to provide users with a more adaptive job management system. The architecture involves consideration of the status of the network when reacting to changes in the system – taking into account the workload on computing resources and the network links when making a meta-scheduling decision. Thus, the architecture provides meta-scheduling of jobs to computing resources and connection admission control, so that the network does not become overloaded.

Performance evaluation shows that ANM can schedule heterogeneous jobs onto computing resources more efficiently than existing literature approaches (namely, Min-min, Max-min, and XSufferage) and conventional meta-scheduling algorithms (that used by GridWay). Besides, it has been compared with a network-aware meta-scheduler, Gridbus. Results show that ANM can make better meta-scheduling decisions, resulting in a better performance from the users' point of view when compared with other meta-schedulers.
Regarding future work, authors are considering the implications of the technique presented in this paper with regard to different contexts, such being Cloud computing. In this case, there should be a tolerance for the time needed to deploy a virtual machine, along with the aforementioned tolerances for the network and CPU time of tasks.
Besides, a combination of Grid and Cloud resources (as in (Kim et al. (2009))) could be used. In this case, depending on the tolerances of each resource, jobs should be mapped to Grid or Cloud resources in order to minimize their completion times.

## 7. References

ATLAS online monitoring and calibration system (2010). Web page at `http://dissemination.interactive-grid.eu/applications/HEP`.

Bobroff, N., Fong, L., Kalayci, S., Liu, Y., Martinez, J. C., Rodero, I., Sadjadi, S. M. & Villegas, D. (2008). Enabling interoperability among meta-schedulers, *Proc. of the 8th Intl. Symposium on Cluster Computing and the Grid (CCGRID)*, Lyon, France.

Buyya, R. & Murshed, M. (2002). Gridsim: A toolkit for the modeling and simulation of distributed resource management and scheduling for grid computing, *Concurrency and Computation: Practice and Experience* 14: 1175–1220.

Caminero, A., Carrión, C. & Caminero, B. (2007). Designing an entity to provide network QoS in a Grid system, *Proc. of the 1st Iberian Grid Infrastructure Conference (IberGrid)*, Santiago de Compostela, Spain.

Caminero, A., Rana, O., Caminero, B. & Carrión, C. (2009a). Performance evaluation of an autonomic network-aware metascheduler for Grids, *Concurrency and Computation: Practice and Experience* 21(13): 1692–1708.

Caminero, A., Rana, O. F., Caminero, B. & Carrión, C. (2009b). A performance evaluation of network-aware grid meta-schedulers, *Intl. Conference on Parallel Processing Workshops (ICPPW)*, Vienna, Austria.

Casanova, H., Legrand, A., Zagorodnov, D. & Berman, F. (2000). Heuristics for scheduling parameter sweep applications in Grid environments, *Proc. of the 9th Heterogeneous Computing Workshop (HCW)*, Cancun, Mexico.

Cirne, W., Brasileiro, F., SauvÃľ, J., Andrade, N., Paranhos, D., Santos-Neto, E., Medeiros, R. & Silva, F. (2003). Grid computing for bag-of-tasks applications, *Proc. of the 3rd Conference on E-Commerce, E-Business and E-Government,*, São Paulo, Brazil.

Czajkowski, K., Kesselman, C., Fitzgerald, S. & Foster, I. T. (2001). Grid information services for distributed resource sharing, *Proc. of 10th Intl. Symposium on High Performance Distributed Computing (HPDC)*, San Francisco, USA.

Fitzgerald, S., Foster, I., Kesselman, C., von Laszewski, G., Smith, W. & Tuecke, S. (1997). A directory service for configuring high-performance distributed computations, *Proc. 6th Symposium on High Performance Distributed Computing (HPDC)*, Portland, USA.

Foster, I. & Kesselman, C. (1997). Globus: A metacomputing infrastructure toolkit, *International Journal of Supercomputer Applications and High Performance Computing* 11(2): 115–128.

Foster, I. & Kesselman, C. (2003). *The Grid 2: Blueprint for a New Computing Infrastructure*, 2 edn, Morgan Kaufmann.

Freund, R. F., Gherrity, M., Ambrosius, S. L., Campbell, M., Halderman, M., Hensgen, D. A., Keith, E. G., Kidd, T., Kussow, M., Lima, J. D., Mirabile, F., Moore, L., Rust, B. & Siegel, H. J. (1998). Scheduling resources in multi-user, heterogeneous, computing environments with SmartNet, *Proc. of the 7th Heterogeneous Computing Workshop (HCW)*, Orlando, USA.

Gentzsch, W. (2001). Sun Grid Engine: Towards creating a compute power Grid, *Proc. of the First Intl. Symposium on Cluster Computing and the Grid (CCGrid)*, Brisbane, Australia.

Globus Projects (2010). Web page at `http://dev.globus.org/wiki/Guidelines`.

GridPP, Real Time Monitor (2010). Web page at `http://gridportal.hep.ph.ic.ac.uk/rtm/`.

Huedo, E., Montero, R. S. & Llorente, I. M. (2007). A modular meta-scheduling architecture for interfacing with pre-WS and WS Grid resource management services, *Future Generation Computing Systems* 23(2): 252–261.

Imamagic, E., Radic, B. & Dobrenic, D. (2005). CRO-GRID: Grid execution management system, *Proc. of 27th Intl. Conference on Information Technology Interfaces (ITI)*, Cavtat, Croatia.

Kim, H., el Khamra, Y., Jha, S. & Parashar, M. (2009). An autonomic approach to integrated HPC Grid and Cloud usage, *Proc. of the 5th Intl. Conference on e Science (e Science)*, Oxford, UK.

LCG Computing Fabric Area (2010). Web page at `http://lcg-computing-fabric.web.cern.ch`.

LCG (LHC Computing Grid) Project (2010). Web page at `http://lcg.web.cern.ch/LCG`.

Litzkow, M. J., Livny, M. & Mutka, M. W. (1988). Condor - A Hunter of idle workstations, *Proc. of the 8th Intl. Conference on Distributed Computer Systems (ICDCS)*, San Jose, USA.

Luther, A., Buyya, R., Ranjan, R. & Venugopal, S. (2005). Alchemi: A .NET-based enterprise Grid computing system, *Proc. of The 2005 Intl. Conference on Internet Computing (ICOMP)*, Las Vegas, USA.

Marchese, F. T. & Brajkovska, N. (2007). Fostering asynchronous collaborative visualization, *Proc. of the 11th Intl. Conference on Information Visualization*, Washington DC, USA.

Massie, M. L., Chun, B. N. & Culler, D. E. (2004). The Ganglia distributed monitoring system: design, implementation, and experience, *Parallel Computing* 30(5-6): 817–840.

Mateescu, G. (2000). Extending the Portable Batch System with preemptive job scheduling, *SC2000: High Performance Networking and Computing*, Dallas, USA.

McCloghrie, K. & Rose, M. T. (1991). Management information base for network management of TCP/IP-based internets:MIB-II, RFC 1213.

Metascheduling Requirements Analysis Team (2006). Final report, available at `http://www.teragridforum.org/mediawiki/images/b/b4/MetaschedRatReport.pdf`.

Roy, A. (2001). *End to End Quality of Service for High End Applications*, PhD thesis, Dept. of Computer Science, University of Chicago.

Sohail, S., Pham, K. B., Nguyen, R. & Jha, S. (2003). Bandwidth broker implementation: Circa-complete and integrable, *Technical report*, School of Computer Science and Engineering, The University of New South Wales.

Stevens, W. R. (1994). *TCP/IP Illustrated: The Protocols*, Addison-Wesley.

Sulistio, A., Cibej, U., Venugopal, S., Robic, B. & Buyya, R. (2008). A toolkit for modelling and simulating Data Grids: An extension to GridSim, *Concurrency and Computation: Practice and Experience* 20(13): 1591–1609.

Tomás, L., Caminero, A., Caminero, B. & Carrión, C. (2010). Using network information to perform meta-scheduling in advance in grids, *Proc. of the Euro-Par Conference.*, Ischia, Italy.

Vázquez, C., Huedo, E., Montero, R. S. & Llorente, I. M. (2010). Federation of TeraGrid, EGEE and OSG infrastructures through a metascheduler, *Future Generation Computer Systems* 26(7): 979–985.

Venugopal, S., Buyya, R. & Winton, L. J. (2006). A grid service broker for scheduling e-science applications on global data Grids, *Concurrency and Computation: Practice and Experience* 18(6): 685–699.

Venugopal, S., Nadiminti, K., Gibbins, H. & Buyya, R. (2008). Designing a resource broker for heterogeneous Grids, *Software: Practice and Experience* 38(8): 793–825.

# 5

# Quantum Encrypted Data Transfers in GRID

M. Dima[1], M. Dulea[1], A. Dima[2], M. Stoica[3] and M. Udrea[3]
[1]*Inst. for Nuclear Physics & Engineering*
[2]*Lairside Laser Center*
[3]*Inst. for Laser & Plasma Physics*
[1,3]*Romania*
[2]*UK*

## 1. Introduction

GRID computing includes applications, some of which are intelligence sensitive (genetics, space, industrial intellectual property, etc) and need to remain confidential. Current security is mostly based based on public (asymmetric) key algorithms (Salomaa, 1996) - hash function algorithms easy to calculate in direct, but estimated as impossible in reverse. The base assumption to this assertion is the difficulty of factorising prime numbers. This received however a serious blow in 1994 (Shor, 1994), when it was shown that (a hypothetical future) quantum computer could rapidly factorise prime numbers via a polynomial algorithm. As such messages could be intercepted and stored today awaiting for the availability of quantum processors, when they could conceivably be deciphered. Evidently, data with short "life-span" (2-5 years) is perfectly safe today, however censi, geological data, etc have long-term implications and need to be adequately protected.
The other main security contender currently in use is the symmetric-key AES encryption (Daemen and Rijmen, 1996-2001 and 2006), that comes in 3 versions of key length 128, 192 and 256 bit (with 10, 12, and 14 rounds, respectively). For AES-128 there is no known attack faster than the $2^{128}$ complexity of exhaustive search. However, AES-192 and AES-256 were recently shown (Biryukov and Khovratovich, 2009) to be breakable by attacks of $2^{176}$ and $2^{119}$ complexities. While these are much faster than the exhaustive search, they are non-practical, and do not to pose a real threat (at the rate the world produces today data, ca. $0.2 \cdot 10^{21}$ bytes/year ($2^{61} \times$ 256-bit ciphertexts) it would take $2^{58} \cong 10^{17}$ years data's worth to recover just one AES key). The US National Security Agency (Hathaway, 2003) stated that "The design and strength of all key lengths of the AES algorithm (i.e., 128, 192 and 256) are sufficient to protect classified information up to the *secret* level." From this assessment and the simple estimates above, it is apparent that given adequate key distribution protection AES cannot be broken - at least not in the next $10^{17}$ years (for 1 key).
The secret key carrier on the other hand needs to be a stable long-term committed technology, that would not come under question any time soon (including from futuristic quantum processor attacks).

### 1.1 Key distribution

In cryptology it was shown (Vernam, 1926) that the use of a hash function with a key of equal length (or greater) than the message can guarantee the safety of the communication.

The problem of such a (symmetrical) key protocol is however the exhaustion of the hash tables - the functions are implemented as tables using random numbers delivered by natural sources (for instance alpha decays). After exhausting the tables, the communication partners need to re-establish contact and exchange a new set of tables. This has come to be known as the Key Distribution Problem.
Quantum Key Distribution (QKD) is secured by the very essence of the quantum nature: attempts to measure in any way quantum states collapses the state into one of its projections. The quantum state cannot be regenerated to its initial state, therefore it is impossible to be cloned and a copy thereof to be kept. The distribution of public quantum keys is thus similar to the Vernam cipher (symmetrical - with secret key). In particular, in Europe this has attracted attention as a means of immunisation against Echelon interception (Willan, 2004).

## 2. Quantum encryption

To transmit keys in quantum format the information can be coded in the various degrees of freedom of the quantum system used – in this case laser light. Laser light offers a number of qualifying degrees of freedom: transverse position/momentum, linear/circular polarisation as well as 2-photon entangled states.

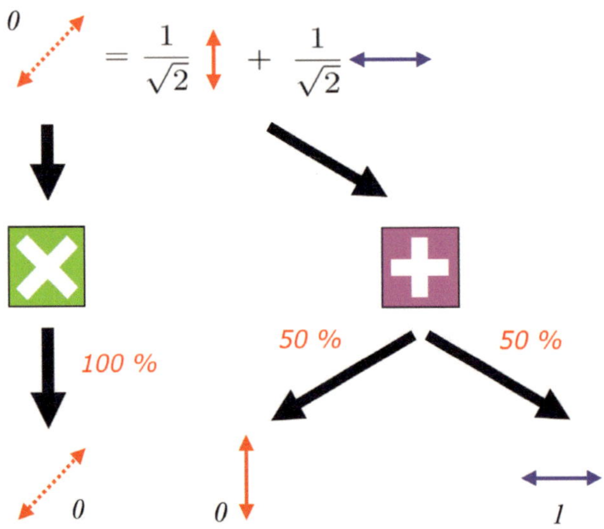


Fig. 1. Measurement of a circular R state in it's eigen basis (giving always the correct result) and in that of its conjugate, linear, basis (giving 50% of the time one state and 50% the other).

Whatever degrees of freedom are used, the central idea is to utilise sets of 2 conjugated degress of freedom. This is because if the receiver does not know in which base the bit was emitted and measures it in the wrong base, the laws of quantum mechanics guarantee an ambiguous outcome, thus conceiling the information. Consider in this respect figure 1 that shows the measurement of circular states in linear polarisation of laser light: $|R\rangle = 1/\sqrt{2}\ |\updownarrow\rangle + 1/\sqrt{2}\ |\leftrightarrow\rangle$ and $|L\rangle = 1/\sqrt{2}\ |\updownarrow\rangle - 1/\sqrt{2}\ |\leftrightarrow\rangle$. Measurement of $|R\rangle$ in the 'x' basis gives everytime the correct answer R since it is its own basis, in which it was produced. Measurement however in the the '+' basis (according to the norms-squared of its decomposition) yields 50% of time the answer ↕ and 50% of time ↔, as the figure shows. For other conjugate quantities, say transverse-coordinate and transverse-momentum, the decomposition gives an infinite series of the conjugate quantity's states: $\sqrt{2\pi}|x\rangle = \int \exp(-ikx)|k\rangle\, dk$. The norms-squared of the decomposition are now all (infinitesimal) equal. This aspect is conjugate-variable dependent. In all cases the fundamental idea of quantum encryption is that without the correct information on the base of the bit sent, its measurement in the base of its conjugate degree of freedom yields an ambiguous result, hence concealing the information sent. Therefore, such a commodity allows the design of a public-key communication protocol that can be implemented maintaining the confidentiality of the key.

There is still one more mention: all said is valid for *single* quantum entities (here photons). If we transmit N photons, the foreseeable interceptor (Eve), can make a statistics for each bit sent. She will observe when she has the wrong basis of figure 1: having enough photons, she divides the bit and sends it through both bases. The one with non-ambiguous statistics is evidently the right one. Hence without faint-photon pulses quantum protocols are rendered decipherable.

### 2.1 Faint-photon pulses

In order to use quantum properties, ensembles of very few quantum objects are necessary, to avoid small numbers of entities to be intercepted and the signal to be detected.

For 2-3 photon pulses interference with the pulse causes the collapse of the quantum states destroying the pulse. The hypothetical eavesdropper, Eve, intercepting pulses sent by Alice to Bob, either destroys them (revealing her presence), or lets them go through. Theoretically even 2-3 photon pulses may allow interception by keeping 1 photon and passing through the other 1-2. Technically that is very demanding - so-called "beam-splitting" attack (Dusek, 1999), and also, as it will be explained below.

A typical setup uses a mono-mode laser, the intensity of which is attenuated at exit to the level of 2-3 photons/pulse. Since the laser line width is almost zero compared to the magnitude of its frequency, the light can be approximated as coherent. Today solid state lasers (in green for instance) have coherence lengths on the order of 100-200 m, and fiber-lasers in the range of km's. Coherence length is the distance over which the light wave has no phase-slips and retains the same frequency: $L = c/n\Delta f$, with $c$ the speed of light, $n$ the index of refraction in the respective medium and $\Delta f$ the frequency width of the laser line. Evidently, for $\Delta f \to 0$, $L \to \infty$ and the laser is 100% mono-chromatic. The distribution of photon number of coherent states is given by a Poisson distribution:

$$p(n) = \frac{\mu^n e^{-\mu}}{n!}, \quad n = 0,1,2,\ldots$$

where $n$ is the number of photons and $\mu$ the average number of photons per pulse. For an attenuated pulse of $\mu = 0.1$, *90.48%* of pulses contain no photons, *9.05%* one photon, *0.45%* two photons, *0.02%* three photons, etc.

It can be seen that the price for security is that of over *90%* of pulses being empty.

Given the corpuscular nature of the signals we equate the probability for a detector of efficiency $\eta$ to produce $m$ photoelectrons in response to the $p(n)$ pulse:

$$p(m) = \sum_{n=m}^{\infty} \binom{n}{m} \eta^m (1-\eta)^{n-m} p(n)$$

The detector does not flag how many photons impacted it, rather it has a probability of producing an electrical output pulse (sum over all possible photo-electron numbers):

$$P = \sum_{m=1}^{\infty} p(m) = 1 - e^{-\eta\mu}$$

For $N$ laser pulses there will be $PN = N_{detected}$ pulses, hence $\eta\mu = -\ ln(1-I_{detected}/I)$. To practically measure this quantity pulses are produced with a convenient (sub-MHz) frequency, attenuated, and measured as intensity vs. the source as the last equation shows. Knowing the detector efficiency $\eta$, the average number of photons/pulse $\mu$ is calculated. The systems have automated DAQ and data processing that controls this level. In the same procedure the attenuation (calibrated at the transmission's initiation protocol) over the optical fiber is calculated and monitored. Interception will be manifest as a rise in this figure, revealing Eve's presence.

### 2.2 Signal coding

The essence of quantum coding relies on chosing the correct measurement basis, a number of conjugate bases being available: transverse position/momentum, orthogonal polarisation bases, etc.

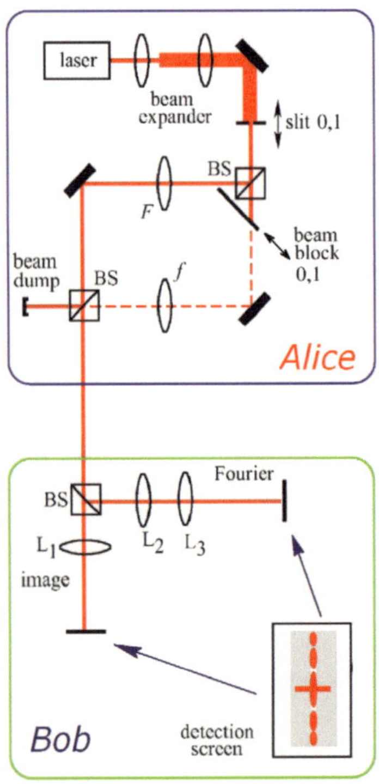


Fig. 2. Experimental setup of quantum key distribution scheme with photon transverse position and momentum.

**Transverse position/momentum coding** - this approach (Lemelle, 2006) encrypts the bits as two discrete positions of a simple slit aperture. In optics a transverse position measurement of a photon is associated with the near field or image plane, while a transverse momentum measurement is associated with the far-field or Fourier plane. Position and momentum measurements of an input field can be performed using simple optical imaging and Fourier systems along with a detector. An illustration of this scheme consists of two stages: preparation (Alice) and measurement (Bob). At Alice's a plane wave illuminates a small slit aperture placed in the input plane, which localises the photon in the transverse plane to within the spatial dimensions of the slit. Because the photon's position is now well defined, it can be considered in a definite transverse position state. In the second part Alice uses a random bit to decide which base (position or momentum) she will use:

- position basis (x): she will use her lens such as to image her slit plane onto Bob's input plane ($f_1^{-1} = d_1^{-1} + d_2^{-1}$), where $f_1$ is the focal length of the coding lens and $d_{1,2}$ the distances slit-to lens and lens to Bob's input plane,
- momentum basis (p): she will use her lens as a Fourier lens system ($f_1=d_1=d_2$) to create the Fourier transform of the slit at Bob's input plane, conducing Bob to chose a momentum eigen state.

In the measurement stage Bob also chooses one of the two measurement bases position or momentum randomply. Bob projects either:

- the (direct) image, by $f_2^{-1}=d_3^{-1}+d_4^{-1}$, where similarly to Alice $f_2$ is the decoding lens, and $d_{1,2}$ the distances input plane to lens and lens to detection screen, or
- the Fourier transform, by $f_2=d_3=d_4$ of his input plane onto his detection plane.

That is: Bob either transports, or Fourier transforms his input, in essence being the inverse of Alice's preparation system.

There are thus four possible (Alice, Bob) configurations: (xx), (xp), (px), and (pp), where "x" is the position basis and "p" the momentum basis.

Bob will have the correct result if his base choice matches Alice's base choice - i.e. only (xx) and (pp) will yield a correct transmission:

- for (xx) or (pp), Bob should detect a photon at the detector plane in a position corresponding to that of Alice's slit aperture. In the (xx) configuration, Alice and Bob implement two imaging systems, that is the image of the slit will be transported to the detection plane. In the (pp) configuration, two consecutive Fourier transforms are applied, returning a coordinate inversion. Thus, aside from this, Bob's detector plane will have the image of the slit position. In summary, when Alice and Bob use the same lens configurations, (xx) or (pp), their combined lens system produces the image of Alice's slit aperture. Consequently, Bob should detect the correct state that Alice has prepared;
- for the (xp) or (px) configurations, there is no correlation between Bob's detected position and Alice's slit position. In these arrangements Bob detects either the image of a Fourier transform or the Fourier transform of an image. The overall detection pattern will be that of a Fourier transform, providing no information on the position of Alice's slit, for the difference between "0" and "1" bits (a transverse position difference) shows up as a phase factor when Fourier transformed. Since detectors provide only amplitude information (phase being lost), precisely the crucial information is obscured, rendering the measurement lost.

The setup described above was implemented by (Lemelle, 2006), illustrating the technique. Although the experiment was performed using an intense laser source (vulnerable to eavesdropping), it allowed the clear illustration of the probability distribution's at Bob's detection plane (in the faint-photon case). This intensity pattern is an illustration of Bohr's complementarity principle playing the crucial role in a faint-photon practical application. The same level of security as with polarization bases, can be achieved if using faint-photons. The experimental setup shown in figure 2 is somewhat more elaborate than the simple 2-lens system above, but offers certain technical advantages.

Alice's setup used a red diode laser was used to illuminate a single thin slit aperture with width a=100 m. Before the slit the beam passed through a 2 beam expander consisting of a 25 and 50 mm lens in confocal arrangement. Alice toggles the slit between positions $s_0$ and $s_1$ using a simple translation stage. In principle, a piezoelectric or similar device driven by a random number generator could be used to toggle the slit position. After the slit there is a typical Mach-Zehnder interferometer with non-polarizing 50–50 beam splitters, with the imaging lens in one arm and the Fourier transform lens in the other. The interferometer allows Alice to switch between x and p encoding by simply choosing which of the arms to block. Alice can then toggle between the imaging arm and the Fourier arm using a simple movable beam block. Because one arm of the interferometer is always blocked, no interferometric stability is required. However, the interference can be exploited to initially ensure that the imaging and Fourier arms are properly aligned. Alice's imaging system is made up of a 250 mm focal length lens f, which creates the image of the slit on Bob's input plane at a distance 1000 mm from the slit in one exit arm of the interferometer. For her Fourier system a 500 mm focal length lens F creates the Fourier transform of the slit on Bob's input plane. The other exit arm is blocked by a beam dump.

Bob's detection system consisted of a 50-50 non-polarizing beam splitter that implemented the random choice between detection bases. In one output of the beam splitter was an imaging system and the other arm a Fourier system. In this proof of principle experiment a digital web-cam was used to photograph the detection screen (ca. 1mm resolution). Therefore the slit's image was magnified. For this reason, Bob's imaging system consisted of a 75.6 mm focal length lens $L_1$ placed so as to create a magnification factor of $M_2$=8. For the Fourier system, a 250 mm focal length lens $L_2$ was used to create the Fourier transform.

The different focal lengths in Alice and Bob's p configurations create a magnification factor of 1/2. To compensate for this magnification factor, an additional 50 mm focal length lens L3 was used to image the Fourier plane onto the detection screen with a magnification factor of about 16, giving an overall magnification factor of 8.

Figure 3 shows the results corresponding to Bob's transverse position measurements configuration. In figure 3a, Alice encoded bit value 0 using slit position $s_0$ and the x configuration. Consequently, Bob detected light in the left region on his position detection screen. In figure 3b Alice sendt bit value 1 using slit position s1 and the x configuration; likewise Bob detected light in the right position of his detection screen. These results show the correlation between the slit position and Bob's detection position when both parties implement x configurations. Figures 3c and 3d show results when Alice encodes slit positions $s_0$ and $s_1$ using momentum encoding. Here photons fall on both detector positions independent of the slit position, indicating no correlation between Alice's preparation and Bob's measurements.

Figure 4 shows digital photos of the results at Bob's momentum detector for the same sequence of measurements as in figure 3. In figures 4a and 4b Alice used x encoding to send slit positions $s_0$ and $s_1$, respectively. No correlation was seen at Bob's momentum detector. In figures 4c and 4d Alice used momentum encoding to send slit positions $s_0$ and $s_1$, and as expected Bob detected photons in the correct positions (observe the "-" sign, inversion, associated with the double-Fourier transform).

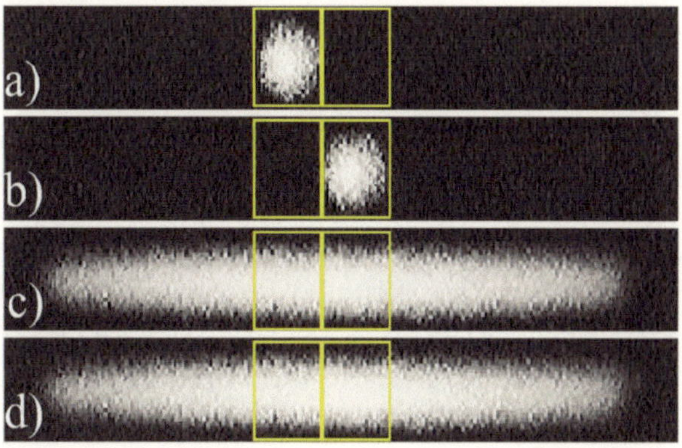


Fig. 3. Results for using position base: (a) bit 0 and (b) bit 1 for Alice encoding in position base, (c) bit 0 and (d) bit 1 for Alice encoding in momentum base.

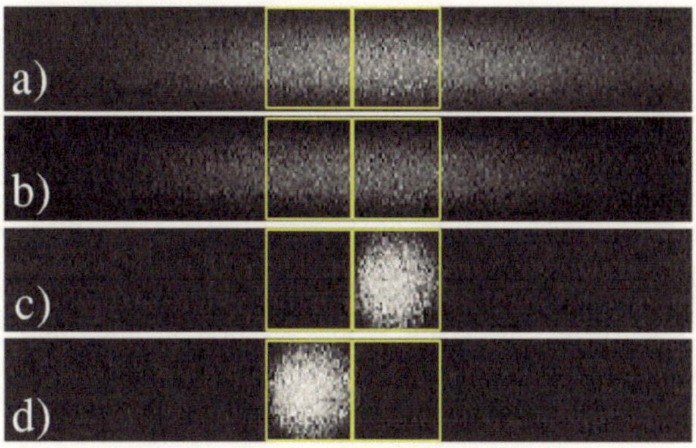


Fig. 4. Results for using momentum base: (a) bit 0 and (b) bit 1 for Alice encoding in position base, (c) bit 0 and (d) bit 1 for Alice encoding in momentum base.

The correlations shown in figures 3a, 3b, 4c and 4d show that Alice can send random bits to Bob, while the random results shown in figures 3c, 3d, 4a, and 4b demonstrate that an eavesdropper Eve will necessarily disturb the system when she guesses the wrong measurement basis. Furthermore, her disturbance will show up in Bob's measurement results. As discussed, for each photon sent, it is necessary for Eve to guess Alice's basis, x or p. After transmission, Eve will know if she guessed correctly or not by listening in on Alice and Bob's classical communication. If she guessed correctly, she will have detected the photon at the correct position and will know the bit that Alice sent. She will have reproduced Alice's original state and sent it to Bob. However, one-half of the time Eve guesses incorrectly, and every photon has an equal probability of being detected at either position, as shown in figures 3c, 3d, 4a and 4b. In this case, Eve has no information regarding the bit sent by Alice and is thus unable to reproduce her original state with certainty. If Alice and Bob calibrate their system correctly, Eve will cause a 25% error rate if she intercepts every photon.

**Polarisation coding** - this approach encrypts the bits in the bases shown in figure 1. Should Bob measure the pulse in the wrong base, he will obtain an ambiguous result. Similar to position-momentum encoding, faint photon pulses are crucial: should there be plenty of photons, the pulse can be divided into two, measured in both bases and retained the result only of the one not ambiguous (the wrong base would have a 50-50% statistic of "0" and "1" photons).

**Phase coding** - this approach encrypts the phase difference in a Mach-Zehnder interferometer as in the setup of (Hendrych, 2002). Alice and Bob each have a phase shifter in one of the arms of the interferometer (figure 5) and by applying suitable combinations of phase shifts, the interference can be tuned to be constructive/destructive (bits 1,0), or (quantum mechanically) random. The probability for a photon from the laser, entering the interferometer, and detected at detector D1 or D2 is: $(1 \pm \cos(\Delta\varphi))/2$ - for the case of zero attenuation and no environmental noise.

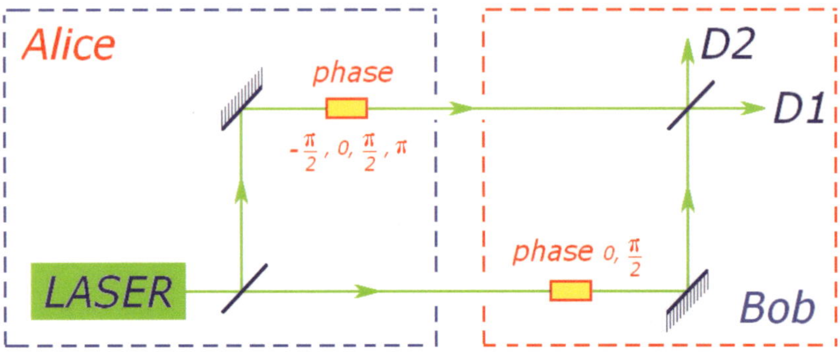


Fig. 5. Quantum encoding of phase difference in a Mach-Zehnder interferometer. For $\Delta\varphi = (0, \pi)$ Bob's base coincides with Alice's and his measurements are exact. For $\Delta\varphi = \pm\pi/2$ his base does not coincide with Alice's and the results of his measurements are stochastic (with the quantum predicted probabilities).

As a typical BB84 protocol implementation, Alice randomly sets one of the four phase shifts $-\pi/2$, 0, $\pi/2$, $\pi$ and Bob also randomly chooses his measurement basis by setting his phase shift 0, or $\pi/2$. When $\Delta\varphi = 0, \pi$, the measurement being performed in the same base, yields bits 1, 0 (constructive, or destructive interference). However, when Bob's base is orthogonal to Alice's base, the outcome can be ambiguous.

Since Alice and Bob are spatially separated, this implementation of would suffer from substantial problems due to environment perturbations, thermal drifts, etc. For the interference not to be washed out, the difference of the optical lengths of the interferometer's arms must stay constant to within a fraction of the wavelength of the used light. Different temperature fluctuations in the two optical fibers result in different changes in their refractive indices and smear out the interference.

To avoid this problem both paths of the interferometer can be launched into the same optical fiber, figure 6.

Such an interferometer comprises of two identical unbalanced interferometers, with path length difference much greater than the coherence length of the laser. Thus altough no interference occurrs in the small interferometers, globally the total system preserves the correct interference. Fiber couplers perform random 50:50 splitting, so photons can go on

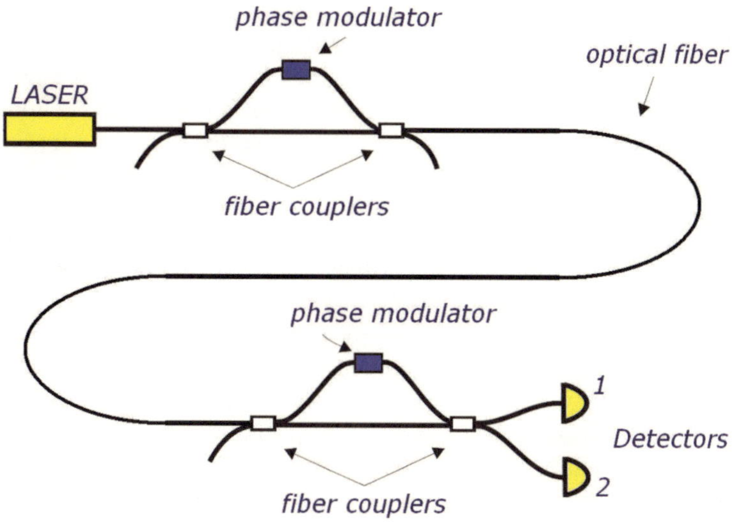


Fig. 6. Environmental perturbations can be eliminated using a time-multiplexing interferometer. In this setup Alice's and Bob's interferometers are identical unbalanced interferometers, whose with path length differences on the order of tens of cm.

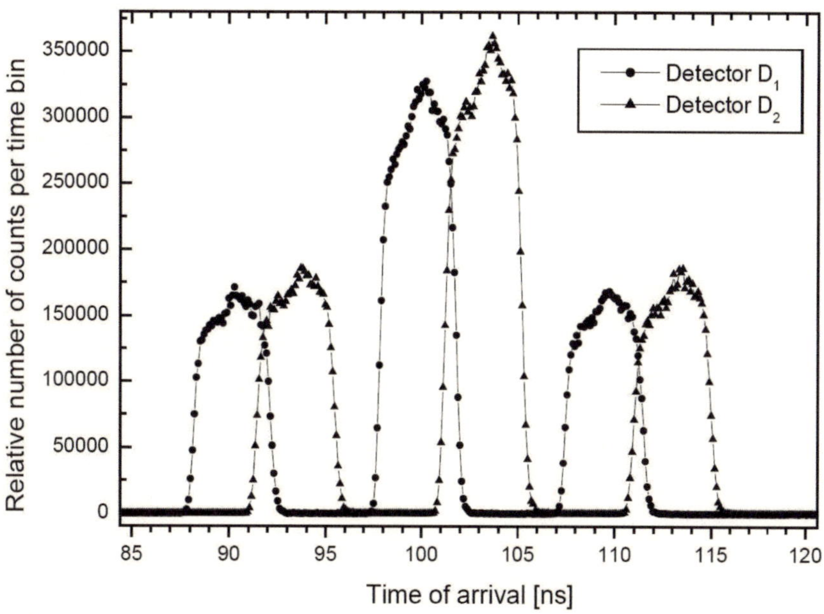


Fig. 7. Time of arrival for pulse in a 15-m time-multiplexing interferometer (circles detector D1, triangles D2). Photons arrive in 3 time windows separated by 10 ns (corresponding to the arm length difference of 2m): the leftmost peak photons taking short-short paths, the rightmost peak photons taking long-long paths. Interference occurs only in the middle (long-short, short-long) time window.

any of the four possible combinations from Alice to Bob: Alice's short path and Bob's short path 25 %, Alice's long path and Bob's short path 25 %, Alice's short path and Bob's long path 25 % and Alice's long path and Bob's long path 25 %. Typicall the length difference between the short and long arms of either interferometer is tens of cm's. Photons arrive at Bob's detectors in three time windows (separated by typically 10 ns - figure 6). There is no interference in the first and third time (short-short and long-long paths), however long-short and short-long paths are indistinguishable - and interfere. This method in effect is an interferometer analogous to that of figure 4, however, at the expense of losing half the photons (on the short-short- and long-long paths) it is possible to eliminate environmental fluctuations by being assured of having both paths of the interferometer equally affected by the latter. What still needs to be stabilised are the small unbalanced interferometers, where the short an long paths are spatially separated. To achieve this, the small unbalanced interferometers can be placed for instance in Styrofoam boxes (Hendrych, 2002).
As an overview on the effects contributing to the widths of the peaks: part is due to the width of laser pulses (4 ns), 0.5 ns to detector jitter and 0.3 ns to processing electronics jitter.
**Entanglement coding** - in this approach the photons are created by shining the laser through a non-linear crystal, producing entangled pairs of photons via spontaneous parametric downconversion. Figure 8 shows that in either polarisation base, the same (maximal) entanglement is present. As Alice (or even a third party - can be Eve !) prepares an entangled pair, she holds her part of the pair, a photon, and sends to Bob his part, the pair photon. When either Bob or Alice detects one's own photon, quantum laws guarantee that the other's photon is in the entanglement correspondent state.

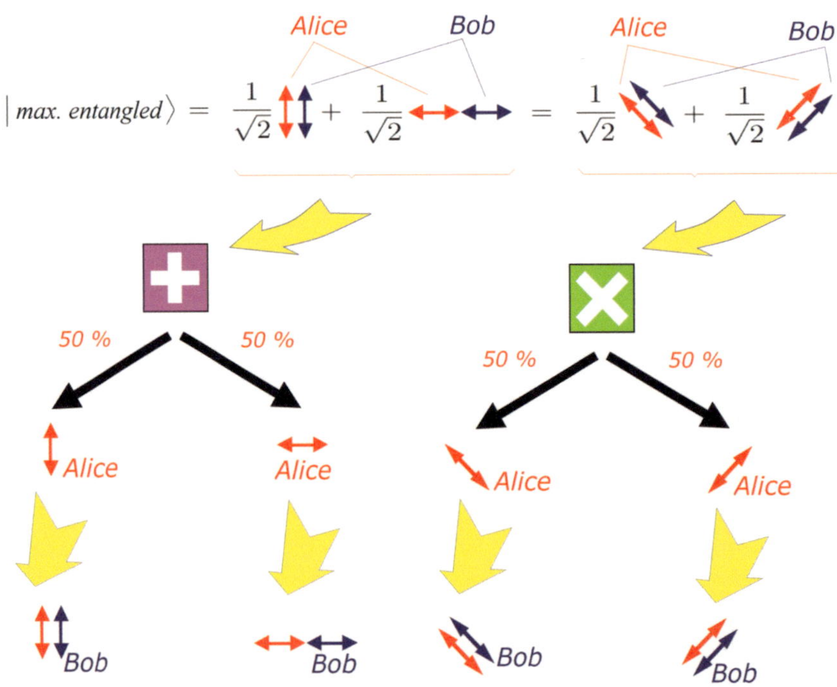


Fig. 8. Collapse of the entangled state by Alice's detection of her photon guarantees that Bob has his photon in the same state of polarisation *and* in the same base.

Any attempt at eavesdropping by Eve destroys the correlated pair in a way that Alice and Bob can detect. Eve cannot gain any information by capturing photons because *the actual information does not exist until Bob or Alice make their measurements*. The act of measuring creates the actual bit (0, or 1) that is to be sent. This is because either of the photons is in a *non*-eigen state for *both* bases (indeed an outstanding feature even for single-particle quantum mechanics !) and the collapse of its wavefunction determines what bit value the measuremtent will be. A remarkable consequence is that the bit's creation basis is decided upon measurement, and that namely by either Alice or Bob. Should the other use the wrong basis, an ambiguous result will ensue.

Should Eve conceive substituting herself for the source of entangled photons and produce 3 entanglement correlated photons, with the extra one held for herself without disturbing Alice or Bob, this will be noticed in the wavelength of the photons. At the single-photon level this translates in a different detection efficiency and non-optimal (path and thermal drift) compensations all equipments have. At the statistical level the wavelength can be measured and the generated keys discarded.

### 2.3 The BB84 protocol

Figure 9 illustrates how Alice transmits to Bob a raw key, how this is sifted and how this is further used to detect communication channel noise/ interference and produce the final key - (Bennett and Brassard, 1984).

Fig. 9. Schematic of the BB84 protocol: the role of conjugate quantum bases (+,×) and outcome both when using the correct and when using the wrong base are shown.

Firstly Alice selects the base for each bit, then decides on the 0,1 value of the bit. She does not tell Bob about the choices, not yet. She then sends the set to Bob, who chooses randomly a base in which to measure the qubits (quantum bits). In figure 8 the fist base is wrong and the result unreliable. The second one is correct and the recorded result faithful to the set sent by Alice ... etc. After the set is received Alice and Bob publicly exchange the information about the bases (and not about the bits). They discard those where Bob was wrong. For the hypothetical intercepter Eve this information is too late. To be in any way relevant she should have intercepted at least 2 photons and have measured one in one base and one in the other. However 2 photons out of a 2-3 photon pulse is too much (moreover, intercepting 1 photon for 1 measurement is likely insuficient).

In case of the **position/momentum** method the BB84 protocol would ensue as follows:

- Before any key bits are transmitted, Alice and Bob align their detectors so that Bob can establish detection positions that correspond to Alice's slit positions. They perform this alignment procedure using (xx) and (pp) configurations.
- Alice generates random bits a1 and a2. She aligns her slit aperture to position s(a1) and prepares either an x eigenstate a2=0 or a p eigenstate a2=1 to Bob's input plane.
- Bob generates a random bit b2, which determines the basis x or p in which he will measure. He detects the photon and records the result as bit b1. If no photon is detected, the run is automatically discarded.
- Alice and Bob repeat steps 2 and 3 until a sufficient number of photons have been transmitted and detected.
- Bob reveals his detection bases x or p for all his measurements using a classical communication channel. They agree to discard all results in which they prepared/measured in conjugate bases.
- Alice and Bob use a subset of the remaining results to check the quality of their correlations and estimate the error rate, which can be used to determine an upper bound on the amount of information possibly available to Eve. If the error rate is too large, Alice and Bob regard transmitted key compromised, they discard it and do not use it in crypting data. They repeat the run.
- If the error rate is acceptable, Alice and Bob use error correction to minimize errors and privacy amplification to minimize Eve's information.

In the of **entangled-photons**, the BB84 protocol takes the following form:

- Alice encodes each random bit value using one of two non-orthogonal polarizations: for example, horizontal (H) or +45° (D) can encode "0", while vertical (V) or −45° (E) can encode "1"
- Bob randomly measures each photon's polarization in either of the two conjugate bases (H/V or D/E) and records the results.
- Then, by conventional public communications Alice and Bob reveal their basis choice (but not the bit value) for each detected event, and sift out the (perfectly correlated) set for which they used the same bases, and discard the uncorrelated, wrong-basis events (approximately half of the detected bits in an ideal system). If Eve intercepts every photon, measures its polarization, and sends an appropriately polarized photon on to Bob, she will induce an error rate of 25–50%. The lower limit is obtained only if Eve makes her measurements in the same bases used by Alice and Bob (or in a basis that lies in the same plane on the Poincare sphere: for example, if Alice and Bob use the (H/V) and (D/E) linear polarization bases, then eavesdropping in any linear polarization basis will yield an error rate of 25%. In contrast, eavesdropping in the left/right (L/R) circular polarization basis will induce an error rate of 50% (Naik, 2000).

It can be seen now how Eve's presence is revealed to Alice and Bob. After obtaining the sifted key, they can sacrifice a small part of the bits to test the noise/error-rate of the communication channel: Alice decides which bits and Bob sends publicly their values. Alice then reports back the BER (bit error rate). If this is above 11% (Lütkenhaus, (1999), should Eve be the reason for this high value, it may be assumed that she has had a starting-to-be-viable chance at gaining information on the transmission. Figure 10 (falling curve) shows the set's discarded fraction as a function of sifted key error rate during information reconciliation (Brassard Salvail, 1993), a protocol to eliminate errors in the set used. Privacy amplification is a method for reducing (and effectively eliminating) Eve's partial information on the transmission. This can be done with a hash function, randomly chosen from a given set of functions, with entry a binary string of length equal to the key and output a shorter string reducing the probability of Eve having knowledge of the new key to a minimal value (calculated as a ratio of the shrinkage factor). Secure transmission is guaranteed for error rate under 11 %.

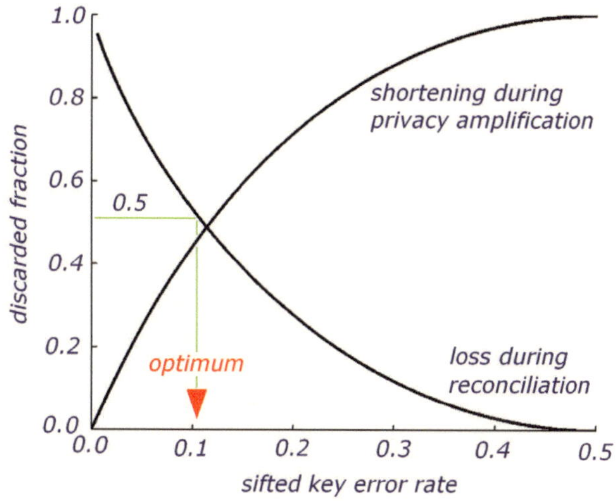


Fig. 10. Losses for Information Reconciliation and Privacy Amplification as a function of sifted key error rate. Secure transmission is guaranteed for error rate < 11%.

## 3. QUANTGRID – Encryption for GRID Applications

It is evident that this encryption technology is attractive to a number of other technologies relying on encrypted communications, such as bank communications, government communications and of course GRID-computing file transfers.

In this respect a test programme was started in the Institute for Nuclear Physics and Engineering (Particle Physics and IT Department) in collaboration with the Institute for Lasers and Plasma Physics and the Polytechnical University (all Bucharest-Romania). The applications under way in the department concern processing data from CERN's LHC experiments, thus large data fluxes are involved. It is known that quantum encryption equipment produces key rates on the order of a few kbps. These need to be amplified in order to be used for the large amounts of data involved. This can be achieved for instance by taking sections from the last transmitted data segment and AES-encrypting them, then using this volume of key as the actual one to do the encryption.

In the following will be described our quantum encryption stand and the software we produced to use in the actual data transmissions of this project (QUANTGRID, 2010).

### 3.2 Quantum encryption unit

A number of component providers (Equipment, 2010) exist on the market, the setup here presented being based on Clavis2 components (ID-Quantique, 2009) from ID-Quantique, which offer the possibility of further configuration modification and future experimentation.

The setup in figure 11 consists of the Bob station (receiver), the Alice station (sender), a 23.845 km (quantum channel) optical line between Alice and Bob for the secret key, 2 dedicated computers handling the Bob and Alice stations and a LAN Ethernet (classical channel) connection between the computers for the encrypted data. The components are described below:

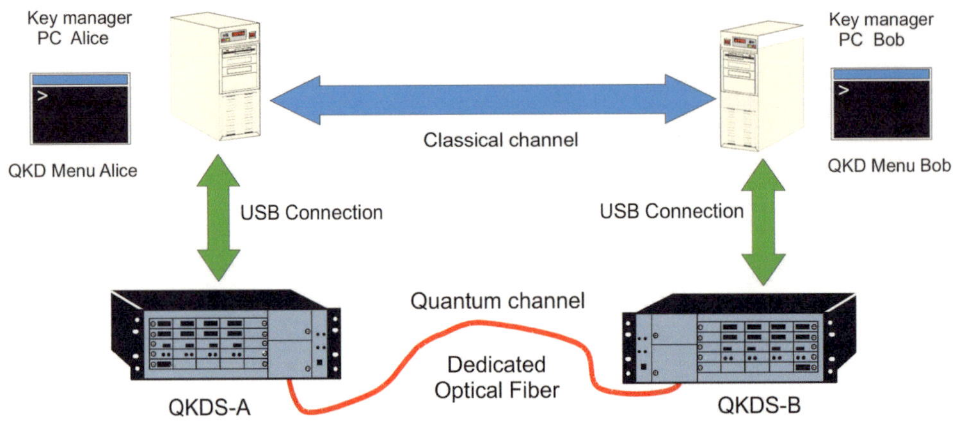


Fig. 11. Communication line setup with two dedicated computers (Bob - receiver and Alice - sender). The quantum channel (23.845 km) is a dedicated optical fiber line, while the classical channel is via LAN Ethernet.

**Bob station** (receiver) - for an auto-compensated setup, the information Alice sends is physically produced by Bob in the form of intense laser pulses that are sent to Alice, reflected back (phase modulated) and detected by Bob as the receiver. After the laser the pulses are split and enter an unbalanced interferometer: one half through the long arm and the other through the short one, after which they are further recombined at an exit phase beam-splitter. On the return way from Alice the pulses take complementary paths and the long arm applies the phase modulation corresponding to Bob's decision for a measurement basis. They then interfere and are detected with the single-photon detectors (avalanche photodiodes in Geiger mode). Polarization maintaining fibers are used throughout.

Components:

- Laser Diode: pulse energy of -17 dBm @ 500ps, pulse duration of 300-2500 ps, pulse power measured with a photodiode
- 2 Photon-Counting Detectors: bias voltage controlled, dead-time on/off and duration (FPGA controlled)
- Phase modulator: with phase voltage control (0, $\pi$)
- Optical Components: circulator, coupler, polarization splitter.

Electronics:

- mainboard - used for handling of high level functions. On-board microcontroller providing USB interface, running temperature regulation, and dedicated PortC and I2C for communication with other electronic components (FPGA and ADC/DAC I2C compatibles, temperature sensor, etc). The FPGA controls 4 different pulsers, DAQ, formatting and storage. An on-board acquisition channel monitors component operations.

- laser, phase modulator and detector boards - dedicated to optoelectronic interfacing, mainly for specific driving functions in accordance to the optoelectronics they drive (gating and/or temperature regulation).

The electronics performs five main tasks:

1. Status monitoring and hardware parameter storage - monitoring of power supplies, APD cooler current/temperature, etc, mainly by the microcontroller.
2. Laser diode control - duration and timing of pulses through an FPGA driven pulser mode (mainboard implemented). Temperature regulation and laser power measurement are performed using the internal photodiode of the laser.
3. Phase modulator control - duration and amplitude setting of phase modulation pulses through an FPGA driven pulser mode (mainboard implemented). Two different states are possible: zero/adjustable amplitude state (state 0/1).
4. Photon-counting detectors control - independent setting of bias voltage for each detector. A current source embedded on the detector board (mainboard microcontroller steered), regulates the detector temperature to $-50^{o}$ C and allows control of the duration and timing of the gates applied on the APD, by sensing avalanches and converting them on FPGA captured detections.
5. Transfer of bit values for key exchange - retrieval of random bits generated by the mainboard embedded random generator. The 2 bits values are sent sequentially to the phase modulator board, for storage in embedded memory together the detector 1/2 counts, then sent to the controlling PC via USB/microcontroller.

Fig. 12. Communication line setup used in the QUANTGRID D11-044 project (Inst. for Laser and Plasma Phys. - Bucharest), with its two dedicated computers (Bob - receiver and Alice - sender). The quantum channel (23.845 km) optical fiber spool is on top of the Bob station. The classical channel linking the computers is local LAN Ethernet.

**Alice station** (sender) – although not directly, physically, producing the pulses, it encodes them by modulating the phase of the second pulse half. The pulses from Bob are split at input by a 10/90 coupler, with the bright part (90%) directed to a classical detector which provides the timing for gating and scrutinizes the incoming signal for intensity variations from potential eavesdroppers (Trojan Horse attack: intense signal injection for phase modulator probing, i.e. - for the sent information). The weak part (10%) is directed into the "quantum emitter": variable optical attenuator (set to guarantee "faint photon" level of the pulses sent to Bob), long delay line (12 or 24 km, preventing spurious detections caused from Rayleigh backscattering), phase modulator (acting on the second half of each pulse) and Faraday mirror (ensuring passive compensation of polarisation mode dispersion effects in the optical link on a round-trip).

Components:

- Variable optical attenuator (dual channel): attenuation 1.5 - 50 dB, channel 1 (at quantum emitter input), channel 2 (in front of the classical detector)
- Classical Detector: bias voltage 30 - 60V, 2 discriminators (detection of Bob's pulses and monitoring of incoming – Trojan Horse attack guard)
- Phase modulator: phase voltage with 4 values ($0, \pi/2, \pi, 3\pi/2$)
- Optical components: delay line, coupler, Faraday mirror.

Electronics:

- mainboard – handling high level functions, it includes a microcontroller providing the USB interface, running a dedicated 8 bit interface to the FPGA and an I2C bus for communications with other electronic components (DAC, ADC, temperature sensor, etc). An FPGA controlling four different pulsers, data acquisition, formatting and storage before sending them to the PC is used. The peripheral boards enclose components with mainly specific driving functions according to the optoelectronic they have to drive (gating and/or temperature regulation), and an acquisition channel which is used to monitor component operations.
- detector and phase modulator boards – dedicated to optoelectronic interfacing, with components having mainly specific driving functions according to the optoelectronics they drive (gating and/or temperature regulation), and an acquisition channel which is used to monitor component operations.

The peripheral boards perform the following tasks:

1. Status monitoring and hardware parameter storage – monitoring of power supplies, temperature and storage for availability to the controlling computer.
2. Variable optical attenuator control – by the two variable optical attenuators. The stepper motor attenuator is controlled through an I2C bus.
3. Classical detector control – used to set bias voltage and threshold levels of the two discriminators connected to detector output. Synchronization output signal of the discriminators is fed back into the high-level electronics.
4. Phase modulation – voltage setting for the four phase values (one for each state) via DAC and multiplexer. Precise timing of the actuation comes from the delay of the timing signal from the classical detector.
5. Transfer of bit values for key exchang – retrieval of random bits generated by the embedded random generator on the mainboard. The 2 bit values are sent sequentially to the phase modulator, there stored on embedded data memory and sent to the controlling PC (through the microcontroller and USB bus).

The actual processes that take place on the equipment are numerous, both units, Alice and Bob, being highly automated. The mode of operation of the hardware is in cycles. During each cycle, a complete frame is produced. A cycle contains the following steps (figure 13):

- **Laser pulse train** - the electronics sends a train of laser pulses (period 200 ns) and produces the laser start signal. The number of pulses is limited by the long delay line enclosed in Alice.
- **Alice sync** - synchronization of Alice's clock to the incoming laser pulse train frequency, producing a clock synchronization signal.
- **Alice phase modulation** - phase modulation (PM) gate is then applied on the second component of each pulse. Phase modulation amplitude is chosen randomly from the four states for each pulse. Phase modulation is applied after a fixed Alice coarse delay versus clock synchronization signal, corresponding to the laser pulse train time of flight through the delay line.
- **Bob phase modulation** - phase modulation gate is applied on the first component of each pulse. Phase modulation amplitude is chosen randomly from two states for each pulse. Phase modulation is applied after a fixed Bob PM coarse delay, corresponding to a roundtrip of the laser pulse train time of flight through the transmission line and Alice. The Bob detector-1 Coarse Delay is used as reference point to compute the Bob PM Coarse Delay.
- **Bob detection** - detector-1 and detector-2 (D1 and D2) gates are applied on the single photon detectors to activate them when encoded weak pulses return. These gates are applied after a variable delay - combination of a coarse delay and a fine delay for each detector - versus laser start signal. These variable delays (for D1 and D2) are determined from the line measurement process, so that the detectors are activated when the laser pulses hit them. These delays are independent for each detector.

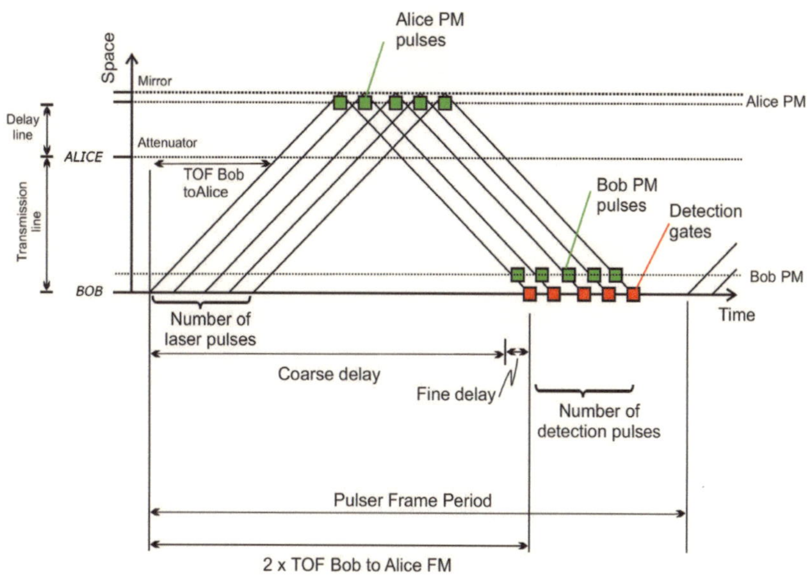


Fig. 13. Time sketch of the processes: Laser pulse train, Alice sync, Alice phase modulation, Bob phase modulation, Bob detection, Next frame, Raw key distillation

- **Next frame** - waiting for the end of the frame period. Next frame cannot be sent if the current frame is not received by Bob entirely.
- **Raw key distillation** - the entire procedure is repeated a number of times until the stop condition applies. Once this state has been reached, the pulser is reset. All measurements (Detection, Alice and Bob Phases) are stored and constitute the raw key. The data is then sent to the controlling computer for distillation and further processing.

### 3.3 Encryption and communications software

We designed 2 C++ packages enabling us to handle socket communications and AES encryption (SXV4 and AXV4, 2008). In particular we are working on applying the two packages in a hopping-sockets configuration in which we constantly change the connection port (based on a number transmitted in the encryption key) as to avoid software surveillance in the target computer:

- **SXV4** - proprietary C++ class for the handle of socket level communications. This gives us a handle close to the hardware level, of interacting with the communication ports
- **AXV4** - proprietary C++ class implementing the FIPS-197 AES standard. This allows us to take control of the procedure and intervene in taking information from intermediate stages in the en/decryption.

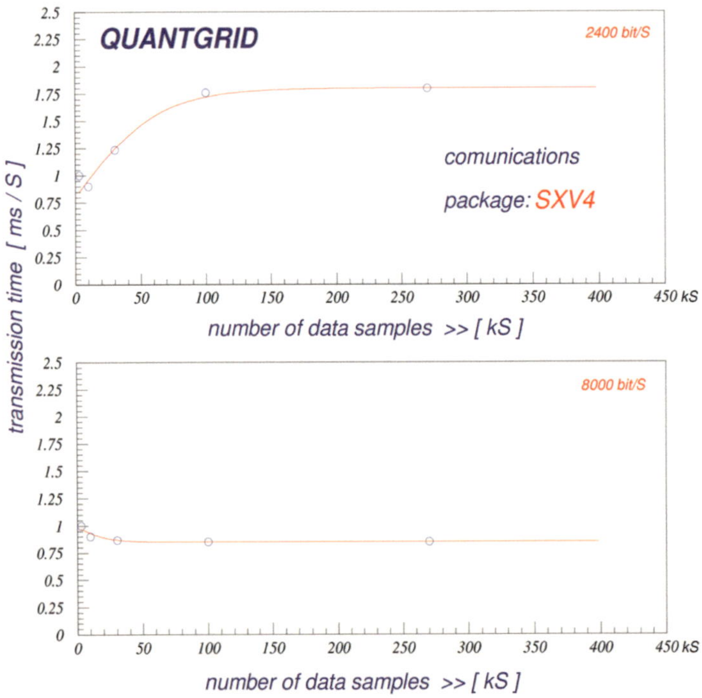


Fig. 14. Server response times package, for 2400 bit/sample and 8000 bit/sample tests. Multiple samples are transmitted for each point on the plots. It can be seen that an optimisation allots high priority to tasks loading the net-card with large data batches, in order to expedite the job, and lessens the priority for small batches of data on the net-card, whether they occur seldomly or frequently.

**SXV4 tests** - we have tested the C++ package on two servers on the same cluster - which is very similar to the configuration quant-modem-to-GRID port, by sending various data samples, of different lengths. Typical transmit-times are presented in figure 14 - function of the number of samples in the same transmit-job. We fitted the server response to saturating functions in order to have an estimate of transmission times for repeated transmissions. A complete map of tests was performed, in the range of 8, 24, 80, 240, 800, 2400, 8000, 24000 bit/sample.

For large samples (over 8000 bit/sample) the transmission time changes from a slowly rising one to a flat (or faintly decreasing) one, on the order of 1 ms/S. This has to do with the optimisation of large data fluxes (in a single connection) on ports.

**AXV4 tests** - we have tested the C++ package as AES is known to be somewhat slow on decryption. Indeed, in our implementation of the FIPS-197 standard we found it to be 5 times slower in decryption over encryption. Also, importantly, whereas for small versus large file sizes the time/character varies within 30% for decryption, for encryption this ratio is roughly a factor of 8 (figures 15 - encryption, and 16 - decryption).

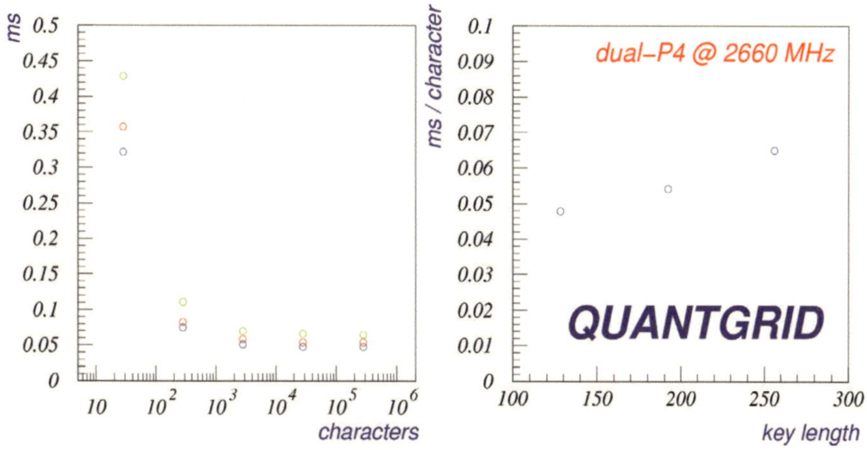


Fig. 15. Performance of AXV4 in encrypting a file function of file size (saturation on the order of 60 μs/character, for file above 2000 characters) - left. Performance function of the key length used (blue = 128 bit, red = 192, green = 256) - right. A linear dependence with key size is observed.

This is important in timing both sender and receiver processes such that they have the proper time in performing the necessary packing/unpacking, switching ports, etc.

Another interesting factor we looked for in the tests was the relative advantage time wise versus the key length used - on a dual-P4 2.66 Pentium machine:

- **128 bit key** - for this key length the average encryption time per character ranges exponentially decreasing from 0.32 ms/character (at 10 characters/file) down to 0.05 ms/character (at 300000 characters/file). For decryption the same numbers are 0.32 ms/character and 0.25 ms/character (a ratio of 1.28 vs. 6.4 for encryption).
- **192 bit key** - for this key length the average encryption time per character ranges exponentially decreasing from 0.36 ms/character (at 10 characters/file) down to 0.06 ms/character (at 300000 characters/file). For decryption the same numbers are 0.39 ms/character and 0.31 ms/character (a ratio of 1.26 vs. 6.0 for encryption).

- **256 bit key** - for this key length the average encryption time per character ranges exponentially decreasing from 0.43 ms/character (at 10 characters/file) down to 0.07 ms/character (at 300000 characters/file). For decryption the same numbers are 0.41 ms/character and 0.37 ms/character (a ratio of 1.10 vs. 6.1 for encryption).

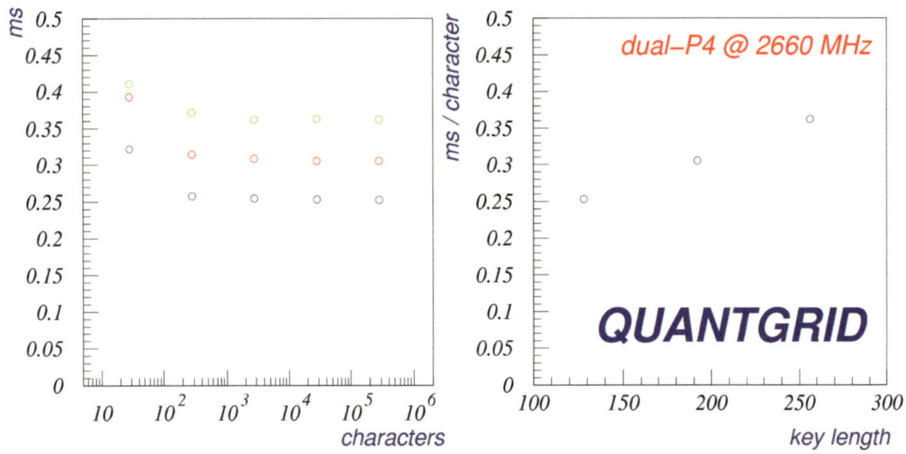


Fig. 16. Performance of AXV4 in decrypting a file function of file size (saturation on the order of 60 μs/character, for file above 2000 characters) - left. Performance function of the key length used (blue = 128 bit, red = 192, green = 256) - right. A linear dependence with key size is observed.

## 7. Conclusion

Quantum encryption is a very promising technology in securing data transfers - as shown, a number of quantum methods being available - each with its own advantages: simpler practical implementation, stability to thermal drift, immunity to eavesdropping, higher key generation rate. So far commercial components exist mostly in the form of polarisation and phase encoding.

Implementation in GRID-computing depends, at the moment at least, on boosting the key generation rate from a few kbps to at least a few 0.1 Mbps. This can be achieved for instance by using the quantum key to AES-encrypt sections of the transmitted data, and then use the resulting volume as key.

The project here presented, QUANTGRID, is a first attempt at using this technology in GRID data transfers. Auxiliary software was developed for embedding quantum keys in the transfers: a proprietary sockets package that allows to hop the communication port on the target machine avoiding surveillance software and an AES encryption package that allows to take control of the procedure and intervene in taking information from intermediate stages in the en/decryption. The project - funded under D11-044 (CNMP-Romania, for the quantum technology) and in part by PN-09370104 (ANCS-Romania, for the GRID technology) - is ongoing.

## 8. References


Salomaa, A. (1990). *Public-Key Cryptography,* Springer-Verlag, ISBN 3540613560, 9783540613565, Berlin, New York, London, Paris, Tokyo, 1996

Shor, P.W. (1994). Algorithms for quantum computation: discrete logarithms and factoring, *Proceedings of Foundations of Computer Science,* pp. 124 - 134, ISBN 0-8186-6580-7, Santa Fe, NM-US, November 1994 , IEEE Computer Society Press, Los Alamitos, CA-US

Daemen J. and Rijmen V. (2006). The Block Cipher Rijndael, in: *Lecture Notes in Computer Science,* 277-284, Springer-Verlag, ISBN 0302-9743, Berlin, Heidelberg; Federal Information Processing Standards Publication 197/Nov-2001 following Section 5131 of the Information Technology Management Reform Act (Public Law 104-106/1996) and Computer Security Act (Public Law 100-235/1987).

Biryukov A. and Khovratovich D. (2009). Related-Key Cryptanalysis of the Full AES-192 and AES-256, *Proceedings of Advances in Cryptology - ASIACRYPT 2009, 15th Intn.'l Conf. on the Theory and Application of Cryptology and Information Security,* pp. 1-18, ISBN 978-3-642-10365-0, Tokyo-Japan, December 2009, Matsui, Mitsuru (ed.), Springer-Verlag Berlin

Hathaway L. (2003). National Policy on the Use of the Advanced Encryption Standard (AES) to Protect National Security Systems and National Security Information.

Vernam G.S. (1926). Cipher Printing Telegraph Systems For Secret Wire and Radio Telegraphic Communications. *Journal of the IEEE,* Vol. 55, pp 109-115

Willan P. (2004). EU seeks quantum cryptography response to Echelon, in *Network World,* of 17.05.2004

Dusek M., Haderka O., Hendrych M. (1999). Generalized Beam-Splitting Attack in Quantum Cryptography with Dim Coherent States, *Opt. Comms.* 169, pp. 103-108

D.S. Lemelle, M.P. Almeida, P.H. Souto Ribeiro, S.P. Walborna (2006). A simple optical demonstration of quantum cryptography using transverse position and momentum variables, *Am. J. Phys.,* Vol. 74, pp 542-546

M. Hendrych (2002), *Experimental Quantum Cryptography;* also M. Dušck, O. Haderka, M. Hendrych, Practical Aspects of Quantum Cryptography, *Book Quantum Communication, Computing, and Measurement 2,* pp. 393-398, ISBN 978-0-306-46307-5, May 2007, Springer-Verlag US

Bennett C.H., Brassard G. (1984). Public Key Distribution and Coin Tossing, *Proceedings of IEEE International Conference on Computers Systems and Signal Processing,* pp. 175-179, Bangalore-India, 1984, IEEE, New York

D.S. Naik, C.G. Peterson, A.G. White, A.J. Berglund, P.G. Kwiat (2000). Entangled State Quantum Cryptography: Eavesdropping on the Ekert Protocol, *Phys. Rev. Lett..,* Vol. 84, pp 4733-4736

Lütkenhaus N. (1999). Estimates for practical quantum cryptography, *Phys. Rev. .* A59, pp. 3301-3319

Brassard G. and Salvail L. (1993). Secret key reconciliation by public discussion, *Proceedings of Advances in Cryptology: Eurocrypt'93,* pp. 410-423, ISBN 3-540-57600-2, Lofthus-Norway, May 1993, Lecture Notes in Computer Science 765, Springer-Verlag Berlin

QUANTGRID (2010) - project D11-044 "QUANTGRID" financed through the National Center for Programme Management (CNMP-Romania)

Equipment (2010) - ID-Quantique (Geneva), MagiQ (Boston), QuintessenceLabs (Canberra), SmartQuantum (Paris)

ID-Quantique (2009) - ID-3100 Clavis2 Components Documentation v1.1, Feb. 2009, © ID-Quantique

SXV4, AXV4 (2008) - QUANTGRID Activity Report 2008.

# 6

# Data Consolidation and Information Aggregation in Grid Networks

Panagiotis Kokkinos and Emmanouel Varvarigos
*University of Patras, Department of Computer Engineering and Informatics Research Academic Computer Technology Institute*
*Greece*

## 1. Introduction

Grids consist of geographically distributed and heterogeneous computational and storage resources that may belong to different administrative domains, but are shared among users by establishing a global resource management architecture. A variety of applications can benefit from Grid computing; among them data-intensive applications that perform computations on large sized datasets, stored at geographically distributed resources. In this context, we identify two important issues: i) data consolidation that relates to the handling of these data-intensive applications and ii) information aggregation, which relates to the summarization of resource information and the provision of information confidentiality among the different administrative domains.

Data consolidation (DC) applies to data-intensive applications that need more than one pieces of data to be transferred to an appropriate site, before the application can start its execution at that site. It is true, though, that an application/task may not need all the datasets at the time it starts executing, but, it is usually beneficial both for the network and for the application to perform the datasets transfers concurrently and before the task's execution. The DC problem consists of three interrelated sub-problems: (i) the selection of the replica of each dataset (i.e., the data repository site from which to obtain the dataset) that will be used by the task, (ii) the selection of the site where these pieces of data will be gathered and the task will be executed and (iii) the selection of the paths the datasets will follow in order to be concurrently transferred to the data consolidating site. Furthermore, the delay required for transferring the output data files to the originating user (or to a site specified by him) should also be accounted for. In most cases the task's required datasets will not be located into a single site, and a data consolidation operation is therefore required. Generally, a number of algorithms or policies can be used for solving these three sub-problems either separately or jointly. Moreover, the order in which these sub-problems are handled may be different, while the performance optimization criteria used may also vary. The algorithms or policies for solving these sub-problems compromise a DC scheme. We will present a number of DC schemes. Some consider only the computational or only the communication requirements of the tasks, while others consider both kinds of requirements. We will also describe DC schemes, which are based on Minimum Spanning Trees (MST) that route concurrently the datasets so as to reduce the congestion that may appear in the future, due to these transfers. Our results brace our belief that DC is an important problem that needs to be addressed in the design of Grids networks, and can lead, if performed efficiently, to significant benefits in terms of task delay, network load and other performance parameters.

Information aggregation relates to the summarization of resource information collected in a Grid Network and provided to the resource manager in order for it to make scheduling decisions. Resource-related information size and dynamicity grows rapidly with the size of the Grid, making the aggregation and use of this massive amount of information a challenge for the resource management system. In addition, as computation and storage tasks are conducted increasingly non-locally and with finer degrees of granularity, the flow of information among different systems and across multiple domains will increase. Information aggregation techniques are important in order to reduce the amount of information exchanged and the frequency of these exchanges, while at the same time maximizing its value to the Grid resource manager or to any other desired consumer of the information. An additional motivation for performing information aggregation is confidentiality and interoperability, in the sense that as more resources or domains of resources participate in the Grid, it is often desirable to keep sensitive and detailed resource information private, while resources are still being publicly available for use. For example, it may soon become necessary for the interoperability of the various cloud computing services (e.g., Amazon EC2 and S3, Microsoft Azure) that the large quantity of resource-related information is efficiently abstracted, before it is provided to the task scheduler. In this way, the task scheduler will be able to use efficiently and transparently the resources, without requiring services to publish in detail their resources characteristics. In any case, the key to information aggregation is the degree to which the summarized information helps the scheduler make efficient use of the resources, while coping with the dynamics of the Grid and the varying requirements of the users. We will describe a number of information aggregation techniques, including single point and intra-domain aggregation and we will define appropriate grid-specific domination relations and operators for aggregating static and dynamic resource information. We measure the quality of an aggregation scheme both by its effects on the efficiency of the scheduler's decisions and also by the reduction it brings on the total of resource information. Our simulation experiments demonstrate that the proposed schemes achieve significant information reduction, either in the amount of information exchanged, or in the frequency of the updates, while at the same time maintaining most of the value of the original information.

The remainder of the paper is organized as follows. In Section 2 we report on previous work. In Section 3 we formulate and analyze the Data Consolidation (DC) problem, proposing a number of DC schemes. In Section 4 we formulate the information aggregation problem and propose several information aggregation techniques. In Section 5 we present the simulation environment and the performance results obtained for the proposed schemes and techniques. Finally, conclusions are presented in Section 6.

## 2. Previous work

The Data Consolidation (DC) problem involves task scheduling, data management and routing issues. Usually these issues are handled separately in the corresponding research papers. There are several studies that propose algorithms for assigning tasks to the available resources in a grid network (Krauter et al., 2002). A usual data management operation in grids is data migration, that is, the movement of data between resources. The effects of data migration in grids have been considered in (Shan et al., 2004). The most common data migration technique is data replication (Rahman et al., 2007) (Rahman et al., 2008) (Dogan, 2009), which is the process of distributing replicas of data across sites. When different sites hold replicas of a particular dataset, significant benefits can be realized by selecting the best replica among them, that is, the one that optimizes a desired performance criterion such as access latency, cost, security, etc (Vazhkudai et al., 2001). Furthermore, the problem of parallel downloading different parts of a dataset from various replica holding resources, as a mean to decrease the download time of that dataset, has been investigated for peer-to-peer networks and the Internet (Byers et al., 1999) (Rodriguez et al., 2002), and also for grid networks (Chang et al., 2008). A number of works consider both task scheduling and data replication issues. The authors in (Ranganathan et al., 2002) suggest that it is better to perform data replication and task scheduling separately, instead of trying to jointly optimize these two operations. In (Elghirani et al., 2007) the authors propose a data management service that proactively replicates the datasets at selected sites, while an intelligent Tabu-search scheduler dispatches tasks to resources so as to optimize execution time and system utilization metrics. The authors in (Bell et al., 2002) (Bell et al., 2003) (Cameron et al., 2004) present the OptorSim simulator and jointly consider task scheduling and data replication for the case where a task requests sequentially a number of datasets. In this case data replication, of a specific dataset to a selected site, is performed when a task requires this dataset for its execution. Also, the authors in (Chakrabarti et al., 2004) propose the Integrated Replication and Scheduling Strategy (IRS) scheduler that combines scheduling and replication strategies. The effective use of the communication/network resources is an important consideration, especially in data grid networks. In (Stevens et al., 2008) a multicost algorithm for the joint time scheduling of the communication and computation resources to be used by a task is proposed. The algorithm selects the computation resource to execute the task, determines the path to be used for routing the single input data, and finds the starting times for the data transmission and the task execution, performing advance reservations.

The Data Consolidation (DC) problem addressed in the present work arises when a task requires before the start of its execution multiple datasets stored at different sites. In this case we believe that it is beneficial for the application to organize the transfers of the datasets concurrently so as to decrease the task's total execution time. Even though this seems like a logical scenario, especially for data-intensive applications, most of the related works seem to ignore it, assuming either that each task needs for its execution only one large piece of data (Ranganathan et al., 2002) (Stevens et al., 2008), or that it requires sequentially a number of datasets (Rahman et al., 2007)(Rahman et al., 2008) (Bell et al., 2002)(Bell et al., 2003) (Cameron et al., 2004). Our work does not consider any specific dynamic data replication strategy; instead, we assume that a dynamic data replication strategy is in place that distributes replicas in the grid, while data consolidation is performed when a task actually requests a number of datasets before its execution. In most cases the task's required datasets will not be located into a single site, and their consolidation to the selected site will be required before task execution. Furthermore, most of the related works do not explicitly examine important issues like the joint replica selection (and estimation of the cost of the transfers) and the joint routing of these replicas (so as to avoid congestion delays that each of the corresponding transfers may cause to each other).

Information aggregation has been previously studied mainly in the context of hierarchical data networks (Lee, 1995), where it is performed on network-related parameters in order to facilitate hierarchical routing. Hierarchical routing is a major issue for data networks, and is important for reducing the memory requirements at the routers (border nodes) for the very large topologies encountered in Internet's infrastructure. A topology is broken down into several layers of hierarchy, thus downsizing the routing tables required, but this comes at the expense of an increase in the average path length. (Kleinrock, Kamoun, 1977) is one of the first works investigating hierarchical routing, where clustering structures are introduced to minimize the routing tables required. Bounds are also derived on the maximum increase in the path length for a given table size. An issue that is central to hierarchical routing is topology information aggregation (Lee, 1995) (Mieghem, 1999). Aggregation techniques in hierarchical topologies try to summarize and compress the topology information advertised at higher levels. In order to perform routing and network resource allocation efficiently, the aggregated information should adequately represent the topology and the characteristics/metrics of the network. Delay and bandwidth are two network-related metrics that are usually aggregated along with the topology. In (Lee, 1995) a number of topology aggregation techniques are presented. An important issue in topology aggregation is the choice of the parameters that are aggregated along with the topology. In (Mieghem, 1999) the parameters that can be aggregated, are distinguished into three classes: additive, min-max and the combination of additive and min-max metrics (multi-criteria). Topology aggregation based on such metrics is investigated in (Bauer et al., 2006), considering only network-related parameters (namely, delay and bandwidth). In the same context (Bauer et al., 2006) presents a topology aggregation scheme that is subject to multi-criteria (delay and bandwidth) constraints. Specifically, a transition matrix is constructed containing the minimum information that describes exactly the traversing characteristics of a domain, that is, the characteristics of the paths connecting border (ingress-egress) node pairs of the domain.

Resource information aggregation in grids has not been studied in detail, despite its practical importance and its impact on the efficiency of the scheduling decisions. Actually, most scheduling algorithms proposed (Krauter et al., 2002) make their decisions using exact resource information. The idea of aggregation has also appeared in sensor networks (Intanagonwiwat et al., 2003), where it is often called data fusion, as a way to reduce the amount of data transferred towards the sink node. Relatively recently, information aggregation appeared as an interesting topic in Peer-to-Peer (P2P) (Renesse et al., 2003) and P2P grid systems (Schulz et al., 2009) (Zhou, Hwang, 2006) (Cai, Hwang, 2007). These works focus on the architecture and on the mechanisms of the system performing the aggregation; on the other hand, in our work we assume that such a mechanism/system is in place and examine the aggregation operations that should be performed for different parameters, the aggregation policies that should be applied and the effects they have on scheduling efficiency. Also, our work applies to all kinds of grids and not specifically to Desktop grids. In addition, resource information aggregation and task scheduling issues have been investigated in a few works, which focus, however, on particular systems and under specific assumptions (Czajkowski et al., 2001) (Muraki et al., 2006) (Rodero et al., 2010). In the Monitoring and Discovery System 2 (MDS2) (Czajkowski et al., 2001) (Muraki et al., 2006) resource management system, information from individual information providers (e.g., resources) is aggregated into collections, where each collection may correspond to a different virtual organization (VO). (Rodero et al., 2010) is a quite recent work where aggregated resource information and scheduling issues are considered. It proposes two aggregation policies (simple and categorized) and two scheduling policies that use the aggregated information. In our work we are interested more in the parameters aggregated, in the operators used and in the policies applied to summarize them, while we use a simple scheduling policy to evaluate the effects of the aggregation on the scheduling efficiency. We also investigate the tradeoffs between the amount of information exchanged, the frequency of updates required, and the quality of the aggregated information. Most importantly, our work is quite more general, and attempts to fill the gap between the topology information aggregation works presented in (Lee, 1995) (Mieghem, 1999) and grid computing.

## 3. Data consolidation

### 3.1 Problem formulation

We consider a grid network, consisting of a set $R$ of $N = |R|$ sites (resources) that are connected through a Wide Area Network (WAN). Each site $r \in R$ contains at least one of the following entities: a computational resource that processes submitted tasks, a storage resource where datasets are stored and a network resource that performs routing operations. There are also a number of simple routers in the network. The path between two sites $r_i$ and $r_j$ has maximum usable capacity equal to $P_{i,j,}$ , defined as the minimum of the path's links capacities and propagation delay equal to $d_{i,j}$.
The computation resource of site $r_i$ has total computation capacity $C_i$, measured in computation units per second (e.g., Million Instructions Per Second - MIPS). Each resource also has a local scheduler and a queue. Tasks arriving at the resource are stored in its queue, until they are assigned by the local scheduler to an available CPU. For the sake of being specific, we assume that the local scheduler uses the First Come First Served (FCFS) policy, but other policies can also be used. We should note that the local schedulers (e.g., Torque scheduler) utilized in the Computing Elements (CE) of a gLite (Laure et al., 2006) powered grid network, use the FCFS policy as their default task queuing policy. At a given time, a number of tasks are in the queue of resource $r_i$ or are being executed in its CPU(s) using a space-sharing policy. The storage resource of site $r_i$ has storage capacity $S_i$, measured in data units (e.g., bytes). Users located somewhere in the network generate atomic (undivisible and non-preemptable) tasks with varying characteristics.
A task needs for its execution $L$ pieces of data (datasets) $I_k$ of sizes $V_{I_k}$ , $k = 1,2,\ldots,L$. A dataset $I_k$ has a number of replicas distributed across various storage resources. The total computation workload of the task is equal to $W$, and the final results produced have size equal to $\Delta$. $W$ and $\Delta$ may depend on the number and size of datasets the task requires. The datasets consolidate to a single site, which we will call the data consolidation (DC) site $r_{DC}$. This site may already contain some datasets so that no transferring is needed for them. The total communication delay that dataset $I_k$ experiences consists of the propagation, the transmission and the queuing delays. The propagation delay of path ($r_i$, $r_{DC}$) is denoted by $d_{i,DC}$ and its usable capacity by $P_{i,DC}$ (minimum capacity available at all intermediate links). A piece of data $I_k$ transmitted over a path ($r_i$, $r_{DC}$) experiences total communication queuing delay $Q_{i,DC}^{Comm}$ , because of other pieces of data utilizing the links of the path. In general the type of transport media used (opaque packet switching, transparent networks such as wavelength routed optical WDM network or OBS, etc), determines whether the queuing delay is counted once at the source (transparent networks) or is accumulated over all intermediate nodes (opaque networks). Finally, a task before starting execution at the DC site experiences a processing queuing delay $Q_{DC}^{Proc}$ , due to other tasks utilizing the resource's computational capacity or already queued.

We assume that a central scheduler is responsible for the task scheduling and data management. The scheduler has complete knowledge of the static (computation and storage capacity, etc) and the dynamic (number of running and queued tasks, data stored, etc) characteristics of the sites. We do not take into account the communication delay of transferring messages between the user and the scheduler and between the scheduler and the resources, since we assume that they are negligible compared to the total execution time of the task, at least for the data-intensive scenarios that we consider in this study.
A task created by a user at site $r_u$, asks the central scheduler for the site where the task will execute. Upon receiving the user's request, the scheduler examines the computation and data related characteristics of the task, such as its workload, the number, the type, and the size of datasets needed, the sites that hold the corresponding datasets etc. The scheduler based on the used Data Consolidation scheme, selects (i) the sites that hold the replicas of the datasets the task needs, (ii) the site where these datasets will consolidate and the task will be executed, and (iii) the routes over which to transfer these datasets. The decisions concerning (i), (ii) and (iii) can be made jointly or separately. Note that the free capacity of the storage resource $r_{DC}$ must be larger than the total size of the datasets that will consolidate:

$$S_{r_{DC}} \geq \sum_{k=1}^{L} V_{I_k} \, . \tag{1}$$

The free storage capacity of a resource includes not only the actual free space, but also the space occupied by datasets that are not used and can be deleted. If needed, the oldest unused datasets are deleted from the DC site (other policies can also be applied, however these are not the focus of this work). If no site is found that fulfils Eq. (1), the corresponding task fails. Otherwise, if Eq. (1) is fulfilled by at least one site, then the scheduler orders the data holding sites to transfer the datasets to this DC site. The scheduler, also, transfer this task to the DC site. The task's execution starts only when both the task and all of its needed datasets have arrived at the DC site. After the task finishes its execution, the results return back to the task's originating user.
Finally, we assume that no dynamic replication strategies operate in the network. A dynamic replication strategy, such as the ones presented in (Dogan, 2009), permits the dynamic movement of data between the storage resources, independently from the various task requests. For example, a popular dataset can be copied to more than one resources so as to be easily accessible when needed. Such strategies are expected to reduce the data transfers required for a DC operation, reducing at the same time the task's execution delay.

### 3.2 Data Consolidation (DC) schemes

In what follows, we present several Data Consolidation (DC) schemes.

#### 3.2.1 Data Consolidation (DC) delays

We assume that the scheduler has selected the data holding sites (replicas), $r_k \in R$, for all datasets $I_k$, $k = 1,\ldots,L$, and the DC site $r_{DC}$. Note that the DC site may already have some pieces of data and thus no transferring is required for these pieces (i.e., $r_k = r_{DC}$ for some $k$). In general, such a data-intensive task experiences both communication ($D_{comm}$) and processing ($D_{proc}$) delays. The communication delay $D_{comm}$ of a task, considering also the delay for transferring the final results from the DC site $r_{DC}$ to the originating user's site $r_u$ is:

$$D_{comm} = D_{cons} + D_{output} =$$
$$\max_{k=1...L}\left(\frac{V_{I_k}}{P_{k,DC}} + Q_{k,DC}^{Comm} + d_{k,DC}\right) + \left(\frac{\Delta}{P_{DC,u}} + Q_{DC,u}^{Comm} + d_{DC,u}\right) \quad (2)$$

where $D_{cons}$ is the time needed for the task's data to consolidate to the DC site $r_{DC}$ and $D_{output}$ is the delay of the output data to be transferred to the originating user's site $r_u$. The computational delay is given by:

$$D_{proc} = Q_{DC}^{Proc} + \frac{W}{C_{DC}}. \quad (3)$$

The total delay suffered by a task is:

$$D_{DC} = D_{comm} + D_{proc}. \quad (4)$$

Note that $Q_{k,DC}^{Comm}$ and $Q_{DC}^{Proc}$ are difficult to estimate since the former depends on the utilization of the network and the latter depends on the utilization of the computation resource. For this reason, we propose a variety of algorithms, some of which assume this information is known, while others do not make this assumption, and we compare their performance.

### 3.2.2 Proposed schemes

As stated before the DC problem consists of three sub-problems: (i) the selection of the repository sites $r_k$ from which the dataset $I_k$, $k$=1,2,...,$L$, will be transferred to the DC site, (ii) the selection of the DC site $r_{DC}$ where the datasets will accumulate and the task will be executed, and (iii) the selection of the paths ($r_k$, $r_{DC}$) the datasets will follow. In general, DC schemes can make these decision based on various criteria such as the computation and storage capacity of the resources, their load, the location and the sizes of the datasets, the bandwidth availability and the expected delay, the user and application behaviours, the price a user is willing to pay for using the storage and computation resources, etc.

In what follows, we propose a number of DC schemes that consider only the data consolidation (*ConsCost*) or only the computation (*ExecCost*) or both kinds (*TotalCost*, *TotalCost-Q*) of task requirements. Algorithms with similar considerations have also been proposed in (Bell et al., 2002) (Bell et al., 2003) (Cameron et al., 2004) that use however different model (sequential access). In the proposed algorithms and in the simulation results that follow, we assume that no output data is returned back to the user and as a result $D_{output}$ is equal to zero. Even though this parameter may be important in some cases, we decided to concentrate our description and our simulation results to the three more important and complex subproblems that comprise the DC problem in Data grids, as described above.

i. ***Random-Random (Rand) scheme:*** In this scheme the data replicas used by a task and the DC site are randomly chosen. The paths are selected using a simple Dijkstra algorithm. This scheme was employed for comparison purposes.
ii. ***Consolidation-Cost (ConsCost) scheme:*** We select the replicas and the Data Consolidation site that minimize the data consolidation time ($D_{cons}$), assuming that the communication queuing delays ($Q_{k,DC}^{Comm}$) are negligible.

Given a candidate DC site $r_j$, we select for each dataset $I_k$ the corresponding data holding site $r_i$ ($I_k \in r_i$) that minimizes the transfer time:

$$\min_{r_i \in R, I_k \in r_i} \left( \frac{V_{I_k}}{P_{i,j}} + Q_{i,j}^{Comm} + d_{i,j} \right), \tag{5}$$

where $R$ is the set of all resources and $d_{i,j}$ the propagation delay between site $r_i$ and $r_j$. Note that in this algorithm we consider the communication queuing delays negligible and thus $Q_{i,j}^{Comm} = 0$. The data consolidation time $D_{cons}$ of candidate DC site $r_j$ is equal to the maximum transfer time of any dataset:

$$D_{cons}(r_j) = \max_{k=1...L} \left( \min_{r_i \in R, I_k \in r} \left( \frac{V_{I_k}}{P_{i,j}} + Q_{i,j}^{Comm} + d_{i,j} \right) \right). \tag{6}$$

In ConsCost scheme we select the DC site ($r_{DC}$) that minimizes the data consolidation time:

$$r_{DC} = \arg\min_{r_j \in R} \left( D_{cons}(r_j) \right). \tag{7}$$

The paths are constructed using the Dijkstra algorithm.

iii. ***Execution-Cost (ExecCost) scheme:*** We select the DC site that minimizes the task's execution time:

$$r_{DC} = \arg\min_{r_j \in R} \left( Q_j^{Proc} + \frac{W}{C_j} \right), \tag{8}$$

while the data replicas are randomly chosen. Since, our focus is more on the communication overhead of the DC problem combined with the execution times of the tasks, we consider the processing queuing delay $Q_j^{Proc}$ of a resource $r_j$ as negligible and that the tasks' workload is known a-priori. In general, it is possible to estimate this delay based on the tasks already assigned to a resource and on the average delay tasks previously executed on it have experienced. Also, regarding the a-priori knowledge of the tasks' workload, there are algorithms that can be used to provide such estimates. On the other hand, if the computation workload of a task is not known a-priori, we can simply choose the resource with the largest computation capacity $C_j$. Finally, in the ExecCost scheme the paths are constructed using the Dijkstra algorithm.

iv. ***Total-Cost (TotalCost) scheme:*** We select the replicas and the DC site that minimize the total task delay. This delay includes the time needed for transferring the datasets to the DC site and the task's execution time. This scheme is the combination of the two above schemes. The paths are constructed using the Dijkstra algorithm.

### 3.2.3 Number of operations for serving a task

Data consolidation is viewed in this paper as a continuous time problem, where the decisions taken for one task affect the decisions taken for the tasks that will arrive in the future and are affected by the decisions taken earlier for previous tasks. In this context, we are interested in the number of operations (complexity) required by the proposed DC schemes. For the Rand algorithm this is polynomial, as it randomly chooses the $L+1$ sites used in the DC operation. Similarly, the ExecCost algorithm complexity is polynomial, since it randomly selects the $L$ data holding sites, while the $r_{DC}$ site is chosen among the $N$ sites of the grid network based on the task execution time criterion. All the other proposed algorithms are based on the ConsCost algorithm. The complexity of these algorithms is determined by the complexity of the ConsCost algorithm, since any additional operations performed by these algorithms. In the ConsCost algorithm, for each candidate DC site, we choose for each dataset the replica site that minimizes its transferring delay. That is, for each dataset, at most all the $N$ sites (assuming that all the sites hold a replica of this dataset) are evaluated as candidates for participating in the DC operation. Then based on the decisions made for all $L$ datasets we calculate the data consolidation time for this particular replica selection and candidate DC site. So, the execution of a shortest path algorithm, with polynomial complexity, is required for each candidate DC site $r_{DC}$. The complexity of Dijkstra's algorithm is $O(N^2)$ in order to find the shortest paths from a single source (the candidate DC site) to all other nodes in a graph. Next, this operation is performed for all the candidates DC sites, that is for all the $N$ grid sites. At the end of the ConsCost algorithm, the $r_{DC}$ site and the corresponding $L$ sites with the minimum data consolidation time (Eq. 7) are selected. Consequently, the total complexity of the ConsCost algorithm, for a single task, is polynomial and equal to $O(N^3)$.

Of course, the polynomial complexity of the ConsCost algorithm is the result of its sub-optimal decisions. The ConsCost algorithm does not optimize the overall consolidation time over all datasets and over all candidate replica sites, whose combinations increase exponentially with the number of sites in the grid network. This can be seen from Eq. (5), where for each dataset the replica site with the minimum transferring delay is chosen, without considering the effect of one choice (one replica's selection) to the other.

In addition, we should note that in this complexity analyses, we do not consider the complexity of the information gathering mechanisms, such as the communication and computation queuing delays in the network.

## 4. Information aggregation

### 4.1 Problem formulation

Our aim is to design efficient and flexible aggregation schemes that can be applied to grids without a significant penalty on the quality of the scheduling (and probably other) decisions taken with the aggregated information. We formulate our problem in a generic way, without assuming grid networks with specific characteristics. The scheduling policies assumed are also relatively simple, since combining our aggregation schemes with a large set of scheduling policies would obscure the focus on the aggregation issues.

We consider a grid consisting of $N$ sites, partitioned according to a hierarchical structure in a total of $L$ domains $D_j$, $j=1,2,\ldots,L$. Each site $i$, $i=1,2,\ldots,N$, has computational and storage capacity $C_i$ and $S_i$, respectively, and belongs to one of the $L$ domains. Site $i$ publishes its resource information as a vector $V_i$ that may contain various parameters:

$$V_i = (C_i, S_i, \ldots).$$

These vectors are collected per domain $D_j$ and are published to a higher level of the hierarchy, in the form of an *information matrix* whose rows are the resource site vectors:

$$M_j = \begin{bmatrix} V_1 \\ V_2 \\ \vdots \\ V_{|D_j|} \end{bmatrix} = \begin{bmatrix} (C_1, S_1, \ldots) \\ (C_2, S_2, \ldots) \\ \vdots \\ (C_{|D_j|}, S_{|D_j|}, \ldots) \end{bmatrix},$$

where $|\cdot|$ denotes the cardinality of a set and $1,2, \ldots, |D_j|$ are the sites contained in domain $D_j$. By performing appropriate operations, to be discussed later, on the information vectors contained in the information matrix, $M_j$ is transformed into the *aggregated information matrix* $\hat{M}_j$.

The grid scheduling problem is usually viewed as a two-level hierarchical problem. At the first level, called *meta-scheduling*, a meta-scheduler allocates tasks to sites, while at the second level, called *local scheduling*, each site schedules the tasks assigned to it on its local computing elements. This is the approach followed by many grid middleware systems, including gLite (Laure et al., 2006), where the Workload Management System (WMS) selects the site where a task will be executed and the local scheduler chooses the Working Node (WN) it will be executed on after reaching that site. Similarly, in our work scheduling is performed at two levels. At the higher level a central scheduler decides the domain $D_j$ a task will be assigned to, and at the lower level a domain scheduler $DS_j$, decides the exact site in the domain where the task will be executed (Figure 1). Information collection and aggregation is performed, similarly, by a two level monitoring system, consisting of a central monitor $CM$ and the domain monitors $DM_j$, $j=1,2,\ldots,L$.

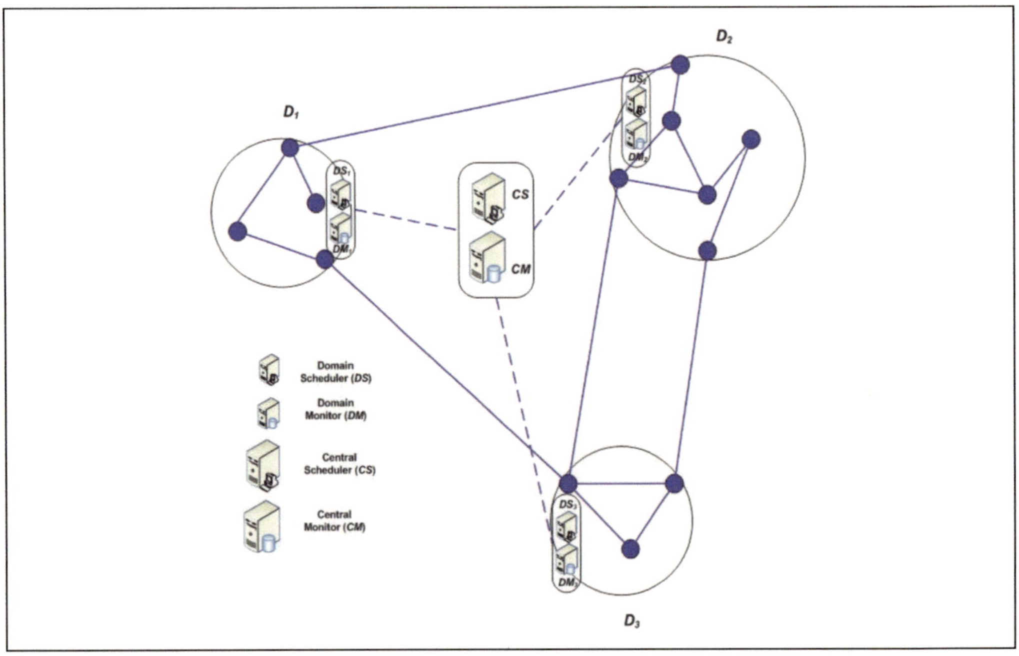


Fig. 1. A two-level hierarchical scheduling and monitoring system. Each domain $j$ has a domain scheduler $DS_j$ and a domain monitor $DM_j$, while there is also a central scheduler $CS$ and a central monitor $CM$.

A user located at some site generates tasks $T_m$, $m$=1,2,…, with computational workload $W_m$, that have to be scheduled and then executed at a resource site.

### 4.2 Information aggregation

In this section we present the resource information parameters of interest, the operators applied and the proposed aggregation techniques.

#### 4.2.1 Operational framework

In Algorithm 2 we present, in pseudocode, the sequence of operations performed by the information collection mechanism and the proposed aggregation scheme.

---

**Algorithm 2** Resource Information Collection & Aggregation

---

1. Each site $i$, $i$=1,2,…,$N$, belonging to some domain $D_j$ periodically or reactively (driven by information changes) publishes its information vector $V_i$ to the domain monitor $DM_j$.
2. Each domain monitor $DM_j$, $j$=1,2,…,$L$, puts together these vectors to form the information matrix $M_j$.
3. Each domain monitor $DM_j$, $j$=1,2,…,$L$, periodically or reactively (when information changes) computes its aggregated information matrix $\hat{M}_j$ and publishes it to the central monitor $CM$.
4. The $CM$ collects the aggregated information matrices.

---

In Algorithm 3 we present the operations performed by a task scheduling scheme that uses the aggregated information.

---

**Algorithm 3** Task Scheduling

---

1. Upon the arrival of a task $T_m$, the central scheduler $CS$ looks at the domain matrices provided by the central monitor $CM$.
2. The central scheduler $CS$ applies an optimization function to the vectors contained in the domain matrices and selects the information vector $V$ that produces the largest value.
3. The $CS$ assigns the task $T_m$ to the domain $D_j$, where the vector $V$ originated from, and forwards the task to the domain scheduler $DS_j$.
4. The domain scheduler $DS_j$ receives the task request and selects the exact site the task will be scheduled on, using exact resource information.

---

Generally, as the number of sites in a domain $D_j$ increases, the amount of information collected by the domain monitors $DM_j$ also increases. Therefore, it is necessary for the information contained in each domain information matrix $M_j$ to be aggregated/ summarized. This is done by performing appropriate associative operations (addition, maximization, etc) on the parameters of the sites' information vectors, in order to transform the information matrix $M_j$ into the *aggregated information matrix* $\hat{M}_j$ which contains a smaller number of vectors than the original matrix. The operators used for summarizing the information depends on the types of the parameters involved. In what follows, we elaborate on the resource parameters of interest, and the associative operators and aggregation techniques proposed. We also present optimization functions that can be applied by the *CS* to select the optimal information vector.

### 4.2.2 Information parameters and aggregation operators

The resource information parameters (both static and dynamic) of interest in this work, the operators used for their aggregation and the benefits we get for different choices of the operators are discussed next:

- The computational capacities $C_i$ of the sites, measured in Millions Instructions per Second (MIPS), in a domain $D_j$ can be aggregated by performing a minimum representative operation, an additive operation or by averaging them:

$$\hat{C}_j = \min_{i \in D_j} C_i, \quad \hat{C}_j = \sum_{i \in D_j} C_i \quad \text{or} \quad \hat{C}_j = \mathop{avg}_{i \in D_j} C_i .$$

  Using the minimum representative operator we obtain the minimum capacity of any site in the domain $D_j$, which would be useful for conservative task scheduling. Using the additive operator we obtain the total computational capacity in the domain, which would be useful for scheduling when a task's workload is divisible, and can be assigned to different resources simultaneously. The minimization, the additive and the average operators (and possibly other operators, such as maximization) could all be used so that a number of capacity related features of the domain are recorded.

- The number of tasks $N_i$ already assigned to the sites can be aggregated over a domain $D_j$ using an additive operation:

$$\hat{N}_j = \sum_{i \in D_j} N_i .$$

  Other operators can also be used, such as the maximum representative or the average number of tasks in the sites of the domain.

- Some tasks require for their execution a number of datasets that may or may not be stored at a given site. If a dataset $k$ exists in site $i$, we set $I_{ik} = 1$; otherwise, we set $I_{ik} = 0$. This parameter is aggregated over all sites in a domain $D_j$ using a boolean OR operator:

$$\hat{I}_{jk} = \mathop{OR}_{i \in D_j}\{I_{ik}\} .$$

  Thus, $\hat{I}_{jk} = 1$ means that there is at least one site in domain $D_j$ that holds dataset $k$.

In any case, the list of parameters and aggregation operators defined above is only indicative of the different options that can be used by the aggregation schemes. Other parameters and operators can also be defined, depending on the needs of the applications and the scheduling algorithms used.

### 4.2.3 Aggregation schemes

In this subsection we present aggregation techniques for reducing the number of vectors in the information matrix $M_j$ of a given domain $D_j$.

**Single Point Aggregation Scheme**

In the *single point aggregation scheme,* the information vectors of the sites in each domain are aggregated into a single information vector. We next show an example of the application of the single point aggregation technique, where the information matrix $M_j$ that has $|D_j|$ rows is reduced to an aggregated information matrix $\hat{M}_j$ that has only one row:

$$M_j = \begin{bmatrix} V_1 \\ V_2 \\ \vdots \\ V_8 \end{bmatrix} = \begin{bmatrix} (C_1, S_1, \ldots) \\ (C_2, S_2, \ldots) \\ \vdots \\ (C_8, S_8, \ldots) \end{bmatrix} \Rightarrow \hat{M}_j = \begin{bmatrix} \hat{V} \end{bmatrix} = \begin{bmatrix} (\hat{C}, \hat{S}, \ldots) \end{bmatrix}.$$

The information transferred to the higher levels is greatly reduced using this aggregation technique, but this happens at the expense of a degradation in the quality of the aggregated information and in the value it has for the resource scheduler.

**Intra-Domain Clustering Aggregation Scheme**

In the *intra-domain clustering aggregation technique,* each domain $D_j$, $j$=1,2,…,$L$, is partitioned into $h_j \leq |D_j|$ intra-domain clusters. For the sites belonging to cluster $l$, $l$=1,2,…,$h_j$, the aggregated vector $\hat{V}_l$ is calculated and sent to domain monitor $DM_j$. The aggregated information matrix $\hat{M}_j$ containing the aggregated information vectors $\hat{V}_l$, $l$=1,2,…,$h_j$, of the clusters, is sent to the higher levels. Various approaches can be used for clustering the sites of a domain. In our work we assume that the sites are clustered randomly.
We next show an example of the application of the intra-domain clustering aggregation technique, where $h_j$ =3 clusters are created in the given domain $D_j$.

$$M_j = \begin{bmatrix} V_1 \\ V_2 \\ \vdots \\ V_7 \\ V_8 \end{bmatrix} = \begin{bmatrix} (C_1, S_1, \ldots) \\ (C_2, S_2, \ldots) \\ \vdots \\ (C_7, S_7, \ldots) \\ (C_8, S_8, \ldots) \end{bmatrix} \Rightarrow \hat{M}_j = \begin{bmatrix} \hat{V}_1 \\ \hat{V}_2 \\ \hat{V}_3 \end{bmatrix} = \begin{bmatrix} (\hat{C}_1, \hat{S}_1, \ldots) \\ (\hat{C}_2, \hat{S}_2, \ldots) \\ (\hat{C}_3, \hat{S}_3, \ldots) \end{bmatrix}.$$

The number of intra-domain clusters per domain influences the amount of information passed to higher levels and the efficiency of the scheduler's decision.

**Reducing Aggregated Information using Domination Relations**

In this subsection we introduce the concept of *dominated resources* to further prune the number of information vectors processed by the domain monitors or the number of aggregated information vectors processed by the central monitor. In particular, we say that the information vector $V_1$ *dominates* information vector $V_2$, if $V_1$ is better than $V_2$ with respect to all the cost parameters. The term "better" is interpreted differently based on the parameters of interest.

For example, consider the information vectors $V_1 = (C_1, S_1, FT_1)$ and $V_2 = (C_2, S_2, FT_2)$. We say that $V_1$ dominated $V_2$ if the following conditions hold:

$$C_1 > C_2,\ S_1 > S_2 \text{ and } FT_1 < FT_2$$

The domination relations can either be applied in the vectors of a domain without any further processing, leading to a standalone aggregation technique, or they can be applied along with the single point and intra-domain aggregation techniques presented earlier.

**Domain Selection Cost Functions**

Upon the arrival of a new task, the central scheduler *CS* selects a proper domain $D_j$ for the execution of the task, and forwards the task request to the corresponding domain scheduler $DS_j$ who assigns it to a specific site in that domain. The *CS* uses aggregated information collected by the central monitor *CM*, while $DS_j$ uses exact resource information in order to make its corresponding scheduling decisions. The *CS* in order to select the appropriate domain for a task's execution (similar are the operations performed by a *DS* so as to select the appropriate site for a task's execution) applies an optimization function to the vectors $\hat{V}$ and the domain giving the optimum value is selected.

## 5. Performance evaluation

### 5.1 Data consolidation

#### 5.1.1 Simulation settings

In our simulations we used a topology derived from the EGEE topology, which consists of 11 nodes and 16 links, of capacities equal to 10Gbps. In our experiments we assume a P2P (opaque) network; the delay for transmitting between two nodes includes the propagation, queuing and transmission delays at intermediate nodes. Only one transmission is possible at a time over a link, so a queue exists at every node to hold the data waiting for transmission.
The size of each dataset is given by an exponential distribution with average $V_I$ (GB). At the beginning of the simulation a given number of datasets are generated and two copies of each dataset are distributed in the network; the first is distributed among the sites and the second is placed at Tier 0 site. The storage capacity of each storage resource is 50% of the total size of all the datasets. Since the storage capacity is bounded, there are cases where a site does not have the free storage capacity required to store a needed dataset. In such a case, one or more of the oldest and unused datasets are deleted until the new dataset can be stored at the resource.
In each experiment, users generate a total of 10.000 tasks, with exponential arrival rates of average value $\lambda$. Unless stated otherwise, we assume $\lambda$=75 tasks/sec (but we also examine other task arrival rates: $\lambda$=50, 75, 100, 125, 150 and 200 tasks/sec). In all our experiments we keep constant the average total data size $S$ that each task requires:

$$S = L \cdot V_I, \tag{10}$$

where $L$ is the number of datasets a task requests and $V_I$ is the average size of each dataset. We use average total data size $S$ equal to 600 GB and examined various ($L$, $V_I$) pair values. In each experiment the total number of available datasets changes in order for their total size to remain the same: 15 TB.
We use the following metrics to measure the performance of the algorithms examined:

- The average task delay, which is the time that elapses between the creation of a task and the time its execution is completed at a site.
- The average load per task imposed to the network, which is the product of the size of datasets transferred and the number of hops these datasets traverse.
- The Data Consolidation (DC) probability, which is the probability that the selected DC site will not have all the datasets required by a task and as a results Data Consolidation will be necessary.

### 5.1.2 Results

Figure 4 shows the DC probability for the Rand, ExecCost, ConsCost and TotalCost schemes, when tasks request different number of datasets $L$ for their execution. The higher the number $L$ of datasets a task requests, the higher is the probability that these datasets will not be located at the DC site, given that the storage capacity of a site is limited. The ConsCost and TotalCost algorithms exhibit smaller DC probability than the Rand and ExecCost algorithms, since the former algorithms select the DC site by taking into account the consolidation delay, which is small for sites holding many or all of the datasets needed by a task. On the other hand, the Rand and ExecCost algorithms select the DC site randomly or almost randomly (as is the case for ExecCost, given that the tasks have negligible computation complexity). As $L$ increases, the probability of not finding all the data at a site increases and converges to 1 for all examined algorithms.

Figure 5 shows the average task delay for the DC algorithms examined. We observe that the algorithms that take the data consolidation delay into account (namely, the ConsCost and TotalCost algorithms) behave better than the algorithms that do not consider this parameter (that is, the Rand and ExecCost algorithms), in terms of the task delay. As the number $L$ of datasets a task requires increases, the average task delays of all the algorithms converge. Specifically, for the ConsCost and TotalCost algorithms the average task delay increases as the number of datasets a task requires increases, since the probability that a DC site will not hold all the data a task needs (i.e., the DC probability) also increases (Figure 4), resulting in more data transfer. In contrast, in the Rand and ExecCost algorithms the average task delay decreases as $L$ increases, because of the decrease in the size of the concurrent transferred datasets $V_I$ (Eq. (10)). Thus, for the Rand and ExecCost algorithms that (almost) randomly select the DC site, the data consolidation time and its impact on the average task delay decreases as $L$ increases.

Figure 6 shows the average network load per task for the various DC algorithms, when tasks request different number of datasets L for their execution. We observe that the algorithms that do not take into account the data consolidation delay (that is, the Rand and ExecCost algorithms) induce, on average, a larger load on the network than the algorithms that do take this into account (ConsCost and TotalCost algorithms). This is because the former algorithms transfer on average more data, over longer paths. Moreover, the decisions made by these algorithms are not affected by the dataset sizes $V_I$ or their number $L$, and as a result they induce on average the same network load. By analyzing our results, we observed that these algorithms transfer on average the same number of bytes over paths of equal on average length, irrespectively of $L$ and $V_I$. The superior performance of ExecCost over that of Rand is because ExecCost assigns tasks to resources in a more balanced way, based on the task execution times. That is, it first assigns tasks to the most powerful resource, where tasks and their datasets are stored until they are executed. When this resource does not have

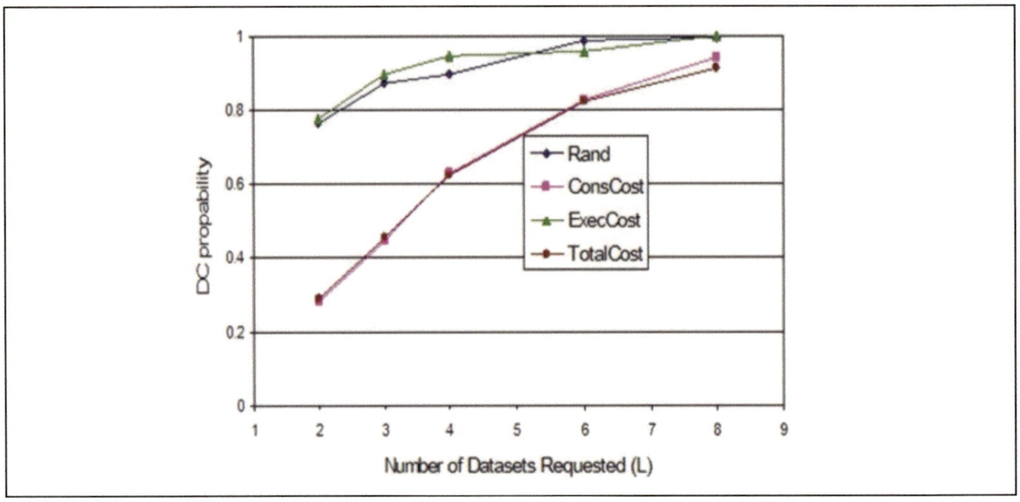


Fig. 4. The DC probability for the Rand, ExecCost, ConsCost and TotalCost DC algorithms, when tasks request a different number of datasets *L* for their execution. The average total data size per task is *S*=600 GB.

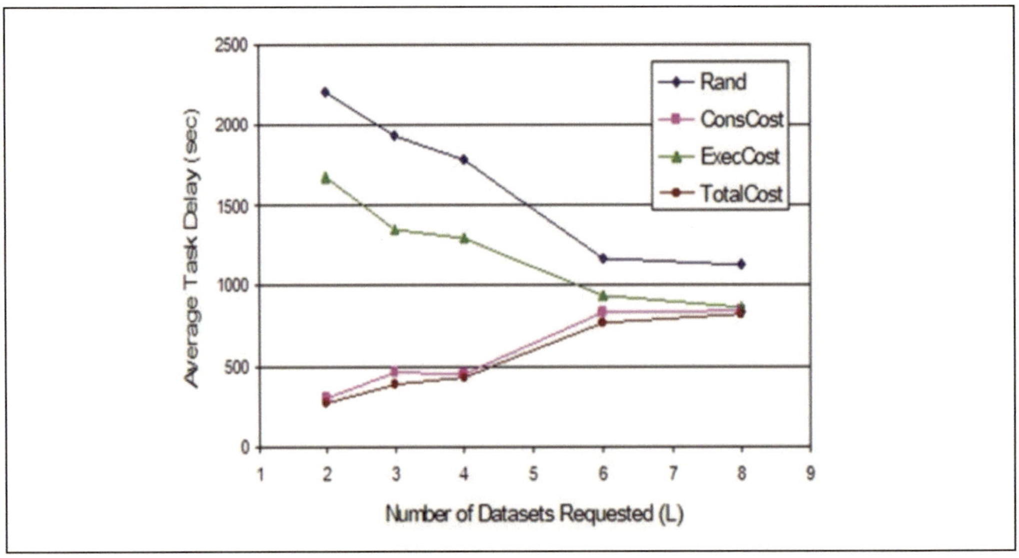


Fig. 5. The average task delay (in sec) for the Rand, ExecCost, ConsCost and TotalCost DC algorithms, when tasks requests a different number of datasets *L* for their execution. The average total data size per task is *S*=600 GB.

sufficient storage capacity to store the dataset of the following tasks, the ExecCost algorithm chooses the second most powerful resource, and so on. At some point this cycle starts (more or less) all over again. In this way, there is a high probability that consecutive tasks will find some of their required datasets in the resource where they are assigned by the ExecCost algorithm. This reduces the network load in comparison to the Rand algorithm. Of course, this property does not appear in the DC metric, since the resource selected by the algorithm changes when it does not have any free space left. The algorithms that take into account the data consolidation delay (namely, the ConsCost and TotalCost algorithm), induce a smaller load on the network. This load increases as the number of datasets L increases, as can be explained by the increasing probability that a DC site will not hold all the required data (Figure 4), and will thus have to transfer more datasets. In addition, these algorithms are affected mainly by the tasks' data dependencies, since their computational load is small (see step 6 in Algorithm 1). Also, the TotalCost and the ConsCost use the same policies for selecting the data replicas and the paths; as a result, both algorithms perform similarly. We should note that in all the experiments performed very few tasks failed (of the order of 4-6 tasks per experiment).

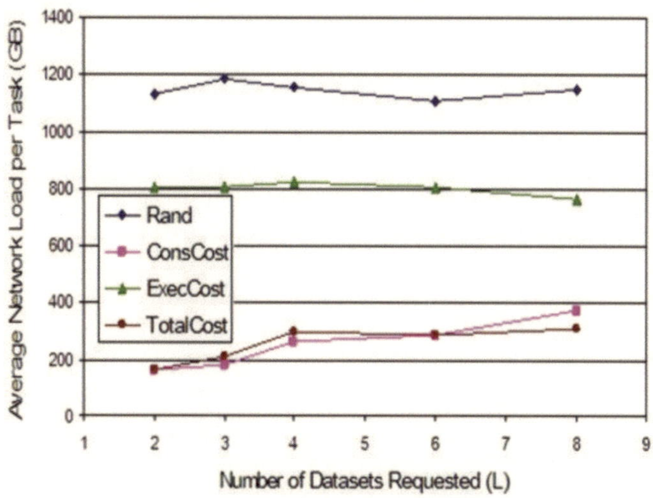


Fig. 6. The average network load per task (in GB) for the Rand, ExecCost, ConsCost and TotalCost DC algorithms, when tasks request a different number of datasets *L* for their execution. The average total data size per task is *S*=600 GB.

### 5.2 Information aggregation

#### 5.2.1 Simulation settings

We consider a number of sites that are randomly grouped into domains, each having an approximately equal number of sites. Site *i* is characterized by its computational capacity $C_i$, measured in MIPS and chosen from a uniform distribution *UC*. In our simulations, tasks are created with exponentially distributed interarrival times with mean *I*, while their workload follows a uniform distribution *UW*. These tasks are submitted to the central scheduler that makes its decisions using either complete or aggregated resource information. In the simulation results we do not consider the effects of the information propagation delay, assuming that resource information (aggregated or not) is not outdated by the time it is used by the scheduler due, to the delay between measuring some parameter and the moment the measured value is available to the scheduler. However, we believe that in practice the aggregation operation can reduce the negative effects of this delay, since summarized information is usually less affected by the change in the values of the parameters measured. Network related issues are not considered in these simulation experiments.

The information vector $V_i$ of site $i$ contains its computational capacity $C_i$ and the number of tasks $N_i$ queued at it:

$$V_i = \{C_i, N_i\} .$$

In case no aggregation is used a new task $T_m$ is assigned to the site $i$ that minimizes

$$\min_i \left\{ \frac{C_i}{N_i} \right\} .$$

In case where aggregation is used then the central scheduler $CS$ uses only the aggregated domain information vectors, and assigns task $T_m$ to the domain $D_j$ that minimizes

$$\min_j \left\{ \frac{\hat{C}_j}{\hat{N}_j} \right\} .$$

Next, the selected domain's scheduler, $DS_j$, receives the task and assigns it to a domain site, having complete knowledge of the information vectors of all the sites in the domain. The assignment again is performed based on the same optimization function:

$$\min_{i \in D_j} \left\{ \frac{C_i}{N_i} \right\} .$$

We implemented and evaluated the performance of the following schemes:

- *FlatCpuTasks*: In this scheme no information aggregation is performed of the sites' computational capacity and number of tasks parameters.
- *MinCpuSumTasks*: In this scheme the information vectors of the sites belonging to the same domain are aggregated (single point aggregation) using the minimum representative and the additive operators, respectively:

$$\hat{C} = \min_i C_i \text{ and } \hat{N} = \sum_i N_i .$$

- *DomMinCpuSumTasks*: This scheme is similar to the *MinCpuSumTasks*, except that domination relations are applied to the vectors of the sites of a domain, before they are aggregated using the single point aggregation scheme.
- *ICMinCpuSumTasks*: This scheme is similar to the *MinCpuSumTasks*, except that the intra-domain clustering aggregation scheme is applied, instead of the single point one, where sites are randomly clustered into intra-domain clusters.

We are interested in evaluating the degree to which the information produced by the proposed aggregation schemes leads to efficient scheduling decisions, while the size and the frequency of the information updates is kept low.

For the evaluation of the MinCpuSumTasks, DominanceMinCpuSumTasks, and ICMinCpuSumTasks aggregation schemes we use the *Stretch Factor* (*SF*), as the metric that measures the scheduling efficiency and in practice the quality of the aggregated information. The *Stretch Factor* (*SF*) is defined as the ratio of the task delay $D$ when the task is scheduled using complete resource information (FlatCpuTasks) over the task delay when an aggregation scheme is used (MinCpuSumTasks, DominanceMinCpuSumTasks, or ICMinCpuSumTasks). The task delay is defined as the time that elapses from the task's submission to the grid until the completion of its execution at a site. A stretch factor metric is also encountered in the hierarchical networks related literature (Lee, 1995), where it is defined as the ratio of the average number of hops (or average delay) between a source and a destination when flat routing is used over the corresponding value when hierarchical routing is used. Table 1 presents the *Stretch Factor* (*SF*) metrics we use in our work. In all cases *SF*≤1, since when a scheduler has complete resource information, it can make better decisions than when this information is aggregated. An aggregation technique is efficient when its corresponding *SF* is close to 1.

| |
|---|
| $SFMinCpuSumTasks = \frac{D_{FlatCpuTaks}}{D_{MinCpuSumTasks}}$ |
| $SFDomMinCpuSumTasks = \frac{D_{FlatCpuTaks}}{D_{DomMinCpuSumTasks}}$ |
| $SFICCpuTasks = \frac{D_{FlatCpuTaks}}{D_{ICMinCpuSumTasks}}$ |

Table 1. The *Stretch Factor* (*SF*) metrics we use in our simulation experiments.

### 5.2.2 Results

Figure 7a presents the *Stretch Factor (SF)* for the MinCpuSumTasks, the DomMinCpuSumTasks and the ICMinCpuSumTasks aggregation schemes when 1000 grid sites are clustered in a variable number of domains and 25000 tasks are created and scheduled. The sites' computational capacity and the tasks' workload follow uniform distributions (*UC* min/max = 10/10000 MIPS and *UW* min/max 1000/10000000 MI respectively). In general, all the stretch factor metrics measured behave similarly, that is, their value first decreases up to some point, after which it starts increasing towards 1. This is because when the number of domains is small, then the number of sites per domain is quite high, increasing the probability that more than one "best" sites or sites similar to the "best" site exist in different domains. This increases the probability that a domain with such a site will be chosen, even if aggregation is used. We represent this probability as $P_{multiple\text{-}best}$, and as our results will indicate it strongly affects the stretch factor; also, by "best" we mean the site that optimizes the metric of interest (task delay, or some other optimization function). Next, as the number of domains increase $P_{multiple\text{-}best}$ decreases and the stretch factors also decrease. After some point, as the number of domains increases and the number of sites per domain decreases, the quality of information produced by the aggregation schemes improves. This is because when there are few sites per domain, the aggregated information better represents the characteristics of its sites.

Comparing the different aggregation policies we observe that the ICMinCpuSumTasks produces the best results, followed by the DomMinCpuSumTasks and the

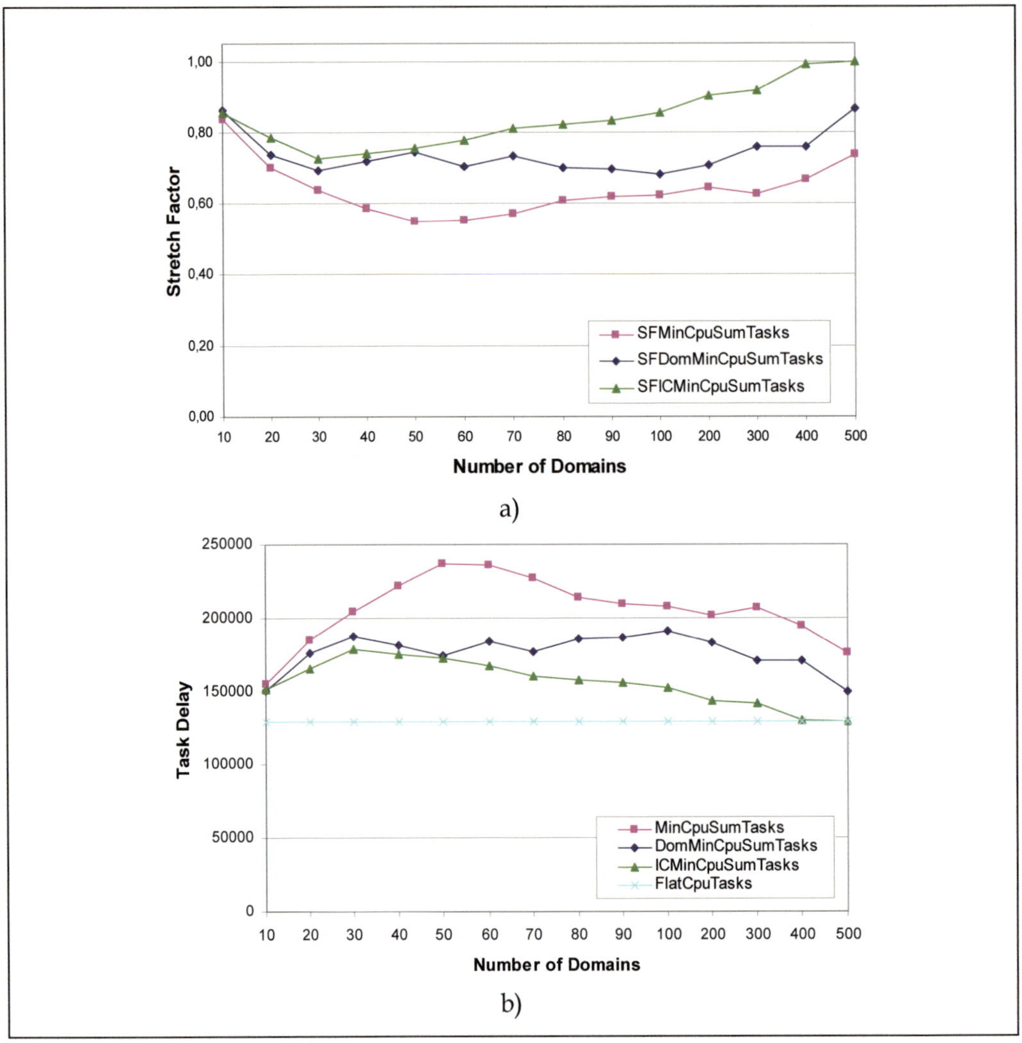


Fig. 7. a) The *Stretch Factor (SF)*, b) the average task delay (in secs) for the MinCpuSumTasks, the DomMinCpuSumTasks and the ICMinCpuSumTasks aggregation schemes, when 1000 grid sites are clustered in a variable number of domains and 25000 tasks are created and scheduled.

MinCpuSumTasks aggregation policies. The ICMinCpuSumTasks aggregation scheme use *h*=5 intra-clusters in each domain and its use leads to better scheduling decisions (as measured by the corresponding stretch factor), however this comes at the cost of increased number of information vectors advertised (Table 2). Reducing the number of intra-domain clusters, reduces the number of information vectors produced, but also reduces the quality of the information provided (as measured by the corresponding stretch factor). In addition, it seems that the domination operation, which discards dominated information vectors, improves the quality of the information provided to the scheduler. In Figure 7b we observe that the average task delay results, using the MinCpuSumTasks, the DomMinCpuSumTasks and the ICMinCpuSumTasks aggregation algorithms, are in accordance with the results presented in Figure 7a. A large task delay indicates that the information produced by the corresponding aggregation scheme, leads the scheduler in wrong task scheduling decisions. We should also note that the average task delay when no information aggregation is applied (FlatCpuTasks) is not affected by the number of domains and this is the reason that it remains static.

Figure 8 illustrates the frequency with which the aggregated information vectors change. Since, our evaluated aggregation schemes consider only one dynamic parameter (that is the number of tasks scheduled in each site), this means that the information vector of a site changes only if a new task is scheduled into it. We observe that the MinCpuSumTasks and ICMinCpuSumTasks aggregation schemes result in a very large number of updates and almost equal, in most cases, to the maximum one. On the other hand using the DomMinCpuSumTasks aggregation scheme, we observe that when the number of domains is small, and as a result many sites exist in each domain, the domination operation achieves in absorbing a large percent of the changes in the sites' information vectors. As the number of domains increases and fewer sites exist in each domain, this capability declines almost linearly.

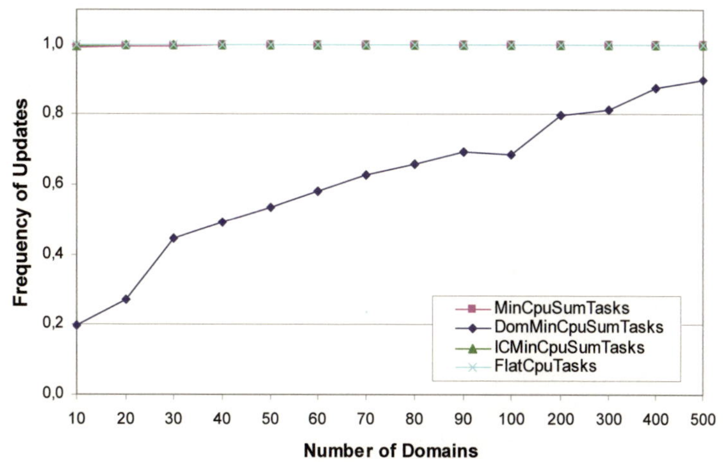


Fig. 8. The frequency of information vector updates for the FlatCpuTasks, the MinCpuSumTasks, the DomMinCpuSumTasks and the ICMinCpuSumTasks aggregation algorithms, when 1000 grid sites are clustered in a variable number of domains and 25000 tasks are created and scheduled.

We also performed several other experiments altering the number of sites, the number of tasks created or their creation pattern. In any case our results and observations were similar to the above.

## 6. Conclusions

In this chapter we examined the Data Consolidation (DC) problem and the application of information aggregation in grid networks. The DC problem arises when a task needs for its execution concurrently two or more pieces of data, possibly scattered throughout the grid network, and consists of three sub-problems: (i) the selection of the repository site from which to obtain the replica of each dataset to be used for task execution, (ii) the selection of the site where these datasets will accumulate and the task will be executed and (iii) the selection of the paths the datasets will follow as they are transferred over the network. These sub-problems can be solved jointly or independently. To the best of our knowledge this is the first time that these issues are jointly considered. We proposed a number of DC schemes, of polynomial number of required operations and evaluated them under a variety of scenarios and choices for the parameters involved. Our simulation results indicated that the DC schemes that consider both the computation and the communication requirements of the tasks behave better than those that consider only one of them. We also investigated for the first time resource information aggregation in grid networks, describing several information aggregation operators and methods. We performed a number of simulation experiments using the stretch Factor (*SF*), defined as the ratio of the task delay incurred when scheduling based on complete resource information over that incurred when an aggregation scheme is used, as the main metric for judging the extent to which the proposed aggregation schemes preserve the value of the information aggregated and assist the scheduler in making efficient decisions. We observed that in many scenarios the proposed schemes enabled efficient task scheduling decisions as indicated by the *SF* achieved, while achieving large information reduction because of the aggregation. We looked into the frequency of information vector updates resulted by the aggregation schemes, and observed that the changes in the dynamic characteristics of the resources will not always propagate to the central monitoring system, since aggregated information vectors sometimes absorb these changes.

## 7. References

K. Krauter, R. Buyya, M. Maheswaran, (2002), A taxonomy and survey of grid resource management systems for distributed computing, Software: Practice and Experience, Vol. 32, No. 2, pp. 135-164, 2002.

H. Shan, L. Oliker, W. Smith, R. Biswas, (2004), Scheduling in Heterogeneous Grid Environments: The Effects of Data Migration, Intl Conference on Advanced Computing and Communication, 2004.

R. Rahman, K. Barker, R. Alhajj, (2007), Study of Different Replica Placement and Maintenance Strategies in Data Grid, IEEE/ACM International Symposium on Cluster Computing and Grid, pp. 171-178, 2007.

R. Rahman, K. Barker, R. Alhajj, (2008), Replica Placement Strategies in Data Grid, Journal of Grid Computing, Springer, Vol. 6, No. 1, pp. 103-123, 2008.

S. Vazhkudai, S. Tuecke, I. Foster, (2001), Replica Selection in the Globus Data Grid, Intl Symp. on Cluster Computing and the Grid, 2001.

J. Byers M. Luby, M. Mitzenmacher, (1999), Accessing multiple mirror sites in parallel: Using Tornado codes to speed up downloads, IEEE INFOCOM, pp. 275-283, 1999.

P. Rodriguez, E. Biersack, (2002), Dynamic parallel access to replicated content in the Internet, IEEE/ACM Transactions on Networking, Vol.10, No.4, pp. 455-465, 2002.

R. Chang, M. Guo and H. Lin, (2008), A multiple parallel download scheme with server throughput and client bandwidth considerations for data grids, Future Generation Computer Systems, Vol. 24, No. 8, pp. 798-805, 2008.

K. Ranganathan, I. Foster, (2002), Decoupling Computation and Data Scheduling in Distributed Data-Intensive Applications, High Performance Distributed Computing Sumposium, pp. 352-358, 2002.

A. Elghirani, R. Subrata, A. Zomaya, (2007), Intelligent Scheduling and Replication in Datagrids: a Synergistic Approach, Symposium on Cluster Computing and the Grid, pp. 179-182, 2007.

W. Bell ,D. Cameron, L. Capozza, A. P. Millar, K. Stockinger, F. Zini, (2002), Simulation of Dynamic Grid Replication Strategies, OptorSim, LNCS, Vol. 2536 , pp. 46-57, 2002.

W. Bell, D. Cameron, L. Capozza, A. Millar, K. Stockinger, F. Zini, (2003), OptorSim: A Grid Simulator for Studying Dynamic Data Replication Strategies, International Journal of High Performance Computing Applications, Vol. 17, No. 4, pp. 403-416, 2003.

D. Cameron, A. Millar, C. Nicholson, R. Carvajal-Schiaffino, F. Zini, K. Stockinger, (2004), Optorsim: a simulation tool for scheduling and replica optimisation in data grids, Computing in High Energy and Nuclear Physics, 2004.

A. Chakrabarti, R. Dheepak, S. Sengupta, (2004), Integration of Scheduling and Replication in Data Grids, LNCS, Vol. 3296 , pp. 375-385, 2004.

T. Stevens, M. De Leenheer, C. Develder, B. Dhoedt, K. Christodoulopoulos, P. Kokkinos, E. Varvarigos, (2008), Multi-cost job routing and scheduling in Grid networks, Future Generation Computer Systems, Vol. 25, No. 8, pp. 912-925, 2008.

A. Dogan, (2009), A study on performance of dynamic file replication algorithms for real-time file access in Data Grids, Future Generation Computer Systems, Vol. 25, No. 8, pp. 829-839, 2009.

L. Kleinrock, F. Kamoun, (1977), Hierarchical routing for large networks. Performance evaluation and optimization, Computer Networks, Vol. 1, No. 3, pp. 155-174, 1977.

W. C. Lee, (1995), Topology aggregation for hierarchical routing in ATM networks, Computer Communication Review, Vol. 25, No. 2, pp. 82-92, 1995.

P. Van Mieghem, (1999), Topology information condensation in hierarchical networks, The International Journal of Computer and Telecommunications, Vol. 31, No. 20, pp. 2115 - 2137, 1999.

D. Bauer, J. Daigle, I. Iliadis, and P. Scotton, (2006), Topology aggregation for combined additive and restrictive metrics, Computer Networks, Vol. 50, No. 17, pp. 3284-3299, 2006.

C. Intanagonwiwat, R. Govindan, D. Estrin, J. Heidemann, F. Silva, (2003), Directed diffusion for wireless sensor networking, IEEE Transactions on Networking, Vol. 11, pp. 2-16, 2003.

R. Renesse, K. Birman, W. Vogels, (2003), Astrolabe: A Robust and Scalable Technology for Distributed System Monitoring, Management, and Data Mining, ACM Transactions on Computer Systems, Vol. 21, No. 2, pp. 164-206, 2003.

S. Schulz, W. Blochinger, H. Hannak, (2009), Capability-Aware Information Aggregation in Peer-to-Peer Grids, Journal of Grid Computing, Vol. 7, No. 2, pp. 135-167, 2009.

R. Zhou, K. Hwang, (2006), Trust overlay networks for global reputation aggregation in P2P grid computing, IPDPS, 2006.

M. Cai, K. Hwang, (2007), Distributed Aggregation Algorithms with Load-Balancing for Scalable Grid Resource Monitoring, IEEE International Parallel and Distributed Processing Symposium, 2007.

K. Czajkowski, S. Fitzgerald, I. Foster, C. Kesselman, (2001), Grid Information Services for Distributed Resource Sharing, IEEE International Symposium on High-Performance Distributed Computing (HPDC), 2001.

K. Muraki, Y. Kawasaki, Y. Mizutani, F. Ino, K. Hagihara, (2006), Grid Resource Monitoring and Selection for Rapid Turnaround Applications, IEICE - Transactions on Information and Systems, Vol. 89, No. 9, pp. 2491 - 2501, 2006.

I. Rodero, F. Guim, J. Corbalan, L. Fong, S. Sadjadi, (2010), Grid broker selection strategies using aggregated resource information, Future Generation Computer Systems, Vol 26, No. 1, pp. 72-86, 2010.

E. Laure, et al., (2006), Programming the Grid with gLite. Computational Methods in Science and Technology, Vol. 12, pp. 33-45, 2006.

# Part 2

# Grid Architectures and Development

# 7

# A GPU Accelerated High Performance Cloud Computing Infrastructure for Grid Computing Based Virtual Environmental Laboratory

Giulio Giunta[1], Raffaele Montella,[1] Giuliano Laccetti[2],
Florin Isaila[3] and Javier García Blas[3]
[1]*University of Napoli Parthenope*
[2]*University of Napoli Federico II*
[3]*University of Madrid Carlos III*
[1,2]*Italy*
[3]*Spain*

## 1. Introduction

Numerical models play a main role in the earth sciences, filling in the gap between experimental and theoretical approach. Nowadays, the computational approach is widely recognized as the complement to the scientific analysis. Meanwhile, the huge amount of observed/modelled data, and the need to store, process, and refine them, often makes the use of high performance parallel computing the only effective solution to ensure the effective usability of numerical applications, as in the field of atmospheric /oceanographic science, where the development of the Earth Simulator supercomputer [65] is just the edge.
Grid Computing [38] is a key technology in all the computational sciences, allowing the use of inhomogeneous and geographically spread computational resources, shared across a virtual laboratory. Moreover, this technology offers several invaluable tools in ensuring security, performance, and availability of the applications. A large amount of simulation models have been successfully developed in the past, but a lot of them are poorly engineered and have been designed following a monolithic programming approach, unsuitable for a distributed computing environment or to be accelerated by GPGPUs [53]. The use of the grid computing technologies is often limited to computer science specialists, because of the complexity of grid itself and of its middleware. Another source of complexity resides on the use of coupled models, as, for example, in the case of atmosphere/sea-wave/ocean dynamics. The grid enabling approach could be hampered by the grid software and hardware infrastructure complexity. In this context, the build-up of a grid-aware virtual laboratory for environmental applications is a topical challenge for computer scientists.
The term "e-Science" is usually referred to computationally enhanced science. With the rise of cloud computing technology and on-demand resource allocation, the meaning of e-Science could straightforwardly change to elastic-Science. The aim of our virtual laboratory is to bridge the gap between the technology push of the high performance cloud computing and the pull of a wide range of scientific experimental applications. It provides generic functionalities supporting a wide class of specific e-Science application environments and

set up an experimental infrastructure for the evaluation of scientific ideas. Our Virtual Laboratory has the ambitious goal to spread elastic and virtually unlimited computing power to scientists belonging to different e-science communities in a transparent and straightforward fashion.

The rest of the chapter is organized as follows: section 2 describes the design and implementation of the application orchestration component. Section 3 is dedicated to the GPU virtualization technique, to the description of key design choices and of some benchmark results, which demonstrate the light impact of our software stack on overall performance; in that section, we also discuss about some high performance cloud computing scenarios depicted by recent gVirtuS enhancements. The need of a high performance file system distributed among virtual machines instances is the main motivation of the section 4; we discuss the design and the implementation of a virtual distributed file system mainly targeted to achieve high performance in dealing with HDF and NetCDF data archives. Our attention on those hierarchical self describing data formats is due to their extensive use in computational environmental science. Hence, section 5 sums up the virtual laboratory software ecosystem and describes the testbed application we have used in order to trim up the implemented features. Finally, the conclusions and future direction in this field are reported in section 6, where the principal guidelines for improving the usability and the availability of the described software components are drown.

## 2. Contextualization and application orchestration

Recently, a multi-disciplinary effort in virtually all science fields led domain specific scientists and computer scientists to work together in order to obtain from the models the best simulation results in the most efficient and reliable way as demonstrated by the tight coupling of computer science and environmental science in data intensive applications [61].

The growth of the many-core technologies could seem to make obsolete one of the traditional goals of the grid computing technology, i.e. the provision of high performance computing capabilities when local resources are not enough. We feel that this point is not correct and that the increase of computing power will continue to follow the increase of the need for it and vice-versa. This means that large scale computing problems can be managed by aggregating and federating many big computing resources and that grid computing can be the underlying technology for resource federation through a virtual organization approach [42].

Currently, the availability of computing and storage resources is a bottleneck in making progress in many fields of science. This suggests that the computing grids have to be elastic, in the meaning of the ability to allocate, for the needed amount of time, as much computing power as needed by the experiment. The cloud computing technology, which is based on hardware virtualization and many-core technologies, provides a suitable environment to achieve such goals. Grid and cloud computing are strictly related and, in many computer science aspects, share some visions and issues, but while the first focuses on aggregation and federation, the last enables the dynamical hosting of computing and storage resources. In this scenario, one can have "clouds on grids" if the virtualization and the dynamical resource provision is managed by a grid middleware. Otherwise, when grid-computing resources are partially (or totally) dynamically allocated on the cloud, one can have "grids on clouds" [24].

Virtual clusters instanced on cloud infrastructures, aggregated using grid computing middleware and leveraging on virtual organizations, suffer from poor message passing performance between virtual machine instances running on the same real machine [74].

Another source of computing power limitation is the impossibility to access hardware specific accelerating devices as GPUs in a fully transparent way [47].
For these reasons, the development of a grid/cloud-aware virtual laboratory for environmental applications is an interesting and a well-know challenge for computer scientists.

### 2.1 The grid and cloud enabling approaches

Making an application capable of working on a grid is a complex process called "grid-enabling". This process could be hampered by the grid software and hardware infrastructure complexity, but, above all, it is strictly related to the application that has to be grid-enabled. Applications characterized by an intrinsic parallelism, where the spatially decomposed domain can be processed without any interaction among computing threads appear to be perfectly suitable for the grid. This is the case, for instance, of parameter sweep based algorithms, very common in computational high-energy physics. Apparently, all parallel applications, which rely on tightly coupled concurrent processes, seem to be unsuitable for grid enabling. Numerical models based on systems of differential equations solved by finite difference or finite elements methods belong to this application class. In the world of parallel computing, these applications can achieve high performance thanks to message passing libraries as PVM [67] and, mainly, MPI [46]. In order to migrate MPI concepts in the grid world, MPICH-G2 [52] permits distributed cluster nodes to be aggregated as a single supercomputing resource. Even though this approach is limited by the connection bandwidth among computing nodes, nevertheless it has been successfully used on production environments deployed on Teragrid [35].

#### 2.1.1 The grid-enabling

In the grid lingo, the job is the processing unit in term of piece of software to be executed and producing a result. A grid-enabled application has to be rearranged as a job or pool of jobs, and, moreover, has to be executed in a shared environment, as a guest on a remote machine, ensuring the management of data staging. First generation grid middleware, such as Condor [68] and Globus 1.x and 2.x [39], considered the job as an executable, with specific computing needs, which is dynamically deployed on a target computing element matching the job needs. Typically, data needed by the job are staged-in on the working machine and then the results staged-out. The user must know the requirements of the application in terms of CPU, memory, disk, and architecture. With the rise of web services technology, the next generation of middleware, such as Globus 3.x [40] and Globus 4.x [41], moved towards a different concept of grid enabled application, i.e. the application must be functionally decomposed and each component has to be exposed to the grid leveraging on a wrapping web service. In this case, the user should search for a computing element offering the needed component and low level details about application's needs are hidden to the user. The application is not deployed on-the-fly and can be managed in a safe, secure, and consistent way, and the main effort for grid enabling consists in designing, developing and implementing a suitable web service interface. The complexity introduced by the web service infrastructure and the latency related to that technology is drown back by the flexibility and the semantic coherence of an application made by components interconnected through web services. The fast development of the web service technology, the poor performance in job submission and the complexity in programming and management called for the last generation of grid middleware Globus 5.x and gLite. Web service technology has been decoupled from authentication, job submission and data management and it is available as a separate tier. A job is executed remotely, using a submission interface, which avoids on-fly deployment.

In our proposed grid infrastructure, we have used the middleware Globus Toolkit version 2.x, 4.x, 5.x (GT2/GT4/GT5), developed within the Globus Alliance and the Open Grid Forum (OGF) with a wide support of institutions belonging to the academia, the government and the business area. The GT4 has been chosen because it exposes its features via web services, using common W3C standards as the Web Service Description Language (WSDL), the Standard Object Access Protocol (SOAP), and the Hyper Text Transfer Protocol (HTTP). More complex features, i.e. service persistence, state and stateless behaviour, event notification, data element management and index services tools, are implemented in a way compliant to that standard. GT4 also supports the GridFTP protocol, an FTP enhanced version, and capable of massive parallel striping and reliable file transfer. Recently, we smoothly migrated under GT5 and explored the interoperability with the EGEE/gLite world.

The application package is the key component of our implementation and is the blueprint of the job execution environment. A framework approach can be used to abstract different application model configurations, by exploiting an object-oriented programming-like methodology. Each application runs in a private custom environment, so that several instances of the same software can be concurrently executed. This approach is based on a repository in which application packages are stored and from where they can be retrieved as instance templates to support a deployment on-the-fly.

A job launcher, invoked as a grid job on a remote machine or locally as well, sets up the virtual private environment and performs the needed stage-in and stage-out operations on the data files. The launching script can be statically installed on the target machine, automatically deployed from the local repository or even staged-in: it represents the job executable file to be run on the target computing-element. This script unpacks the application package, downloaded from a repository or copied from a local directory, unpacks and inflates input data, runs the actual application executable and, finally, deflates results. The framework produces logs based on a XML schema that allows a straightforward parsing.

The resource specification is performed by a description XML file, following the Job Submission Description Language schema [23]. The submitted job is described by specifying the executable path, the current working directory, the files to be staged-in before the execution and staged-out after the job run. All files are named using full-qualified URLs, with protocol details from the target machine. In order to simplify the process of grid enabling and then the application execution as a job, we implemented a custom resource specification pre-processor for the definition of jobs, which relies on an advanced method of labelling and placeholders parsing and evaluation, macro based code explosion and late binding capabilities.

### 2.1.2 The cloud-enabling

While the grid-enabling process is well defined, the concept of cloud enabling is still under drawing. NIST defines cloud computing as a pay-per-use model for enabling available, convenient, on-demand network access to a shared pool of configurable computing resources that can be provisioned and released with minimal management effort or service provider interaction [55]. Within the cloud paradigm, server time and network storage can be provisioned to the user in an on-demand self-service fashion without requiring human interaction. Resources are made available over the network and ubiquitously accessed through standard mechanisms such as thin or thick client platforms. According to current demand, computing resources (both physical and virtual) are dynamically assigned and reassigned to serve all users that generally have no control or knowledge over the exact location of the provided resources. The computing resources can be elastically provisioned to scale up and released to scale down: the set of resources appears to be infinite (infinitive computing) [25].

Any kind of software, including operating systems and applications can be deployed and then run on the best matching computing resource that is provided for rent to the user. The user doesn't manage the underlying cloud infrastructure, but has control over operating systems, storage and applications. This is the so-called Infrastructure as a Service (IaaS) and could be considered as the lowest level in a cloud oriented infrastructure stack [33]. The next level is the Platform as a Service (PaaS, where the user has control over the deployed applications and possibly the application hosting environment [71]. The highest level of the stack is the Software as a Service (SaaS): one can use the provider's applications running on a cloud infrastructure from various client devices through a client interface such as a Web browser (e.g., web-based email). The user can modify only some application configuration parameters, but doesn't manage or control the underlying cloud infrastructure [54].

If the cloud infrastructure is owned by a single organization and is used only inside that organization, then it is a "private cloud". A cloud is a "community cloud" when the infrastructure is shared by several organizations. In e-science applications, "hybrid clouds" are becoming popular.

In our context, resources include storage, processing, memory, network bandwidth, and virtual machines. Since a virtual laboratory is designed to serve the world of computational science, a hybrid cloud solution appears to be the most suitable grid deployment. Cloud-enabled software has to take full advantage of the cloud paradigm by being service oriented with a focus on statelessness, low coupling, modularity, and semantic interoperability or encapsulated in a virtual machine image and executed as a virtual machine instance.

Experience in grid enabling application may be useful in order to design and implement cloud enabling guidelines, especially concerning the virtual laboratory software components. An object-oriented approach, yet followed in grid enabling, may be replicated in this more complex scenario. The process could be divided in two main steps. First, the application package is deployed in a virtual machine image and then, once the virtual machine is instanced, the application performs its lifecycle. The deployment of an application on a virtual machine image could be a complex task if the main goal is the cloud infrastructure best resource allocation. We have developed a software tool specifically designed to help and partially automate the creation of application appliances. Our Virtual Machine Compiler (VMc) produces a XML description of the needed virtual machine in order to run a generic piece of software in a virtualized environment with minimal resources for achieving a required performance. Once installed and configured by the user, the application is executed in a full featured virtual machine under the control of the VMc, that evaluates the disk and memory needs and, above all, the needed services and libraries. The application lifecycle is managed by an abstract framework in which the user can implement software components performing specific actions, such as answering to events fired when the virtual machine is up and running, or before the application is going to be executed (in order to implement data staging-in), or during the application run (for example for progress status notification), or even when the application finished (for the staging-out of the results) and the virtual machine instance is ready to be shouted down. The VMc output is a XML file which contains the software and hardware requirements needed by the application. This output can be converted to platform-specific installation/configuration file (as the Fedora/RedHat/CentOS kickstart file). The VMc output will be used in the virtual machine image creation using commonly available open source software packages. Finally, the application environment is cloned on the virtual machine image and made ready to be executed within a software appliance. This process is far from being completely automatic, but, once performed successfully, it is no more in charge to the user. The computational scientist has just to instantiate the virtual machine and wait for results. In case of distributed memory parallel programs, the tool helps to automatically set up two virtual machine images, one for the head node and the other for the computing node, and all the other needed features, such as the shared file system, user authentication and message passing interface libraries.

### 2.2 Application orchestration

In many scientific applications, the final result is obtained by assembling different components executed as jobs on remote machines as workflows [70]. Each component could be related to its previous/next component as data producer or data consumer, defining a so-called computational pipeline, with one job for one component.

For example, let us consider this simple application:

1. A regional-scale atmospheric model waits until data can be downloaded from a specified service.
2. It acquires the boundary and initial conditions from a global-scale forecast, and runs for a specified time period.
3. When data are ready to be processed, another job, which simulates an ocean circulation model, uses atmospheric data as boundary conditions.
4. When this second job finishes its computing task, the produced data are consumed by another job which simulates the wind driven sea wave propagation and forecasts the wave height/period and their direction fields.
5. At last, the user retrieves all pipelined outputs produced by all models.

This scientific application could be implemented via shell scripts and middleware specific job submission tools, specifying the target machine in the script.

The Globus Toolkit grid middleware provides job submission tools via web services (4.x), pre-web services (2.x) and web services-independent (5.x) infrastructure without any support for job flow scheduling and resource broking. Other grid technologies offer a full support of direct acyclic graph job workflow with conditional branches, recovery feature and graphic user interfaces. Our custom software solution provides domain scientists with a full configurable grid and cloud-computing tool, which minimizes the impact of the computing infrastructure.

In a hybrid grid/cloud infrastructure scenario, the shell script instantiates virtual machines, without concerning about where to execute the computation but the needed computing resources.

This approach, though operatively correct, presents many disadvantages. The user must know many details about the script programming language, the job submission, the system environment setup, and, if the computing resources are virtualized, even about the virtual machine lifecycle and the interaction with instances. The developed code is tightly coupled to its application and any change to the job behaviour or model configuration affects the entire application. In case of complex job fluxes, like in a concurrent ramification context, for example when a weather simulation model forces both wave propagation and oceanic circulation models, the control code may grow in complexity and data consuming/production relationships could be hard to implement, since several synchronization issues arise. Moreover, this kind of approach is potentially insecure because the user must be logged into the system to run a script, and this scenario is not applicable in the case of an interactive application on a web portal.

### 2.2.1 Orchestration components design and implementation

The orchestration component design has been driven by the goal of disclosing to the final user the power of a hybrid grid/cloud infrastructure and hiding technical details.
The virtual laboratory main component is the Processing Unit (PU). The PU may be seen as a black box feed by input data, performing a computation task and producing output data. In a grid-computing environment, the PU could be considered as a job submitted to a grid machine matching the computational needs. In a dynamical infrastructure as a service cloud, the PU can be totally embedded in a virtual machine image and deployed to be executed using the requested computing resources. To the user of the virtual laboratory, the view has completely changed: the cloud elasticity permits to consider computing resources as potentially infinite. In our architecture stack, the PU represents the highest level of interaction component and leverages on the cloud management software components.

### 2.2.2 JaClouX, a cloud independent Java API

Different cloud infrastructure systems, such as Amazon AWS, Open Nebula, Open Stack, Eucalyptus, etc, offer similar services through different web service interfaces, so a cloud-aware component is needed in order to manage virtual machine instances on different clouds. JaClouX (Java bindings for Cloud eXtensions) [9] is a unified application program interface to the cloud written in Java and it represents a fundamental change in the way clouds are managed, breaking the barriers among proprietary, closed clouds and open scientific clouds. JaClouX is our cloud management component; it is independent of the underlying cloud software and interacts with other components as Images, Instances, Locations, and Sizes. Moreover, JaClouX is cloud-aware thanks to a plug in architecture. The support to any cloud software can be added by just implementing a new Driver component. Respect to other similar APIs, such as libcloud [13] and JClouds [8], JaClouX provides some enhanced specific features for storage and high performance computing.
While most cloud software manage virtual machine images and instances in a quite similar way, the storage and other high level services turn out to be different among the various cloud solutions. For example, AWS offers the Simple Storage Service (S3) implemented in Eucalyptus as Walrus. The Eucalyptus storage controller provides a service similar to the AWS Elastic Block Storage (EBS). The OpenNebula stack does not provide S3-like services, but leverages on shared network file systems on which the virtual machine instances are attached. JaClouX's Driver component provides an abstraction of both S3 and EBS using the Simple Storage Component (SSC) and the Elastic Block Component (EBC). The Driver component can provide the missing cloud features by software emulation.
The Virtual Computing Cluster (VCC) component permits the dynamical creation of high performance computing cluster on-demand. A VCC is defined specifying the virtual machine image for the head and the compute nodes and the number of working nodes

instances. VCC manages the user authentication and the execution authorization in a coherent fashion deploying automatically, if needed, the grid security infrastructure components. The virtual network file system permits to the head node user to execute on working nodes using secure shell and perform some other operation in the distributed memory parallel programming ecosystem. VCC takes in charge file system related issues abstracting the low level implementation especially regarding the distributed parallel file system. Last but not the least, VCC interacts with the cloud scheduler, where possible, in order to locate the virtual computing nodes in the most effective and high performance way: i. e. groups of computing nodes belonging to the same virtual cluster can be allocated on the same real machine, so MPI optimization for virtual networks can be used in the best way; in a similar way, virtual working nodes needing for GPGPU acceleration support are spawn on the real hardware achieving the best possible computing effort.

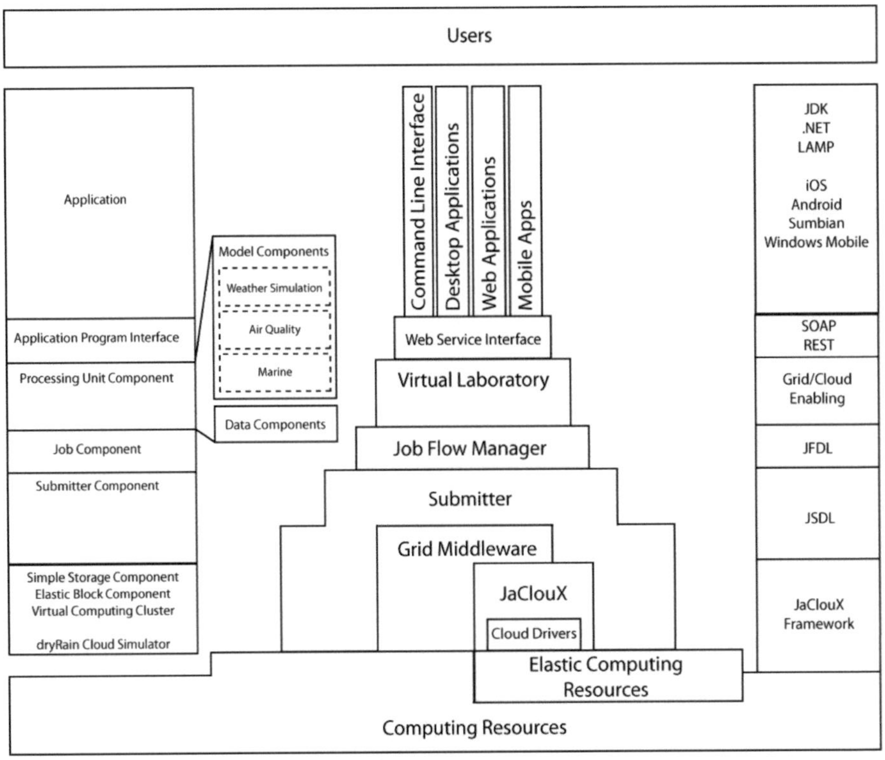


Fig. 1. The Virtual Laboratory big picture. On the right the component stack schema. In the centre area the component interactions/dependences diagram. On the right the main technologies used each application tier.

### 2.2.3 Managing the application workflow

The automation of scientific processes in which tasks are structured based on their control and data dependencies are defined as *scientific workflows*. Scientific applications on Grids gain several advantages following the workflow paradigm. The ability to build dynamic applications, which orchestrate distributed resources using resources that are located in a particular domain, accelerates the advance in knowledge in many scientific fields. The workflows permit to increase the throughput or reduce execution costs spanning the execution of scientific software on multiple administrative domains to obtain specific processing capabilities. The highest advantage in the workflow technology application in e-Science is in the integration of multiple teams involved in management of different parts of the experiment promoting inter and cross organization collaborations [48]. With the advent of the cloud technology applied to computational sciences the potential importance of scientific workflows increased: the scientist is in the power of allocate all the needed computing power doesn't caring about the effective availability.

In order to enhance flexibility and to minimize the impact on the grid configuration, we have implemented a software component for scientific workflow management. The Job Flow Manager (JFM) component is an evolution of the previously developed Job Flow Scheduler [26] improved with the cloud computing and the on demand virtual computing cluster support. The JFM component plays a key role in the grid application orchestration. Using this tool the entire complex, multi branch, grid application can be configured through a XML file. JFM takes care of submitting jobs to computing nodes without concerning whether the target machine is a real computing resource or a virtual computing node dynamically allocated on demand on a cloud. The JFM have been designed in a modular fashion and does not depend on the actual grid middleware or cloud ecosystem.

The main JFM role is the submission of jobs or virtual machine instances creation to the propter computing resource abstracting the Processing Unit in our virtual laboratory component stack. The Submitter Component (SC) is a piece of software dealing with the grid middleware and/or with the cloud infrastructure interface. As previously stated, the jobs are formally described with an extension of the JSDL, providing syntactic and semantic tools for job description in terms of virtual machines instances. The user may create virtual computing resources and instantiate them when needed. We defined a XML schema, called Job Flow Definition Language [59] so one can define virtual laboratory experiments as XML files. Thanks to the interaction between the JFM and the SC components, the submitted job could face as a classical grid job wrapped an executable on a remote machine or an application appliance to instantiate, run and destroy on a cloud computing provided resource. The SC is the software interface connecting the PU with the computing resource. We have designed the Submitter component abstracting virtually any kind of remote execution technology including HPC, grid or cloud (via JaClouX).

In the virtual laboratory an experiment is an aggregated of Processing Units, each of them, connected with the others in a direct acyclic graph, draws the computing steps as the nodes of the experiment graph.

The Virtual Lab and the Job components (VLC, JC) represent our playground for scientific workflows form an higher point of view and interacts with the user interface (VLC) and with Submitter component (JC). In particular, the Job component takes in charge the list of the jobs to be completed before the actual processing unit is executed and the list of jobs to be submitted when the PU work eventually ends up.

Finally, VLC provides a friendly user interface through a desktop client, a mobile app, an interactive or batch console or even a web application (Figure 1).

## 3. GPGPU virtualization

Recently, scientific computing has experienced on general purpose graphics processing units using massive multi core processors available on graphics devices in order to accelerate data parallel computing tasks. One of the most successful GPU based acceleration system is provided by nVIDIA and relies on the CUDA programming paradigm and tools [16]. Currently, in the world of high performance computing clouds, virtualization does not allow the use of accelerators as CUDA based GPUs in a transparent way. This happens because of the communication between virtual and real machines, of the communication between guest and host on the real machine side, and of the issues related to the vendor specific interface (on the virtual machine side). The use of the GPGPUs massive parallel architecture in scientific computing is still relegated to HPC clusters. A serious limitations exist on the overall potential performances of an on-demand instanced high performances computing cluster and, in general, on the use of cloud computing infrastructure as an high performance computing system based on elastically allocated resources.

### 3.1 gVirtus architecture and design

gVirtuS (GPU Virtualization Service) is our result in GPGPUs transparent virtualization targeting mainly the use of nVIDIA CUDA based accelerator boards through virtual machines instanced to accelerate scientific computations [45].

The basic virtualization idea is based on a split driver approach [37] in which a front-end is deployed on the virtual machine image and a back-end is hosted on the real machine. The communication technology between the front and the back-ends is a key component in order to achieve high performances. The front-end and the back-end layers implement the uncoupling between the hypervisor (which has in charge the control of the acceleration device) and the communication layer. A key property of the proposed system is its ability to execute CUDA kernels with an overall performance similar to that obtained by real machines with direct access to accelerators. This has been achieved by developing a component that provides a high performance communication between virtual machines and their host, and implements an efficient data transfer between the guest VM's application, which use the kernel, and the GPU, which runs it.

On the front-end side, the component packs the API invocation, recovers the result values and automatically translates host and device memory pointers. This approach permits to enforce the isolation overcoming some hardware-related specific limitations. On the front-end a CUDA library stub imitates the real CUDA library implementation interacting with the back-end in a transparent way. This architectural scheme makes evident an important design choice: the GPU virtualization is independent of the hypervisor.

The approach can naturally be extended to a wide range of devices designed to work in a non-virtualized environment, but the overhead introduced by the system can be prohibitive for HPC applications without an efficient and reliable high performance communication system between guest and host machines. Due to the potentially large size of the input/output data of a CUDA kernel, this is particularly relevant for the GPU accelerators that span many pages of contiguous memory. Our effort was mainly aimed at delivering a GPU virtualization suitable for the performance requirements of current HPC scientific applications and to develop CUDA API as much as possible hypervisor and communicator independent, but the hypervisor proprietary virtual/real machine communication technology affects deeply the over all performances.

In the world of virtualization and cloud computing some hypervisors reached the status of standard *de facto*:

- Xen [21] is a hypervisor that runs directly on the top of the hardware through a custom Linux kernel. Xen provides a communication library between guest and host machines, called XenLoop, which implements a low latency and wide bandwidth TCP/IP and UDP connection both among virtual machines running on the same host and virtual machine and host machines. XenLoop can reduce latency up to a factor of 5 and can increase efficiency up to a factor of 6. Moreover, it is application transparent and implements an automatic discovery of the supported virtual machines [73]. We excluded Xen from our test-bed because there is no official support of nVIDIA driver for this hypervisor.

- VMWare [19] is a commercial hypervisor running at the application level. VMWare provides a high performance communication channel between guest and host machines, called VMCI (Virtual Machine Communication Interface), leveraging on a shared memory approach. VMWare offers a datagram API to exchange small messages, a shared memory API to share data, an access control API to control which resources a virtual machine can access and a discovery service for publishing and retrieving resources [20].
- KVM (Kernel-based virtual machine) [10] is a Linux loadable kernel module now embedded as a standard component in most of Linux distributions, with a full virtualization support. KVM offers a high performance guest/host communication component called vmChannel. This component exposes a set of fully emulated inter virtual machines and virtual/real machine serial ports and network sockets, based on a shared memory approach. Unfortunately, most of the promising vmChannel features are not yet fully implemented [11].

The use of the TCP/IP stack to permit the communication between virtual machines and a real machine is common feature in virtualization. This approach is not only hypervisor independent, but deployment independent too: the virtual resource consumer and the real producer can be on physical different computing elements. This is a cool feature, especially if in the field of cloud computing, but the introduced overhead is unacceptable for HPC applications. Nevertheless the use of TCP/IP could be interesting in some deployment scenarios where the size of the computing problem, the network performances and, above all, the GPU acceleration justify the general overhead.

In order to be hypervisor and communication technology independent, we designed a fully pluggable. It is an independent communication channel and allows the communicator change through a simple configuration file. Moreover, if a new kind of communicator is implemented, it can be plugged in without any change in the front-end and the back-end layer.

CUDA accelerated applications interact with the front-end CUDA library in a standardized manner. The CUDA library instead of dealing directly with the real nVIDIA hardware interacts with our GPU virtualization front-end. The front-end, using the communicator component, packs the library function invocation and sends it to the back-end. The back-end deals with the real nVIDIA hardware using the CUDA driver; it unpacks the library function invocation and suitably maps memory pointers. Then it executes the CUDA operation, retrieves the results and sends them to the front-end using the communicator. Finally, the front-end interacts with the CUDA library by terminating the GPU operation and providing results to the calling program. Any accesses to the GPU is routed via the front-end/back-end layers under control of a management component, and data are moved from GPU to guest VM application, and vice versa.

This design is hypervisor independent, communicator independent and even accelerator independent, since the same approach could be followed to implement different kinds of virtualization. The platform is designed to emulate future heterogeneous many-core chips comprised of both general and special purpose processors (Figure 2).

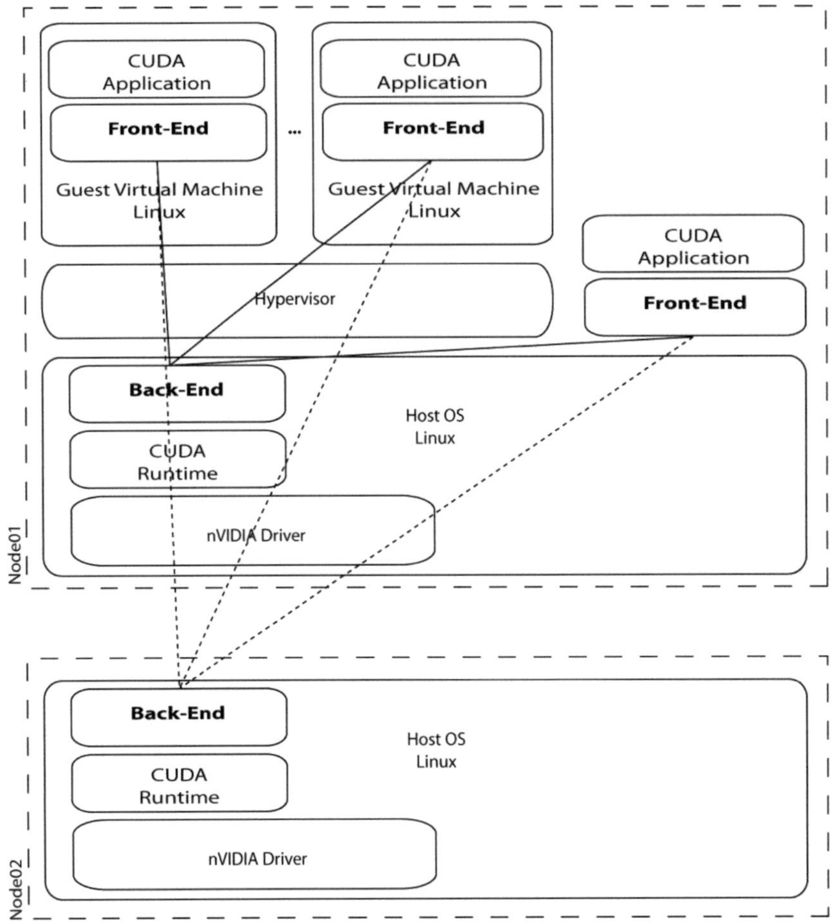


Fig. 2. The gVirtuS schema. In the single node deployment scenario the CUDA application can interact with the back-end with, or without, the hypervisor interaction. If the back-end is on a different computing node (cluster deployment scenario), then the application can be accelerated by GPGPUs devices physically installed on different machines. The actual performances (and benefits) depend of the application, the problem size and the network bandwidth.

### 3.2 gVirtus implementation

The implementation, in C++, is related to an x86-based multi-core hardware platform with multiple accelerators attached via PCIe devices, running Linux as both host and guest operating system. According to the underlying idea of high performance cloud computing applications, we implemented the virtual accelerator in a hypervisor independent fashion and in a fully configurable way. In particular, we focused on VMware and KVM hypervisors. The GPU is attached to the host system and must run its drivers at a privileged level that can directly access the hardware. Memory management and communication methods for efficient sharing of the GPU by multiple guest VMs, have to be implemented at the same run level.

We implemented a wrapper stub CUDA library with the same interface of the nVIDIA CUDA library. Our library performs some processing and passes parameters to the lower level components. The library currently implements all function calls synchronously and is able to manage multiple application threads. Since the source code of both library and driver are strictly closed, the wrapper library running in the guest virtual machine intercepts CUDA calls made by an application, collects arguments, packs them into a CUDA call packet, and finally sends the packet to the front end. The front-end driver manages the connections between the guest virtual machine and the host machine. It uses the services offered by the communicator component to establish event-based channels through both sides, receiving call packets from the wrap CUDA library, sending these requests to the back end for execution over a shared call buffer and relaying responses back to the wrap CUDA library.

We designed and implemented a component to achieve a high performance communicator working with the KVM hypervisor: vmSocket. This component exposes Unix Sockets on virtual machine instances thanks to a QEMU device connected to the virtual PCI bus. The device performs register based I/O operations using dynamically allocated memory buffers.

We focused on concentrating most components on the guest machine side, in order to make reusable as many components as possible. On the host side, the back end mediates all accesses to the GPU and it is responsible for executing the CUDA calls received from the front end and for returning the computed results. Once a call has been executed, it notifies the guest and passes the results through the connector component. The back end has been implemented as a user-level module to avoid the additional runtime overhead of multiple accesses to the user space CUDA memory. This component converts the call packets received from the front end into CUDA function calls; notice that it is the wrap CUDA library host side counterpart. Finally, the nVIDIA CUDA library and the driver interact with the real device.

GPU based high performance computing applications usually require massive transfer of data between host (CPU) and device (GPU) memory. In a non-virtualized environment, a memory copy operation invoked by a CUDA application copies data between host memory and GPU memory, managed by the nVIDIA driver. This can be avoided by making a call to the CUDA API enabling the allocation of host-mapped GPU memory, and implies zero-copy of data. In a virtualized environment the virtual machine isolation adds another layer between the CUDA application working in the guest memory and the CUDA device.

In our implementation there is no mapping between guest memory and device memory because the gVirtuS backend acts in behalf of the guest running virtual machine, then device memory pointers are valid in the host real machine and in the guest as well. In this way the front end and the back end sides interacts in a effective and efficient way because the memory device pointers are never de-referenced on the host side of the CUDA enabled software (with gVirtuS the host side is the guest virtual machine side): CUDA kernels are executed on our backend side where the pointers are fully consistent. Exists a sort of pointers mapping between backend and frontend sides managed by the backend due to support the execution of CUDA function via the vmSocket channel. When a CUDA function have to be invoked on the device, the stub CUDA library interact with the front end. The front end prepares a package containing the name of the function to be invoked and the related parameters. The front end/back end communication handles three kinds of

parameters: automatic scalar variables, host memory pointers and device memory pointers. The serialization function packs the scalar variables without any modification, uses the value pointed by the pointer for each host memory pointer and considers as unsigned 64 bits long integer each device memory pointer. The de-serialization function works in an analogue, but opposite way when the communication is from the backend to the frontend.
Sharing memory between virtual and real machines could be a strange feature in the world of cloud computing where the isolation among VM instances and computing resource is a primary goal. Nevertheless in the high performance cloud computing context this feature could be extremely limiting: using shared memory a MPI communication channel could implement transparently a latency free network among virtual computing nodes without any change to the distributed memory parallel software. In order to achieve better performances in our GPU virtualization we designed and implemented the VMShm component. VMShm ensures high performance memory block copying between guest and host system using an implementation approach similar to vmSocket via the PCI-e virtual driver.
We compared and contrasted many hypervisor/communicator configurations (VMWare: VMCI/tcp, KVM-QEMU: vmSocket/tcp) and, using standard CUDA SDK benchmark programs, demonstrated our GPU virtualization (KVM-QEMU with vmSocke) achieves performances not so much different than the GPU with no virtualization [45].

### 3.3 Cloud deployment

As mentioned above, we have designed and implemented the gVirtuS GPU virtualization system with the primary goal of using GPUs in a private computing cloud for high performance scientific computing. We have set up a department prototypal cloud computing system leveraging on the Eucalyptus open source software. Eucalyptus, developed at the University of Santa Barbara in California [], implements an Infrastructure as a Service (IaaS), as it is commonly referred to. The system gives users the ability to run and control entire virtual machine instances deployed across a variety of physical resources in the same way the Amazon Web Service infrastructure works [1]. Eucalyptus enables users familiar with existing Grid and HPC systems to explore new cloud computing functionalities while maintaining access to existing, familiar application development software and Grid middleware. In particular we were interested in setting up high performance computing clusters on-demand, leasing the resources upon an existing infrastructure [72]. In our test aimed at assessing the performance of gVirtuS in a high performance computing cloud system, we have used an Intel based 12 computing nodes cluster, where each node is equipped with a quad core 64 bit CPU and an nVIDIA GeForce GT 9400 video card with 16 CUDA cores and a memory of 1 Gbyte.
We carried out an experiment focused on the gVirtuS behaviour in a private cloud, where the GPUs are seen as virtual computing nodes building a virtual cluster dynamically deployed on a private cloud [66]. We developed an *ad-hoc* benchmark software implementing a matrix multiplication algorithms. This software uses a classic memory distributed parallel approach. The first matrix is distributed by rows; the second one by columns, and each process have to perform a local matrix multiplication. MPICH 2[] is message-passing interface among processes, whereas each process uses the CUDA library to perform the local matrix multiplication.
The evaluation process results show that the gVirtuS GPU virtualization and the related sharing system allow an effective exploitation of the computing power of the GPUs [45]. We

note that without such component the GPUs could not be seen by the virtual machine and it would be not possible to run this experiment on a public or private cloud hosting an dynamic (on demand) virtual cluster using, for example, JaClouX features.

## 4. High performance parallel I/O

The needs of scientific applications have driven a continuous increase in scale and capability of leading parallel systems [7]. However, the improvement in rates of computation has not been matched by an increase in I/O capabilities. For example, earlier supercomputers maintained a ratio of 1GBps of parallel I/O bandwidth for every TFLOP, whereas in current systems 1GBps for every 10 TFLOPS [22] is the norm. This increased disparity makes it even more critical that the I/O subsystem is used in the most efficient manner. Scalable I/O has been already identified as a critical issue for PFLOP systems. Future exascale systems forecasted for 2018-2020 will presumably have O(1B) cores and will be hierarchical in both platform and algorithms [17]. This hierarchy will imply a longer path in moving data from cores to storage and vice-versa, resulting in even higher I/O latencies, relative to the rates of computation and communication in the system. The GPGPU-based systems introduce an additional level into this hierarchy, making a high-performance low-latency solution for file accesses even more necessary.

An additional contribution of this chapter is to extend our previous work on designing and implementing multiple level parallel I/O architectures for clusters [50] and supercomputers [51] to virtualized GPGPU-based cloud architecture in order to improve the file access performance (I/O latency and throughput) of parallel applications.

Our proposed solution is based on a multi-tier hierarchy as depicted in Figure 3, the parallel I/O architecture is organized on six tiers: application, application I/O forwarding, client-side cache, aggregator I/O forwarding, I/O node-side cache and storage. In the figure we show the components of the parallel I/O architecture and on the margins, we depict how the logical components map on physical nodes.

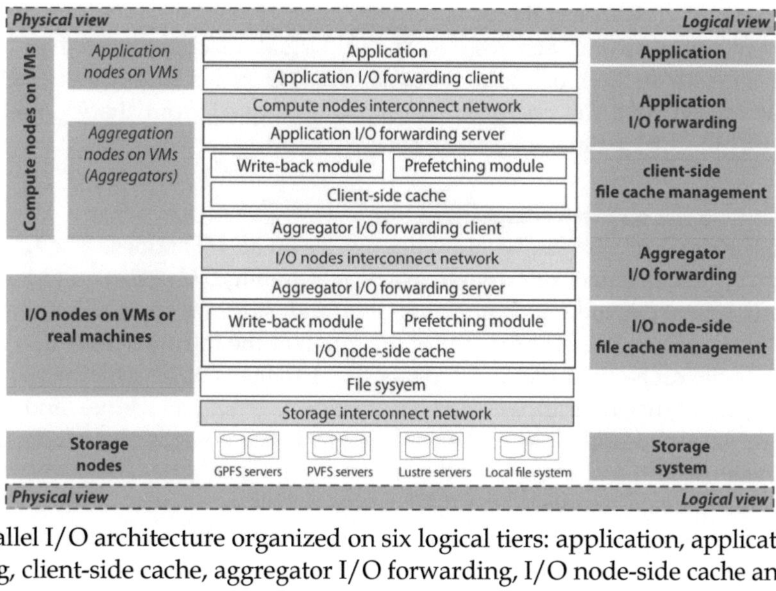


Fig. 3. Parallel I/O architecture organized on six logical tiers: application, application I/O forwarding, client-side cache, aggregator I/O forwarding, I/O node-side cache and storage.

### 4.1 Application tier.

From a parallel I/O perspective applications run on virtual machines and access the file systems through file interfaces such as MPI-IO or POSIX. As described in section, the CUDA calls of the applications running on virtual machines are intercepted in forwarded in zero-copy fashion to the guest machine where they are processed by the CUDA run time. The transfers between main memory and GPGPU memory as well as GPGPU processing can be completely overlapped by completely overlapped with the service of file system calls.

### 4.2 Application I/O forwarding tier.

Application I/O forwarding tier resides on all application nodes and has the goal of forwarding the file accesses to the next tier through the compute nodes interconnect network. The forwarding is done on-demand, when the application issues the file access. This forwarding tier leverages VMSocket and VMShm in order to achieve high performance in intra virtual machines interactions.

### 4.3 Client-side file cache management tier.

The client-side file cache module resides on the memory of virtual machines and has the role of aggregating small file access requests from several application processes running on virtual machines and performing the file access on behalf of them. The application accesses the client-side cache through the application I/O forwarding tier. i.e. through VMSocket. The objective of client-side file cache module is to provide the management of a file cache close to the applications and to offer efficient transfer methods between the applications and I/O subsystem. The main tasks of the module are buffer management and asynchronous data staging, including write-back and prefetching modules. This module is generic, is network- and file system-independent and is common for both cluster and supercomputer architectures. The client-side cache management tier absorbs the writes of the applications and hides the latency of accessing the I/O nodes over interconnect networks.

### 4.4 Aggregator I/O forwarding tier.

Aggregator I/O forwarding tier resides on all virtual machines and has the goal of forwarding accesses at file block granularity to the I/O nodes through vmSocket library. The communication with the compute nodes are decoupled from the file system access, allowing for a full overlap of the two operations.

### 4.5 I/O node-side file cache management tier.

The I/O node-side file cache management tier resides on all I/O nodes. The I/O nodes can run either on virtual machines or on a real machine. Running I/O nodes on virtual machines bring benefit when the load is highly variable and starting or shutting down virtual machines can contribute to adapt the cost of operation of the infrastructure. The objective of I/O node-side file cache module is to provide the management of a file cache close to the storage and offer efficient transfer methods between virtual machines and the storage system. The I/O node-side file cache management tier absorbs the blocks transferred asynchronously from the client-side cache through the aggregator I/O forwarding client, and hides the transfers between the I/O nodes and file systems. An I/O thread is responsible for asynchronously accessing the file systems by enforcing write-back and prefetching policies.

### 4.6 Storage system tier.

The file system components run on dedicated file servers connected to storage nodes through the storage interconnection network. The storage system provides the persistent storage service and can be any file system providing a VFS (virtual file system) interface. The I/O node-side file cache management tier provides an agile and elastic proxy layer that allows the performance of the file systems to scale up with the load generated by the applications.

### 4.7 Data staging.

The architecture presented in the previous sections scales both with the computation and I/O requirements of the applications but at the cost of a hierarchical organization of file caches. In order to make an efficient use of hierarchy of file caches our solution employs a multiple level data staging. The first file level caching is deployed on virtual machines of the applications and have the role improving the performance of the accesses to the file systems by overlapping the GPGPU and processor cores computation with I/O transfers between computational virtual machines and I/O nodes. The I/O servers manage the second level of distributed caching at I/O nodes. File blocks are mapped to I/O servers and each server is responsible for transferring its blocks to and from the persistent storage. In order to hide the latency of file accesses, data staging acts in coordination both on virtual machines and on I/O nodes. The data staging consists of two flows corresponding to the write and read operations.

#### 4.7.1 Multiple-level write-back.

After a file write is issued on a virtual machine, data are pipelined from compute nodes through the I/O nodes to the file systems. The application I/O forwarding tier transfers the application write request to the client-side cache management tier. The cached file blocks are marked dirty, the application is acknowledged the successful transfer and is allowed to continue. The responsibility of flushing the data from client-side cache to I/O node over the I/O network belongs to a write-back module on a virtual machine. On the I/O node a write-back module is in charge of caching the file blocks received from the compute nodes and flushing them to the file system over the storage network. The write-back policies are based on a high/low water-mark for dirty blocks. The high and low water marks are percentages of dirty blocks. The flushing of dirty blocks is activated when a high water mark of blocks is reached. Once activated the flushing continues until the number of dirty blocks falls below a low water mark. Blocks are chosen to be flushed in the Least Recently Modified (LRM) order. In order to efficiently hide the latency, coordination along the pipeline is necessary. In a previous work we made an extensive evaluation of coordination strategies for Blue Gene supercomputers [51]. The evaluation of this coordination for GPGPU clouds is subject of current research.

#### 4.7.2 Multi-level prefetching.

The file read pipeline involves transfers from storage through storage nodes and I/O nodes toward the compute nodes. Our prefetching solution for GPGPU clouds proposes two prefetching modules on the computing virtual machines and I/O nodes, each of which enforcing its own prefetching policy. The prefetching mechanism is leveraged in both cases by an I/O thread.

Our prefeching solution leverages the characteristics of the stream processing model of the GPGPU applications [32]. In GPGPU applications the kernel operations define unambiguously both the input and output data. We exploit this information for issuing early prefetching requests on the computing virtual machines. This approach activates the prefetching pipeline in our architecture and allows the overlapping of GPGPU computing and prefetching for future computations. The evaluation of this solution is subject of current research.

## 5. The virtual laboratory

A domain scientist can use the Virtual Laboratory through a desktop, web or command line client application. An experiment is designed by connecting processing units in a data producer/consumer schema represented as a direct acyclic graph. The scientist can configure and run his experiment selecting and assembling each component from a palette or submitting a JFDL file to the Virtual Laboratory Engine.

Our virtual laboratory is specialized (but not limited to) environmental modelling experiments and applications. Starting in 2003, we run operationally a weather and marine forecast grid application integrating weather, sea wave propagation, ocean circulation and air quality models and offering products, focused on the Bay of Naples (Italy) reaching a nested ground resolution of about one kilometre. Common citizens, via a web portal interface or smart-phones apps, consume the application products. We have used this application as test bed to evolve our laboratory till the actual state of the art of a fully elastic-Science approach.

Relying on our grid-enabled components, we implemented real world applications based on the close integration between environmental models, environmental data acquisition instruments and data distribution systems glued by the hybrid grid/cloud computing technology.

### 5.1 Laboratory's virtual components

The virtual laboratory is designed in order to provide computing support to any kind of experiment deployable as a scientific workflow. Our packaged framework for grid enabling legacy software components simplifies the process of including additional grid components. In the current implementation, the processing units black-boxing the computing models are based on the cloud-enabling scheme. In this way, distributed memory parallel models, i.e. weather models, are executed on a dynamically created computing cluster or on a real HPC cluster as well, just changing an experiment parameter. As previously stated, we focused our interest in environmental modelling, grid and cloud enabling the needed components for all around coupled forecasts, simulations and scenario analysis: weather, air quality, ocean currents and sea waves models. Over the last decade, we implemented several environmental models. Some of them are currently used in our virtual laboratory production; others have been substituted with more up to date components.

### 5.2 Weather simulation components

Weather models are the main driver in this kind of experiments and applications, so we grid enabled the MM5 (Mesoscale Model 5) [56] and the WRF (Weather and Research Forecasting model) [57], the latter beingcurrently our first source of operational weather forecasts. It is a mesoscale numerical weather prediction system designed to serve both operational

forecasting and atmospheric research needs. It features multiple dynamical cores, a 3-dimensional variational data assimilation system, and a software architecture allowing for computational parallelism and system extensibility. WRF provides to operational forecasting a model that is flexible and efficient computationally, while offering the advances in physics, numerical solution of equation and data assimilation contributed by the research community. WRF allows researchers the ability to conduct simulations reflecting either real data or idealized configurations. WRF is suitable for a broad spectrum of applications across scales ranging from meters to thousands of kilometres. WRF is modular and its components could be parted in pre-processing, computing and post-processing units.
We grid enabled WRF in order to run each model anywhere on the grid and/or even on the cloud. The components available on our virtual laboratory wrap the Geogrid for terrain preparation, the Ungrib for initial and boundary condition processing and the Metgrid for initial data interpolation over spatial domains. This components could be run on serial or parallel target computing elements, while the Real component, for input data preparation, and the Wrf component, i.e. the model itself, have to be run on parallel computing elements. In particular, Wrf (version 3.2 and beyond) could be executed using a GPU equipped parallel computing cluster dynamically instanced on a cloud resource supporting a gVirtuS based GPGPU virtualization. The post-processing components wrap over standard ARW-POST features and custom developed coupling software.

### 5.3 Air quality components

Air quality models permit to produce air pollution forecasts maps and have to be fed by emission models of primary chemical pollutants. Currently, we use CHIMERE [29] which integrates both models. It is a multi-scale model primarily designed to produce forecasts of the concentration of ozone, aerosols and other pollutants. The model performs long-term simulations, entire seasons or years, for emission control scenarios and what-if hypothesis studies. CHIMERE runs over meso to urban scale making possible advanced simulation analysis thanks to many different options. It is a powerful research tool for testing parameterization hypotheses.
The CHIMERE grid enabling process deals with the LAM management in order to deploy, boot and destroy computing nodes. The cloud enabled version of CHIMERE makes straightforward the model execution as a virtual laboratory processing unit instance: the HPC cluster, dynamically created and managed, hides the whole distributed memory message passing interface environment using pre-configured *ad hoc* virtual machine images. Moreover, the virtual laboratory offers tools for WRF/CHIMERE coupling in the data components suite.
In the past, we developed the PNAM (Parallel Naples Airsheld Model) [28], we integrated the STdEM Spatio-temporal distribution Emission Model [27] and grid enabled CAMx (Comprehensive Air quality Model with eXtension)[2].

### 5.3 Marine components

Currently, the ocean modeling components of our virtual laboratory primarily consist of the WW3 (WaveWatch III) [69] sea-wave propagation model. WW3 is a third generation wave model developed at NOAA/NCEP as an evolution of the WAM model [34]. It differs from its predecessors in many important points such as the governing equations, the model structure, the numerical methods and the physical parameterizations. It is a wave-modelling framework, which allows for easy development of additional physical and numerical approaches. WW3 solves the random phase spectral action density balance equation for wave-number direction spectra. The implicit assumption of this equation is that properties of medium (water depth and current) as well as the wave field itself vary on time and space scales that are much larger than the variation scales of a single wave. Some source term options for extremely shallow water (surf zone) have been included, as well as wetting and drying of grid points. Whereas the surf-zone physics implemented so far are still fairly rudimentary the wave model can now be applied to arbitrary shallow water.

Our WW3 grid enabling process involved the development of several pre-processing and post-processing components especially related to the model coupling and the offline nesting implementation. We developed from scratch the specific components for the domain setup (CreateDomain), a sort o Geogrid equivalent for WW3, GrADS2WW3 for weather model coupling (it works with both MM5 and WRF) and the Configuration Helper component that simplifies the model setup.

Previously, for shallow water simulation, we grid-enabled the SWAN [31] in order to be coupled with WW3 and to obtain a more reliable simulation of the waves in the surf zone.

In our virtual laboratory we made available to environmental scientists two ocean dynamics models: the ROMS[63], Regional Ocean Model System, and the POM [30] (Princeton Ocean Model). The first is very well engineered, modular, suitable for an implementation on parallel distributed memory machines, and supports nesting features in order to increase the domain resolution over specified areas. POM is a simple-to-run but powerful model, able to simulate a wide-range of problems: circulation and mixing processes in rivers, estuaries, shelf and slope, lakes, semi-enclosed seas and open and global ocean. The model is a sigma coordinate, free surface ocean model with embedded turbulence and wave sub-models, and wet-dry capability. We enhanced it in a parallel version with nesting capabilities (POMpn) [44].

The POM grid enabling process required a complete revision of the code in order to implement user provided cases. In particular, we had to implement the components needed to set up spatial domains, initial and boundary conditions. An interface to a seasonal database has also been implemented to support open basins real case simulations.

### 5.4 Data components

Our virtual laboratory provides several processing unit components for data acquisition. The NCEPDataProvider retrieves real time weather forecast initial and boundary conditions from NOAA NCEP [14], thanks to a daemon component, completely decoupled from the grid; the ECMWFDataProvider [3] performs an on-demand download, from the ECMWF repository, of historical data for scenario and what-if analyses; the DSADataProvider performs an on-demand download of processed data. Weather stations, cams, ocean surface current radars and wind profilers are interfaced to laboratory components using the Abstract Instrument Framework and the grid enabled Instrument Service [58]. A data sink component has been developed to store and provide to users environmental multidimensional data [60].

Currently, we are working on a MET [49] grid-enabled version in order to provide a standard tool for model evaluation.

The virtual laboratory includes some data visualization tools as grid-enabled wraps on standard world spread software as GrADS [6], Vapor[18] and Ferret[4].

### 5.5 Operational grid application

We have used the Virtual Laboratory components to develop a grid application for producing weather and marine forecasts in both operational and on-demand mode, where several simulation models, data acquisition, conversion, and visualization software are coupled. The application workflow is simple: the starting event is produced either by an on-demand user request or by an initialization data availability signal, in an operational environment; then, the weather forecast model is initialized, and the output data is rendered by a presentation software and concurrently consumed by other models, such as ocean dynamics, sea wave propagation or air quality models; then each application branch proceeds on separate thread (Figure 4).

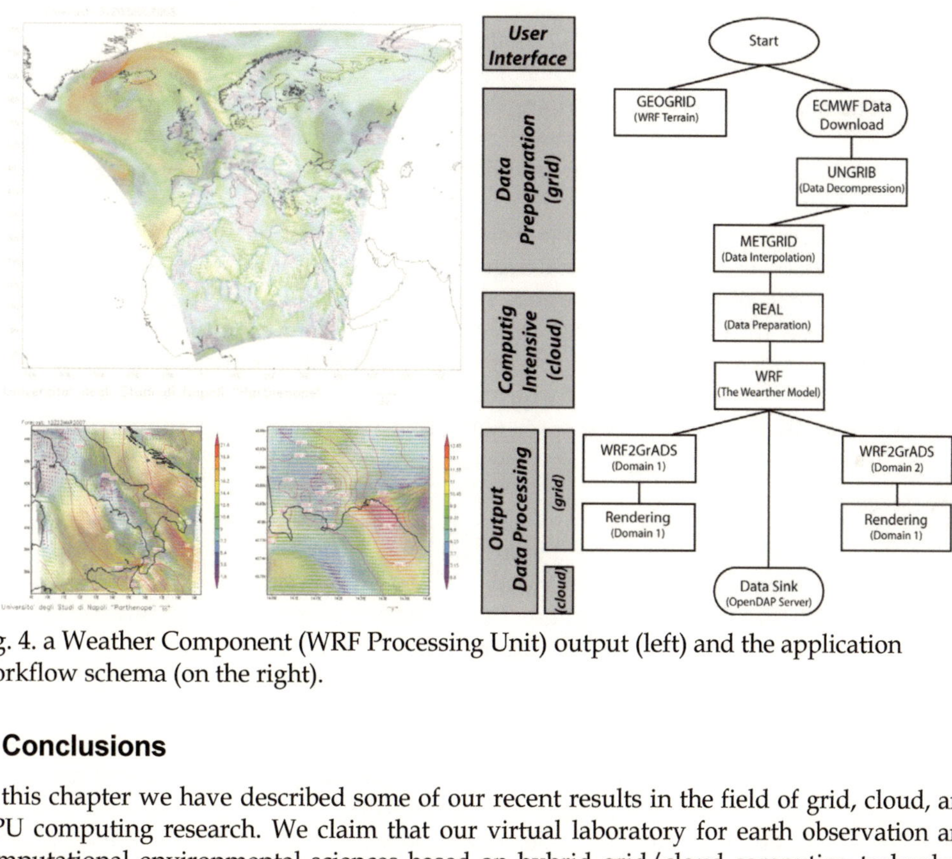


Fig. 4. a Weather Component (WRF Processing Unit) output (left) and the application workflow schema (on the right).

## 6. Conclusions

In this chapter we have described some of our recent results in the field of grid, cloud, and GPU computing research. We claim that our virtual laboratory for earth observation and computational environmental sciences based on hybrid grid/cloud computing technology can be a useful tool in both research and operational applications, and we have shown how to develop a complex grid application dedicated to operational weather, marine and air quality forecasts on nested spatial domains.

The virtual laboratory is an elastic-Science environment. It provides GPGPU acceleration thanks to a GPU virtualization and sharing service. This service is realized by the gVirtuS component. It enables a virtual machine instance, running in a high performance computing cloud, to properly exploit the computing power of the nVIDIA CUDA system. In discussing the architecture of our framework, the adopted design and implementation solutions, and the key communication component, we stressed the main features of gVirtuS: the hypervisor independence, the fully transparent behaviour and, last but not the least, its overall performance. We have reported elsewhere [45] the results of an extensive test process to assess how gVirtuS performs in different and realistic setups. gVirtuS leverages on our previous works on high performance computing grids, and our interest in the apparently poor performing TCP communicator is related to other more complex deployment schemes. For example, a private cloud could be set up on a massive multi-core cluster, hosting general-purpose virtual machine instances and GPU powered computing elements for compute-intensive scientific applications.

Another important issue we have addressed in this paper is a scalable parallel I/O system for data intensive GPGPU applications. We have designed a scalable parallel I/O architecture based on a hierarchy of caches deployed on the computing virtual machines and on the I/O system backend, close to the storage. In order to hide the latency of file accesses inherent in a hierarchical architecture, we proposed a multiple level data staging strategy. The multiple level I/O pipelining in a data staging approach maps suitably to the characteristics of stream computing model, which exposes the inputs and outputs of the kernel computation, an important piece of information that can be leveraged by parallel I/O scheduling strategies.

Several scientists for different kinds of one-shot or operational applications currently use the Virtual Laboratory environment we designed and implemented. The weather forecast application we described in this chapter, deployed in its first version in 2003, runs in operational mode with a few maintenance operations, except components or grid/cloud middleware upgrades. All performed results are interactively published at a web portal http://dsa.uniparthenope.it/meteo (the actual URL could change: a redirect to elsewhere could be expected) and used by several scientists, local institutions and common users.

## 7. References


[1] Amazon Web Services. http://aws.amazon.com

[2] CAMx Comprehensive Air Quality Model with eXtensions. http://www.camx.com

[3] ECMWF European Centre for Medium Range Weather Forecast. http://www.ecmwf.int

[4] Eucalyptus, the open source cloud platform. http://open.eucalyptus.com

[5] Ferret data visualization and analysis. http://ferret.wrc.noaa.gov/Ferret

[6] GrADS Grid Analysis and Display System. http://www.iges.org/grads

[7] International Exascale Software Project. http://www.exascale.org.

[8] jclouds an open source framework that helps you get started in the cloud and reuse your java development skills. http://www.jclouds.org

[9] JaClouX (Java bindings for Cloud extensions) project at UniParthenope open source lab web portal. http://osl.uniparthenope.it/projects/jacloux

[10] KVM kernel based virtual machine. http://www.linux-kvm.org

[11] KVM VMChannel. http://www.linux-kvm.org/page/VMchannel_Requirements

[12] LAM/MPI local area multicomputer. http://www.lam-mpi.org

[13] libcloud a unified interface to the cloud. http://incubator.apache.org/libcloud

[14] MPICH 2 high performance and widely portable message passing interface. http://www.mcs.anl.gov/research/projects/mpich2

[15] NCEP/NOAA National Centres for Environment Prediction, National Oceanic and Atmosphere Administration. http://www.ncep.noaa.gov

[16] NVIDIA CUDA Zone. http://www.nvidia.com/cuda
[17] Top 500 list. http://www.top500.org
[18] Vapor, Visualization and Analysis Platform for Ocean, Atmospheric and Solar Research. http://www.vapor.ucar.edu
[19] VMWare. Virtualization software for desktop, servers and virtual machines for public and private cloud solutions. http://www.vmware.com
[20] VMWare. Virtual Machine Communication Interface. http://pubs.vmware.com/ vmci-sdk/VMCI_intro.html.
[21] Xen hypervisor. http://www.xen.org
[22] Ali N., P. Carns, K. Iskra, D. Kimpe, S. Lang, R. Latham, R. Ross, L. Ward, and P. Sadayappan. Scalable I/O Forwarding Framework for High-Performance Computing Systems. In Proceedings of IEEE Conference on Cluster Computing, New Orleans, LA, September 2009.
[23] Anjomshoaa A., F. Brisard, M. Drescher, D. Fellows, A. Ly, S. McGough, D. Pulsipher, A. Savva. Job Submission Description Language (JSDL) Specification, Version 1.0. GFD-R.136. Open Grid Forum, 28-Jul-2008.
[24] Armbrust M.,A. Fox, R. Griffith, A. D. Joseph, R. H. Katz, A. Konwinski, G. Lee, D. A. Patterson, A. Rabkin. I. Stoica, M. Zaharia. Above the Clouds: A Berkeley View of Cloud Computing. Electrical Engineering and Computer Sciences University of California at Berkeley, Technical Report No. UCB/EECS-2009-28, http://www.eecs.berkeley.edu/Pubs/TechRpts/2009/EECS-2009-28.html, February 10, 2009.
[25] Armbrust M.,A. Fox, R. Griffith, A. D. Joseph, R. H. Katz, A. Konwinski, G. Lee, D. A. Patterson, A. Rabkin. I. Stoica, M. Zaharia. A view of cloud computing. Commun. ACM 53, 4 (Apr. 2010), 50-58, 2010.
[26] Ascione I., G. Giunta, R. Montella, P. Mariani, A. Riccio: A Grid Computing Based Virtual Laboratory for Environmental Simulations. Euro-Par 2006 Par-allel Processing, (W.E. Nagel, W.V. Nagel, W. Lehner, eds.) LNCS 4128, Springer (2006) 1085–1094.
[27] Barone G., D'Ambra P., di Serafino D., Giunta G., Montella R., Murli A., Riccio A.: An Operational Mesoscale Air Quality Model for the Campania Region. Annali Istituto Universitario Navale (2000) - 179-189, 2000.
[28] Barone G., D'Ambra P., di Serafino D., Giunta G., Murli A., Riccio A.: Parallel software for air quality simulation in Naples area. J. Environ. Manag. & Health (2000) 209–215, 2000.
[29] Bessagnet B., A.Hodzic, R.Vautard, M.Beekmann, S.Cheinet, C.Honoré, C.Liousse and L.Rouil, Aerosol modeling with CHIMERE - preliminary evaluation at the continental scale, Atmospheric Environment, 38, 2803-2817, 2004
[30] Blumberg, A.F., Mellor, G. L.: A description of a three-dimensional coastal ocean circulation model. Three-Dimensional Coastal ocean Models, edited by N. Heaps, American Geophysical Union, 1987.
[31] Booij, N., Holthuijsen, L.H., Ris, R.C.: The SWAN wave model for shallow water. Int. Conf. on Coastal Engineering., Orlando, USA (1996) 668–676, 1996.
[32] Buck I., Foley T., Horn D., Sugerman J., Fatahalian K., Houston M. and Hanrahan P. Brook for GPUs: stream computing on graphics hardware. In Proceedings of SIGGRAPH 2004.

[33] Buyya, R., Chee Shin Yeo and Venugopal, S. Market-Oriented Cloud Computing: Vision, Hype, and Reality for Delivering IT Services as Computing Utilities. HPCC '08. 10th IEEE International Conference on High Performance Computing and Communications, 2008.
[34] Cardone V. J., J. A. Greenwood et al. The WAM model - a third generation ocean wave prediction model. J. of Phys. Oceanog., 18, 1775-1810, 1988.
[35] Dong S., G. E. Karniadakis, N. T. Karonis. Cross-Site Computations on the TeraGrid Computing in Science and Engineering, pp. 14-23, September/October, 2005.
[36] Evangelinos C. and Chris N. Hill. Cloud Computing for parallel Scientific HPC Applications: Feasibility of Running Coupled Atmosphere-Ocean Climate Models on Amazon's EC2. Proceeding of CCA-08, Cloud Computing and its Applications, University of Illinois in Chicago, 2008.
[37] Fagui Liu, Wei Zhou and Ming Zhou. A Xen-Based Data Sharing & Access Controlling Method. Third International Symposium on Intelligent Information Technology Application, 2009. IITA 2009. , vol.3, no., pp.7-10, 21-22 Nov. 2009.
[38] Foster I., C. Kesselman and S. Tuecke. The Anatomy of the Grid: Enabling Scalable Virtual Organizations. International J. Supercomputer Applications, 15(3), 2001.
[39] Foster I. The Grid: A New Infrastructure for 21st Century Science. Physics Today, 55(2): 42-47, 2002.
[40] Foster I., C. Kesselman, J. Nick, S. Tuecke. Grid Services for Distributed System Integration. Computer, 35(6), 2002.
[41] Foster I. Globus Toolkit Version 4: Software for Service-Oriented Systems. IFIP International Conference on Network and Parallel Computing, Springer-Verlag LNCS 3779, pp 2-13, 2006.
[42] Foster I., Z. Yong, R. Ioan and L. Shiyong: Cloud Computing and Grid Computing 360-Degree Compared. Proceedings of Grid Computing Environments Workshop, 2008. GCE '08
[43] Giunta G., R. Montella, P. Mariani, A. Riccio. Modeling and computational issues for air/water quality problems: A grid computing approach. Il Nuovo Cimento, 28, 2005.
[44] Giunta G., P. Mariani, R. Montella, and A. Riccio. pPOM: A nested, scalable, parallel and fortran 90 implementation of the princeton ocean model. Envirnonmental Modelling and Software, 22:117–122, 2007.
[45] Giunta G., R. Montella, G. Agrillo, and G. Coviello. A gpgpu transparent virtualization component for high performance computing clouds. In P. D'Ambra, M. Guarracino, and D. Talia, editors, Euro-Par 2010 - Parallel Processing, volume 6271 of Lecture Notes in Computer Science, chapter 37, pages 379-391. Springer Berlin / Heidelberg, Berlin, Heidelberg, 2010.
[46] Gropp, W. 2009. MPI at Exascale: Challenges for Data Structures and Algorithms. In Proceedings of the 16th European PVM/MPI Users' Group Meeting on Recent Advances in Parallel Virtual Machine and Message Passing interface (Espoo, Finland, September 07 - 10, 2009). M. Ropo, J. Westerholm, and J. Dongarra, Eds. Lecture Notes In Computer Science. Springer-Verlag, Berlin, Heidelberg, 3-3, 2009.
[47] Gupta, V., Gavrilovska, A., Schwan, K., Kharche, H., Tolia, N., Talwar, V., and Ranganathan, P. 2009. GViM: GPU-accelerated virtual machines. In Proceedings of the 3rd ACM Workshop on System-Level Virtualization For High Performance

Computing (Nuremburg, Germany, March 31 - 31, 2009). HPCVirt '09. ACM, New York, NY, 17-24., 2009.

[48] Hoffa C., Mehta G., Freeman T., Deelman E., Keahey K., Berriman B. and Good, J. On the Use of Cloud Computing for Scientific Workflows. eScience '08. IEEE Fourth International Conference on eScience, 2008.

[49] Holland L., J. H. Gotway, B. Brown, and R. Bullock. A Toolkit For Model Evaluation. National Center for Atmospheric Research Boulder, CO 80307

[50] Isaila F., Garcia Blas F. J., Carretero J., Wei-keng Liao, Choudhary A. A scalable MPI implementation of an ad-hoc parallel I/O system. International Journal of High Performance Computing Applications, 2010.

[51] Isaila F., Garcia Blas F. J., Carretero J., Latham R., Ross R. Design and evaluation of multiple level data staging for Blue Gene systems. In IEEE Transactions of Parallel and Distributed Systems, 2010.

[52] Karonis N., B. Toonen, and I. Foster. MPICH-G2: A Grid-Enabled Implementation of the Message Passing Interface. Journal of Parallel and Distributed Computing, 2003.

[53] Larsen, E. S. and McAllister, D. Fast matrix multiplies using graphics hardware. In Proceedings of the 2001 ACM/IEEE Conference on Supercomputing (Denver, Colorado, November 10 - 16, 2001). Supercomputing '01. ACM, New York, NY, 55-55, 2001.

[54] Lizhe Wang, Jie Tao, Kunze M., Castellanos A.C., Kramer D. and Karl W. Scientific Cloud Computing: Early Definition and Experience. HPCC '08. 10th IEEE International Conference on High Performance Computing and Communications, 2008.

[55] Mell P. and T. Grance. The NIST Definition of Cloud Computing, National Institute of Standards and Technology. Version 15. Information Technology Laboratory, July 2009.

[56] Michalakes, J., T. Canfield, R. Nanjundiah, S. Hammond, G. Grell: Parallel Implementation, Validation, and Performance of MM5. Parallel Supercomputing in Atmospheric Science. World Scientific, River Edge, NJ 07661 (1994)

[57] Michalakes, J., J. Dudhia, D. Gill, T. Henderson, J. Klemp, W. Skamarock, and W. Wang, 2004: "The Weather Reseach and Forecast Model: Software Architecture and Performance,"to appear in proceedings of the 11th ECMWF Workshop on the Use of High Performance Computing In Meteorology, 25-29 October 2004, Reading U.K. Ed. George Mozdzynski, 2004.

[58] Montella R., G. Agrillo, D. Mastrangelo and M. Menna. A Globus Toolkit 4 based instrument service for environmental data acquisition and distribution. In Proceedings of the Third international Workshop on Use of P2p, Grid and Agents For the Development of Content Networks (Boston, MA, USA, June 23 - 23, 2008). UPGRADE '08. ACM, New York, NY, 21-28, 2008.

[59] Montella R., Giunta G. and Laccetti G. A Grid Computing Based Virtual Laboratory for Environmental Simulations. Parallel Processing and Applied Mathematics. Lecture Notes in Computer Science, Volume 4967/2008, 951-960, 2008.

[60] Montella R., Giunta G. and Laccetti G. Multidimensional Environmental Data Resource Brokering on Computational Grids and Scientific Clouds. Handbook of Cloud Computing, Part 4, 475-492, 2010.

[61] Montella R., Foster I. Using Hybrid Grid/Cloud Computing Technologies for Environmental Data Elastic Storage, Processing, and Provisioning. Handbook of Cloud Computing, Part 4, 595-618, 2010.

[62] Nurmi D., Wolski R., Grzegorczyk C., Obertelli G., Soman S., Youseff L. and Zagorodnov D. The Eucalyptus Open-Source Cloud-Computing System. In Proceedings of the 2009 9th IEEE/ACM international Symposium on Cluster Computing and the Grid (May 18 - 21, 2009). CCGRID. IEEE Computer Society, Washington, DC, 124-131, 2009.

[63] Powell B. S., H. G. Arango, A. M. Moore, E. Di Lorenzo, R. F. Milliff and R. R. Leben. Real-time Assimilation and Prediction in the Intra-Americas Sea with the Regional Ocean Modeling System (ROMS) . Dynamics of Atmospheres and Oceans, 2009.

[64] Raj, H. and Schwan, K. 2007. High performance and scalable I/O virtualization via self-virtualized devices. In Proceedings of the 16th international Symposium on High Performance Distributed Computing (Monterey, California, USA, June 25 - 29, 2007). HPDC '07. ACM, New York, NY, 179-188, 2007

[65] Sato, T. The earth simulator: roles and impacts. Parallel Computing 30, 12 (Dec. 2004), 1279-1286, 2004.

[66] Sotomayor B., K. Keahey, I. Foster: Combining Batch Execution and Leasing Using Virtual Machines. ACM/IEEE International Symposium on High Performance Distributed Computing 2008 (HPDC 2008), Boston, MA. June 2008.

[67] Sunderam V. S. PVM: A Framework for Parallel Distributed Computing. Concurrency: Practice and Experience, 2, 4, pp 315--339, December, 1990.

[68] Thain D., T. Tannenbaum, and M. Livny. Distributed Computing in Practice: The Condor Experience. Concurrency and Computation: Practice and Experience, Vol. 17, No. 2-4, pages 323-356, February-April, 2005.

[69] Tolman. H.L.: A third-generation model for wind waves on slowly varying, unsteady and inhomogeneous depths and currents. J. Phys. Oceanogr. , 21 (1991) 782–797, 1991.

[70] Yu J. and Buyya R. A taxonomy of scientific workflow systems for grid computing. SIGMOD Rec. 34, 3 (Sep. 2005), 44-49. 2005.

[71] Vaquero, L. M., Rodero-Merino, L., Caceres, J., and Lindner, M. A break in the clouds: towards a cloud definition. SIGCOMM Comput. Commun. Rev. 39, 1 (Dec. 2008), 50-55, 2008.

[72] Vecchiola C., Suraj Pandey, Rajkumar Buyya. High-Performance Cloud Computing: A View of Scientific Applications. Parallel Architectures, Algorithms, and Networks, International Symposium on, pp. 4-16, 2009 10th International Symposium on Pervasive Systems, Algorithms, and Networks, 2009

[73] Wang, J., Wright, K., and Gopalan, K. XenLoop: a transparent high performance inter-vm network loopback. In Proceedings of the 17th international Symposium on High Performance Distributed Computing (Boston, MA, USA, June 23 - 27, 2008). HPDC '08. ACM, New York, NY, 109-118, 2008.

[74] Zhelong Pan, Xiaojuan Ren, Eigenmann, R. and Dongyan Xu. Executing MPI programs on virtual machines in an Internet sharing system. Parallel and Distributed Processing Symposium, 2006. IPDPS 2006. 20th International, vol., no., pp.10 pp., 25-29 April, 2006.

8

# Using Open Source Desktop Grids in Scientific Computing and Visualization

Zoran Constantinescu[1] and Monica Vladoiu[2]
[1]*ZealSoft Ltd.*
[2]*PG University of Ploiesti*
*Romania*

## 1. Introduction

Scientific Computing is the collection of tools, techniques, and theories required to develop and solve on a computer, mathematical models of problems in science and engineering, and its main goal is to gain insight of such problems (Heat, 2002; Steeb et al., 2004; Hamming, 1987). Generally, it is difficult to understand or communicate information from complex or large datasets generated by scientific computing methods and techniques (computational simulations, complex experiments, observational instruments etc.). Therefore, support of Scientific Visualization is needed, to provide techniques, algorithms, and software tools that are necessary to extract and display properly important information from numerical data. Complex computational and visualization algorithms normally require large amounts of computational power. The computing power of a single desktop computer is not sufficient for running such complex algorithms, and, traditionally, large parallel supercomputers or dedicated clusters were used for this job. However, very high initial investments and maintenance costs limit the large-scale availability of such systems. A more convenient solution, which is becoming more and more popular, is based on the use of non-dedicated desktop PCs in a desktop grid computing environment. Harnessing idle CPU cycles, storage space and other resources of networked computers, to work together, on a particularly computational intensive application, perform this job. Increasing power and communication bandwidth of desktop computers provides for this solution as well.

In a Desktop Grid (DG) system, the execution of an application is orchestrated by a central scheduler node, which distributes the tasks amongst the worker nodes and awaits workers' results. It is important to note that an application only finishes when all tasks have been completed. The attractiveness of exploiting desktop grid systems is further reinforced by the fact that costs are highly distributed: every volunteer supports her resources (hardware, power costs and Internet connections), while the benefited entity provides management infrastructures, namely network bandwidth, servers and management services, receiving in exchange a massive and otherwise unaffordable computing power. The typical and most appropriate application for desktop grid comprises independent tasks (no communication exists amongst tasks) with a high computation to communication ratio (Domingues, Silva & Silva, 2006; Constantinescu, 2008). The usefulness of desktop grid computing is not limited to major high throughput public computing projects. Many institutions, ranging from academics to enterprises, hold vast number of desktop machines and could benefit from exploiting the idle cycles of their local machines. In fact, several studies confirm that CPU idleness in desktop machines averages 95% (Domingues, Silva & Silva, 2006; Constantinescu, 2008; Vladoiu & Constantinescu, 2009b).

In the work presented in this chapter, the central idea has been to build a desktop grid computing framework and to prove its viability by testing it in some scientific computing and visualization experiments. We present here QADPZ, an open source system for desktop grid computing, which enables users from a local network or even Internet to share their resources. It is a multi-platform, heterogeneous system, where different computing resources from inside an organization can be used. It can also be used for volunteer computing, where the communication infrastructure is the Internet. QADPZ supports the following native operating systems: Linux, Windows, MacOS and Unix variants. The reason behind the native support for multiple operating systems, and not only for one (Unix or Windows, as other systems do), is that, often in real life, this kind of limitation restricts very much the usability of dekstop grid computing.

QADPZ provides a flexible object-oriented software framework that makes it easy for programmers to write various applications, and for researchers to address issues such as adaptive parallelism, fault-tolerance, and scalability. The framework supports also the execution of legacy applications, which for different reasons could not be rewritten, and that makes it also suitable for other domains as business. It also supports either low-level programming languages as C and C++ or high-level language applications, like for example Lisp, Python, and Java, providing the necessary mechanisms to use such applications in a computation. Consequently, users with various backgrounds can benefit from using QADPZ. The flexible, object oriented structure and the modularity of the system allows improvements and further extensions to other programming languages to be made easily.

We have developed a general-purpose runtime and an API to support new kind of high performance computing applications, and therefore to benefit from the advantages offered by desktop grid computing. We show how distributed computing grid extends beyond the master-worker paradigm, typical for such systems, and provide QADPZ with an extended API which supports in addition lightweight tasks creation and parallel computing, using the Message Passing Interface paradigm (MPI). The C/C++ programming language is directly supported by the API. QADPZ supports parallel programs running on the desktop grid, by providing and API in the C/C++ language, which implements a subset of the MPI standard. This extends the range of applications that can be used in the system to already existing MPI based applications, like for example parallel numerical solvers, from computational science, or parallel visualization algorithms. Another restriction of existing systems, especially middleware based, is that each resource provider needs to install a runtime module with administrator priviledges. This poses some issues regarding data integrity and accessibility on providers computers. The QADPZ system tries to overcome this by allowing the middleware module to run as a non-privileged user, even with restricted access, to the local system (Constantinescu, 2008; Vladoiu & Constantinescu, 2008a).

QADPZ provides also low-level optimizations, such as on-the-fly compression and encryption for communication. The user can choose from different algorithms, depending on the application, improving both the communication overhead imposed by large data transfers and keeping privacy of the data. The system goes further, by providing an experimental, adaptive compression algorithm, which can transparently choose different algorithms to improve the application. QADPZ support two different protocols (UDP and TCP/IP) in order to improve the efficiency of communication (Constantinescu, 2008; Constantinescu & Vladoiu, 2009a). Free availability of the source code allows its flexible installations and modifications based on the individual needs of research projects and institutions. In addition to being a very powerful tool for computationally-intensive research, the open-source availability makes QADPZ a flexible educational platform for numerous small-size student projects in the areas of operating systems, distributed systems, mobile agents, parallel algorithms, and others. Moreover, free or open source software constitutes a natural choice for modern research, as well, because it encourages integration, cooperation and boosting of new ideas, in a very effective way (Cassens & Constantinescu, 2003; Constantinescu, 2008).

QADPZ has been built in top of an extended master-worker conceptual model. The extensions and refinements to the original master-worker paradigm concern mainly both the reduction of the time consumed for delays in communications and the increase of the period of time in which the workers perform computations. This goal is achieved by making use of different methods and techniques. The most important of them are as follows: pulling or pushing of work units, pipelining of the work-units at the worker, sending more work-units at a time, adaptive number of workers, adaptive timeout interval for work units, multithreading, redundant computation of the last work-units to decrease the time to finish, overlapped communication and computation at both the workers and the master, and use of compression to trim down the dimension of messages (Constantinescu 2008; Vladoiu & Constantinescu 2008b). Our work has also shown that that the use of desktop grid computing should not be limited to only master-worker type of application, but it can be used also for more fine-grained parallel applications, in the field of scientific computing and visualization, by performing some experiments in those domains. Thus, we have used QADPZ in several experiments: geophysical circulation modelling, fluid flow around a cylinder, both simulation and visualisation and so on (Constantinescu, 2008; Constantinescu & Vladoiu, 2009a). It is worth to mention that to the present QADPZ has over a thousand four hundred users who have download it, and that many of them use it for their daily tasks. They constantly give feedback on the system, ask for support in using it for their research and development tasks, or discuss about it in specialized discussion forums. QADPZ is also actively used in universities where students get work assignments based on its features (Constantinescu, 2008; QADPZ, 2010).

The chapter structure is as follows: the second section reveals other major desktop grid environments, such as BOINC, distributed.net, Condor and XtremWeb, along with examples of both desktop grids generated with their support and projects that use these environments. The third section describes briefly the QADPZ system. It starts with a justification for our endeavour to build a new DG system, and continues with the main capabilities of QADPZ, and with the improvements of the master-worker model implemented in the system. Within the next section, some scientific and visualization experiments performed with QADPZ's support are presented: geophysical circulation modelling within the Trondheim fjord, fluid flow around a cylinder - simulation and fluid flow around a cylinder - visualization. In the last section we will present some conclusions and some future work ideas that aim to improve both the conceptual model and the QADPZ system. We also invite the interested enthusiastic developers in the open-source community to join our development team and we appreciate any kind of feedback.

## 2. Related work

In high-throughput computing or desktop grid systems, pooled resources are used to achieve high throughput on a set of compute jobs. Such systems permit large numbers of machines to be added as a single resource in a higher-level grid system, achieving this way significant benefits in reduced management effort and grid complexity (Foster & Kesselman, 2003). Desktop Grids (DGs) evolve in two major directions: institution- or enterprise-wide desktop grid computing environment, and volunteer computing. The former, usually called simply desktop grid (or local DG, or LAN-based DG), refers to a grid infrastructure that is confined to an institutional boundary, where the spare processing capacity of an enterprise's desktop PCs are used to support the execution of the enterprise's applications. User participation in such a grid is not usually voluntary and is governed by the enterprise's policy. Applications like CONDOR, Platform LSF, DCGrid and GridMP are all such examples (Mustafee & Taylor, 2006).

The later is an arrangement in which volunteers provide computing resources to various projects that use those resources to perform distributed computationally intensive applications and/or storage. Volunteers are typically members of the general public who own Internet-connected PCs. Organizations such as universities and businesses may also volunteer the use of their computers. Projects are generally academic and are concerned with scientific research. Though, there are notable exceptions, such as GIMPS (GIMPS, 2010) and distributed.net (distributed.net, 2010), two major projects that are not academic. In fact, GIMPS (Great Internet Mersenne Prime Search), which started in 1996, has been the first volunteer computing project ever (BOINC, 2010). Other early projects include distributed.net, SETI@home (Seti@home Classic, 2010), and Folding@home (Folding@home, 2010).

Several aspects of the project/volunteer relationship are worth to be noticed (BOINC, 2010): (1) volunteers are truly anonymous - even though they may be asked to register and supply information as the email address, there is no way for a project to link them to a real-world identity; (2) due to their anonymity, volunteers are not accountable to projects – for example, if a volunteer misbehaves in some way, the project cannot take any action against that volunteer; (3) volunteers are ought to trust that projects will provide applications that will not damage their computers or invade their privacy, will be truthful about both work that is performed by its applications and use of the resulting intellectual property, and will follow proper security practices, so that the projects will not be used as vehicles for malicious activities. Desktop grid differs from volunteer computing in several aspects. First, the computing resources can be trusted, namely one can assume that the workstations do not usually return results that are wrong either intentionally or due to hardware malfunction, and that they do not falsify credit. Hence there is typically no need for redundant computing. Moreover, there is no need for using screensaver graphics and, in fact, it may be desirable that the computation is completely invisible and out of the control of the PCs' users. Furthermore, client deployment is typically automated (BOINC, 2010).

### 2.1 SETI@home - BOINC

SETI, or the Search for Extraterrestrial Intelligence, is a scientific effort seeking to determine if there is intelligent life outside Earth. One popular method that the SETI researchers use is *radio SETI*, which involves listening for artificial radio signals coming from other stars. Previous radio SETI projects have used special-purpose supercomputers, located at the telescope, to do the bulk of data analysis. In 1995, a new idea was proposed to do radio SETI using a virtual supercomputer composed of large numbers of Internet-connected computers (SETI@home Classic, 2010). SETI@home, developed at the University of California in Berkley, is a radio SETI project that allows anyone with a computer and an Internet connection to participate. The method they use to do this is based on a screen saver that can go get a chunk of data from a central server over the Internet, analyse that data, and then report the results back. When the computer is needed back by its user, the screen saver instantly gets out of the way and it only continues its analysis when the computer is not used anymore. The program that runs on each client computer looks and behaves like a captivating screen saver. It runs only when the machine is idle, and the user can choose from several different colourful and dynamic "visualizations" of the SETI process. The data analysis task can be easily broken up into little pieces that can all be worked on separately and in parallel. None of the pieces depends on the other pieces, which makes large deployment of clients and computations over the Internet very easy.

The SETI@home project has not been evolving without problems. For all the media attention and public interest that it has got, funding has not been forthcoming. The SETI@home project has been devised for a very specific problem, as described above. There was no general framework for the system, which could have been used by other types of applications, and, therefore it became SETI@home Classic. When new funding has become available for the BOINC project, the SETI@home project was rewritten for the new framework and it became the new SETI@home/BOINC in 2005. BOINC is open-source software that can be used for both volunteer computing and desktop grid computing. It presents the following features: project autonomy, volunteer flexibility (flexible application framework, security, server performance and scalability), source code availability, support for large data, multiple participant platforms, open and extensible software architecture, and volunteer community related characteristics. BOINC has been designed to support applications that have large computation requirements, large storage requirements, or both. The main requirement of the application is that it shall be divisible into a large number (thousands or millions) of jobs that can be executed independently. In addition, to benefit from volunteered resources, a project needs to be appealing for the general public and needs to have a low data/compute ratio (BOINC, 2010).

As a *quasi-supercomputing platform*, BOINC has about 495,000 active host computers worldwide that process on average about 3 PetaFLOPS per day as of October 2010 (Wikipedia, 2010a; BOINC stats, 2010), which is more than the processing power of the fastest existing supercomputer system (Jaguar - Cray XT5), with a sustained processing rate of 1.759 PetaFLOPS (Wikipedia, 2010; Meuer, 2010).

There are many BOINC-based projects that are active around the world. Some are based at universities and research laboratories, while others are run by companies or individuals. The research areas of the problems to be solved vary from mathematics (e. g. ABC@home, NFS@home, SZTAKI Desktop Grid, Rectilinear Crossing Number, primaboinca etc.), cryptography (e. g. Enigma@home and PrimeGrid), biology and medicine (e. g. GPUGrid.net, POEM@HOME, SIMAP, docking@home, Malariacontrol.net etc.), to earth sciences (e. g. Climateprediction.net and Virtualprairie), astronomy (e.g. SETI@home, Cosmology@Home, Orbit@home, Milkyway@home etc.) and so on (BOINC, 2010).

### 2.2 distributed.net

A very similar project is the distributed.net project (Constantinescu, 2008; distributed.net, 2010). It takes up challenges and run projects which require a lot of computing power.

The collective computing projects that have attracted the most participants have been attempts to decipher encrypted messages. RSA Security, a commercial company has made public a number of cryptographic puzzles, and has offered cash prizes for those who would have solved them. The company's aim has been to test the security of their own products and to demonstrate the vulnerability of the encryption schemes they considered inadequate (Hayes, 1998).

Another type of project, which involves a lot of computing power, is the Optimal Golomb Ruler (OGL). Essentially, a Golomb Ruler is a mathematical term given to a set of whole numbers where no two pairs of numbers have the same difference. An Optimal Golomb Ruler is just like an everyday ruler, except that the marks are placed so that no two pairs of marks measure the same distance. OGRs can be used in various real world situations, including sensor placements for X-ray crystallography and radio astronomy. Golomb rulers can also play an important role in combinatorics, coding theory and communications. The search for OGRs becomes exponentially more difficult as the number of marks increases, being a *NP complete* problem (distributed.net, 2010).

The focus of the distributed.net project is on very few specialized computing challenges. Furthermore, the project only releases the clients' binary code and not the server code, making impossible the adaptation of this to other types of projects.

### 2.3 Condor

Condor is a High Throughput Computing (HTC) environment that can manage very large collections of distributively owned available computing resources. It is being developed at the department of Computer Science, University of Wisconsin, Madison. Condor delivers large amounts of computational power over a long period of time, usually weeks or months. In contrast, High Performance Computing (HPC) environments deliver a tremendous amount of compute power over a short period of time. In a high throughput environment, scientists and engineers are more interested in how many jobs they can complete over a long period of time instead of how quick an individual job can complete. Hence, HTC is more concerned to efficiently harness the use of all available resources (Condor, 2010).

The Condor environment has a layered architecture that provide for a powerful and flexible suite of resource management services for sequential and parallel applications. Condor is a workload management system that is focused on computationally intensive jobs, and offers a job queuing mechanism, a scheduling policy, a priority scheme, and resource monitoring and management. Users can submit their serial or parallel jobs to the system, which places them into a queue, schedule them to be run based on a policy, carefully monitors their progress, and finally informs the user upon completion (Constantinescu, 2008; Condor, 2010).

Condor provides a powerful resource management mechanism by matchmaking resource owners with resource consumers. This is crucial to any successful HTC environment. This mechanism implements a very elegant design, called ClassAds, that works similarly to the newspaper classified advertising want-ads. All the machines in the system's pool advertise in a resource offer ad their resource properties, such as available RAM memory, CPU type, CPU speed, virtual memory size, physical location, current load average etc. When submitting a job, a user needs to specify a resource request ad, which defines both the required and a desired set of properties that are needed to run that job. Hence, Condor acts as a broker by matching and ranking resource offer ads with resource request ads, and by making certain that all the requirements in both ads are fulfilled. During this process,

Condor also considers several layers of priority values: the priority assigned to the resource request ad by the user, the priority of the user which submitted that ad, and the desire of the machines in the pool to prefer certain types of ads over others (Condor, 2010).
There are various Condor-based grids around the world, for example Greedy@EFPL, a desktop grid platform (called Greedy Pool) that runs at Federal Polytechnic School of Lausanne, and supports various mono-processors jobs (Grid@EFPL, 2010; Thiemard, 2008; Jermini, 2010), and a very large condor pool available at University College of London, which is used for several UK eScience projects, such as eminerals within molecular simulations of environmental issues domain (Wilson, 2004; eMinerals, 2010). Condor is used also at his "home university" from Wisconsin in several scientific projects such as genomics, IceCube Neutrino Observatory, Collider Detector at Fermilab etc. (Paradyn/Condor Week Presentations, 2008). Another interesting approach consists in using Condor inside a Blackboard learning management system for archiving Blackboard courses, reducing this way the time needed by 65% (Hoover, Dobrenen & Trauner, 2009).

### 2.4 XtremWeb, a open source platform for desktop grids

XtremWeb is a open source software that provide for build lightweight desktop grids by gathering the unused resources of desktop computers (CPU, storage, network), which is developed by IN2P3 (CNRS), INRIA and Universisty Paris XI. The working principle is that any participant can volunteer his computing resources, as in BOINC, but can also use other participants' available resources. Thus, participants may register new applications and data and may submit new computational jobs, provided that they are entitled to (advances in DGs, 2010). XtremWeb allows multi-users, multi-applications and cross-domains deployments, by harnessing volatile resources spread over LAN or Internet and putting them to work as a runtime environment that executes highly parallel applications. XtremWeb may be customised for a wide range of applications (bag-of tasks, master/worker), of computing requirements (data, CPU or network-intensive) and of computing infrastructures (clusters, desktop PCs, multi-LAN) (XtremWeb, 2010).
The designers of XtremWeb place the system somewhere between *pure desktop grid system, a la Condor and pure Volunteer Computing system, a la BOINC* (XtremWeb, 2010). XtremWeb relies on a pull model (workers pull tasks from the server), whilst Condor relies on a push model (the matchmaker selects the best machine to run the job and push the job on it). Moreover, with XtremWeb, each user or node has the ability (if authorized) to submit a job. When using BOINC, only the projects are able to create tasks and insert new applications (XtremWeb, 2010).
Several deployments are available for XtremWeb, for instance the XtremWeb-CH project that aims at building an effective Peer-To-Peer system for high performance computing, based on a completely symmetric model where nodes are both providers and consumers, or XWHEP (XtremWeb for High Energy Physics), a desktop grid computing platform capable of deploying and run user applications on the available computinf resource. Various projects use these desktop grid platforms. For instance, NeuroWeb and Virtual EZ Grid in medical domain, and From-P2P in public computing are all based on XtremWeb-CH (XtremWeb-CH, 2010). XWHEP middleware is currently used by the DGHEP, EDGI, DEGISCO, IDGF, and EDGeS projects (XWHEP, 2010). It is worth to mention that there is also a constant endeavour to create an integrate grid infrastructure that seamlessly put together a variety of desktop grids based either on BOINC, or on XtremWeb, around the

world, within the EDGeS (Enabling Desktop Grids for e-Science) umbrella (EDGeS, 2010; Cardenas-Montes et al., 2008; He et al., 2010).

## 3. The QADPZ system

Using the idle computational resources from the existent desktop computers in a organization or connected to the Internet is not a new idea, though the use of such distributed systems, especially in a research environment, has been limited because both the lack of supporting applications and the numerous challenges regarding security, management, and standardization. This section includes a brief description of the QADPZ system, starting with a justification for our endeavour to develop a new DG platform, and continuing with both the main QADPZ capabilities and the improvements of the master-worker conceptual model that is implemented in the system.

### 3.1 Why to develop a new desktop grid system?

A fair question to ask is why we have taken into consideration the development of a new desktop grid system instead of using an existent one. One reason is that many of the existing systems at the time when the QADPZ project started were highly specialized in a very limited set of computationally challenging problems, and hence they did not allow the execution of a general application. For example, SETI@home has been developed having one specific goal: the analysis of data from telescopes; similarly, distributed.net aimed to test the vulnerability of some particular encryption schemes. Moreover, at the time of the development, the source code of the available desktop grid systems was generally not available, therefore making difficult the extension or analysis of any new, non-standard application. Commercial systems such as Entropia, Office Grid and United Devices offered a lot of useful features, but they were not free. On the other hand, the available open source systems, like XtremWeb, BOINC, Condor, were limited in functionality. Furthermore, very few existing systems provided for making specific considerations with respect to the challenges of computationally intensive applications, especially those of scientific computing and visualization. Systems like BOINC and Bayanihan allowed only task parallelism, where there was no communication whatsoever between the running tasks during a computation, nevertheless most computationally intensive applications need such communication (Constantinescu, 2008; Vladoiu & Constantinescu, 2008a).

Many of today's networks are heterogeneous, thus requiring a distributed computing system with both support for various architectures and different type of operating systems. The Java language provides the incentives for such requirements, and many Java-based systems emerged: JXTA, Bayanihan, XtremWeb, Javelin. There were very few systems that supported different architectures and operating systems in native mode - e.g. Condor and BOINC. There were also systems, which run only on one type of operating system, either Windows or Unix, therefore limiting their usability in heterogeneous environments - for instance, Entropia. In addition, most of the existing systems usually had a complicated deployment procedure, requiring high-level, privileged access to the desktop computers and that made very hard to use such systems on a larger scale, and also complicated the further maintenance of computers - e.g. Condor and Globus Toolkit (Constantinescu, 2008; Vladoiu & Constantinescu, 2008a; Vladoiu & Constantinescu, 2009a).

### 3.2 QADPZ capabilities

When the QADPZ project has been started we had to come up with a set of capabilities that a desktop grid computing system should provide in order to successfully support computationally intensive applications. Back then, QADPZ has been foreseen as being friendly, flexible and suitable to a variety of needs. Therefore, we have created an open architecture able to evolve in pace with the needs and challenges of the continuously changing real world. The main functional capabilities of the system concern resource sharing and management, job management, heterogeneity, simple installation and maintenance, support for parallel programming, network support, autonomy, performance measurements, multi-project use, and on-line/off-line support (Constantinescu, 2008; Vladoiu & Constantinescu, 2009a).

The most important resources that need to be shared are the idle computational cycles of the desktop machines that contribute to the system. Other kind of resources, like storage space, may be shared as well. The system is able to manage efficiently the available shared resources; though, the owners of the desktop computers that share resources keep control of them, and are able to both define use policies and retract some resources on their will. The users may submit computational jobs to the system, which will be executed using the shared computational cycles; there is also possible to monitor and control job executions. The system may be deployed on a network of heterogeneous desktop computers, with different architectures (Intel, RISC, etc.) and different operating systems (UNIX type, Windows, Mac OS). It is the responsibility of the user who submits the jobs to provide the appropriate binary files for execution on different platforms. QADPZ is able to work both in a LAN environment and in the Internet. Two families of protocols are available for communication: TCP/IP and UDP/IP. The system supports different parallel programming paradigms, for example both task- and data-parallelism.

The system is easy to install on a large number of computers in a network, and further maintenance of the installed programs it is be minimal. QADPZ is able to deal with its own complexity, by supporting different autonomic features: self-healing, self-management, self-knowledge, self-configuration, self-optimisation (Constantinescu, 2003). QADPZ is able to provide information about its performances, which could be used for better usage of the available resources. It also provide for multi-project use. Many projects have downtime and shortage of tasks, and participation in multiple projects helps to cope with projects' downtime. The system provides support for both batch and interactive type of applications. In a batch setting, the user submits jobs that will be executed at a later time, when resources become available. In contrast, interactive jobs provide real-time feedback of the execution, and the user can inspect the partial result, and interact with the execution of the application.

The QADPZ user interface provides for monitoring and controlling of the behaviour of the system, and the programming interface allows different user applications to interact with the system. Both interfaces satisfy requirements with regard to personalization (different levels of access for various users, according to their personal skills and preferences), job management (a simple, platform independent, graphical user interface that allows submission, monitoring and control of different computational jobs), and resource sharing (a simple, intuitive graphical user interface, which allows the control of shared resources).

QADPZ complies also with non-functional requirements that mainly concern object oriented programming, for its well-known advantages, and open source development, which is a natural choice for modern research, as it encourages integration, cooperation and boosts new ideas (Cassens & Constantinescu, 2003; Constantinescu, 2008).

### 3.3 QADPZ architecture

The QADPZ system has a centralized architecture, based on the client-server model, which is the most common paradigm used in distributed computing. The paradigm describes an asymmetric relationship between two processes, one of which is the client, and the other is the server. Generally, applications based on this paradigm involve multiple clients, however they can involve one or multiple servers. In our case, the server manages the computational resources available from the desktop computers, by offering services, which can be used by other processes. *The client* is a process that needs those services in order to accomplish a certain work. It sends a request to the server, in which it asks for the execution of a concrete task that is covered by some particular service. Usually, the server carries out the task and sends back the result to the client (Constantinescu, 2008; Vladoiu & Constantinescu, 2009a).

In our situation, the server has two parts: a single master that accepts new requests from the clients, and multiple slaves, which handle those requests. The system consists of three types of entities: master, client, and slave (Fig. 1). Each computer that contributes with computing power to the system is called *a slave*, and runs a small background process in the form of a UNIX daemon or as a Windows system service. The process can be run with the privileges of an ordinary user, it does not need administrative rights. This process is responsible for reporting the computer's resources and the status to a central server, *the master*. It also accepts computational requests from the master, downloads the corresponding binaries and data files for the tasks, executes the task, and then uploads the result files when finished. The slave also downloads the task to be executed together with the input data, and starts the computation. The presence of a user logging into a slave computer is automatically detected and the task is killed or moved to another slave to minimize the disturbance of the regular computer users (Constantinescu, 2008; Vladoiu & Constantinescu, 2009a).

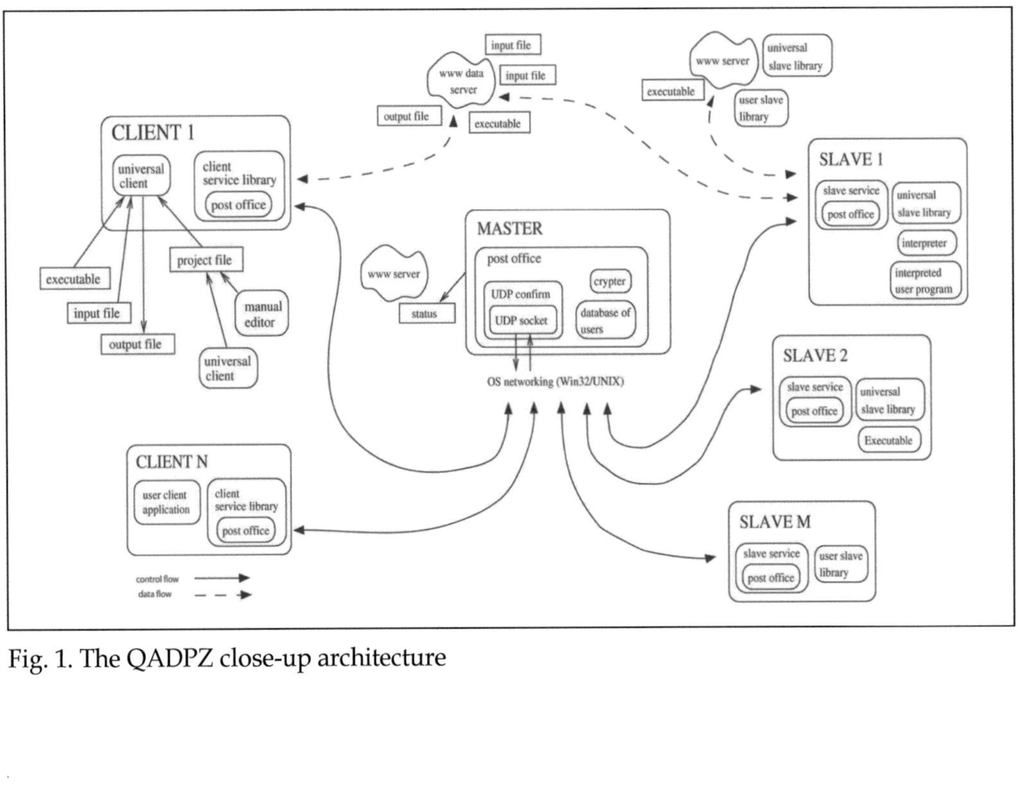


Fig. 1. The QADPZ close-up architecture

The control and data flow in the system are separated. The data files (represented by binary, input, and output files) that are necessary to run the applications are not sent to the master. They are stored on one or more data servers. The smallest independent execution unit of the QADPZ is called *a task*. To facilitate the management, multiple tasks can be grouped into *jobs*. Different types of jobs can be submitted to the system: programs written in scripting languages (e.g. LISP, Java, or Python), legacy applications and parallel programs (MPI). A job can consist of independent tasks, which do not require any kind of communication between them. This is usually called task parallelism. Jobs can also consist of parallel tasks, where different tasks running on different computers can communicate with each other. Inter-slave communication is accomplished using a MPI subset.

The current implementation of QADPZ considers only one central master node. This can be an inconvenience in certain situations, when computers located in different networks are used together. However, our high-level communication protocol between the entities allows a master to act as a client to another master, thus making possible to create *a virtual master* that consists of independent master nodes, which communicate with each other.

### 3.4 Improved master worker model

Our conceptual model is based on the master-worker paradigm that is built on the observation that many computational problems can be broken into smaller pieces that can be computed as one or more processes in parallel. That is, the computations are fairly simple consisting of a loop over a common, usually compute-intensive, region of code. The size of this loop is usually considered to be long. In this model, a number of worker processes are available, each being capable of performing any one of the steps in a particular computation. The computation is divided into a set of mutually independent work units by a master node. Worker nodes then execute these work units in parallel. A worker repeatedly gets a work unit from its master, carries it out and sends back the result. The master keeps a record of all the work units of the computation that it is assigned to perform. As each work unit is completed by one of the workers, the master records the result. Finally when all the work units have been completed, the master produces the complete result. The program works in the same way irrespective of the number of workers available - the master just gives out a new work unit to any worker who has completed the previous one (Constantinescu, 2008; Vladoiu & Constantinescu, 2008b).

The most important part of parallel programming is to map out a particular problem on a multiprocessor environment. The problem must be broken down into a set of tasks that can be solved concurrently. There are two different ways of decomposing a parallel problem, based on the way and time when the work-units are created: static or dynamic. In the case of *static decomposition* the master generates all the work-units in the beginning of the computation, while in *dynamic decomposition* the computation starts with a small number of work-units, and later new work-units are created, depending on the results of already executed work-units. Moreover, the master can create or delete dynamically work-units. After decomposing the problem, the work-units need to be distributed to the work-units, or scheduled for execution. The key to making a parallel program work well is to schedule their execution so that the load is balanced between the processing elements. Distribution of work-units to the workers can be of two types: static or dynamic. In the former case, the master processor decides on the distribution of work at the start of the computation, by assigning the work-units to the workers, and in the latter the distribution of work-units varies between workers as the computation proceeds.

QADPZ uses an improved version of the master-worker model, which is based on an algorithm with dynamic decomposition of the problem and dynamic number of workers. The improvements regard the performance of the original model by increasing the time workers are doing computations, and decreasing the time used for communication delays. This is achieved by using different techniques, such as using pulling or pushing of work units, pipelining of the work-units at the worker, sending more work-units at a time, adaptive number of workers, adaptive timeout interval for work units, multithreading, redundant computation of the last work-units to decrease the time to finish, overlapped communication and computation at the workers and the master, and use of compression to reduce the size of messages (Constantinescu, 2008; Vladoiu & Constantinescu, 2008b).
In the original master-worker model, each time a worker finishes a work-unit, it has to wait until it receives the next work-unit for processing. If this communication time is comparable with the time needed for executing a work-unit, the efficiency of the worker is reduced very much. The master-worker model uses the pull technology, which is based on the *request/response paradigm*. The user (the worker) is requesting data from the publisher (the master). The user is the initiator of the transaction. In contrast, a push technology relies on the *publish/subscribe/distribute paradigm*. The user subscribes once to the publisher, and the publisher will initiate all further data transfers to the user. In this model, the worker doesn't send any more requests for work-units. Instead, it first announces its availability to the master when it starts, and the master is responsible for sending further work-units. The workers just wait for work-units, and process them when received. At the end of each work-unit, it sends back the results to the master. The master will further send more work-units to the worker. This moves all decisions about initiating work-units transfers to the master, allowing a better control and monitoring of the overall computation.
The worker efficiency increases if we reduce the total time spent in waiting for communication. One way to do that is to use work-units pipelining at the worker, thus making sure that the worker has a new work-unit available when it finishes the processing of the current work-unit. In the beginning, the master sends more than one work-units to the worker, then after each received result, sends another work-unit to be queued on the worker. The worker does not need to wait again for a new work-unit from the master after sending the result, the next work-unit being already available for processing. If the communication time is too large, the pipeline will eventually become empty and the worker will need to wait for new work-units. To overcome this situation, the master needs to send more than one work-units per each message. The master starts by sending a message containing more than one work-unit, and then keeps sending messages as long as the pipeline is not full. Each time it receives a result, it sends another work-unit, to compensate the decreasing number of work-units from the pipe. If the worker sends only one result per message back to the master, and the master sends only one new work-unit, then, eventually the pipeline will become empty. In order to prevent that, the worker will need to send back more results at a time.
In a heterogeneous environment based on idle desktop computers, the total number of workers available could be changing during the computation. New workers can register to the master, and other can become temporarily unavailable. The master controls the total number of workers used for computation, since it is the one sending out work-units to the workers. If necessary, the master can choose not to use all the available workers for computation, only a few of them. The master can become a bottleneck, either when there are a lot of workers, which connect to get work-units and send results back or it could be caused

by too much communication. QADPZ uses an adaptive algorithm to choose the number of workers, based on performance measures and estimates of execution times for work-units and communication times for sending and receiving messages. The number of workers is automatically reduced if the efficiency of the computation decreases. We employ a heuristic-based method that uses historical data about the behavior of the application. It dynamically collects statistical data about the average execution times on each worker.

## 4. QADPZ-supported scientific computing and visualization experiments

Scientific Computing (or Computational Science) is concerned with using computers to analyze and solve scientific and engineering problems, by constructing mathematical models and numeric methods and techniques to tackle the involved issues. The Scientific Computing's approach is to gain understanding, mainly through the analysis of mathematical models implemented on computers (Wikipedia, 2010b). As Richard Hamming has observed many year ago, "the purpose of computing is insight, not numbers" (Hamming, 1987). Scientific Computing programs often model real-world changing conditions, such as weather, air flow around a plane, automobile body distortions in a crash, the motion of stars in a galaxy, an explosive device, etc. Such programs might create a 'logical mesh' in computer memory where each item corresponds to an area in space and contains information about that space that is relevant to the model. For example in weather models, each item might be a square kilometre, with land elevation, current wind direction, humidity, temperature, pressure, etc. The program calculates the likely next state based on the current one, in simulated time steps, solving equations that describe how the system operates, and then it repeats the process to calculate the next state (wiki). Scientists and engineers develop software systems that implement the mathematical models of the studied systems and run these programs with various sets of input parameters. These models require massive amounts of calculations, usually floating-point, and need huge computing power to be run. Supercomputers, computer clusters, grid computing, or desktop grids can supply the necessary computational and storage resources.

Following further the idea of Hamming, Scientific Visualization could help overcome the dilemma of having information, but not the right interpretation for it. Interactive computing and visualization could provide an invaluable support during the scientific discovery process, as well as a useful tool for gaining insight into scientific anomalies or computational errors. Scientists and engineers need a more helpful alternative to numbers. Paraphrasing another well-known idea, *a image is worth a thousand .. numbers*, the use of images has become the needed alternative. The ability of scientists to visualize complex computations and simulations is essential to ensure the integrity of the analysis, to give insights, and to communicate about them with others. Scientific Visualization is concerned with presenting data to users by means of images, and seeks ways to help users explore, make sense of, and communicate about data. It is an active research areas, drawing on theory in information graphics, computer graphics, human-computer interaction and cognitive science (McCormick, 1987).

Some of the domains and directions in which Scientific Computation and Visualization are able to give valuable insight are listed here: engineering, computational fluid dynamics, finite element analysis, electronic design automation, simulation, medical imaging, geospatial, RF propagation, meteorology, hydrology, data fusion, ground water modeling, oil and gas exploration and production, finance, data mining/OLAP, numerical simulations, orbiting satellites returning earth resource, military intelligence, astronomical data, spacecraft sending planetary and interplanetary data, earthbound radio astronomy arrays, instrumental arrays recording geophysical entities, such as ocean temperatures, ocean floor features, tectonic plate and volcanic movements, and seismic reflections from geological strata, medical scanners employing various imaging modalities, such as computed transmission and emission tomography, and magnetic resonance imagery.

Further on in this section, we presents some of the scientific and visualization experiments we have performed to prove the viability of the QADPZ system: a real world problem: geophysical circulation modeling within the Trondheim fjord, fluid flow around a cylinder - simulation and fluid flow around a cylinder - visualization.

### 4.1 Real world problem: Trondheim fjord

With the growing concern for environmental and ecological issues, and the increasing number of occurrences of serious pollution episodes, geophysical circulation modelling is a more and more important area of research. This relates to problems of different scales, from global issues to more local ones about water pollution in coastal areas, estuaries, fjords, lakes, etc. Analysis of these specific problems is based on the prediction of the flow circulation and transport of different materials, either suspended in water or moving along the free surface or the bottom. The numerical model of this complex phenomenon is based on a finite element formulation, because the finite element flexibility is beneficial for applications in restricted waters, where the topography is usually complex. The Navier-Stokes equations give the basic mathematical formulation (Utnes & Brors, 1993).

A map of Trondheimsfjorden, a typical Norwegian fjord that is located on the coast of central Norway, is shown in Fig. 3a. Detailed topographical data are used to interpolate the depth data to the element mesh. The horizontal element mesh is shown in Fig. 3b. It consists of 813 biquadratic elements with 3683 nodes, and there are 17 levels in the vertical direction with fine grading close to the bottom boundary. This grid is assumed to be detailed enough to describe the main flow field of the Trondheim fjord (Constantinescu 2008; Constantinescu & Vladoiu, 2009b). Shading the discretized cells according to the value of the scalar data

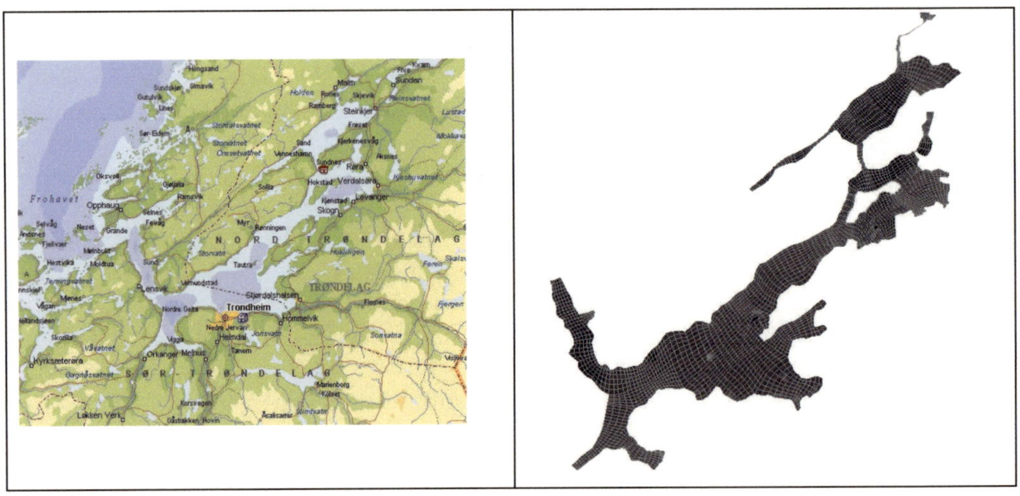

Fig. 3. a) Map of the Trondheim fjord b) Grid of the Trondheim fjord

field does colour coding. The colour allocation is linearly graduated for improved appreciation of continuum data. Using directed arrows also represents the velocity vector field (Figure 4 to Figure 5).

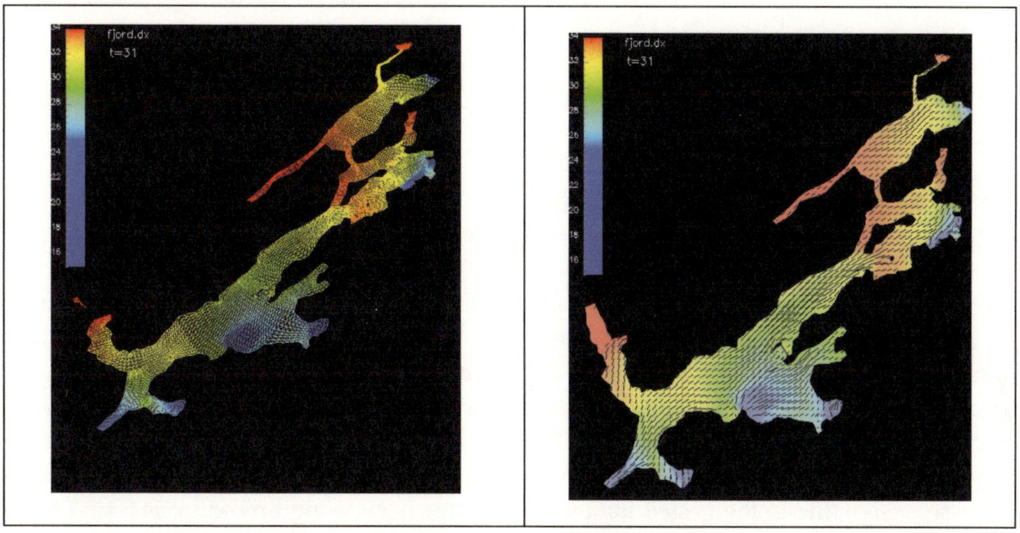


Fig. 4. Grid colored by salinity concentration (max 34 ppt - parts per thousand - mg/l)

Note. Color by salinity concentration - 3D model with isosurface representation

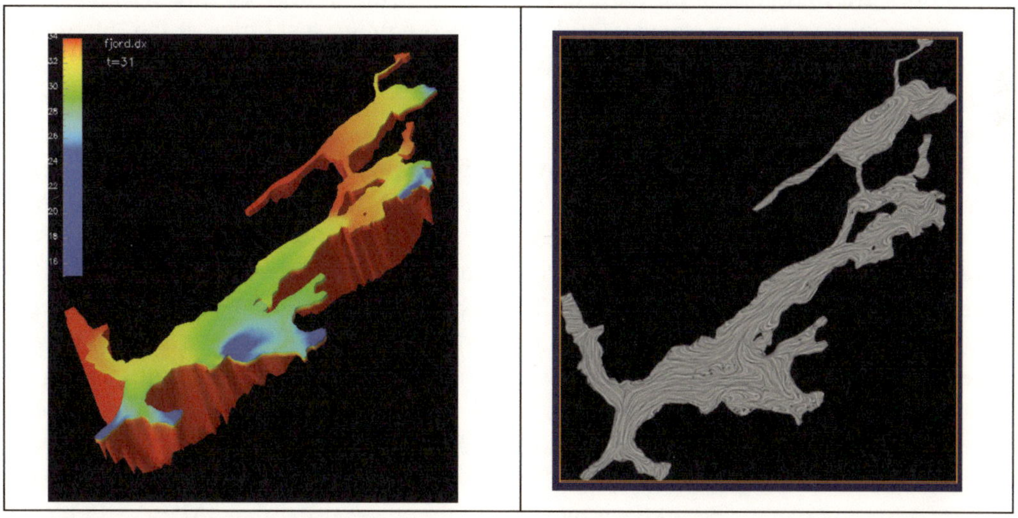


Fig. 5. a) Trondheim fjord model b) Velocity vector field - LIC representation

Large vector fields, vector fields with broad dynamic ranges in magnitude, and vector fields representing turbulent flows can be hard to visualize efficiently using common techniques such as drawing arrows or other icons at each data point or drawing streamlines. Drawing arrows of length proportional to vector magnitude at every data point can generate cluttered and confusing images. In areas of turbulence, arrows and streamlines can be difficult to interpret (Merzkirch, W. 1987; Forsell, 1994; Smits & Lim, 2000). Line Integral Convolution (LIC) is a powerful technique for imaging and animating vector fields. The image is created beginning with a white noise that is then convoluted along integral lines of the given vector field. That creates a visible correlation between image pixels that lie on the same integral line. The local nature of the LIC algorithm recommends a parallel implementation, which could, in principle, compute all pixels simultaneously. This would provide interactive generation of periodic motion animations and special effects (Cabral & Leedom, 1993; Forssell & Cohen 1995).

### 4.2 Fluid flow around a cylinder – simulation

In this sub-section we present some experiences with running a typical Computational Fluid Dynamics problem in QADPZ environment. The numerical method for solving the incompressible Navier-Stokes equations is used in a test case for the system. An evaluation of the performance of the system is presented, by comparing it with running the same simulation on a typical dedicated cluster environment.

To solve the incompressible Navier-Stokes equations we have used a version of the well-known projection method, in which equations for the velocity components and pressure are solved sequentially at each time step. Solving the discretized, fully coupled equations can be very expensive due to the nested iterations, and this decoupling procedure is found to be computationally efficient for transient problems, particularly for higher Reynolds numbers. In general, the separation of pressure and velocity can be performed on both the continuous equations and the discretized equations. While the latter is attractive due to the straightforward interpretation of boundary conditions, these methods give a significantly more complicated pressure equation and we therefore prefer a splitting at the differential level. The Galerkin finite element method is used to discretize in space. The pressure is fixed in one node to ensure a unique solution, and has homogeneous Neumann conditions on all boundaries.

Implementation of the flow solver has been done in C++ using the object oriented numerical library Diffpack. In fact, a parallel version of Diffpack was used, which is based on the MPI standard for communication. Linux has been used as our development platform. An MPI library with a subset of the most used MPI calls has been implemented on top of QADPZ's communication protocol. This QADPZ-MPI library allows us to use QADPZ as a straightforward replacement communication system for the MPI based Diffpack library. A series of tests have been performed on a dedicated cluster of 40 PCs, with Athlon XP 1.46GHz CPU, 1 GByte memory, and 100 MBps network interconnection between nodes, running a Linux distribution. First, we used the original implementation of the solver's software (which uses MPICH as a parallel communication protocol) to run the cluster version of the simulation. Second, we recompiled the solver using the QADPZ-MPI library to create the distributed computing version of the simulation. The solver was run using exactly the same computers of the cluster (i.e. identical hardware setup). A third test case used a pool of 8 computers with similar hardware specifications, that were ordinary desktop PCs from our labs together with other computers connected to our LAN. Simulations were done in two different times of the day: during the night, when network traffic in the LAN is minimal, and during working hours, when the LAN traffic is significant.

The first set of results shows the simulation of some time steps of an oscillating flow around a fixed cylinder in three dimensions. The grid had 81600 nodes and was made of 8-node isoparametric elements, while the coarse mesh (used for pressure preconditions) had approximately 2000 nodes. The resulted execution times are presented in Fig. 6. We run the same simulation in three different parallel settings for the underlying MPI library: (1) the MPICH library from the Argone National Laboratory, (2) the QADPZ MPI library using LZO based compression for communication, and (3) the QADPZ MPI library using bzip2 based compression for communication. The second set of results presented here is from corresponds to simulating some time steps of an oscillating flow around a fixed cylinder in three dimensions. The grid had 307296 nodes and was made of 294912 elements (8-node isoparametric). A coarse grid was used for pressure preconditioning, which had 2184 nodes and 1728 elements. Three sets of simulations were done, using respectively, MPICH, PVM and QADPZ-MPI as communication library. For each set of simulation, a maximum of 16 processors (Athlon AMD 1.466 GHz) have been used. Running times were between around 240 minutes (1 processor) and 18 minutes (16 processors). Speedup results from these simulations, presented in Fig. 7, show that the performance of our system is comparable with other similar systems based on the message-passing interface.

The advantages of using our system are as follow: the installation of the slave on the computational nodes is extremely easy, only one executable file and one configuration file are needed; moreover, no root or administrator access is necessary. Upgrade of the slaves is done automatically from the master, without any administrator intervention. Also, there is no need for a shared file system, since each of the slaves is downloading by itself the necessary files. The slaves systems may have different operating systems, and there is no need for remote access to them (by using the rsh/ssh type of protocols).

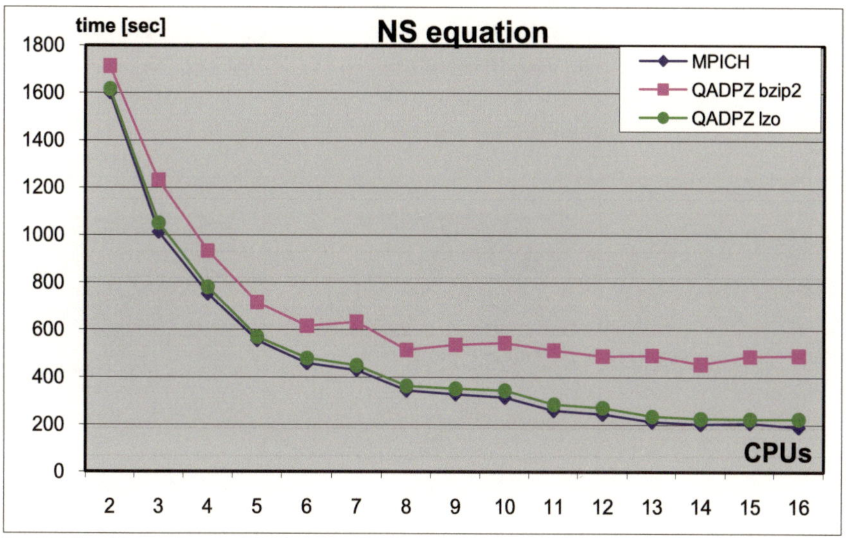


Fig. 6. Execution times for the solver

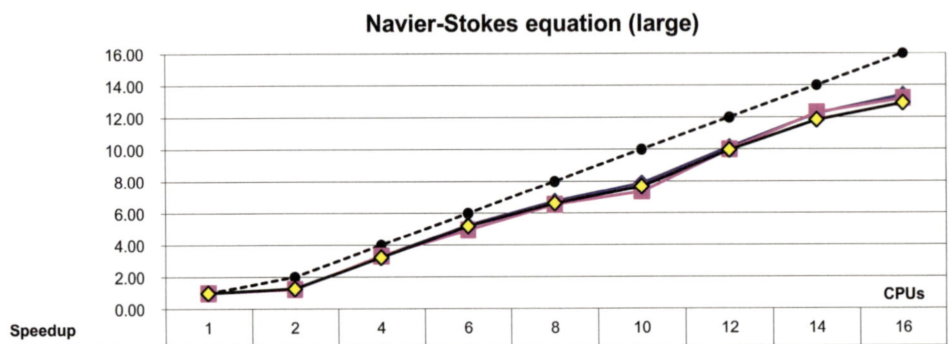


| Speedup | 1 | 2 | 4 | 6 | 8 | 10 | 12 | 14 | 16 |
|---|---|---|---|---|---|---|---|---|---|
| S - ideal | 1.00 | 2.00 | 4.00 | 6.00 | 8.00 | 10.00 | 12.00 | 14.00 | 16.00 |
| S - mpich | 1.00 | 1.28 | 3.27 | 5.24 | 6.74 | 7.88 | 10.14 | 12.24 | 13.39 |
| S - pvm | 1.00 | 1.24 | 3.32 | 4.95 | 6.54 | 7.36 | 9.99 | 12.29 | 13.18 |
| S - qadpz | 1.00 | 1.28 | 3.22 | 5.20 | 6.63 | 7.68 | 9.96 | 11.84 | 12.89 |

Fig. 7. Speedup for the simulation

### 4.3 Fluid flow around a cylinder - visualization

The results correspond to some time steps of an oscillating flow around a fixed cylinder in three dimensions. The second experiment is with three cylinders. The grid had 81600 nodes and was made of 8-node isoparametric elements, while the coarse mesh (used for pressure preconditioning) had approximately 2000 nodes. As in the previous case, numerical simulation was done by using the Navier Stokes equations. In the Fig. 8a the 2D domain grid is represented using triangular elements, and the colouring is done using the pressure scalar field. Fig. 8b is a real life experimental image for Re=26 (Van Dyke, 1982), and Fig. 8c is a simulation image using LIC vector field representation for Re=20. Two simulations with one and three cylinders are presented, respectively, in Fig. 9 and Fig. 10.

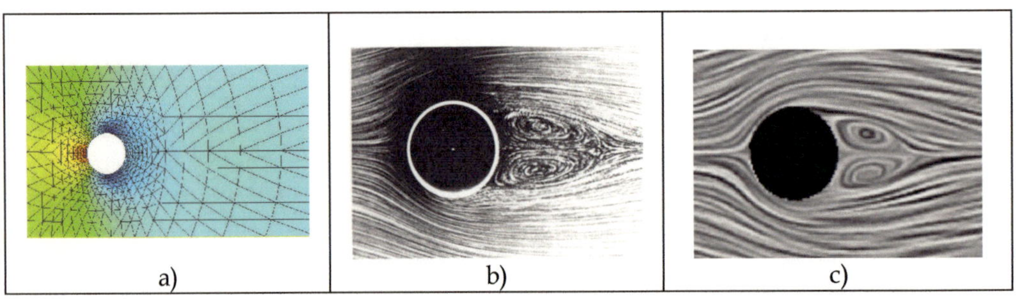


Fig. 8. Flow around cylinder: a) grid b) measurement c) simulation

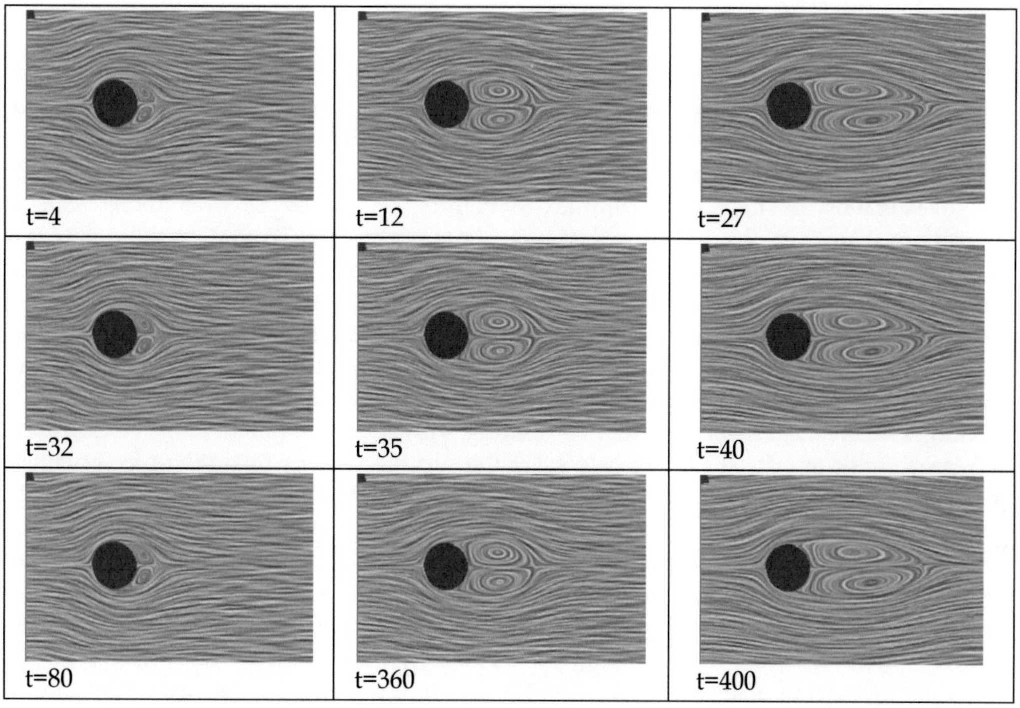


Fig. 9. Flow around cylinder: Simulation experiment for Re=100 at different time steps.

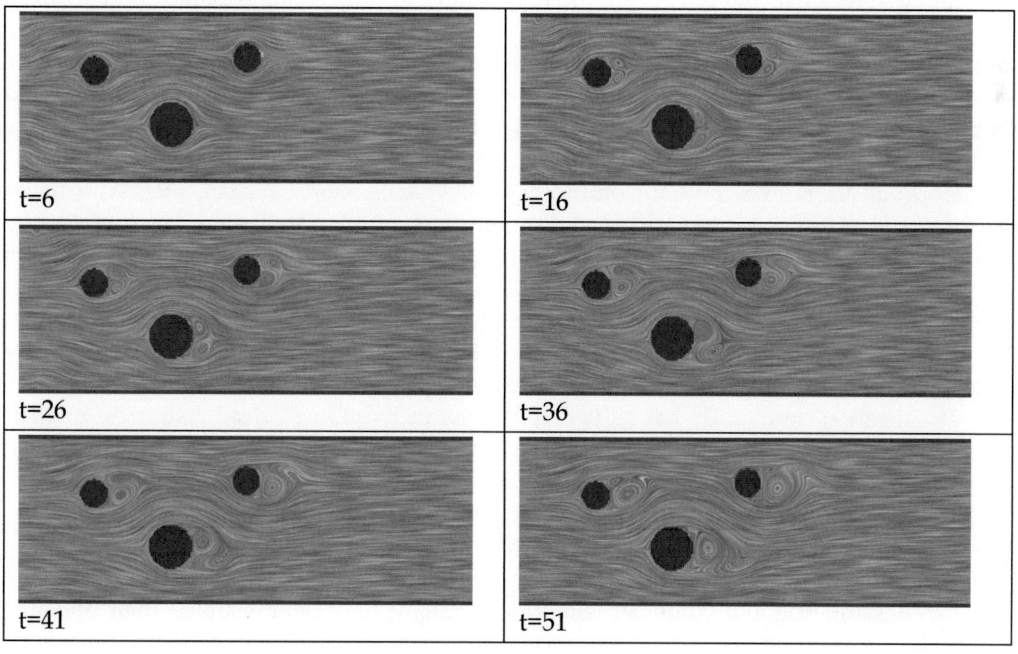


Fig. 10. Flow around cylinder: Simulation experiment for Re=100 at different time steps, with 3 cylinders

## 5. Conclusions and future work

The nowadays advances in information and communication technology, especially commodity computing, supercomputing and grid computing enable every scientist or engineer to have access to an advanced simulation kit of tools that makes analysis, product development, and design more optimal and cost effective. Further, that will make possible the investigation of incredibly complex dynamics by means of ever more realistic simulations. However, this brings with it huge amounts of data. To analyze these data it is crucial to use software tools, which can visualize multi-dimensional data sets, despite the difficulties inherent to this process. Scientific breakthroughs are enabled by insight, and, better visualization of an issue provides for a better understanding of the underlying science, and often for the discovery of something profoundly new and unexpected. The most exciting potential of visualization is the insight gained and the mistakes caught by spotting visual inconsistencies while computing. Advanced capabilities for visualization may prove to be as critical as the existence of the supercomputers themselves for scientists and engineers, and also for specialists in other domains. Better visualization tools might enhance human productivity and improve efficiency in several areas of science, industry, business, medicine, government and society in general. Visualization has the potential to *put the scientist into the computing loop and change the way the science is done* (McCormick, 1988).

Moreover, today everyone can produce their own computer graphics, with easy-to-use software integrated into various computer applications that makes charts and plots an obligatory element of many electronic documents. More professional packages offer in turn complex techniques for visualization of higher dimensional data. Visualization has thus become ubiquitous. Scientists are becoming familiar with desktop programs capable of presenting interactive molecular graphics. Bioinformatics, cheminformatics, and medical imaging use heavily such visualization engines for both interpreting lab data and training purposes (Wright, 2007). Furthermore, nowadays data visualization techniques are commonly used to provide business intelligence, for instance performance metrics and indicators may be displayed on interactive digital dashboards, and business executives rely on these software applications to monitor the status of business results and activities.

Therefore, all users of Scientific Computing and Visualization have an interest in better hardware, software and integrated systems, and much of what has being developed so far has been shared by a number of scientific and engineering projects up to a point, and with very large costs that were accessible only to large research facilities (e.g. SGI visualization servers and large PC clusters). Then the gaming industry has made a breakthrough, under the pressure of the gamers who have requested more and more graphical power, by developing very high performance graphics cards, at very low costs (commodity hardware). The visualization community has shifted to the use of these low-priced resources for their visualization tasks and progressively more PC-based visualization results have been obtained. However, gaming graphics hardware is not well suited for scientific computing and visualization, leading to a fundamental rethinking of how high-end systems are built as designers attempt to apply to large scale (interactive) rendering the clustered computing techniques that have revolutionized HPC (Constantinescu, 2008).

By now, desktop grid and volunteer computing systems have demonstrated their potential to supply more computing power to science and other in need domains than any other type of computing, and have therefore proved themselves as a viable solution to this problem. The benefits will increase over time due to the laws of economics, which states that consumer electronics (PCs and game consoles) will progress faster than any specialized products, and that there will be an abundance of them. Nevertheless, desktop grid computing and volunteer computing are still under heavy conceptualization, research and development. There are still many aspects to clarify and solve: security issues, scheduling, volatile environment, sabotage-tolerance, integration with Grid, decentralization, peer to peer aspects etc.

The core idea of the work presented in this chapter has been to provide a desktop grid computing framework and to prove its viability by testing it in some Scientific Computing and Visualization experiments. We presented here QADPZ, an open source system for desktop grid computing, which enables users from a local network or Internet to share their resources. It is a multi-platform, heterogeneous system, where different computing resources inside an organization can be used. It can also be used for volunteer computing, where the communication infrastructure is the Internet. The system is currently used for research tasks in the areas of large-scale scientific visualization, evolutionary computation, simulation of complex neural network models, and other computationally intensive applications. It is also in use for educational purposes in universities around the world.

Further on we present some future work ideas that aim to improve both the conceptual model and the QADPZ system, as they are meant to make QADPZ more compliant with the requirements for a successful desktop grid and, therefore, more useful for its users. First, we consider inclusion of checkpointing, as many large-scale parallel problems require such support, because running a parallel application for hours or even days and loosing all results due to one failing node is unacceptable. Another feature to be added with high priority is handling of the restart of the master computer. In the current version of the system, each job needs a different client process, and currently we consider extending the client functionality to allow a single client instance to optionally connect to multiple masters and handle multiple jobs. Improved support for user data security is envisaged as well; computation results data can be encrypted and/or signed so that the user will be ensured that the received data is correct. Data integrity is another important issue, which is especially useful in an open environment (such as Internet). For faster performance, slave libraries will be cached at slave computers - in the current version, they are downloaded before each task is started. Moreover, slave computers will provide a flexible data storage available to other computers in QADPZ. Users are ought to be provided with different scheduling algorithms to choose from, according to the type of their problem.

Future developments of the system include more complete implementation of the MPI layer and development of a complete library of the collective communication routines. Our current implementation does not support collective communication, only the MPI_COMM_WORLD communicator. However, a complete library of such communication routines can be written entirely using the point-to-point communication functions and a few auxiliary functions. Current QADPZ's implementation is limited to a small subset of the MPI standard. It contains only the most used functions, as it has been developed to support only testing and evaluation of parallel communications. Another future work idea we consider is adding a set of transparent profiling tools for evaluating performance of different components. This is an important issue in compute-intensive applications, especially when running parallel applications. Dynamic balancing of the workload can be used for tackling this issue. The current user interface to the system is based on C++. Possible extensions of the system would be different interfaces for other languages, e.g. Java, Perl, Tcl or Python.

This can easily be done, since the message exchanges between different components of the system are based on an open XML specification.

The current implementation of the system is made considering only one central master node. This can be an inconvenience in certain situations, where computers located in different networks are used together. The master node can also be subject to failures, both software and hardware, and therefore a more decentralized approach is necessary. However, the basic elements are already in place as our high-level communication protocol between the entities, especially between the client and master, allows a master to act as a client to another master, thus making possible to create a distributed master that consists of independent master nodes, which communicate with each other, i.e. some sort of *virtual master*. Approaches from peer-to-peer computing will be used for implementing such a decentralized approach. Future desktop grid infrastructure are ought to be *decentralized, robust, highly available, and scalable,* while efficiently mapping application instances to available resources in the system (Berman et al., 2003). However, current desktop grid computing platforms are typically based on a client-server architecture, which has inherent shortcomings with respect to robustness, reliability and scalability. Fortunately, these problems can be addressed as well through the capabilities promised by new paradigms and techniques in P2P systems. By employing P2P services, our system could allow users to submit jobs to be run in the system and to run jobs submitted by other users on any resources available in the system, essentially allowing a group of users to form an ad-hoc set of shared resources, moving this way towards a P2P architecture. Interconnection with a grid computing environment is another goal, as desktop grid computing is not to evolve outside the Grid, but connected closely with it, inside it.

During the last decades, technologies have become commoditized and will continue to evolve in this direction to such a degree that we will be able to afford to have a tremendous number of them in the environment, providing for a commensurately powerful interconnected infrastructure to support for e-science in particular, and for e-society in general. The quality of provided services will improve constantly, as the infrastructure will become more autonomous and will strengthen its capabilities of self-configuring, self-optimizing, self-healing, self-protecting, and, why not, self-programming. In our opinion, desktop grids have revealed their huge potential to support computationally intensive applications, and to solve other significant real-world problems, being an invaluable part of this future infrastructure. In the near future we will find them enabling millions of users to collaborate and solve unimaginably sophisticated problems, having this way an important contribution to scientific research, and, even more important, to the directions of this research. Finally, improvements of their day to day life may and will come up as a result of this active participation of people to science.

## 6. References


Berman F., Fox G. & Hey A.J.G. (2003). *Grid computing: making the global infrastructure a reality*, Wiley, ISBN 978-0470853191, New York

BOINC. (2010). Open Source Software for Volunteer Computing and Grid Computing, available at http://boinc.berkeley.edu, accessed September 2010

BOINCstats. (2010). Statistics for BOINC, available at http://www.boincstats.com, accessed September 2010

Cabral, B. & Leedom, L. C. (1993). Imaging Vector Fields Using Line Integral Convolution. *Proceedings of the 20th Annual Conference on Computer Graphics and Interactive Techniques SIGGRAPH 1993,* pp. 263-270, ISBN 0-89791-601-8, August, 1993, Anaheim, CA, ACM Press, New York

Cardenas-Montes, M., Emmen, A., Marosi, A. C., et al. (2008). EDGeS: bridging Desktop and Service Grids, *Proceedings of the 2nd Iberian Grid Infrastructure Conference (IBERGRID 2008)*, pp. 212-224, ISBN 978-84-9745-288-5, Porto, Portugal, May, 2008, NETBIBLO, A Coruna, Spain

Cassens J. & Constantinescu Z. (2003). Free Software: An Adequate Form of Software for Research and Education in Informatics?, *Proceedings of LinuxTag 2003 Conference,* Karlsruhe, Germany, July, 2003

Condor. (2010). Condor High Throughput Computing, available at http://www.cs.wisc.edu/condor, accessed September 2010

Constantinescu, Z. (2003). Towards an Autonomic Distributed Computing System, *IEEE DEXA Workshop on Autonomic Computing Systems (ACS'2003),* Prague, Czech Republic, September, 2003, IEEE Computer Society Press

Constantinescu, Z. (2008). *A Desktop Grid Computing Approach for Scientific Computing and Visualization,* PhD Thesis, Norwegian Univ. of Science and Technology, ISBN 978-82-471-9158-3 Trondheim, Norway

Constantinescu Z., Vladoiu M. (2009a). A Solution for Improving Communications in Desktop Grid Systems, *BMIF Journal - Bulletin of PG University of Ploieşti, Series Mathematics, Informatics, Physics,* Vol. LXI, No. 2, December, 2009, pp. 27-32, ISSN 1224-4899, e-ISSN 2067-242X

Constantinescu Z., Vladoiu M. (2009b). Experimenting with Visualization on Desktop Grids, *BMIF Journal - Bulletin of PG University of Ploieşti, Technical Series,* Vol. LXI, No. 3, June 2009, pp. 255-260, ISSN 1224-8495

Distributed.net. (2010). Distributed.net available at http://boinc.berkeley.edu, accessed September 2010

Domingues, P.; Silva, J. G. & Silva, L. (2006). Sharing Checkpoints to Improve Turnaround Time in Desktop Grid Computing, *Proceedings of 20th Int. Conf. on Advanced Information Networking and Applications (AINA 2006),* Vol. 1, pp. 301-306, Viena, Austria, April 2006, IEEE Computer Society Press, Los Alamitos, California

EDGeS. (2010). Enabling Desktop Grids for eScience, available at http://www.edges-grid.eu, accessed September 2010

eMinerals. (2010). Environment from the Molecular Level - a NERC eScience testbed project, available at http://www.eminerals.org, accessed September 2010

Folding@home. (2010). Folding@home distributed computing, available at http://folding.stanford.edu, accessed September 2010

Forssell, L. K. (1994). Visualizing Flow Over Curvilinear Grid Surfaces Using Line Integral Convolution, *Proceedings of IEEE Visualization '94,* pp. 240-247, ISBN 0-8186-6626-9, Washington D.C., October, 1994, IEEE Computer Society Press

Forssell, L. K. & Cohen, S. D. (1995). Using line integral convolution for flow visualization: curvilinear grids, variable-speed animation, and unsteady flows, *IEEE Transactions on Visualization and Computer Graphics*, Vol. 1, No. 2, June, 1995, pp. 133-141, ISSN 1077-2626

Foster, I. & Kesselman, C. (2004). *The Grid: Blueprint for a New Computing Infrastructure*, Morgan Kaufmann Publishers, ISBN 978-1558609334, Boston, USA

GIMPS. (2010). Great Internet Mersenne Prime Search, available at http://www.mersenne.org, accessed September 2010

Grid@EFPL. (2010). Greedy Pool desktop Grid, available at http://greedy.epfl.ch, accessed September 2010

He H., Fedak G., Kacsuk P. et al. (2010). Extending the EGEE Grid with XtremWeb-HEP Desktop Grids, *Proceedings of the 2010 10th IEEE/ACM International Conference on Cluster, Cloud and Grid Computing*, pp. 685-690, ISBN 978-0-7695-4039-9, Melbourne, Australia, May 2010, IEEE Computer Society Press Washington, DC, USA

Hoover, S., Dobrenen, K. & Trauner, M. (2009). Project Blackbird: Deploying Condor in a Blackboard Environment, *EQ EDUCAUSE Quarterly Magazine*, Vol. 32, No. 3, 2009, *ISSN* 1528-5324, available online at http://www.educause.edu/EDUCAUSE+Quarterly/EDUCAUSEQuarterlyMagazineVolum/ProjectBlackbirdDeployingCondo/182625, accessed September 2010

Jermini, P. (2010). Building a Condor Desktop Grid and its exercises, *Swiss Grid School 2010*, June, 2010, Lugano, Switzerland, available online at http://greedy.epfl.ch/articles/building-condor-grid-sgs10.pdf, accessed September 2010

Hamming, R. W. (1987). *Numerical Methods for Scientists and Engineers*, Dover Publications, 2nd edition, ISBN 978-0486652412 , Mineola, New York

Hayes, B. (1998). Collective Wisdom, *American Scientist*, Vol. 86, No. 2, March, April, 1998, pp. 118-122, ISSN 0003-0996

Heath, M.T. (2002). *Scientific Computing: an Introductory Survey*, McGraw-Hill, ISBN 978-0072399103, Boston

McCormick, B. H. (1988). Visualization in Scientific Computing, *ACM SIGBIO Newsletter*, Vol. 10, No. 1, March, 1998, pp. 15-21, ISSN 0163-5697

Merzkirch, W. (1987) *Flow visualization*, 2nd Edition, Academic Press, ISBN 978-0124913516, Orlando, Florida, USA

Meuer, H.W. (2010), Top500 Supercomputer Sites Report, 35th Edition, June 2010, available at http://www.top500.org, accessed September 2010

Mustafee, N. & Taylor, S. J. E. (2006). Using a desktop grid to support simulation modelling, *Proceedings of 28th International Conference on Information Technology Interfaces (ITI 2006)*, pp. 557-562, ISBN 953-7138-05-4, Dubrovnik, Croatia, June, 2006, Zagreb's University Computing Centre SRCE, Zagreb, Croatia

Paradyn/Condor Week. (2008). Paradyn/Condor Week - Condor Presentations, Madison, Wisconsin, United States of America, April-May, 2008, available at http://www.cs.wisc.edu/condor/PCW2008/condor_presentations.html, accessed September 2010

Seti@home Classic. (2010). The Search for Extraterrestrial Intelligence, available at http://seticlassic.ssl.berkeley.edu, accessed September 2010

Seti@home. (2010). The Search for Extraterrestrial Intelligence - the current Seti@home project, available at http://setiathome.ssl.berkeley.edu, accessed September 2010

Smits, A. J. & Lim, T. T. (2000). *Flow visualization: techniques and examples*, Imperial College Press, ISBN 978-1860941931, London, UK

Steeb, W.-H.; Hardy, Y.; Hardy, A. & Stoop, R. (2004). *Problems & Solutions In Scientific Computing With C++ And Java Simulations*, World Scientific Publishing Company, ISBN 978-9812561121, Singapore

Thiemard, M. (2008). On the Usage of a Desktop Grid - Greedy@EPFL, *Symposium on High Performance Computing Methods (HPCM)*, June, 2008, Lausanne, Switzerland, available online at http://greedy.epfl.ch/articles/hpcm-0608.pdf, accessed September 2010

QADPZ. (2010). Quite Advanced Distributed Parallel Zystem, QADPZ's homepage on sourceforge, available at http://qadpz.sourceforge.net, accessed September 2010

Utnes, T. & Brors, B. (1993). Numerical modelling of 3-D circulation in restricted waters, *Applied Mathematics Modeling*, Vol. 17, No. 10, October, 1993, pp. 522-535

Van Dyke, M. (1982). *Album of Fluid Motion*, Parabolic Press, ISBN 0-915760-03-7, Stanford, California, USA

Vladoiu, M. & Constantinescu Z. (2008a). A Taxonomy for Desktop Grids from Users Perspective, *Proceedings of ICPDC 2008 - the 2008 International Conference of Parallel and Distributed Computing, a Conference of World Congress on Engineering 2008 (WCE 2008)*, Vol. I., pp. 599-604, ISBN 978-988-98671-9-5, London, UK, July, IAENG

Vladoiu, M. & Constantinescu Z. (2008b). An Extended Master-Worker Model for a Desktop Grid Computing Platform (QADPZ), *Proceedings of 3rd International Conference on Software and Data Technologies (ICSOFT 2008)*, Vol. I, pp. 169-174, ISBN 978-989-8111-51-7, Porto, Portugal, July, 2008, INSTICC, Setubal, Portugal

Vladoiu, M. & Constantinescu Z. (2009a). Development Journey of QADPZ - A Desktop Grid Computing Platform, *International Journal of Computers, Communications & Control (IJCCC)*, Vol IV, No. 1/2009, pp 82-91, ISSN 1841–9836; E-ISSN 1841–9844

Vladoiu, M. & Constantinescu Z. (2009b). Availability of Computational Resources for Desktop Grid Computing, *BMIF Journal - Bulletin of PG University of Ploieşti, Series Mathematics, Informatics, Physics*, Vol. LXI, No. 1, June, 2009, pp. 43-48, ISSN 1224-4899

Wikipedia. (2010a). Berkeley Open Infrastructure for Network Computing, available at http://en.wikipedia.org/wiki/Berkeley_Open_Infrastructure_for_Network_Computing, accessed September 2010

Wikipedia. (2010b). Wikipedia - The Free Encyclopedia's page on Computational Science, available at http://en.wikipedia.org/wiki/Computational_science, accessed September 2010

Wilson, P., Emmerich, W. & Brodholt, J. (2004). Leveraging HTC for UK eScience with Very Large Condor Pools: Demand for Transforming Untapped Power into Results, *Proceedings of the UK e-Science Programme All Hands Meeting (AHM 2004)*, pp. 308-315, ISBN 1-904425-21-6, Nottingham, UK, August-September, 2004, EPSRC, Swindon, UK

Wright H. (2007). *Introduction to Scientific Visualization*, Springer, ISBN 978-1846284946

XtremWeb. (2010). The Open Source Platform for Desktop Grids, available at http://www.xtremweb.net, accessed September 2010
XtremWeb-CH. (2010). The Volunteer Computing Middleware, available at http://www.xtremwebch.net, accessed September 2010
XtremWeb-HEP. (2010). Desktop Grid for High Energy Physics, available at http://www.xwhep.org, accessed September 2010

# 9

# Security in the Development Process of Mobile Grid Systems

David G. Rosado[1], Eduardo Fernández-Medina[1] and Javier López[2]
[1]*University of Castilla-La Mancha. GSyA Research Group, Ciudad Real*
[2]*University of Málaga. Computer Science Department, Málaga*
*Spain*

## 1. Introduction

Grid computing has emerged to cater the need of computing-on-demand (Jana et al., 2009) due to the advent of distributed computing with sophisticated load balancing, distributed data and concurrent computing power using clustered servers. The Grid enables resource sharing and dynamic allocation of computational resources, thus increasing access to distributed data, promoting operational flexibility and collaboration, and allowing service providers to scale efficiently to meet variable demands (Foster & Kesselman, 2004).

Security is considered as the most significant challenge for Grid computing (Humphrey et al., 2005), due to the fact that resources are shared between organizations; expensive resources, that may go from computers and other hardware facilities, to potentially valuable, sensitive and confidential data files.

In recent years the mobile computing community has been successful in utilising academic and industry research efforts to bring products to the commercial market. We have seen a proliferation of consumer electronic devices taking advantage of wireless technology enrich our daily lives with increased productivity thanks to higher connectivity.

At first glance, it seems that the marriage of mobile wireless consumer devices with high-performance Grid computing would be an unlikely match. After all, Grid computing to date has utilised multiprocessors and PCs as the computing nodes within its mesh. Consumer computing devices such as laptops and PDAs are typically restricted by reduced CPU, memory, secondary storage, and bandwidth capabilities. However, therein lies the challenge. The availability of wirelessly connected mobile devices has grown considerably within recent years, creating an enormous collective untapped potential for resource utilisation. To wit, recent market research shows that in 2008, 269 million mobile phone and 36 million smartphone (Gartner, 2009) were sold worldwide, and that in 2006, 17 million PDAs (Gartner, 2007) were sold worldwide. Although these individual computing devices may be resource-limited in isolation, as an aggregated sum, they have the potential to play a vital role within Grid computing (Phan et al., 2005).

On the other hand, the idea of developing software through systematic development processes to improve software quality is not new. Nevertheless, there are still many information systems such as the Grid Computing ones, that are not developed through methodologies adapted to their most differentiating features (Kolonay & Sobolewski, 2004). That is to say, generic development processes are used to develop specific systems without taking into consideration either the subjacent technological environment or the special features and particularities of these specific systems.

Additionally, the growing need for constructing secure systems, mainly due to the new vulnerabilities derived from the use of the Internet and that of the applications distributed in heterogeneous environments, encourages the scientific community to demand a clear integration of security into the development processes (Bass et al., 2004; Breu et al., 2003; Haley et al., 2006; Jürjens, 2005; Lodderstedt et al., 2002; Mouratidis & Giorgini, 2006). The main reason is that security aspects are only considered at the implementation stages causing that security solutions are not perfectly coupled with the design and the rest of requirements of the system (Artelsmair and Wagner, 2003; Mouratidis & Giorgini, 2006).

Therefore, the goal of the paper is to define a systematic development process for Grid systems that supports the participation of mobile nodes and incorporates security aspects into of all sofware lifecycle will thus play a significant role in the development of systems based on Grid computing. The reasons that led us to focus on this topic are several: Firstly, the lack of adequate development methods for this kind of systems since the majority of existing Grid applications have been built without a systematic development process and are based on ad-hoc developments (Dail et al., 2004; Kolonay & Sobolewski, 2004), suggests the need for adapted development methodologies (Giorgini et al., 2007; Graham, 2006; Jacobson et al., 1999; Open Group, 2009). Secondly, due to the fact that the resources in a Grid are expensive, dynamic, heterogeneous, geographically located and under the control of multiple administrative domains (Bhanwar & Bawa, 2008), and the tasks accomplished and the information exchanged are confidential and sensitive, the security of these systems is hard to achieve. And thirdly, because of the appearance of a new technology where security is fundamental together with the advances that mobile computation has experienced in recent years that have increased the difficulty of incorporating mobile devices into a Grid environment (Guan et al., 2005; Jameel et al., 2005; Kumar & Qureshi, 2008; Kwok-Yan et al., 2004; Sajjad et al., 2005).

The rest of paper is organized as follows: In section 2, we will present the related work. In section 3, we will define the proposed development process with the models used and activities and tasks. In section 4 we will apply the proposed process to a real case showing the results obtained. We will finish by putting forward our conclusions as well as some research lines for our future work in section 5.

## 2. Related work

There are some proposals which try to integrate security into the software development process, even from the first stages, but however, none of them are defined for Grid Computing based systems. For instance, authors in (Steel et al., 2005) present a methodology for the integration of the security on software systems. This methodology is based in the Unified Process (Kruchten, 2000) and it is called Secure Unified Process (SUP). The problem is that it only offers a solution to a very high level without offering "practical mechanisms" (e.g. Grid-specific security artifacts or a security architecture of reference) that permits to implement his approach in a short space of time and with minimal effort. Other approach (Jurjens, 2001; Jurjens, 2002; Jürjens, 2005) concentrates on providing a formal semantics for UML to integrate security considerations into the software design process. UMLSec is more focused on access control policies and how these policies can be integrated into a model-driven software development process (Mouratidis et al., 2005). This aspect is important but is very specific and it is applicable only to certain stages of the development process. Other approach is CLASP (Comprehensive, Lightweight Application Security Process) that is an activity-driven, role-based set of process components guided by formalized best practices (Graham, 2006). CLASP suggests a number of different activities across the development lifecycle in order to improve security, but does not define a whole development process only the activities which can be integrated into any development process. Finally, AEGIS (Appropriate and Effective Guidance for Information Security) (Flechais et al., 2003) is a secure software engineering method that integrates security requirements elicitation, risk analysis and context of use, bound together through the use of UML. This approach is the only approach found in which the authors attempt to apply the methodology to Grid systems, although they do not explain how to do this, and do not define guides and practices for capturing specific security aspects in Grid systems.

On the other hand, there are numerous approaches related to Grid architectures, middleware, infrastructures, projects, and so on, such as OGSA (Foster et al., 2002) that is a specification that defines a set of concepts, rules, features, properties, services, capacities and behaviour for implementing Grid Computing applications, but it does not indicate the steps and methods to develop for obtaining a Grid application. Other approach is UNICORE (Uniform Interface to Computing Resources) (Romberg, 2002) which develops a software infrastructure for seamless access to distributed supercomputer resources. The problem is that does not support either dynamic environment or mobile devices. The gLite approach (EGEE Middleware Design Team, 2004) provides a framework for building Grid applications tapping into the power of distributed computing and storage resources across the Internet. These security features are sufficient for many Grid applications, but insufficient when the applications are more complex and even more when mobile devices are included in the application as Grid resources. Also, the Legion project, developed at the University of Virginia, is an attempt to provide GRID services that create the illusion of a virtual machine. This architecture does not support the dynamic behaviour of the Grid.

Finally, some of the most interesting approaches for the incorporation of mobile devices into Grid systems are: LEECH (Leveraging Every Existing Computer out tHere) (Phan et al., 2005) that takes into account security aspects for wireless network and mobile devices through the proxy which serves as an intermediary between mobile devices and the Grid. This proxy must additionally be protected to safeguard Grid systems with mobile devices so that is a weak spot by the attackers. Mobile-To-Grid (Jameel et al., 2005; Kalim et al., 2005; Sajjad et al., 2005) is other approach that defines a middleware which permits heterogeneous mobile devices access to Grid services. This approach treats mobile devices like external elements and the security must be implemented outside the Grid environment. Other of the approaches is the Surrogate approach wich defines a middleware that will allow handheld devices, e.g. PDA units, to interact with Grid services while inducing minimal burden on the device itself (Riaz et al., 2005). Security to Grid level is not considered, only to gateway level that is not sufficient for the complexity of Mobile Grid systems with thousand of mobile resources and different VOs and domains. Finally, the Akogrimo architecture (Access to Knowledge through the Grid in a Mobile World) (The AKOGRIMO project) is intended to support business process designs that both support and take advantage of dynamic, mobile services and users. This approach defines a design and implementation solution for Grid with mobile devices but it is not development guides or methodologies to apply these solutions of controlled and systematic way.

Therefore, after studying and analyzing each of the approaches related to the development and security in Mobile Grid computing, we conclude that the existing proposals are not specific enough to provide a complete solution of security under a systematic development process for Mobile Grid environments. This is due to the fact that none of the approaches defines a systematic development process for this specific kind of systems that incorporates security from the earliest stages of the development. Moreover, the existing security approaches to Mobile Grid computing are more focused on offering a technological solution than on the requirements and design. Neither of them offers solutions that integrate mobile devices as own resources of the Grid under a global security environment.

## 3. Secure development process

### 3.1 Overview

This process is designed for building software systems based on Mobile Grid computing with security aspects. It is a process which builds, from initial requirements and needs of Mobile Grid systems, a secure executable software product. It is not a process for including only security in a development process but it is a development process in itself incorporating security aspects during all the process.

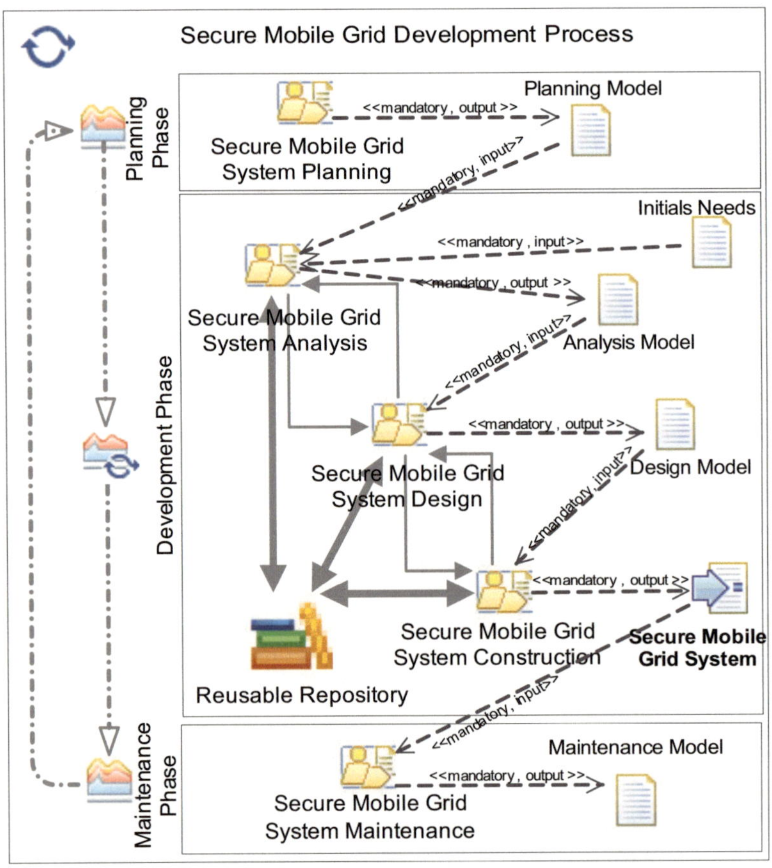


Fig. 1. Development process for secure Mobile Grid systems with SPEM 2.0

The structure of the process which we propose follows the classical cycle (see Fig. 1), in which we find a planning phase, a development phase including analysis, design and construction and finally a maintenance phase. However, the proposed process is specially designed for this kind of systems because we consider their particular aspects and features in each of the activities of the process

Our systematic process of development is an iterative and incremental process. An iterative approach refers to the cyclic nature of the process in which activities are repeated in a structured manner and proposes an understanding of the problem through successive refinements, and an incremental growth of an effective solution through several versions. Thus, in each iteration of the process, new and necessary characteristics can be added and extended so that a complete final design is obtained. Also, it is a reusable process in the sense of the utilization of artifacts built in others executions of this process or in previous iterations which have been validated and tested and that improve the quality of the new artifacts built and save developers' time and effort.

### 3.2 Models of the process

This section presents the defined models identified for the process and which are necessary for carrying out the different activities and tasks. These models are: i) an extension of UML (GridUCSec-profile) to define Grid use cases that include security use cases and misuse cases oriented to the characteristics of Mobile Grid systems, and that are used in the analysis activity (Rosado et al., 2009a; Rosado et al., 2010b; Rosado et al., 2010c); ii) the reference security architecture used in the design activity, which ensures the fulfillment of the security requirements for these systems and that is service-oriented (Rosado et al., 2010a; Rosado et al., 2010d); iii) the association rules model between security requirements and security services for identifying what services are necessary for fulfilling what requirements, and it is used in the design activity when the security services are defined; and finally, iv) the reusable elements of the repository that are used in the different tasks of the process and that help us build artifacts in an easy, fast and reliable way (Rosado et al., 2009a; Rosado et al., 2009b).

### 3.3 Activities of the process

As we have seen above, the process consists of 3 phases, planning, development and maintenance. The phases of planning and maintenance are common phases which any development of information systems has to define, so we move on a generic development process to carry out the activities and tasks of these phases. Thus, our work focuses on defining what is really specific and differentiating in developing systems based on Grid computing, the development phase. This phase consists of three activities, analysis, design and construction, and each of them defines the specific tasks necessary, the artifacts to be used, and the steps to take to analyze, design and build specific information systems as Mobile Grid systems are.

#### 3.3.1 Analysis activity

Analysis focuses on ensuring that the system's security and functional requirements are elicited, specified and modelled. In our approach, this activity is driven by use cases and supported by the reusable repository. This obtains, builds, defines and refines the use cases of the secure Mobile Grid systems which represent the functional and non-functional requirements of this kind of systems. Both the wide set of elements which are common to these systems and that are stored in the repository, such as secure Mobile Grid use cases, interaction diagrams, UML profiles, templates, etc., and the GridUCSec-profile model aforementioned, help the analyst define all the requirements (functional and non-functional, and security in particular) and build the necessary diagrams with which to complete the analysis activity from beginning to end.

The analysis activity is based on use cases in which we define the behaviour, actions and interactions with those implied by the system (actors) to obtain a first approach to the needs and requirements (functional and non-functional) of the system to be constructed. This activity is supported by repositories in which several types of elements appear: Firstly, the elements that have been developed in earlier stages; secondly, those that have been built at the beginning of the process and finally, those that come from other executions of the process from which we have obtained elements that can be reused by other applications. Reuse is appropriate here thanks both to the common features of applications based on Grid computing (CPU intensive, data intensive, collaborative and so on) and to the fact that these applications use mobile devices. Therefore, we must abstract all the common features (by analyzing the main features of Grid applications and constructing, for example, generic use case diagrams in which all these common features are represented) and make them available for the process (through the repository) in order to be able to use the common elements in any activity and adapt them to our needs.

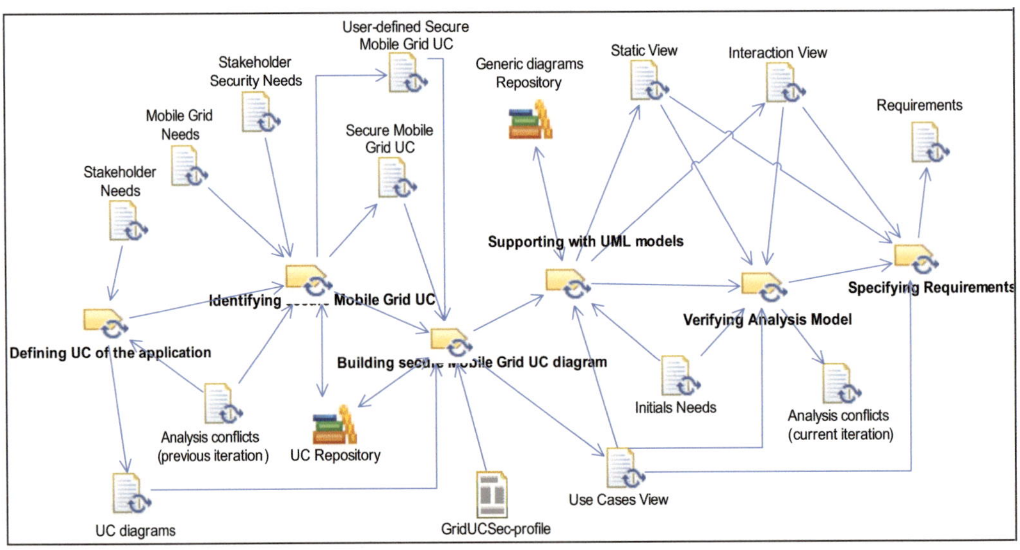


Fig. 2. Tasks and artifacts of the Secure Mobile Grid System Analysis activity

The analysis activity is composed of tasks which build use case diagrams and specifications to obtain the analysis model in which the requirements are defined. This activity produces internal artifacts which are the output of some tasks and the input of others. Fig. 2 shows a graphical representation of the analysis activity tasks using SPEM 2.0 diagrams. Initially, in the "Defining UC of the application" task, we define the functional use cases of the application identified from the stakeholder needs and study the interactions with the user without considering the specific aspects of Mobile Grid environments. Next, in the

"Identifying secure Mobile Grid UC" task, we study the security aspects of the application within the Mobile Grid context and identify the possible security use cases and misuse cases that can be reused from those defined in the repository, for the system in development. Once the use cases have been identified and defined, we build the overall use case diagram (or diagrams) in which we define the relationships between all the use cases and actors previously identified, and we describe the information from all the diagram's elements by following a new UML profile for Mobile Grid use cases. We can also reuse and integrate some diagrams with common features of the repository which have been previously built for Mobile Grid environments. This is carried out in the "Building secure Mobile Grid UC diagram" task. In the "Supporting with UML models" task, we complete the analysis model with different UML models such as the sequence and collaboration diagrams according to use cases and scenarios, or class diagrams for an initial structural description of the system from the use cases diagrams built in previous tasks. Then, in the "Verifying Analysis model" task, we have to verify that the artifacts have been correctly generated and the possible conflicts or errors in the analysis model have to be identified and analyzed for their subsequent refinements and corrections in next iterations of this activity. Finally, the "Specifying Requirements" task consists of the formal definition of the requirements identified in previous tasks (functional requirements and non-functional requirements including security) in natural language (though a template of requirements specification will be defined in the future).

### 3.3.2 Design activity

Design focuses on ensuring that the system's security and functional requirements are fulfilled, covered and validated with the design, on the one hand, of a security architecture, and the other hand, of a software architecture. In our approach, this activity is supported by a reference security architecture which covers and fulfills the security requirements of the Mobile Grid system specified in the analysis activity. This reference security architecture is instantiated to a concrete security architecture (depending on the security requirements required) and is integrated with the software architecture designed (using a generic development process as the Unified Process), obtaining a Secure Software Architecture for Mobile Grid systems which is an input artifact for the construction activity.

The design activity is centred on building the secure software architecture of the system through UML views, services and a reference security architecture stored in the repository. The design activity is centred on architecture that is the main element of the system and, on the one hand, it covers the necessities and requirements identified and specified in the analysis activity, and on the other hand, it serves as a guide in the next activity of system construction. The designed software architecture will be a secure architecture because we have incorporated a security architecture for this kind of systems into the general software architecture fullfiling with the security requirements specified in the previous activity. This activity is supported by repositories in which several types of elements appear: Firstly, the elements that have been developed in earlier stages; secondly, those that have been built at the beginning of the process and finally, those that come from other executions of the process from which we have obtained elements that can be reused by other applications. A reference security architecture has been defined in the repository for its use together with UML diagrams for the system construction.

The design activity is composed of tasks which build the software architecture, the security architecture and their specifications with different views and using architectural elements of the repository, obtaining the design model where the architecture is defined. Fig. 3 shows a graphical representation of the design activity tasks using SPEM 2.0 diagrams. Initially, the "Designing Mobile Grid Software Architecture" task designs a software architecture following the steps, methods and techniques of the typical development processes (as the Unified Process (Jacobson et al., 1999), TOGAF (Open Group, 2009), etc.) using UML diagrams, views and realizations of use cases from the use cases model and analysis model defined in the analysis activity for Mobile Grid systems. The "Designing Mobile Grid Security Architecture" task defines the security architecture using the reusable elements of the repository and following the security Requirement-Service association rules of use cases to security services from the use cases of the analysis model. The reusable elements are generic elements which should be instantiated and integrated into the security architecture that is built with the help of security patterns. Once we have built both the software architecture and the security architecture, now we have to build and define the final architecture that is the security architecture integrated into the software architecture defining the relationships between elements (classes, collaboration, sequence, objects, diagrams, etc.), obtaining the secure Mobile Grid software architecture. This is executed in the "Designing/Integrating Secure Mobile Grid Software Architecture" task. Next, in the "Specifying Secure Mobile Grid Software Architecture" task, the final architecture built is specified using natural language or the IEEE 1471-2000 standard (IEEE, 2000). Last, in the "Validating and Verifying Secure Mobile Grid Software Architecture" task, the architecture obtained in the previous task has to be validated with the requirements specified in the analysis activity and the traceability between artifacts has to be verified, and the possible conflicts or errors in the design have to be identified and analyzed for their subsequent refinements in next iterations of this activity.

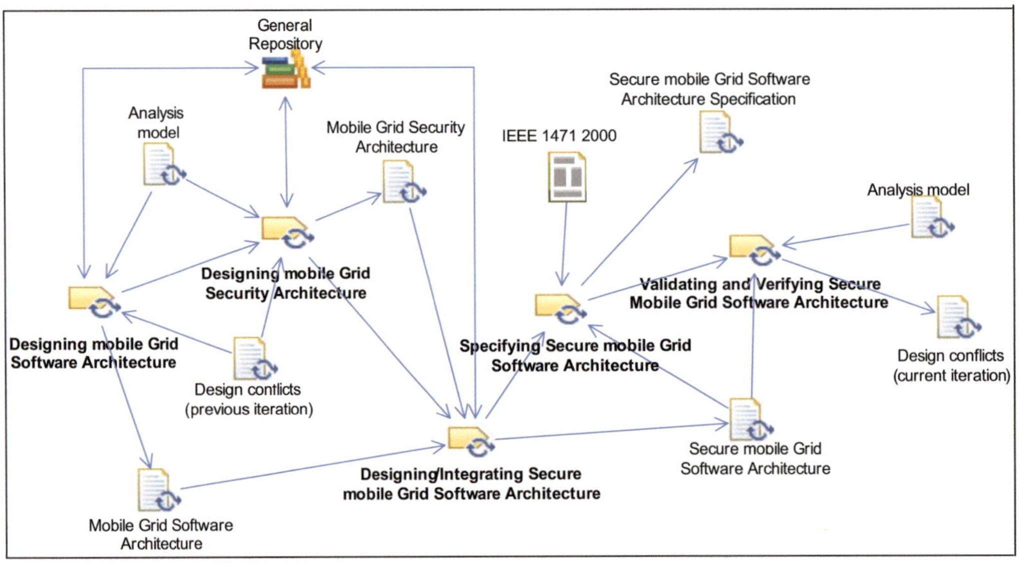


Fig. 3. Tasks of the Secure Mobile Grid System Design activity

### 3.3.3 Construction activity

Construction focuses on implementing the elements designed in the previous activity using a technological platform for the building of Grid systems. Mainly, the goal of this activity is to generate code of services and interfaces of the secure software architecture and to configure and compile files, data, packages, interfaces and classes under a Grid platform which gives life to the design and makes the system available for users, resources and organizations to be able to communicate between them sending tasks and obtaining information from the Grid.

The construction activity is centred on implementing the architecture designed in the design activity through a technological platform for Grid computing previously studied whose tools and libraries can be obtained from the implementation repository. The construction activity consists of implementing the designed architecture (interfaces, components, classes, etc.) under a technological environment related to Grid computing and supported by mobile computing. This environment will be installed and configured so that it helps us implement the design model with the tools, mechanisms, methods and libraries available in the selected technological environment. In the repository the most used tools to build this kind of systems together with common services implemented in different programming languages, generated in other executions of the process are available. The aim of this activity is to obtain the final product, the secure Mobile Grid system, depending on a specific technological environment for Grid computing.

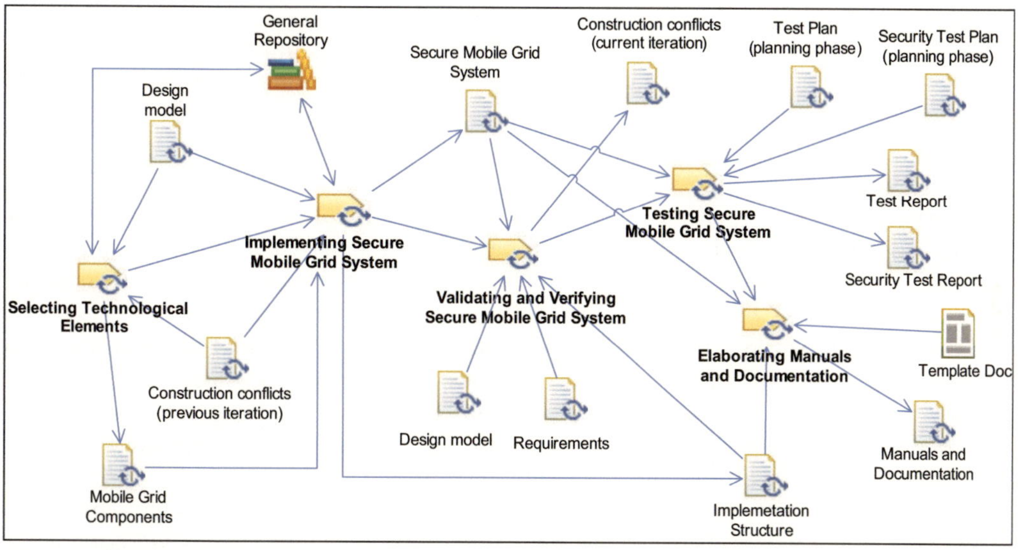


Fig. 4. Tasks of the Secure Mobile Grid System Construction activity

The construction activity is composed of tasks which implement the designed secure software architecture for obtaining an executable final product with the help of the tools and technologies available for Mobile Grid computing. Fig. 4 shows a graphical representation of the construction activity tasks using SPEM 2.0 diagrams. Initially, the "Selecting Technological Elements" task refers to study and analyze the different current technological approaches for Grid computing (Globus, gLite, PERMIS, VOMS, etc.) and choose the most appropriate that facilitates the implementation of the system. This choice together with the tools requirements and features are defined in the Mobile Grid Components artifact. The "Implementing Secure Mobile Grid System" task is the main task of this activity and converts the design elements into executable and deployed components running in different resources of different organizations. To implement the secure software architecture, we must take into account the chosen technological components and the specified aspects in the design activity. Once we have implemented the services interfaces, classes, services and protocols under the technological environment, we will generate executable code (files, packages, executable classes, objects, etc.) which represents the designed architecture and that offers solutions to the necessities and requirements initially raised, especially of security, for this kind of systems. Also, we must describe and indicate, in the implementation structure artifact, the decisions of implementation carried out as the generated files of a class, the relations between files and packages, the final deployment structure, what services interfaces and operations are being implemented and with what programming language, used communications protocols, exchanged messages format, standards and specifications used, and so on. Then, with the implemented architecture, the design model and the requirements, in the "Validating and Verifying Secure Mobile Grid System" task we validate that the system implementation fulfills and covers the requirements and we verify the right traceability from design to implementation. The tests and security tests of all components of the implemented system have to be checked in the "Testing Secure Mobile Grid System" activity, obtaining the possible failures and issues not considered in previous activities and which are important for protecting the system and for ensuring that the system is reliable and robust. Finally, we elaborate, in the "Elaborating Manuals and Documentation" activity, all the necessary documentation on how we have designed and implemented the application (decisions, configurations, tools requirements, files, languages, etc.) and the manuals of development for its maintenance and updateness, and user and execution manuals.

### 3.4 Prototype tool

To help in the building of use cases diagrams following the UML extension aforementioned, we have developed a tool, SMGridTool (Secure Mobile Grid Environments Tool) which provides a simple, automatic and intuitive way of building use cases diagrams especially designed for Secure Mobile Grid systems. This tool is focused on the construction and definition of secure Grid use cases diagrams, and on the management of the repository that stores reusable artifacts which can be reused in the construction of diagrams.
SMGridTool performs automatically the validation of the use cases diagrams, checking the constraints defined by the GridUCSec-profile for each use case and relationship. The tool automates the analysis activity of the development process for Secure Mobile Grid Systems, but our objective is that in future versions it will also support the design activity. To facilitate the user the completion of this activity, the prototype offers an easy to use graphic interface supported by Microsoft Visio controls for building diagrams. The use of Microsoft Visio 2007 activex controls also provides an easy way to reuse diagrams, export to other formats like images or xml files, and many more advantages.
In short, the SMGridTool has been developed to facilitate building and managing specific use cases diagrams for Mobile Grid environments which are necessary for carrying out an exhaustive and deep analysis of the needs and requirements of this kind of systems.

## 4. Case study

The real case study selected to apply the process is the media and journalism application that is a pilot Grid application of GREDIA, which is an FP6 project funded by the European Union and that provides a Grid application development platform, which will enable the integration of secure Grid middleware for managing mobile services and allowing mobile devices to participate in a protected data Grid as service providers, in a peer-to-peer manner, where journalists and photographers make their work available to a trusted network of peers at the moment it is produced, either from desktop or mobile devices. This pilot will bring together the market orientation and pervasiveness of mobile communication technology with the promise of a dynamically concerted use of resources and services provided through Grid infrastructures.

We want to build a system that will cater for the reporter who is on the move with lightweight equipment and wishes to capture and transmit news content. This user needs to safely and quickly upload the media to a secure server to make it easier for others to access, and to avoid situations where his/her device's battery dies or another malfunction destroys or makes his/her media unavailable.

To develop this pilot application, we will use an iterative and incremental approach so that for the end of the iterations cycle, we have developed the final product. Therefore, in a first iteration, that is shown here, we must select a part of the aims and goals of the system, of an acceptable size, so that we can apply the different activities and tasks to this part of the system and we can obtain reasonable artifacts, even a reduced version of the product. In the next iterations, that have been omitted here, this part of the system will be refined and extended with new elements and the process will again be applied to obtain a new version of the product. In the last iteration, the process will be applied to the whole system obtaining the final product.

In this case, we will describe the first iteration of the process for a set of initial needs, not all, and we will obtain in the analysis activity the functional and security requirements of the case study using the defined model GridUCSec-profile and the SMGridTool which help us build security use cases diagrams for Mobile Grids. The set of requirements have to be incorporated into the secure software architecture in the design activity and later, we will implement from this architecture, a first version of the product. We will put more emphasis on the part of security that is the original of this process omitting the software part that is generally built making use of other generic development processes.

### 4.1 Application of the analysis activity

The aim of this first iteration in the analysis activity is to define a set of requirements of the system (most of them) through the use cases diagrams built with the help of the SMGridTool and the repository of reusable elements of the process. We mainly focus on security requirements but without forgetting the rest of requirements.

#### Task A1. Defining UC of the application

Based on the initial needs and the scenarios defined for the media sector, a set of use cases have been identified along with a first level analysis. It is certainly expected that these will be refined during the design and construction activities according to a continuous feedback loop to be finalised with the final delivery of the Grid system, and with the subsequent iterations of the process. These use cases identified are: Add/edit Mobile user; Login to the system; Formulate the 'news' task; Notify Human Resources of task assignment; Search for news; Get query results; Record audio/video; Create news item; Submit news item; Join a Community; Review news item; Archive news item; Approve news item; Annotate news item; Assign news item publishing position; Display breaking news.

**Task A2. Identifying secure Mobile Grid UC**

Once we have identified the functional use cases of the application, now, we must identify all the use cases and security use cases for the Grid system that are related to the functional use cases of the application. These use cases for the Grid system include Grid use cases, security use cases, Grid security use cases, misuse cases and mobile use cases together with Grid actors and Misactors, all of them defined with the GridUCSec-profile. We use the reusable artifacts of the repository where many of these use cases for Grid systems and diagrams that can be easily used in this application and that help us obtain use cases, actors and associations that are necessary in this application are defined.

**Step A2.1. Identify generic Grid UC for the application.** We must act on the repository of Grid use cases to identify the generic Grid use cases that are needed to extract and that are related to the use cases defined in the previous task. To define the Grid use cases we will use the GridUCSec-profile defined as a model of the process and using the repository where a large set of Grid use cases are defined, we can build the Grid use case diagram, with the SMGridTool, where security use cases and misuse cases oriented to Mobile Grid are present. In the repository we have a set of generic use cases which have a common behaviour for any Grid systems and have been identified in other executions of the process and that can be used in this application. We select some of these generic Grid use cases that have relation with the functional use cases identified previously and are show in Fig. 5.

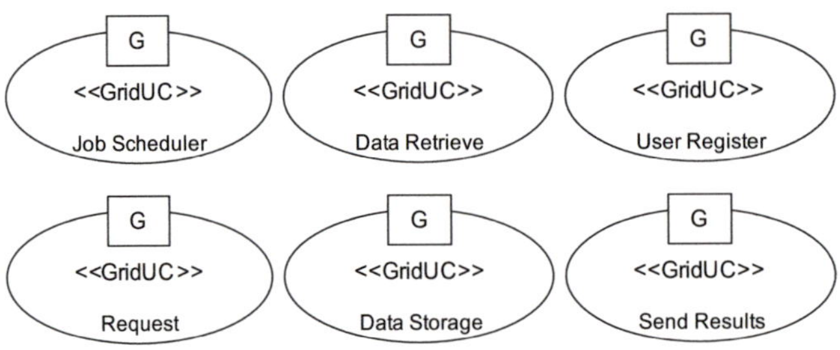


Fig. 5. Generic Grid Use Cases of the repository

These generic Grid use cases are defined based on the GridUCSec-profile, so that in the repository, we have all information related to these Grid use cases. For example, the information related to the "Job scheduler" Grid use case stored in the repository is shown in Fig. 6.

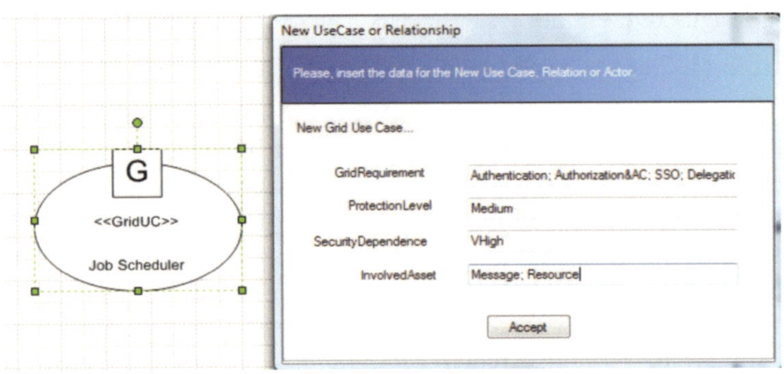


Fig. 6. Defining Tagged Values for "«GridUC» Job Scheduler" with SMGridTool

**Step A2.2. Identify security Assets of the application in a Mobile Grid environment.** In Mobile Grid environments we can identify a set of generic assets that we must protect for obtaining a secure Grid system, which are the following: User and system data (stored, transmitted); Identity information; Credentials (private keys, passwords); Accounting; CPU-/Storage-/Mobile devices-/Network-resources; General system.

In this first iteration of our case study, we define the most important assets related to the use cases aforementioned that we must protect and that are the reference for the identification of threats, attacks and security use cases. These assets are: Personal information about the journalist or editors; Media information used: photos, articles, recordings, videos, intellectual property rights; Exchange information: messages, queries, transactions.

**Step A2.3. Identify Threats, Attacks and Risks of the application in a Mobile Grid environment.** The set of threats and attacks that can occur in a Mobile Grid system is similar to that produced in a distributed system by adding those occurring in the mobile environment with wireless network and limited resources. Examples of threats are unauthorized disclosure of information, attacks to the content of a message through wireless links, denial-of-service attacks, network authentication related attacks, physical node attacks, alteration of information, and so on. In this first iteration, we can identify several possible types of threats to Information: Unauthorized access to Grid system; Unauthorized disclosure and alteration of information; Masquerade.

**Step A2.4. Identify the Security UC and Misuse cases from the repository.** Once we have defined the most significant threats and major assets to be protected in this first iteration, we start with the identification, definition and incorporation of security use cases and misuse cases for the application. In the repository, the main security use cases for Mobile Grid environments, and misuse cases that capture the behaviour of the main threats identified in these environments are defined. We can identify those security use cases and misuse cases that fit in with the attacks and threats for this application identified in the previous step.

In this first iteration, the misuse cases that we have found in the repository and that fit in with the threats identified for this application are: Alteration info, Disclosure info, Unauthorized access and Masquerade.

With these misuse cases, we can identify security use cases that mitigate them observing the information offered by the repository for security use cases and the diagrams defined where we can see the relationships of mitigation between security use cases and misuse cases. In case that the required use cases are not in the repository we can define them and specify relationships as it is convenient.

We find in the repository the security use cases (including Grid security use cases and Grid actors) that are related to the misuse cases identified. These security use cases are: Authenticate, Authorize access, Ensure Confidentiality and Ensure Integrity.

**Step A2.5. Security Assessment.** Finally, it is necessary to assess whether the threats are relevant according to the security level specified by the security objectives. Therefore we must estimate the security risks based on the relevant threats, their likelihood and their potential negative impacts, in other words, we have to estimate the impact (what may happen) and risk (what will probably happen) to which the assets in the system are exposed. We must therefore interpret the meaning of impact and risk. In Table 1 we define the impact and risk for some of the threats identified previously. We are going to evaluate risk and impact with five possible values: Very Low, Low, Medium, High and Very High. The likelihood of a threat could be: Very Frequent (daily event), Frequent (monthly event), Normal (once a year), Rare (once in several years).

As we can see in Table 1, all threats have to be dealt with because they cause a high or very high value of risk in the worst case, therefore, misuse cases that represent these threats must be studied and analyzed in this first iteration and will take part of the Grid use cases diagram that we will build in the next task.

| **Threat** | **Unauthorized access to Grid system** | |
|---|---|---|
| *Impact* | MEDIUM if the authorization privileges are very limited (i.e. only reading). | VERY HIGH if the opposite is the case |
| *Attack* | Unauthorized access | |
| *Probability* | Normal | Normal |
| *Risk* | HIGH | VERY HIGH |
| **Threat** | **Unauthorized alteration of information** | |
| *Impact* | LOW if there is no personal information modified | HIGH if the opposite is the case |
| *Attack* | Modification of information | |
| *Probability* | Frequent | Frequent |
| *Risk* | LOW | HIGH |

Table 1. Assessment of Impact and Risk

**Task A3. Building secure Mobile Grid UC diagram**

After identifying functional use cases of the application, generic Grid use cases related, misuse cases that represent the threats identified and security use cases that protect from those threats, we are able to build the overall use cases diagram and to define the relationships between them following the UML GridUCSec-profile and using the SMGridTool which help us build the diagram and manage the repository where there are defined use cases diagrams that we can incorporate into the overall diagram.

In previous tasks, we have been studying and analyzing artifacts of the repository (use cases) that define common features for Grid environments and that can be usable for this specific application, as it is. These reusable artifacts have been identified and used in the previous tasks in an isolate way resolving the tasks suggested and obtaining concrete results of the application analysis. Now we have to add all these defined artifacts to the use cases diagram of the application and define the relationships, according to the GridUCSec-profile, between functional use cases, generic Grid use cases, security use cases and misuse cases.

All use cases and relationships defined in the overall diagram have associated a set of properties and values that indicate the behaviour, function and semantic of each use case and relationship. These properties may be already predefined for reusable use cases in the repository, or have to be defined by the developer within the diagram identifying specific properties of each use case and the different relationships between them.

These properties are defined with the GridUCSec-profile model that has been elaborated for capturing the specific features and values of the use cases for Mobile Grid systems. As the overall diagram is complex to define here, we will describe a sub-diagram for showing how the GridUCSec-profile is used in the definition of the use cases and relationships involved. Fig. 7 shows a sub-diagram of the overall diagram which will be used for describing its elements according to the GridUCSec-profile model.

The "«GridSecurityUC» Authenticate" models the authentication service of the application and is responsible for protecting the "Login" UC and for mitigating the "«MisuseCase»

Unauthorized access" misuse case which threatens the "Login" UC. The "«GridSecurityUC» Authorize access" models the authorization service and is responsible for protecting the "«MobileUC» Search news" UC, for mitigating the "«MisuseCase» Unauthorized access" misuse case and for permitting the execution of "Login" and "«GridUC» Request". We also have the "«MisuseCase» Alteration info" misuse case that threatens the modification or alteration of the information exchanged in the messages every time that a request is sent to the system. This threat is mitigated by the "«GridSecurityUC» Ensure Confidentiality" and "«GridSecurityUC» Ensure Integrity" UCs which are part of the reusable sub-diagram stored in the repository. Finally, the "«MobileUC» Search News" UC is identified as a mobile UC due to the possible mobility of the user who requests information from the system from the mobile devices. This mobile UC includes the "«GridUC» Request" UC which is responsible for making the request in a secure manner.

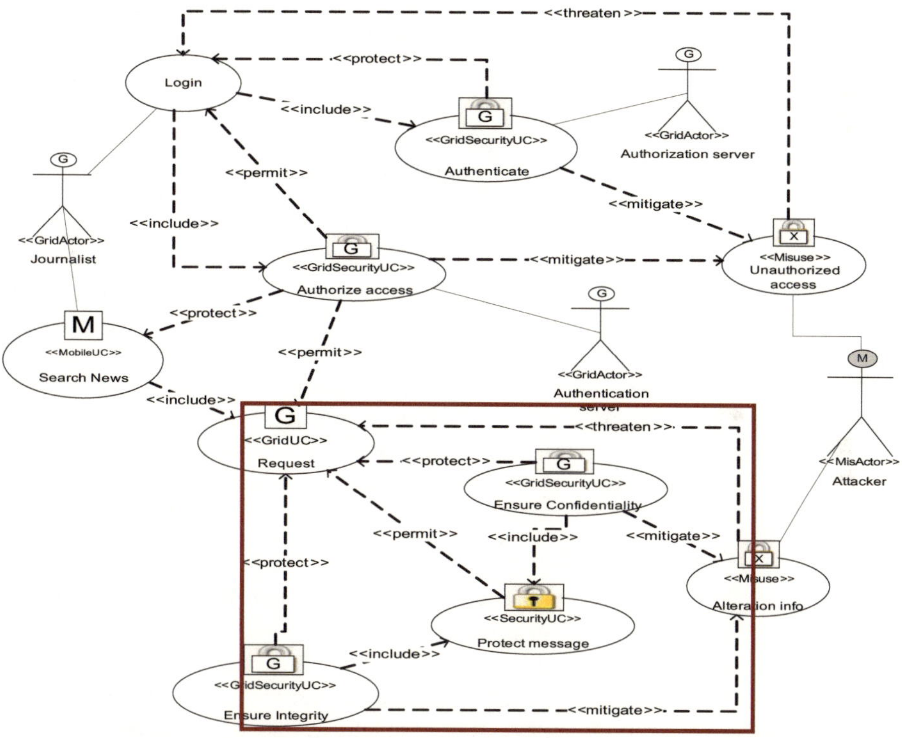


Fig. 7. Sub-diagram of the overall diagram of the application

In order to build the resulting diagram, we have used a reusable UCs diagram (framed sub-diagram shown in Fig. 7) which is available in the repository and is defined by using our UML profile, to model a common scenario that ensures confidentiality and integrity of a request in Grid environments, which our application requires. This sub-diagram shows how the "«GridUC» Request" UC is protected, through «protect» relationships, by the "«GridSecurityUC» Ensure Confidentiality" and "«GridSecurityUC» Ensure Integrity" security UCs which mitigate the "«MisuseCase» Alteration info" misuse case that threatens "«GridUC» Request". It also establishes a «permit» relationship from the "«SecurityUC» Protect message" security UC, meaning that once the message is protected, the request can be carried out.

Last, we should validate this diagram checking if the relationships between use cases are well defined and there is not redundancy or faults. This can be made in a first iteration or can go refining in successive iterations of this task when we add new use cases and relationships. This validation is automatic using the SMGridTool that is responsible for controlling the constraints of the use cases, the relationships between elements and that the possible values selected are within the range specified in the GridUCSec-profile.

The output artifact of this task is Use Cases View which contains all use cases diagrams generated in this task and the description of each use case, actor and relationship defined within the diagram.

**Task A4. Supporting with UML models**

UML models as interaction diagrams are used in this task for completing the capture of requirements and their dynamic behaviour. With these models we can define the actions between actors and use cases, and the flow of events produced between the elements of the diagram. With UML models we want to complete the definition of use cases knowing better the behaviour of the system and all the involved elements for refining the use cases model with new aspects identified thanks to these UML models.

In the repository there is a defined set of generic interaction diagrams which are related to reusable use cases. So we can instantiate these generic diagrams for the specific use cases of this application. In this first iteration, we have identified the Grid security use case called "«GridSecurityUC» Ensure Integrity" of the reusable repository, which has also a generic sequence diagram associated that we have to instantiate with the actors involved in this scenario. To finish this task, besides of interaction diagrams, other diagrams that completely define the behaviour of the use cases and facilitate the specification of requirements are defined. In this step, we will follow the analysis stage of the Unified Process, which defines classes diagrams, use case realizations, and initially describes packages and development diagrams which will be used and refined in the design activity.

The output artifacts of this task are: Static view whit diagrams generated applying the Unified Process, and Interaction view with the sequence and collaboration diagrams associated with the use cases and scenarios.

**Task A5. Verifying Analysis model**

Once the artifacts have been defined, we must verify that they have been correctly generated, that is, that the UML diagrams, such as for example the sequence diagram for message integrity, define the correct elements involved in the use case or in a scenario of use cases, in this case, the "«GridSecurityUC» Ensure Integrity" use case. This verification should also be made with the remaining diagrams and guides by the use cases defined in this activity.

**Task A6. Specifying requirements**

This is the last task of analysis activity and it specifies the set of requirements extracted from the use cases identified during all the previous tasks obtaining a description of functional and non-functional requirements of the system. This description should indicate all elements involved in the definition of requirements together with the interactions between use cases and actors and the attributes of these elements. All this information has been generated in previous tasks through use cases models using the GridUCSec-profile and with UML models. Here we define the requirements in natural language but we know that there are templates for the definition of requirements where the main characteristics of the models generated in this activity can be summarized and formally described in a document which will be part of the analysis model in future works. This task is carried out through review meetings by involved stakeholders in this task and the artifacts elaborated in previous tasks.

**Step A6.1. Specify functional requirements.** The functional requirements together with the related use cases can be clustered into the following categories: Network specific requirements; File and database management requirements; Query and retrieval requirements; User Interface requirements; Requirements for providing miscellaneous functionality.

**Step A6.2. Specify security requirements.** The security requirements are distinguished according to the different security services. They relate to safeguarding the accuracy and completeness of data and processing methods and the prevention of unauthorized entities to access and modify data. A first vision of security requirements that can be extracted from the functional use cases and security use cases of the application are: System requires authentication mechanisms for user identification; Users are classified into groups; System needs to give the capability to the administration users to define user group access permissions; Users can access to specific content based on their role; System uses data encryption; Single authentication process is required for accessing the functionality of the system. These security requirements extracted from use cases together with the security requirements that are defined in the security use cases can be specified into the following general categories: Data confidentiality; Trust and reputation; Authorisation and access control; Data integrity and authenticity; Authentication.

**Step A6.3. Specify non-functional requirements.** Based on the general requirements identified in (Fenkam et al., 2002; Jacob et al., 2005; Manish Parashar et al., 2005), this step presents the non-functional requirements, which should be considered during the development of the Grid system: Performance; Scalability/Expandability; Resource Management Capabilities; Semantic Grouping of Information; Availability; Security; Fairness; Robustness, Fault Detection and Recovery; Maintainability; Portability; Distribution; Usability; User interface; System stability; Deployment.

The output artifacts of this task are: "Requirements" artifact that defines all requirements (functional and non-functional) specified in this task, and "Analysis conflicts" artifact that identifies the possible conflicts or errors found in the specification of requirements and in the building of the use cases diagrams. This last artifact will be an input artifact for the subsequent iterations of this activity, but we have found none.

### 4.2 Application of the design activity

With these requirements, in the design activity, we can design the secure software architecture which covers all these requirements (functional, non-functional and those of security). The software architecture has been omittied for simplicity, and we focused on the reference security architecture specifically defined for the process.

**Task D1. Designing Mobile Grid Software Architecture**

This task defines the software architecture of the system using traditional methods and mechanisms of software engineering as the Unified Process, OPEN, OpenUP, etc. The software architecture is designed from functional requirements and use cases of the application that have been analyzed following the techniques and guides offered by some development processes but its input artifact is the analysis model elaborated in the previous activity of this process.

The output artifact is a software architecture oriented to Mobile Grid systems (that we have omitted here).

**Task D2. Designing Mobile Grid Security Architecture**

This task defines the security architecture where all security aspects of the application are taken into account. The aim of this task is to design a security architecture whose services and components cover the security requirements and needs for this case study and can be integrated with the software architecture designed in the previous task.

The input artifact is the analysis model with all use cases and requirements specified in the analysis activity.

**Step D2.1. Find architecturally significant security UC.** In this first iteration of the process, we are working with a reduced set of security use cases for simplicity, so that the same security use cases identified in the analysis activity will be selected for developing the different tasks of the design activity of the process. These security use cases selected are: Authenticate, Authorize access, Ensure Confidentiality, and Ensure Integrity. Each one of these security use cases are associated with some or many security services of the reference security architecture which will be identified in the next step.

**Step D2.2. Relate Security UC – Security Services.** Following the association rules defined for this process between security requirements and security services, we have that the security services to consider for the security architecture of this application from the security use cases identified in the previous activity are: Authorization, Authentication, Credential Management, Identity Management, Trust Management, Confidentiality and Integrity. We cannot forget the Grid Security Policy service and the Mobile Policy service which are needed to manage the different policies of the system. These security services are obtained of the relationship with the security requirements which are defined as tagged values in the GridUCSec-profile.

**Step D2.3. Instantiate Reference Security Architecture.** Each security use case is associated with one or more security requirements, and the security services associated with these security use cases cover the security requirements represented by these security use cases. Therefore, the aim is to obtain a set of security services which cover and take into account the security requirements represented by the four security use cases. In Fig. 8 we can see the set of security services necessary for fulfilling the security requirements specified in the first iteration with the four security use cases selected.

**Step D2.4. Define security policies.** Security policies must be defined for the services identified in the previous step and they must indicate the security rules allowed for each service along with protocols, mechanisms, attributes, etc., admitted by the service. The policies are stored in one or more LDAP repositories distributed throughout the Grid system but always available online.

We must have security policies associated with each Grid security service of the instantiated architecture (for example, the security policy of the authorization service); we must also define security policies for messages exchanged between services, or inbound to the system (for example, each message must be protected against attacks on the integrity and confidentiality of the message body); and we must define security policies for inter-, intra-organizational partnerships (the sending of messages should be protected from attacks on privacy, integrity, confidentiality, and the sender entity must be trusted).

Grid Security Policies govern and control the overall security of the Grid system and are associated with the security services, with inter-, intra- organizational partnerships, with

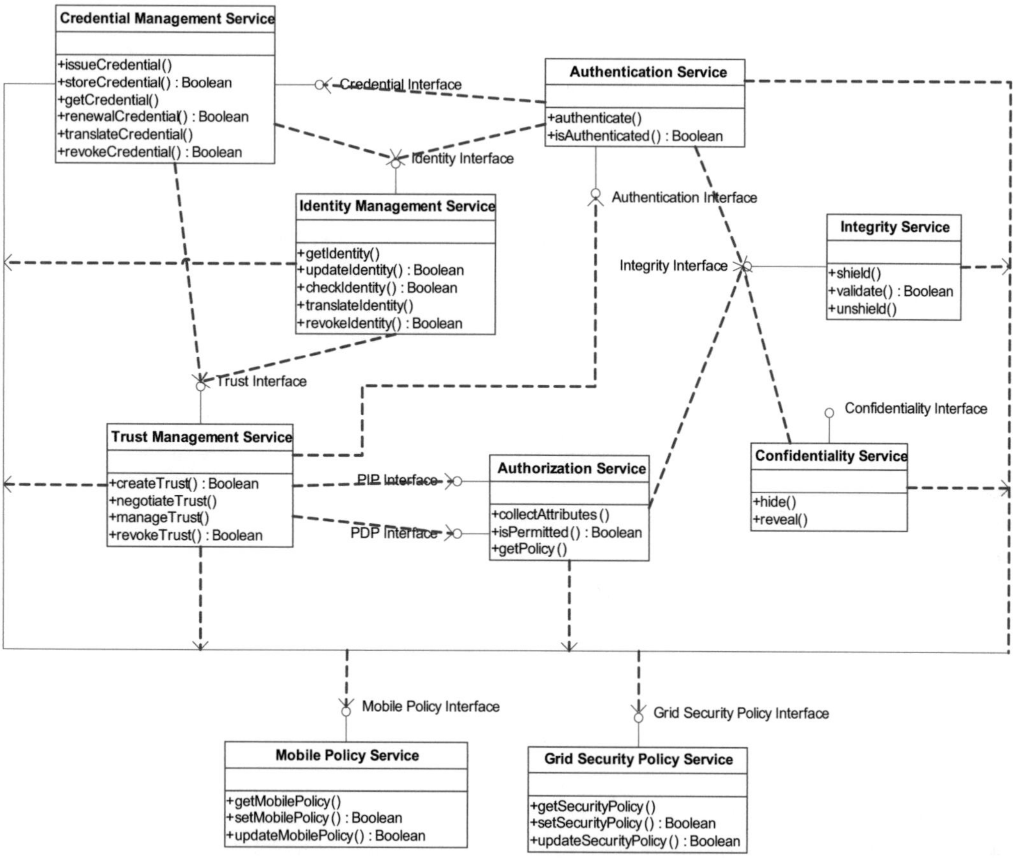


Fig. 8. Services and interfaces of Security Architecture instantiated for this case study

communication and exchange of information between resource users and Grid entities. Mobile Policies govern the use of mobile devices and wireless communications by establishing rules, standards, norms and advices of how resources must act on the mobile environment, protect their data, communicate via protocols, sending data, etc.

The output artifact is a part of the security architecture designed from the set of use cases selected and with the help of the reference security architecture.

**Task D3. Designing/Integrating Secure Mobile Grid Software Architecture**

This task cannot be applied because for this case study we have omitted the part of the software of the architecture and we cannot see how the integration is carried out. Basically we have to define how the various elements of the system, software architecture and security architecture, potentially constructed at different times, should be brought together into a single architecture, a secure software architecture.

Elements of the security architecture should be integrated into the software architecture because many software elements have to make use of the security elements, and the security elements have to act over the software elements to provide security in the system. Therefore, we must define the relations between these elements through the interfaces of the services, defining the protocols and mechanisms of exchange, policies, permissions and constraints.

Moreover, the static, dynamic and deployment views of all these elements of the secure software architecture are very useful to understand and know better the architecture and the interactions between all its elements when the decisions of implementation are made in the implementation activity. These views are defined using traditional methods with the secure software architecture as input artifact.

**Task D4. Specifying Secure Mobile Grid Software Architecture**

Systems Architect and Security Architect created an initial version of the document of secure software architecture in which all the information outlined in the previous points is widespread. This document follows the basic points of the document specifying the functional architecture consistent with IEEE 1471-2000 adding new players, views, views, and packages of views of security.

**Task D5. Validating/Verifying Secure Mobile Grid Software Architecture**

This task validates and verifies the designed architecture. We can only validate and verify the security architecture that is that we are developing in this case study. The analysis model with the specified use cases and requirements and the architecture designed in this task are the input artifacts to validate and verify the architecture.

**Step D5.1. Validate designed architecture.** Using as input the document of specification of secure software architecture (although in this case study we will only have the security architecture, the software architecture has not been shown), the process of validating the security architecture was done through review meetings by the involved roles in this task and it was found that the security architecture response to the needs of involved stakeholders and, moreover, it is integrated without any impact into the designed software architecture.

**Step D5.2. Verify design model.** It was verified that the traceability between requirements and services designed through the rules of association was successfully performed. Therefore, artifacts of the activity analysis are needed as input to the design activity and are the basis for developing the artifacts of the design model.

**Step D5.3. Identify, study and analyze conflicts.** In addition, it was observed that this architecture was not in conflict with any other non-functional requirements, and that all elements designed in this iteration were well integrated and there was no irregularity or inconsistency.

### 4.3 Application of the construction activity

Finally, in the construction activity, a possible implementation of the elements previously designed is carried out. In this first iteration, we can implement a set of elements of the designed architecture that are independent of the rest of elements or with little relationships for being implemented in an isolated way.

**Task C1. Selecting Technological Elements**

This task defines the technological environment that we must use in order to implement the system with the help of tools and libraries oriented to Grid computing.

**Step C1.1. Study Grid middleware, tools and libraries.** Within the Gredia project, a series of tools and platforms to develop the different proposals that are being carried out with reference to Grid systems and mobile devices are being used. These same tools will be used here for their perfect integration into GREDIA and because they are the most used and appropriate for these systems. This tool is Globus toolkit which provides software tools that make it easier to build computational grids and grid-based applications. Also PERMIS and VOMS can be used as security infrastructure for authorization and access control, and Java CoG kits that is a tool which provides the implementation in Java of some components of Globus toolkit.

**Step C1.2. Install and Configure Grid environment.** With this set of tools and libraries identified we can begin the installation and configuration in a way that all components are available under the same platform. Globus defines a wide set of manuals and documentation[1] for the installation and configuration of GT4, such as the quickstart guide and the administrador's guide where the steps to carry out for that GT4 is implemented and prepared to its use are indicated. The Java CoG Kit provides convenient access to Grid middleware through the Java framework. The version 4.1.2 of the Java CoG Kit has been released and guides, manuals and documentation are available to be downloaded[2]. Finally, PERMIS[3] will be used as an authorization infrastructure integrated into the Globus toolkit[4] that helps us implement the authorization service designed in the previous activity. The Java libraries, PERMIS package, Globus toolkit, XML files, LDAP repository, policy files, etc. are the output artifacts of this task.

**Task C2. Implementing Secure Mobile Grid System**

For this first iteration, we will only consider the authorization service because we believe it is the most comprehensive one that takes into account many aspects of the technologies chosen and that requires more effort to install and configure. We have as input artefact, just one element of the design model (the authorization service, we have omitted the rest) and all grid components identified and installed previously. The Authorization service has two interfaces, PIP interface and PDP interface. The first has one operation that is collectAttributes() and the latter has two operation that is isPermitted() and getPolicy(). Globus provides the ideal framework for the authorization and permits us to create our own authorization framework. We have to implement the PDP interface and PIP interface of our authorization service. Globus shows how we can change and implement our own PDPs and PIPs into the Globus platform.

The authorization service of the reference security architecture designed in the design activity defines one operation for PIP interface and two operations for PDP interface. All these operations define a set of parameters that Globus uses and implements. Therefore, if we define the interfaces of Globus for the security services of the architecture, we can easily implement a robust authorization service. This activity belongs more to the programming field than to the research field, which is out of the scope of this paper to get and to implement Java code for security services.

As output artifacts, we obtain a part of the secure Mobile Grid system artifact (the part corresponding to the implementation of the authorization service), and the implementation structure of the authorization service.

**Task C3. Validating and Verifying Secure Mobile Grid System**

This task validates and verifies that the system which is being built fits to the requirements and follows a right traceability of artifacts during the development. We need as input

[1] www.globus.org/toolkit/docs/4.0/

[2] www.cogkit.org/release/4_1_2/

[3] http://sec.cs.kent.ac.uk/permis/

[4] http://sec.cs.kent.ac.uk/permis/integrationProjects/GT.shtml

artifacts the security requirements (because the rest of requirements are not dealt with here) specified for the elements selected in the design, the part of the design model developed, the structure of how the authorization service has been implemented and the own authorization service (classes and packages).

**Step C3.1. Validate implemented system.** In this first iteration we can only validate the components that have been implemented because the end system has not been constructed yet. We can validate that the security services of authentication, authorization, confidentiality and integrity which have been designed in the previous activity are implemented with security mechanisms that carry out the protection of the system complying with a set of requirements specified in the analysis activity. In this case the implemented services cover authentication, mutual authentication, confidentiality, integrity, trust, interoperability, flexibility and single sig-on. These implemented services help us fulfill other requirements but must be supported with more security services that will be implemented in the next iterations. When the system is totally built, apart from validating elements which have not been validated yet, it validates the whole set of elements, i.e. how the elements relate and interact to provide more security and cover more requirements.

**Step C3.2. Verify construction model.** We verify that the implemented services, interfaces and any other element have followed the methods and techniques indicated in the process ensuring the traceability between artifacts thus justifying that all artifacts previously defined in the process are necessary for achieving the aim of implementation.

**Step C3.3. Identify, study and analyze conflicts.** In a first iteration in which a few elements are selected for their development incompatibilities or errors do not generally appear. It is in the latest iteration in which all elements are implemented and integrated when we can identify a greater number of them. We declare that all elements implemented in this iteration were well built and there was no irregularity or inconsistency with the rest of elements.

#### Task C4. Testing the Secure Mobile Grid System

The tests of the system are carried out once the system has been completely built. Nevertheless in this first iteration we have implemented the authorization service into Globus that can be tested. As this case study is focused on the part of security, we only have security elements implemented, such as the authorization service; therefore the test must be carried out over this element.

These tests consist in adding users, roles and policies to the system and perform calls to the Grid services requesting the access to some data or execution of a simple job (information appeared in the security test plan and test plan of the planning activity of the process). In these tests, we must study some cases where the authorization service permits access (returning PERMIT) and other cases in which access is denied (returning DENY) to check their correct implementation and logical functioning. For the authorization service we can confirm that the tests obtained the expected result.

The output artifacts indicate the tests executed adding to the reports the results obtained from a set of input data, and their valoration.

#### Task C5. Preparing Manuals and Documentation

This task defines the manuals and documentation of development, configuration, installation and user but once the system has been completely developed, therefore until the last iteration it is not recommendable to elaborate them due to the possible changes and refinements of the system.

## 5. Conclusion

This paper has proposed a development process for secure Mobile Grid systems (SecMobGrid), which enables to develop in a systematic and secure way a Grid system with mobile devices incorporating security from the earliest stages of development and based on the reuse of artifacts which have been generated in the different applications of the process.
This is an iterative and incremental process and exploits the reusability of the different artifacts that are generated during the process. This process is composed of several activities and among them, we can highlight the following: the analysis activity where all system requirements (especially security requirements) are captured and specified basing on specific use cases, which are defined using a UML profile (GridUCSec-profile); the design activity focused on the construction of a security architecture for this kind of systems from the reference security architecture developed that defines the minimum set of security services covering all possible security requirements that can be specified in mobile Grid systems; and the construction activity that is in charge of the implementation of the system using the existing tools for the development of Grid systems.
Moreover, the prototype tool called "SMGridTool" that gives automated support for the development of the tasks of the analysis activity of the SecMobGrid process is presented. Finally, in order to validate and improve the SecMobGrid development process, the result of its application to a case study of a real Mobile Grid system is offered.
As future work, we will concrete and refine the generic tasks of the used development processes that have been incorporated into the SecMobGrid process. We will refine and improve the parameters and tagged values of the GridUCSec-profile for capturing the most important aspects and features of Mobile Grid systems and we will improve the reference security architecture for that the security aspects considered in the analysis activity through the GridUCSec-profile can easily be incorporated as parameters into the interfaces of the security architecture, into the definition of policies of the system or into the decisions of implementation. Finally, we will carry out new case studies for a continuous improvement of the SecMobGrid process in other Grid environments and dominions.

## 6. Acknowledgments

This research is part of the following projects: QUASIMODO (PAC08-0157-0668), SISTEMAS (PII2I09-0150-3135) and SEGMENT (HITO-09-138) financed by the "Viceconsejería de Ciencia y Tecnología de la Junta de Comunidades de Castilla-La Mancha" (Spain) and FEDER, and MEDUSAS (IDI-20090557), BUSINESS (PET2008-0136) and PEGASO/MAGO (TIN2009-13718-C02-01) financed by the "Ministerio de Ciencia e Innovación (CDTI)" (Spain). Special acknowledgment to GREDIA (FP6-IST-034363) funded by European Commission.

## 7. References

Artelsmair, C. and R. Wagner, 2003. Towards a Security Engineering Process. *The 7th World Multiconference on Systemics, Cybernetics and Informatics*, Orlando, Florida, USA.

Bass, L., F. Bachmann, R. J. Ellison, A. P. Moore and M. Klein, 2004. "Security and survivability reasoning frameworks and architectural design tactics." *SEI.*

Bhanwar, S. and S. Bawa, 2008. Securing a Grid. *World Academy of Science, Engineering and Technology.*

Breu, R., K. Burger, M. Hafner, J. Jürjens, G. Popp, V. Lotz and G.Wimmel, 2003. Key issues of a formally based process model for security engineering. *International Conference on Software and Systems Engineering and their Applications.*

Dail, H., O. Sievert, F. Berman, H. Casanova, A. YarKhan, S. Vadhiyar, J. Dongarra, C. Liu, L. Yang, D. Angulo and I. Foster, 2004. Scheduling In The Grid Application Development Software Project. *Grid resource management:state of the art and future trends*: 73-98.

EGEE Middleware Design Team. (2004). "EGEE Middleware Architecture." from https://edms.cern.ch/document/476451/.

Fenkam, P., S. Dustdar, E. Kirda, G. Reif and H. Gall, 2002. Towards an Access Control System for Mobile Peer-to-Peer Collaborative Environments. *Eleventh IEEE International Workshops on Enabling Technologies: Infrastructure for Collaborative Enterprises (WETICE'02).*

Flechais, I., M. A. Sasse and S. M. V. Hailes, 2003. Bringing Security Home: A process for developing secure and usable systems Workshop on New Security Paradigms. Ascona, Switzerland, ACM Press: 49--57.

Foster, I. and C. Kesselman, 2004. *The Grid2: Blueprint for a Future Computing Infrastructure.* San Francisco, CA, Morgan Kaufmann Publishers; 2 edition.

Foster, I., C. Kesselman, J. M. Nick and S. Tuecke, 2002. The Physiology of the Grid: An Open Grid Services Architecture for Distributed Systems Integration. Open Grid Service Infrastructure WG, Global Grid Forum.

Gartner. (2007). "Gartner Says Worldwide PDA Shipments Top 17.7 Million in 2006." Gartner Press Release, from http://www.gartner.com/it/page.jsp?id=500898.

Gartner. (2009). "Gartner Says Worldwide Mobile Phone Sales Declined 8.6 Per Cent and Smartphones Grew 12.7 Per Cent in First Quarter of 2009." Gartner Press Release, from http://www.gartner.com/it/page.jsp?id=985912.

Giorgini, P., H. Mouratidis and N. Zannone, 2007. Modelling Security and Trust with Secure Tropos. *Integrating Security and Software Engineering: Advances and Future Visions.* H. M. a. P. Giorgini, Idea Group Publishing: 160-189.

Graham, D. (2006). "Introduction to the CLASP Process." from https://buildsecurityin.us-cert.gov/daisy/bsi/articles/best-practices/requirements/548.html.

Guan, T., E. Zaluska and D. D. Roure, 2005. A Grid Service Infrastructure for Mobile Devices. *First International Conference on Semantics, Knowledge, an Grid (SKG 2005),* Beijing, China.

Haley, C. B., J. D. Moffet, R. Laney and B. Nuseibeh, 2006. A framework for security requirements engineering. *Software Engineering for Secure Systems Workshop,* Shangai, China.

Humphrey, M., M. R. Thompson and K. R. Jackson, 2005. "Security for Grids." *Lawrence Berkeley National Laboratory. Paper LBNL-54853.*

IEEE, 2000. Recommended Practice for Architectural Description of Software-Intensive Systems (IEEE Std 1471-2000). . New York, NY, Institute of Electrical and Electronics Engineers: 29.

Jacob, B., M. Brown, K. Fukui and N. Trivedi, 2005. *Introduction to Grid computing,* IBM Redbooks.

Jacobson, I., G. Booch and J. Rumbaugh, 1999. *The Unified Software Development Process*, Addison-Wesley Professional.

Jameel, H., U. Kalim, A. Sajjad, S. Lee and T. Jeon, 2005. Mobile-To-Grid Middleware: Bridging the gap between mobile and Grid environments. *European Grid Conference EGC 2005*, Amsterdam, The Netherlands, Springer.

Jana, D., A. Chaudhuri and N. B. Bhaumik, 2009. "Privacy and Anonymity Protection in Computational Grid Services." *International Journal of Computer Science and Applications* 6(1): 98-107.

Jurjens, J., 2001. Towards Development of Secure Systems Using UMLsec. *Fundamental Approaches to Software Engineering (FASE/ETAPS)*.

Jurjens, J., 2002. UMLsec: Extending UML for Secure Systems Development. *5th International Conference on the Unified Modeling Language (UML)*, Dresden, Germany.

Jürjens, J., 2005. *Secure Systems Development with UML*, Springer.

Kalim, U., H. Jameel, A. Sajjad and S. Lee, 2005. Mobile-to-Grid Middleware: An Approach for Breaching the Divide Between Mobile and Grid. *4th International Conference on Networking*, Reunion Island, France, Springer.

Kolonay, R. and M. Sobolewski, 2004. Grid Interactive Service-oriented Programming Environment. *Concurrent Engineering: The Worldwide Engineering Grid*, Tsinghua, China, Press and Springer Verlag.

Kruchten, P., 2000. *The Rational Unified Process: An Introduction*, Addison-Wesley.

Kumar, A. and S. R. Qureshi, 2008. Integration of Mobile Computing with Grid Computing: A Middleware Architecture. *2nd National Conference on Challenges & Opportunities in Information Technology (COIT-2008)*, Mandi Gobindgarh, India.

Kwok-Yan, L., Z. Xi-Bin, C. Siu-Leung, M. Gu and S. Jia-Guang, 2004. "Enhancing Grid Security Infrastructure to Support Mobile Computing Nodes." *Lecture Notes in Computer Science* 2908/2003: 42-54.

Lodderstedt, T., D. Basin and J. Doser, 2002. SecureUML: A UML-Based Modeling Language for Model-Driven Security. *5th International Conference on the Unified Modeling Language (UML), 2002*, Dresden, Germany, Springer.

Manish Parashar, Zhen Li, Hua Liu, Vincent Matossian and C. Schmidt, 2005. Enabling Autonomic Grid Applications: Requirements, Models and Infrastructure. *Self-star Properties in Complex Information Systems*, Springer. 3460: 273-290.

Mouratidis, H. and P. Giorgini, 2006. *Integrating Security and Software Engineering: Advances and Future Vision*, Idea Group Publishing.

Mouratidis, H., P. Giorgini and G. Manson, 2005. "When security meets software engineering: A case of modelling secure information systems." *Information Systems* 30(8): 609-629.

Open Group. (2009). "TOGAF™ Version 9 -- The Open Group Architecture Framework." from http://www.opengroup.org/architecture/togaf9-doc/arch/.

Phan, T., L. Huang, N. Ruiz and R. Bagrodia, 2005. Chapter 5: Integrating Mobile Wireless Devices Into the Computational Grid. *Mobile Computing Handbook*. M. Ilyas and I. Mahgoub, Auerbach Publications.

Riaz, M., S. L. Kiani, A. Shehzad and S. Lee, 2005. Bringing Handhelds to the Grid Resourcefully: A Surrogate Middleware Approach. *Computational Science and Its Applications – ICCSA 2005*, Singapore, Lecture Notes.

Romberg, M., 2002. "The UNICORE Grid Infrastructure." *Scientific Programming* 10(2): 149-157.

Rosado, D. G., E. Fernández-Medina and J. López, 2009a. Applying a UML Extension to build Use Cases diagrams in a secure mobile Grid application. *5th International Workshop on Foundations and Practices of UML, FP-UML 2009*, Gramado, Brasil, LNCS 5833.

Rosado, D. G., E. Fernández-Medina and J. López, 2009b. Reusable Security Use Cases for Mobile Grid environments. *Workshop on Software Engineering for Secure Systems, in conjunction with the 31st International Conference on Software Engineering*, Vancouver, Canada.

Rosado, D. G., E. Fernández-Medina and J. López, 2010a. "Security Services Architecture for Secure Mobile Grid Systems." *Journal of Systems Architecture. Special Issue on Security and Dependability Assurance of Software Architectures* (article in press).

Rosado, D. G., E. Fernández-Medina, J. López and M. Piattini, 2010b. "Analysis of Secure Mobile Grid Systems: A Systematic Approach." *Information and Software Technology* 52: 517-536.

Rosado, D. G., E. Fernández-Medina, J. López and M. Piattini, 2010c. "Developing a secure mobile Grid system through a UML extension." *Journal of Universal Computer Science* (to be published in 2010).

Rosado, D. G., E. Fernández-Medina, J. López and M. Piattini, 2010d. "Systematic Design of Secure Mobile Grid Systems." *Journal of Network and Computer Applications* (under review).

Sajjad, A., H. Jameel, U. Kalim, S. M. Han, Y.-K. Lee and S. Lee, 2005. AutoMAGI - an Autonomic middleware for enabling Mobile Access to Grid Infrastructure. *Joint International Conference on Autonomic and Autonomous Systems and International Conference on Networking and Services - (icas-icns'05).*

Steel, C., R. Nagappan and R. Lai, 2005. Chapter 8.The Alchemy of Security Design Methodology, Patterns, and Reality Checks. *Core Security Patterns:Best Practices and Strategies for J2EE™, Web Services, and Identity Management*, Prentice Hall PTR/Sun Micros: 1088.

The AKOGRIMO project. from http://www.akogrimo.org/.

# Part 3

## Grid Enabled Applications

# 10

# Grid Computing for Artificial Intelligence

Yuya Dan
*Matsuyama University*
*Japan*

## 1. Introduction

This chapter is concerned in grid computing for artificial intelligence systems. In general, grid computing enables us to process a huge amount of data in any fields of discipline. Scientific computing, calculation of the accurate value of $\pi$, search for Mersenne prime numbers, analysis of protein molecular structure, weather dynamics, data analysis, business data mining, simulation are examples of application for grid computing. As is well known that supercomputers have very high performance in calculation, however, it is quite expensive to use them for a long time. On the other hand, grid computing using idle resources on the Internet may be running on the reasonable cost.

*Shogi* is a traditional game involving two players in Japan as similar as chess, which is more complicated than chess in rule of play. Figure 1 shows the set of *Shogi* and initial state of 40 pieces on 9 x 9 board. According to game theory, both chess and *Shogi* are two-person zero-sum game with perfect information. They are not only a popular game but also a target in the research of artificial intelligence.

Fig. 1. Picture of *Shogi* set including 40 pieces on a 9 x 9 board. There are the corresponding king, rook, knight, pawn, and other pieces. Six kinds of pieces can change their role like pawns in chess when they reach the opposite territory.

The information systems for *Shogi* need to process astronomical combinations of possible positions to move. It is described by Dan (4) that the grid systems for *Shogi* is effective in reduction of computational complexity with collaboration from computational resources on the Internet. A solution to next move problems as artificial intelligence systems will be discussed in more detail in the chapter.
The chapter introduces the history and current state of computer *Shogi* systems, and the applicaion of grid computing for thinking routines for next move problems, then proposes an idea of the interaction between human and grid computing in game theory. Moreover, we suggest possibility of the human grid computing for artificial intelligence systems. It is described that the present situation of computer *Shogi* systems and the possibility of the human grid computing which assists the position evaluation function with human intuition. Proposed model in the chapter seems to be applied to any other efficient systems. The wisdom of crowds can make up qualitatively for grid systems essentially based on the concept of Web 2.0. While the design of the human grid computing is only proposed, the development and the implementation of that are left open.
In the autumn of 2010, the grid system for *Shogi* is going to challenge against a human expert player of *Shogi*. The system is not human grid system, however, it is the first time to collect computing resources in order to play against a human expert player. We will also discuss the battle between human and computers in *Shogi*. Not only the human grid computing organized by amateur *Shogi* players but also the grid computing system constructed on the Internet may win against *Meijin* before 2015, when we predict as the X day.

## 2. Background

Grid computing is a great tool in order to solve problems in complex systems, because computing resources including Central Processing Unit (CPU), main memory, strage and so on are rich with a reasonable cost.
Grid technology is applied to large-scale computing, such as numerical simulation and data analysis not only in the academic research but also in the business world. Numerical simulation enables virtual experimentation on computers such as collision of rigid body, weather forecast in hydrodynamics, economic phenomenon, and so on. Data analysis is intended for huge amounts of data even for data mining with the purpose of marketing. SETI@home (22) is the most famous project for an application of data analysis by grid technology. At the present time, many computers are connected to the internet. The efficiency of machines has made remarkable progress more than we could possibly use their all resources. Idle resources of a large number of computers on the internet can realize high performance computing equivalent to supercomputers. We can say that we have already had an inexpensive supercomputer on the Internet.
We can use mathematics only for a simple model, however, cannot apply our hand-writing calculation to more complicated problems that have a large number of variables to be solved. In particular, combinatorial optimization has a difficult structure of problem that takes a very long time to finish searching the optimal solution. In other words, it is likely that we can solve the difficult problems with high performance computing beyond hand-writing calculation.
Natural sciences have been based the framework of mathematics to describe phenomena in the physical world. Newton formulated the law of motion with differential equations, and Einstein proposed the equation of gravitational fields with the concept of geometry. Almost all of the models of natural phenomena can be described for the corresponding ordinary or

partial differential equations, so that we can analytically solve the equation with initial state and boundary conditions.

On the other hand, there are many unsolved models of differential equations even in the classical physics. Since a certain class of models is not solvable analytically, we calculate the alternative numeric solution with hand-writing approximation or computers. For example, the Navier-Stokes equation is a system of partial differential equations which describes the motion of a compressive and incompressive fluid in fluid mechanics. The equation is essentially nonlinear, and we can obtain no explicit solution to initial data. We can only calculate the numerical solution using finite element method etc.

Newton succeed in solving two body problems in gravitational fields, however, he were faced the difficulty in solving many body problems in the same framework. Differential equations know the motion of the Sun and the Earth interacting by gravitation, they cannot provide the clear solution with fundamental functions to the problem of the motion of the Sun, the Earth and the Moon exactly. We know the reason why mathematical analysis has these limitation in the existence of chaos which often appear in the nonlinear phenomena.

In the latter half of twentyth century, scientific comupation was made in a variety of fields. The contemporary sciences are based on theories, experiments and computational matter.

According to the progress of computers, we can use a large scale of computation for artificial intelligence based on the model of natural sciences. Althogh early reseaches of artificial intelligence failed to realize the ideas, supercomputers enables the models in artificial intelligence with high performance computing. Moreover, the number of computers on the Internet has grown like hotcakes, we obtain another choice for grid computing. There is possibility of high performance grid computing for artificial intelligence than cluster system in the present time.

In the following sections, we describe the history of research in artificial intelligence, construction of grid computing, and the application to the battle against human intelligence. What are we able to do by grid technology? In other words, what does grid technology enable to do anything impossible so far? An answer proposed in the work of Dan (4) is to implement computer Shogi systems as artificial intelligence by human-computer interactions. That is another solution to the difficulty of astronomical combinations to be processed by only grid technology.

## 3. Artificial intelligence systems

### 3.1 History

Information scientists and engineers have struggled for realization of artificial intelligence, since Shannon (19) sugested the possibility of computer chess program with evaluating functions, which pointed out that a typical chess game involved about $10^{120}$ possible moves. It seems natural to let computers get hold of intelligence, and that we want to use computer resources instead of human labor. In fact, Shannon made the suggestion not only of computer chess, but also about design of electric circuit, translation from one language to another, strategic decisions in simplified military operations, and so on. Development of computer chess systems has been equipped with great academic interest to researchers in artificial intelligence.

John McCarthy and Marvin Minsky organized a summer workshop at Dartmouse College in 1956. There are ten researchers interested in the study of machine intelligence, artificial newral networks and automata theory. The Dartmouse workshop gave birth to a new science called artificial intelligence.

| Year | Event |
|---|---|
| 1950 | Shannon proposed computer playing program |
| 1956 | Dartmouse workshop |
| 1970 | North American Computer Chess Championship |
| 1986 | Computer Shogi Association founded |
| 1997 | Deep Blue defeated Garry Kasparov |
| 2002 | 3-Hirn System in Shogi |
| 2009 | Council System in Shogi |
| 2010 | Akara came out for a grid system |

Table 1. History of Artificial Intelligence Research

The first working computer *Shogi* program was written in 1974 by a research group supervised by Takenobu Takizawa (20). The program did not cope well with the game-tree complexity, so it could only play at the level of beginners.

After that, the Computer Shogi Association (CSA) founded as a society for the study of computer *Shogi* programming in 1986. The CSA has motivated the leading researchers in the field and provided place to exchange ideas at academic symposiums such as the series of Game Programming Workshops.

Of course, the scope of research in artificial intelligence has not been limited to computer chess and *Shogi*. In that time, researchers have struggled the other problems in expert systems for medicine, artificial neural networks, pattern recognition, optimization or automation, classification, etc. However, it is not enough to run programs which need a plenty of resources on the computers in decades ago. Research in artificial intelligence have taken progress according to the progress of computing performance.

It follows from Moore's law that the densiy of semiconducters in electronic circuits grows two times for twelve to eighteen months. Since the throughput of computing is approximately proportional to the density of semiconducters, the program or software on artificial intelligence obtains higher performance in future, even if we do not anything else. Hence, we will have more effective performance when we brush up the algorhithm or discover new algorithm for solving difficuties in the research of high performance computing including artificial intelligence.

Table 1 shows the history of main events in the artificial intelligence researches.

### 3.2 Deep blue

Shannon's dream came true after a half of a century. The most remarkable epoch-making event for artificial intelligence occurred in May 1997 when the chess machine Deep Blue, developed by IBM research team, defeated world chess champion Garry Kasparov in an exhibition six-game match. This was a major success for computer game-playing and a milestone in the history of computer sciences.

Deep Blue is a parallel system with optimized algorithms designed for carrying out chess game tree searches. The system was composed of a 30-node IBMRS/6000 SP computer and 480 single-chip chess search engines, with 16 chess chips per SP processor. The SP system consists of 28 nodes with 120 MHz P2SC processors, and 2 nodes with 135 MHz P2SC processors. The nodes communicate with each other via a high speed switch. All nodes have 1 GB of Random Access Memory (RAM), and 4 GB of disk. The system ran the AIX 4.2 operating system.

The chess chips in Deep Blue are each capable of searching 2 to 2.5 million chess positions per second, and Deep Blue in total can examine and evaluate up to 200 million chess positions per second. The system can search a game tree to a depth of between six and twelve plies

Fig. 2. Initial position on board in Shogi (Japanese chess)

to a maximum of forty plies in some situation, although the system speed varied widely, depending on the specific characteristics of the positions being searched. No one in the world can win against the strongest computer chess system even on ordinary PC at the present time. See Campbell et. al. (2), IBM web site (6), Hsu (9), Newborn (16) and (17) in detail for Deep Blue.

### 3.3 Difference between chess and *Shogi*

On the other hand, computer systems for *Shogi*, often referred to as Japanese chess, are behind those of chess in intelligence. *Shogi* is also a two-person zero-sum game with perfect information as chess. Iida, Sakuta and Rollason in (10) described the current state of the art for this game.

Let us consider the difference between chess and *Shogi*. First, Chess has an 8x8 board, while *Shogi* has an 9x9 board. There are 6 different pieces in chess, while there are 8 different kinds of pieces in *Shogi*. In chess each player has 32 pieces in total (16 pieces each), while in shogi each player has a total of 40 pieces (20 pieces each).

Second, in chess only the pawn is allowed to promote, otherwise in shogi promotion is allowed for 6 different kinds of pieces.

Third, difference between shogi and chess is the possibility of reusing pieces in shogi. When a piece is captured, the piece does not disappear from the game, but is put next to the board.

Finally, one of the crucial difference between chess and *Shogi* is the complexity of game-trees, which is significantly higher in *Shogi* than in chess. Captured pieces may be brought into play again by the player who captured the piece. Because *Shogi* has the ability to return captured pieces in hand from the opponent to the board, it generates a great number of combinations of each possible position in comparison with chess.

After all, *Shogi* has more spacious in game trees than chess does.

### 3.4 Game tree analysis

In order to solve next move problems, which returns the optimal move to given position, we analyze the game tree of position transition. The basic method is to find the solution for a player to win even if the opposite player will do the best. However, it is impossible to run full-width search to some sufficient depth. In fact, *Shogi* has $10^{219}$ possible search of game trees, while chess has $10^{123}$ in average. Table 2 shows comparison of complexity in Checker,

| Game | Checker | Chess | *Shogi* | Go |
|---|---|---|---|---|
| Branching Factor | 2.8 | 35 | 80 | 250 |
| Average Game Length | 70 | 80 | 115 | 150 |
| Complexity | $10^{31}$ | $10^{123}$ | $10^{219}$ | $10^{360}$ |

Table 2. Comparison of game-tree complexity in checker, chess, *Shogi*, Go

Chess, *Shogi* and *Go*, sorted by the average number of branching factor, average game length and game-tree complexity.
The game tree of *Shogi* is a graph of infinite number of vertices connected by directed egdes, which begin the root, that is, the vertix corresponds to the initial position. In order to solve next move problems, we should estimate the leaves where one player is check-mated. The game of *Shogi* finishes the state of check-mated, All most of ordinary routes of game tree from the root have end points.
For the average number of branching factor $B$ and average game length $L$, the average search space that can be expected in a game is estimated by $B^L$. More precisely, the exact one is

$$G = \prod_{j=1}^{L} B(j) = B(1) \cdot B(2) \cdot \cdots \cdot B(L) \tag{1}$$

where $L$ denotes the average game length and $B(j)$ the number of branching factor of $j$-th ply for $j = 1, 2, \ldots, L$. We know that $B(1) = 30$ and $B(2) = 30$ in *Shogi*, and $B(j)$ for $j \geq 3$ depends on the previous move and the present position. $B(j)$ becomes small when check-mated. It is known that *Shogi* has an average branching factor of about 80, and that the maximum branching factor is 593. It is also known that a game of *Shogi* takes about 115 plies on average, and that the maximum game length (in actual games) is more than 500 plies. See Matsubara et. al. (14) for *Shogi*, Allis (1) for the other games in detail.
Therefore, computer systems for *Shogi* have a long way to go before they will be able to offer a serious challenge to *Meijin*, a human champion of *Shogi*. In the newest research, it is expected that computer *Shogi* systems will defeat *Meijin* in 2015 at the earliest.

## 4. Computer *Shogi*

### 4.1 Algorithm for computer *Shogi*

The core algorithms for thinking routine of computer *Shogi* systems are analysis of the game tree and pruning using the alpha-beta method from min-max tree for evolutionary sequence of positions. These method to solve next move problems are similar to chess and other games. Given position information including array of pieces on the board, pieces in hands and the next player, the position evaluation function returns the value of the position forward several steps.
When initial position is given, all legal hands of the next player are genarated, say $h_1$ and $h_2$ for the hands. Then possible positions are $P_1$ and $P_2$ respectively. In order to select the best hand, all legal hands of the opposite player are genarated by recursive call. It is thought that players do their best, therefore the next hand will be selected by the min-max method under the restriction of finite moves.
Although a computer program seeks as many positions as possible, almost all of the evolutionary sequence seems not to be valid clearly even for amateur players. Full-width search algorithm can make sure a limited number of combination like checkers, resources of computer *Shogi* consume waste of time in many cases.

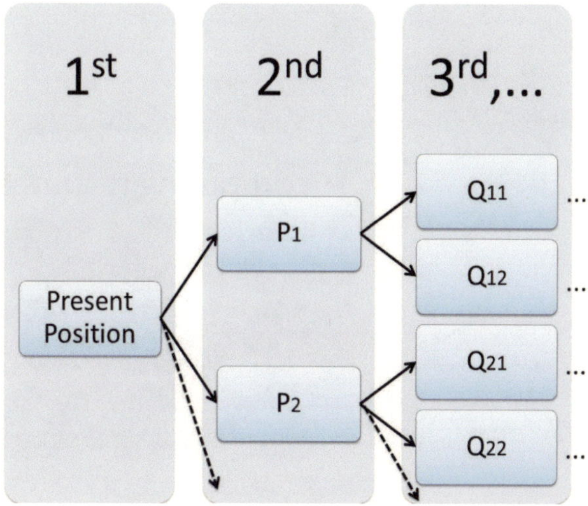


Fig. 3. Game trees present a evolutionary sequence of positions at playing games

There is a pseudo-code for the thinking routine of min-max method by recursive call in the appendix.

### 4.2 Position evaluation functions

We use position evaluation functions when we want to know or jugde which player is advantageous. Position evaluation functions return values from the status of position including array of pieces on the board, pieces in hands and the next player given as arguments. Position evaluation function are defined almost as static evaluation functions, constructed by heuristic process. These functions have a large number of parameters, so that these parameters are optimized automatically from the playing before. Machine learning is a method in artificial intelligence for the optimization.
The value for each pieces on the board is important factor to estimate the position. It may be different in time or position, we never know optimal values.
Let $f$ be a real-valued (may take $\pm\infty$) function:

$$f : (p, h, t) \mapsto \mathbb{R} \cup \{\pm\infty\}, \tag{2}$$

where $p$ denotes the array of position of all pieces on the board, $h$ pieces in the hand of both players, $t$ which is the next turn. $\pm\infty$ mean the status of check mated for each player, which is used in the program like this: For every evaluated real number $v$, $v < \infty$ and $-\infty < v$. The game ends up when the value of $f$ takes $\pm\infty$, although a player decrare to finish the game before that in the real play.
In fact, position evaluation functions are also a function of "time". Opening game, middle game and end game are different each other in evaluation, computers feel difficulties in the evaluation of middle game. They are not good at overlooking on the board in the global point of view, however, almost perfect opening game for a huge scale of databases and end game for logical thinking.

### 4.3 *Shogi* using grid computing

Marsland and Popowich (13) proposed the parallel implementation of the alpha-beta search algorithm of game trees on distribution systems as a methematical model.

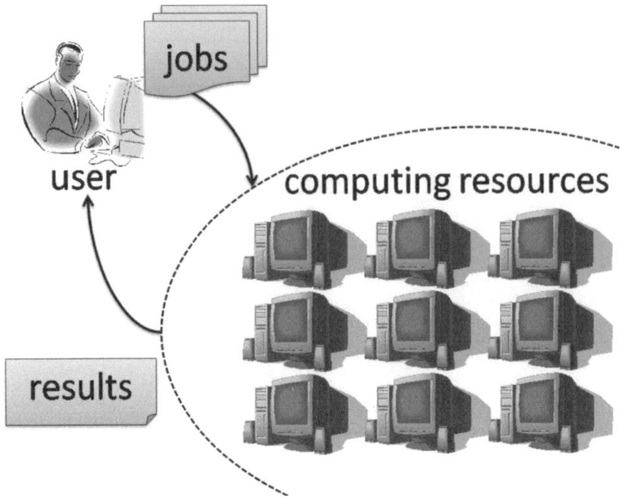


Fig. 4. A grid system is like a supercomputer but uses with computational resources on the Internet.

Grid computing is a possible technology solution for deeper search of the algorithms for computer *Shogi* systems. The system constructed by grid computing brings its forces into high throughput as super computers by a set of usual individual computers connected to the Internet. Although each computer does not have so high performance, the total performance of the connected computing resources surpasses super computers, when each individual computer is properly allocated to appropriate jobs.
If initial state of the *Shogi* position has $B$ possible hands, one more deeper search will become possible by the $B$ grid computers, two more deeper search by the $B^2$ grid computers. In general, the performance of grid systems improves at most logarithmically as $N$ more deeper search needs $B^N$ grid computers, regardless of bottleneck of job assignment.
On the other hand, $T = G/\rho$ where $G$ in (1) is the number of node of game tree and $\rho$ is the ability to calculate the position evaluation function per unit time, say $\rho = 200,000,000$ for Deep Blue.
Grid computing attains high throughput in enormous search of the optimized solution, however, it keeps bottleneck that the case of clearly misdirected search is not different from that without grid computing. Logarithmical improvement is hopeless for the full-width search in playing *Shogi*. Therefore, the other way to solve the problem is desired, which excludes clearly misdirected searches before evaluating the positions.
Figure 5 shows a next move problem in the Meijin title match held on 17 June, 2008. In the real play, Yoshiharu Habu use a pieces in hand near opposite King on the board which is not so easy, but there are many misdirected plies seen even if amateur Shogi players. So far computers cannot recognize the difference between promising and misdirected ply. They only can judge the amount of values of current position by calculating position evaluation functions.

#### 4.4 Human grid computing

3-Hirn System (8) is to selecte the opinion of 2 advisors by one person. Advisors may be computers. This system is proposed for chess by Althofer in 1980, which is stronger than the person who is selecting one of the opinions proposed by two other advisors.

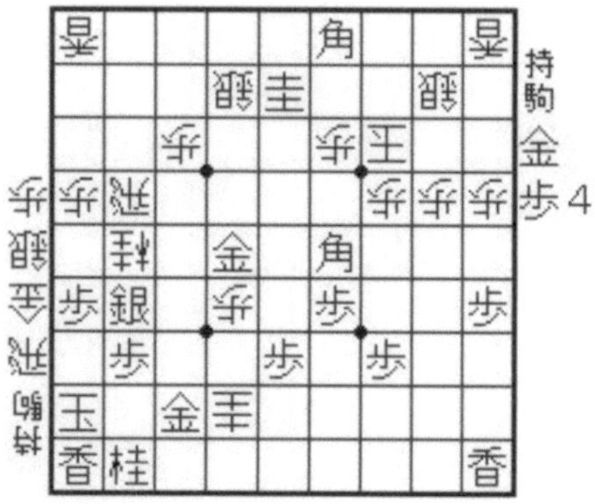

Fig. 5. The Next Move Problem

The 3-Hirn System is an example of interaction of human and computers, which is extended for a counsil system on playing game (7).
The computer Shogi by grid systems throws jobs to client computers on the internet. Such client computers run the position evaluation functions, as they display the process and the result of calculation, and then return the value of the evolutionary sequence of positions back to the grid server. It improves efficiency in enormous search of the next move, if amateur Shogi players in front of the screens dismiss negative results.
When an amateur Shogi player $j$ can dismiss negative results per unit time, and we denote by $\rho_j$. For the average time $T$ to think one ply, total possible positions are reduced to

$$G - \sum_{j=1}^{M} T\rho_j \tag{3}$$

where $M$ is the number of amateur Shogi players, regardless of the correctness. This formula means we can reduce total possible positions from $G$, as $M$ is large and $\rho_j$ is small.
Therefore, we conclude the relation

$$T\left(\rho + \sum_{j=1}^{M} \rho_j\right) = G. \tag{4}$$

It should be remarked that $\rho_j << \rho$ for $j = 1, 2, \cdots, M$.
On the other hand, evaluation system for human intuition is indispensable. All of human intuition are not always wise as we know. It is necessary for human grid systems that the judge of amateur Shogi players is evaluated by achievements. The position evaluation functions include the information who judge the negative results as arguments.
Instead of human assisted system, the proposed system has possibility of realizing high-performance intelligence ever.

## 5. Implementation environment

Although there are lots of computing resources on the Internet, we do not use that without the permission of their owners. The performance of grid systems depends on the number of computational resources on the Internet.

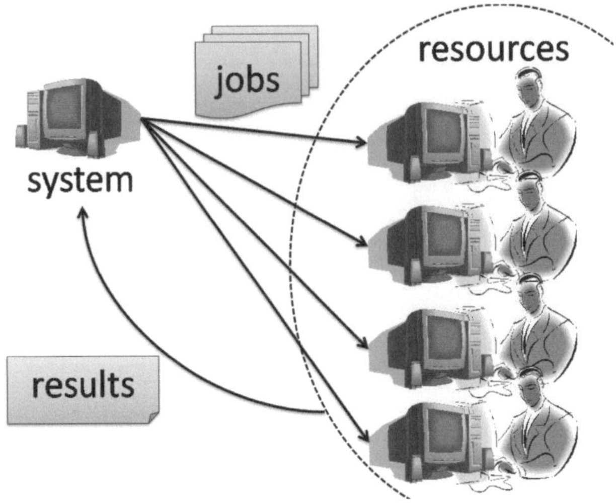


Fig. 6. Human Grid

Let us consider the number of computing resources constructed for grid systems, following from the discusstion on the growth of social networks according to Dan (5). We will use a mathematical model of diffusion on social networks.

Let $N$ be the total number of the computing resources on the Internet to be estimated which is a positive constant for a while in our discussion, $n(t)$ be the number of active computing resources for use which is also a function of time $t$. The inequality

$$0 \leq n(t) \leq N \tag{5}$$

holds for any $t$ in $\mathbb{R}$. According to the property of growth and the assumption that active ones does not run away from the grid system constructed, it can be supposed that $n(t)$ increases as $t$ goes.

Continuation can extend $n(t)$ be a continuous function of $t$ from the domain of integers. According to the process, the probability of the growth is proportional to both $n(t)$ and $N - n(t)$. We can estimate the increase rate of active people as follows:

$$\frac{dn(t)}{dt} = \lambda n(t) \left(N - n(t)\right) \tag{6}$$

with a positive constant $\lambda$. In the right hand side of this equation, teh terms $n(t)$ and $N - n(t)$ denotes incoming and outgoing effect respectively. The differential equation (6) is derived from our model for the growth of the number of computing resources on the Internet.

Then, we obtain from the form of separation of variables,

$$\frac{1}{N}\left(\frac{1}{n(t)} - \frac{1}{n(t) - N}\right) dn = \lambda\, dt. \tag{7}$$

Integrating both side of the equation, we have

$$\frac{1}{N} \log \left| \frac{n(t)}{n(t) - N} \right| = \lambda t + C \tag{8}$$

with a integral constant $C$. This means

$$\frac{n(t)}{N - n(t)} = e^{\lambda N(t-t_0)}, \tag{9}$$

where

$$t_0 = -\frac{C}{\lambda N} \tag{10}$$

which is determined by initial conditions. Finally, we can solve $n(t)$ as

$$n(t) = \frac{N}{1 + e^{-\lambda N(t-t_0)}}, \tag{11}$$

which is known as one of the logistic curves. It should be remarked that $n(t)$ is equal to $N/2$ when $t = t_0$ and $n(t)$ is equal to $N$ when $t \to \infty$. From the differential equation (6), $n(t)$ increases the most rapidly when $t = t_0$.

If the total number of the Internet is not constant, say does increase, then we should consider another differential equation for the spread of grid computing. We can extend (refDifferentialEquation) to more general expression:

$$\frac{dn(t)}{dt} = \lambda n(t) \left(N(t) - n(t)\right), \tag{12}$$

where N(t) is not a constant, but the function of $t$. We cannot solve the equation above analytically, all we have to do is the numeric calculation using computers to obtain the approximate solutions.

Because of the comparison of growth rates, that is,

$$\frac{dn(t)}{dt} = \lambda n(t) \left(N(t) - n(t)\right) \geq \lambda n(t) \left(N - n(t)\right), \tag{13}$$

it is easy to prove that the solution to the equation (12)

$$n(t) \geq \frac{N}{1 + e^{-\lambda N(t-t_0)}}, \tag{14}$$

if $N(t) \geq N$ for $t \in \mathbb{R}$. We can expect that the population $n(t)$ is greater or equal to the above eatimation.

## 6. Akara 2010

It is a difficult question what a computer is even for the human experts in computer science and philosophy.

Akara 2010 is a grid or cluster system for Shogi as the project of 50th anniversary of Information Processing Society in Japan (IPSJ). It is constructed for a council system of four different Shogi programs on 169 Intel Xeon CPUs with 676 cores in the University of Tokyo as a cluster system. The computers are usually used for the class of exercises for the students at the university, which is not constructed for the particular purposes in high performance computing.

The name of Akara stands for $10^{224}$ in Japanese, which is the around the number in average of possible moves for one game of Shogi. We, researchers in artificial intelligence, were expected

that Akara might be the first information system for winning against the professional human Shogi player.
On the other hand, Ichiyo Shimizu is the top of the woman Shogi players who takes the match against Akara 2010. She is not the top or the champion in Shogi, however, if Akara 2010 win against her, then Akara series will be permited to challenge the strongest Shogi player. The goal of the project is the day when Akara defeats the human Shogi champion as Deep Blue did in 1997. Since Akara won against Shimizu, we can see the challenge with Akara 2011 in the next chance.
On 11th October in 2010, Akara 2010 defeated Shimizu in 86 plies. Three hours to think are given to both of them.

## 7. Concluding remarks

The chapter suggests the progress of the grid computing and the possibility of human grid computing for artificial intelligence systems for Shogi. It is described that the present situation of computer Shogi systems and the possibility of the human grid computing which assists the position evaluation function using human intuition. In the most advanced systems, position evaluation functions are constructed by the parameters which are determined by the technology of machine learning. We can see that the next move problems are the optimal combinatorial ones under the rules of Shogi.
According to the history of computer chess, advances not only in hardware but also in software algorithm enable the breakthrough for artificial intelligence. It is the time that we expect to consider the challenge from the computer in formal. Deep Blue had an extreme performance in the search of game trees in chess specially for the human champion, so that the full-width search was very efficient at the challenge to Kasparov.
We also introduced Akara 2010 in the project of game computing in Japan, which is expected as the first computer program to win against the human champion of Shogi. Computing performance have grown up in the exponential rate of Moore's law, so that it is certain to exceed the strength of human abilities, although the information systems for Shogi need to process astronomical number of combinations of possible positions to move.
Cluster computing is gathering the computing resources efficiently, where we can expect the linear growth of performance proportional to the number of computers in cluster system. Grid computing has difficulties in the growth of performance efficiently, however, we expect to gather a large number of computing resources in the Internet. Grid computing faces at the limitation we estimated in the theory of growth, or logistic curve generalized.
On the other hand, human grid computing cannot be a pure artificial intelligence system. However we expect the reduction of the game tree search or investigation in Shogi. Human intuition or global viewpoint is blind at the clearly misdirected search.
The wisdom of crowds can make up qualitatively for grid systems essentially based on the concept of Web 2.0. While the design of the human grid computing is proposed, the development of that remains open.
The human grid computing organized by amateur Shogi players may win against Meijin before 2015. We can also expect that the grid or cluster system Akara defeats series the Meijin in recent future.

## 8. Acknowledgement

The author would like to thank Dr. Peter Dell, Dr. Hitoshi Okada and Prof. Shiro Uesugi for useful suggestions and improvements on the earlier version of the work at the ITeS workshop of the 2008 International Symposium on Applications and the Internet (SAINT 2008) in Turku, Finland. He also thanks Takehiro Moriya for fruitful discussion on the most advanced grid computing technology.

## 9. References

[1] L. V. Allis, *Searching for Solutions in Games and Artificial Intelligence,* Ph.D. thesis, University of Limburg, Maastricht. (1994)
[2] M. Campbell, A. J. Hoane Jr., F. Hsu, "Deep Blue," *Artificial Intelligence,* Vol. 134, Iss. 1–2, pp. 57–83. (2002)
[3] Condor, http://www.cs.wisc.edu/condor/
[4] Y. Dan, "Reduction of misdirected search in game trees by human grid computing," Journal of Informatics and Regional Studies, pp. 35–42. (2009)
[5] Y. Dan, "Modeling and simulation of diffusion phenomena on social networks," to apear in *Proceedings of 2011 Third International Conference on Computer Modeling and Simulation (ICCMS 2011).*
[6] Deep Blue (IBM), http://researchweb.watson.ibm.com/deepblue/
[7] M. Hanawa, T. Ito, (in Japanese) "The Council System on Playing Game," *The third simposium of entertainment and cognitive science.* (2009)
[8] T. Hashimoto, M. Sakuta, H. Iida, "3-Hirn System: The First Results in Shogi," *Game Programming Workshop in Japan,* pp. 57–64. (2002)
[9] F. Hsu, *Behind Deep Blue,* Princeton University Press, New Jersey. (2002)
[10] H. Iida, M. Sakuta, J. Rollason, "Computer Shogi," *Artificial Intelligence,* Vol. 134, Iss. 1–2, pp. 121–144. (2002)
[11] D. E. Knuth, R. W. Moore, "An Analysis of Alpha-Beta Pruning," *Artificial Intelligence,* Vol. 6, No. 4, pp. 293–326. (1975)
[12] D. N. L. Levy, M. Newborn, *All about Chess and Computers,* Computer Science Press. (1982)
[13] T .A. Marsland, F. Popowich, "Parallel game-tree search," *IEEE Transactions on Pattern Analysis and Machine Intelligence,* Vol. PAMI-7, No. 4, pp. 442–452. (1985)
[14] H. Matsubara, K. Handa, (in Japanese) "Some Properties of Shogi as a Game," *Proceedings of Artificial Intelligence,* Information Processing Society of Japan, Vol. 96, No. 3, pp. 21–30. (1994)
[15] H. Matsubara, H. Iida, R. Grimbergen, "Chess, Shogi, Go, natural developments in game research," *ICCA Journal,* Vol. 19, No. 2, pp. 103–112. (1996)
[16] M. Newborn, *Kasparov Versus Deep Blue: Computer Chess Comes of Age,* Springer-Verlag, New York. (1997)
[17] M. Newborn, *Deep Blue: an artificial intelligence milestone,* Springer-Verlag, New York. (2003)
[18] T. O'Reilly, "What Is Web 2.0," http://www.oreillynet.com/pub/a/oreilly/tim/news/2005/09/30/what-is-web-20.html
[19] C. E. Shannon, "Programming a computer for playing chess," *Philosophical Magazine,* Vol. 41, pp. 256–275. (1950)
[20] T. Takizawa, (in Japanese) "Report on Computer-Shogi Grand Prix in 1999," *Journal of Computer Shogi Association,* Vol. 12, pp. 39–41. (1999)
[21] H. Yamashita, "Algorithm of move generation in a shogi program," *Proceedings of The Game Programming Workshop,* Computer Shogi Association, pp. 134–138. (1994)
[22] SETI@home, http://setiathome.ssl.berkeley.edu/

[23] IPSJ project of computer Shogi, http://www.ipsj.or.jp/50anv/shogi/index2.html
[24] Komazakura, http://komazakura.shogi.or.jp/vscomshogi/kifu/

## 10. appendix

```
int thought( int Level, int *Board, int NextPlayer, int *BestMove )
{
  int i, j;
  int n;
  int CriticalValue, value;
  int BetterMove, MoveList[594];
  int CheckMate = isCheckMated( Board, NextPlayer );
  int x, y;
  int koma;

  if( CheckMate != 0 )
    return CheckMate * ( Level + 1 ) * 32;

  n = GenerateMove( Board, NextPlayer, MoveList );
  if( n == 0 )
    return EvaluatePosition( Board );

  if( Level == 0 )
    return n;

  BetterMove = MoveList[0];
  CriticalValue = -1<<16;
  for( i = 0; i < n; i++ ){
    koma = MoveTo( Board, MoveList[i], k );
    value = k * thought( Level - 1, Board, NEXT( k ), BestMove );
    if( value > CriticalValue ){
      CriticalValue = value;
      BetterMove = MoveList[i];
    }
    Board[MoveList[i] / 256] = Board[MoveList[i] % 256];
    Board[MoveList[i] % 256] = koma;
  }

  *BestMove = BetterMove;
  return ( ( k == SELF ) ? 1 : -1 ) * n;
}
```

# 11

# Grid Computing for Fusion Research

Francisco Castejón and Antonio Gómez-Iglesias
*Laboratorio Nacional de fusion. CIEMAT*
*Spain*

## 1. Introduction

Fusion could be an environmentally and socially acceptable source of energy for the future, since it does not emit greenhouse gases or creates long term radioactive wastes. Moreover, fusion reactors will be intrinsically safe, since the losing of the optimum operational parameters will cause the stopping of the fusion reactor.
Nevertheless, fusion still presents several open problems that need to be overcome before the commercial fusion is available. So, fusion research needs to give answers to those open questions and experiments and theory developments must be carried out. The latter require a large computing capacity.
Since the needed temperatures for fusion to occur are of the order of hundred millions of degrees the matter will be in plasma state in fusion reactors. And plasmas are very complex systems to study, especially if they suffer the effect of the confining magnetic field of the device. Fusion research is concentrated on studying the properties of plasmas, which require a large computing effort. The problem is that plasma physics includes in fact almost all the physics since a lot of disciplines are playing a role in understanding plasmas. Plasmas are self-organised and complex systems that exhibit a non-linear behaviour and that require kinetic theory and fluid theory, both including electromagnetic equations, to be understood. So it is possible to find a wide diversity of applications and code to be run.
Specifically, the ITER [1] (International Tokamak Experimental Reactor) project will show a new range of plasma parameters that are outside the present experiments and simulations and will also present some new phenomena that have never been observed. Especially relevant are those related to burning plasmas, i. e., to the plasmas heated by alpha particles that are born in the fusion reactions. But ITER will not be the only device relevant for fusion that will be built in the next future. The large superconductor stellarator Wendelstein 7-X [2] that will be in operation by the end of 2014 in the IPP-Max Planck Institute of Greifswald, a city in the North of Germany, will need also a large computational effort to understand its plasmas. Both supercomputers and computing grids are needed for these activities.
The long term objective in fusion research modelling is to "build" a numerical tokamak and a numerical stellarator, which implies the full knowledge of the relevant physical phenomena that happens in a fusion device, including plasma physics itself, the properties of plasma waves, and plasma-wall interaction (PWI). These numerical fusion reactors could help to save a lot of money since all the scenarios and exploitation regimes that can be expected in fusion reactors can be simulated before doing the experiments. In this way, it would be also possible to teach future fusion reactor operators by the use of numerical

simulators. The achievement of this knowledge is a challenging task that needs the understanding of all basic plasma phenomena and of all the physical phenomena that will happen in the reactor. Beyond this knowledge, it is necessary to have enough computation power to describe all these processes that can interact one another. Other important simulation field is the research on fusion materials. The materials needed for fusion reactors are still under discussion and a wide range of properties must be fulfilled. Especial attention must be paid to the effects of the neutron radiation on the material properties.

Hence, the most relevant tasks for the fusion modelling can be summarized as: first of all, it is necessary a full understanding of the physically relevant phenomena that will happen in a reactor, inside the plasma but also in the walls and in all the complex systems that will be installed. Second, the necessary tools for ITER and Wendelstein 7-X exploitation must be developed. Third, the quest for a numerical fusion reactor needs a large effort in the fields of software and hardware development.

With these tasks in mind, all the large scale computing tools available are necessary: computing grids and high performance computers (HPC). The latter have been customarily used for plasma modelling by fusion community from a long time ago, while grids are used in fusion only recently. In fact, grid activities for fusion research started as a pilot experience in 2004, in the frame of EGEE project [3]. After the EGEE projects work, EUFORIA project [4], which bridges the fusion, the grid and HPC communities, appears as a logic prolongation of these activities.

Beyond the use of computing grids and HPCs, it is necessary to establish workflows among applications that can run on heterogeneous computational environments and can deal with different plasma models and phenomena.

The remainder of the paper is organised as follows. In Section 2 a general discussion on fusion applications porting is presented. Section 3 is devoted to the description of the serial applications that were ported in the beginning of the grid-fusion activities and to their scientific production. Section 4 is devoted to show the use of genetic algorithms in the grid for fusion research. The results of porting a Particle-in-Cell (PIC) code are shown in Section 5. Section 6 shows a complex workflow between an application running in a shared memory computer and grid applications. Finally, Conclusions come in Section 7.

## 2. Fusion on the grid: the strategy

From the beginning of fusion computation on the grid up to now, the range of plasma physics topics that are being investigated by means of grid technologies has been widened, and so have the techniques that have been developed to work on fusion on the grid [5]. The strategy that has been used in order that grid computing is extended in fusion community is to start porting those applications that can be easily gridifyed because of their distributed nature, and still can give physically relevant results. This is what we call "the demonstration effect": it was necessary to show that grid computing is useful for the fusion community. With this objective, we have identified embarrassingly parallel applications that are composed of a huge number of identical processes, as a first step. The codes that are based on Monte Carlo techniques or on input parameter scans are clearly of this type: both are serial and do not need any communication between the CPUs, so they are perfectly suited to run on the grid. Once ported, the applications were exploited scientifically. After these two types of applications have been ported, others with more complexity have been identified. In these cases, more complicated workflows appear. Remarkably, a PIC code that requires more communication among CPUs has been ported. And, as another important example, an application to optimise the stellarator configuration based upon genetic algorithms has been also implemented.

Beyond considering the extension of the grid use to different types of applications, it is necessary to consider the application of these techniques to different research topics relevant for fusion reactors. This is why it could be necessary to make an especial effort in porting applications to the grid, although they could not be fully appropriated for this distributed architecture. From the core of the reactor to the edge, very different research fields can be identified. The plasma dynamics can be studied both by fluid and kinetic theories. The first ones consist of solving continuity-like and conservation equations in the presence of the three-dimensional background magnetic field, while the second consist of studying the properties of the individual plasma particles. The fluid equations must be solved using finite differences or even finite element techniques, so they are not, in principle, the most appropriated for the grid, while the kinetic approach problems can be easily ported to the grid, as has been done with the application ISDEP [6]. Another kinetic code that estimates collisional transport from a totally different point of view is DKES (Drift Kinetic Equation Solver) code, which solves the drift kinetic equation for the distribution function under several approximations [7].

Plasma heating can be performed experimentally by several methods, but there are two of them that can be modelled by means of grid technologies: electron heating by a microwave beam, which can be simulated by the estimate of a large number of rays as it is performed with the TRUBA code [8], and neutral beam injection (NBI) that can be simulated by means of the Monte Carlo code FAFNER [9]. The plasma wall interaction and the edge transport can be simulated by means of the use of a Monte Carlo code like EIRENE [10], a widely distributed code for plasma-wall interaction studies, or by a PIC code like BIT1 [11].

The Magnetohydrodynamic (MHD) equilibrium and stability are also important disciplines since they study the dynamics of the geometry of the magnetic trap. The main application that estimates the equilibrium is VMEC (Variational Moment Equilibrium Code), which has been also ported to the grid in the frame of the stellarator optimization. Finally, some material research codes should be considered in order to include the simulation of the reactor structure behaviour in the grid simulations. We are thinking of neutron Monte Carlo codes as a first option.

A key development is the building of complex workflows among applications that can run on different architectures including grid and HPCs. Several examples of those workflows are shown.

## 3. Embarrassingly parallel applications

As has been stated above, the serial applications of embarrassingly parallel nature were chosen as the first ones to be ported. The main of them are described below.

### 3.1 The ISDEP code

The ISDEP (Integrator of Stochastic Differential Equations for Plasmas) code is used to estimate transport properties of fusion devices by following independent particle trajectories in the plasma, according to the well-known movement equations in the guiding centre approximation. This problem is perfectly suited to the grid, since all the particle trajectories are independent and can be solved separately in the nodes of the computing grid. As a first step we solved these equations in the TJ-II stellarator, which has a very complicated geometry, without collisions [12]. The effects of collisions have been included by adding a stochastic term. Typically $10^7$ ions must be followed to obtain representative results and Monte Carlo techniques are used: Particles are distributed randomly, according to the experimental density and ion temperature profiles, considering a Maxwellian distribution function in velocity space. The next step could be to add Langevin Equations for heating and turbulence. An example of orbit in the real 3D Stellarator geometry takes 10 s CPU time in a single processor, totalling $10^7$ s for one million of particles. The total distribution function can be obtained at a given position and requires about 1 GB data and 24 h x 512 CPUs. An example of several trajectories, together with the coil structure of TJ-II, is shown in Figure 1. The use of the grid for these calculations has allowed us to obtain the 3D collisional ion fluxes without any approximation on their diffusive nature or on the orbit size of the trajectories. This is an excellent example of application to be run on the grid, since all the ions can be run independently and the accuracy of the results can be increased just by adding more calculated ions, distributed initially according to the density and temperature of the background plasma.

This application has been used to open a new line of research consisting of studying the particle and heat flux onto the vacuum chamber walls. Once the flux structure is known it is possible to develop strategies to minimize the flux and to reduce the possible hot spots in the chamber [13].

More recently, the problem has been converted in a non-linear one by allowing the background plasma to change by the influence of the test particles [14]. The non-linear version of the application elapses about 35 times more CPU time than the linear one, but allows the study of the plasma evolution. This task can be accomplished only due to the grid computing capabilities.

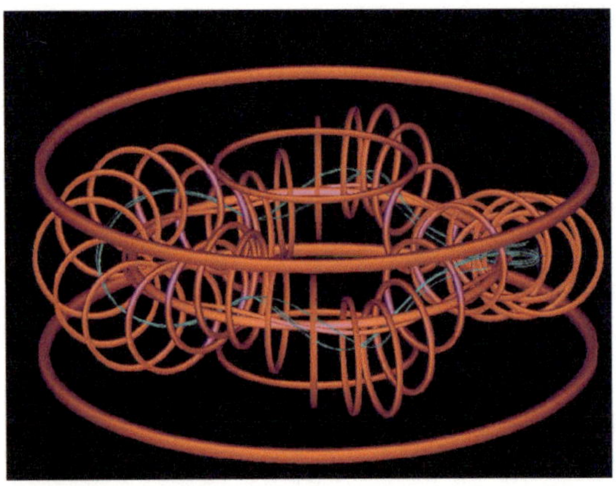

Fig. 1. Ion trajectories and TJ-II

### 3.2 Microwave heating: the MaRaTra application

The microwave beam for plasma heating can be simulated by a bunch of independent rays with different wave numbers. The trajectories of every ray are estimated by solving their Hamiltonian equations. A single weakly relativistic ray takes about 10 minutes in a 3D plasma confinement device. The microwave beam is simulated by 100-200 rays in the usual situations, where electromagnetic waves are used to heat the plasma. Nevertheless, there is

a special case of plasma heating that requires the use of a much larger number of rays in order to simulate the microwave beam behaviour. In these cases about (100-200 rays) x (100-200 wave numbers) ~$10^5$ rays can be needed to have a good description of the plasma behaviour. This type of waves is known as electron Bernstein waves, which are characterised by being approximately polarised along the propagation direction. The ray tracing TRUBA [8] has been used to simulate the behaviour of this type of waves in a complex system like TJ-II.
The TRUBA code has been ported to the grid using the Gridway metascheduler [15] to perform massive ray tracing. The application that runs on the grid is called MaRaTra (Massive Ray Tracing) [16]. MaRaTra has been used, for instance, to design the hardware system for launching the waves in TJ-II stellarator and for more complicated works. Figure 2 shows examples of ray trajectories performed with MaRaTra.

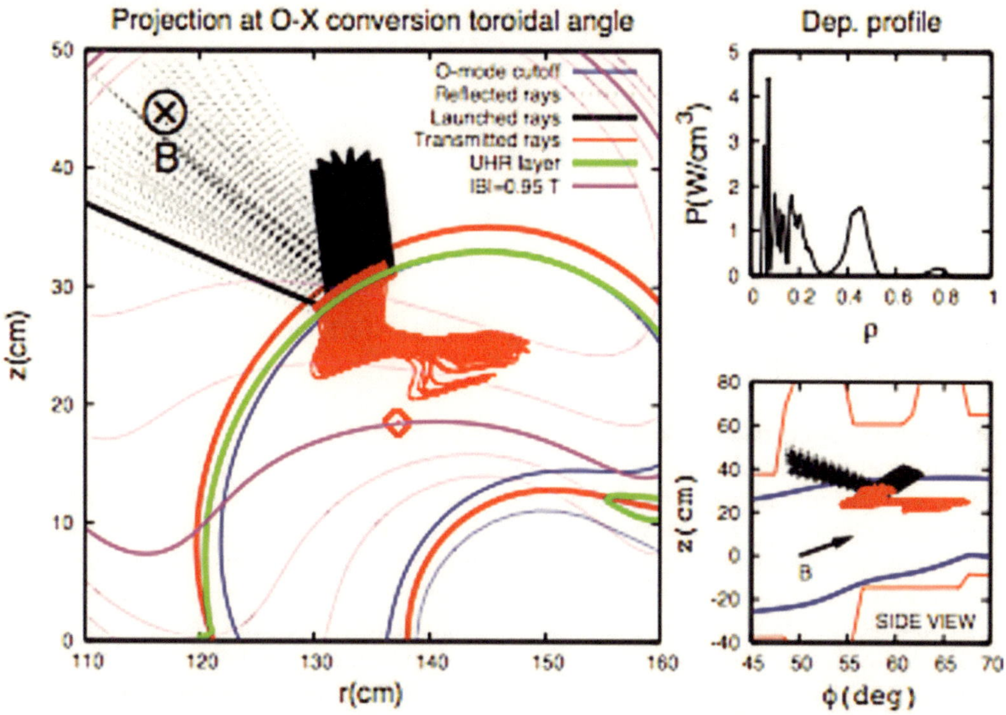


Fig. 2. Ray trajectories in TJ-II plasma (side and top views) and power deposition profile of 100 rays.

### 3.3 NBI heating: FAFNER2 on the grid

NBI (Neutral Beam Injection) heating system is commonly used in large and medium size plasma fusion devices. This heating system consists of launching energetic neutral particles that can penetrate into the magnetic field device colliding with the plasma species. The collisions will ionize the incoming hot neutrals that will deposit their energy in the plasma.
The properties of this heating system and the different phenomena that are produced inside the plasma must be estimated using a Monte Carlo code that takes into account the cross-sections of all the possible processes. FAFNER2 code is the common tool that is used in the

fusion community to perform this kind of calculations. Every neutral trajectory is estimated in a single CPU of a computing element of the grid and the birth points in the 5D space (3D in real space plus 2D in velocity space) of ions are calculated.
Putting all the results together, it is possible to study the fractions of heat that go to ions and to electrons, the direct losses, and the fraction of neutral particles that go through the plasma without colliding. It will be possible to establish connection between FAFNER2 and other codes described above like ISDEP, the ion kinetic transport code, which will allow us to study the confinement of fast ions. Figure 3 shows the escape points of the fast particles as coming from FAFNER2 calculations after followed their trajectories using ISDEP. We have observed similar advantages in porting FAFNER to the grid as the ones achieved with ISDEP.

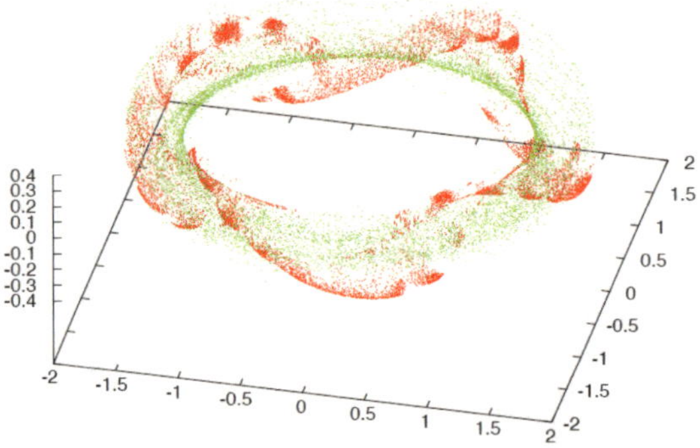


Fig. 3. Escape points of the fast ions as coming from FAFNER2 calculations after following their trajectories using ISDEP.

### 3.4 Standard neoclassical calculations: the DKES code

The ion kinetic transport code ISDEP is useful to estimate the ion collisional transport in different magnetic configurations without any assumption either on the diffusive nature of transport, on the energy conservation, or on the typical orbit size. But, presently, the electric field cannot be estimated by the code and must be supplied by experimental measurements. Therefore, it can be necessary to use a standard tool to estimate the transport in a way in which the electric field can be calculated self-consistently. This can be done using the standard neoclassical transport code DKES (Drift Kinetic Equation Solver), which is very common among the stellarator community. DKES estimates the mono-energetic transport coefficients, valid for a single particle of given energy, which must be convoluted with the Maxwellian distribution function of the particles (ions and electrons) in order to obtain the final coefficients for all the plasma species. Every mono-energetic coefficient must be estimated on a single node of the grid. Once a large number of values are obtained for different plasma parameters (namely electric potential and collisionality) the final transport coefficients can be estimated. The density and temperature gradients are ingredients to obtain the fluxes and, from the latter, the electric field can be calculated. In this way, it is possible to predict the electric field in a magnetic confinement device, which could be compared with the experimental results.
The use of the grid for running DKES code allows us to obtain a well calculated monoenergetic coefficients as a function of the input parameters, thus allowing a more precise estimation of the matrix of coefficients.

## 4. Improving the magnetic configuration by means of metaheuristics. The VMEC code

Although ITER will be a tokamak, the stellarator configuration must be taken into account as an alternative for the fusion reactor. Stellarators are steady state devices and are free from disruptions, which are the main caveats of the tokamak configuration. Nevertheless, the problem is that there is not a unique stellarator configuration that can be proposed as a candidate for the reactor. On the opposite, there exist a lot of different stellarator concepts (different magnetic configurations) available nowadays. The optimization based on the knowledge of stellarator physics is mandatory in order that stellarator community can propose a single candidate for a reactor. The optimization can be performed numerically by variation of the magnetic field parameters. The magnetic configuration, given by the flux surfaces and the magnetic field structure, is described by Fourier series. The strategy is to vary the Fourier coefficients and compute the so obtained "new stellarator" on a separate processor, which takes about 40 minutes, using the customary code VMEC (Variational Momentum Equilibrium Code). The outermost magnetic surface can be described by about 120 Fourier modes. The optimization criteria can be:

- Minimizing Neoclassical Transport and Bootstrap current.
- Equilibrium and plasma stability at high plasma pressure.

Metaheuristics can be used to select the optimum configuration for given target functions. An important point is to carefully select the target function or to include more than one in order to have a stellarator optimized under several criteria. The optimization process was performed in a supercomputer in this case. As a first step, we minimise the drift velocity of the particles, which in principle would imply the improvement of the confinement of the device. The target function that describes such drifts depends on the magnetic field structure and must be estimated using the VMEC output. This one will be the fitness function for all our algorithms. To obtain the magnetic field, it is mandatory to execute the following workflow:

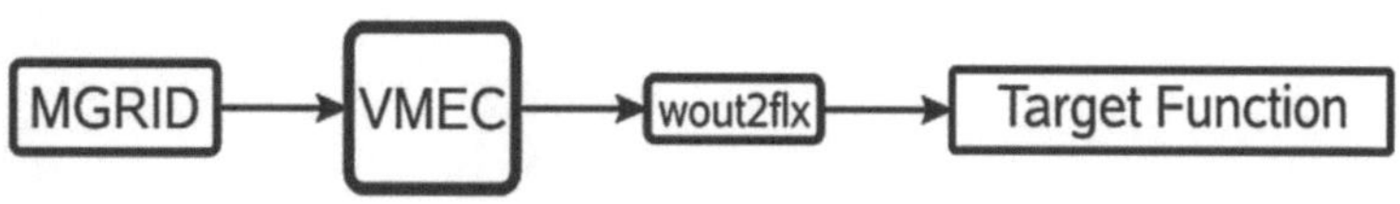


This workflow takes 45 minutes for optimal configurations and 1'5 hours on average when we are performing our optimisation process.

### 4.1 Tested genetic algorithms

Several genetic algorithms (GA) are being investigated to perform this task. The first GA uses recombination to form new populations. All the population elements are chosen by using a tournament selection of a size of two and the worst one of the pair is randomly crossed with values of the best individual.

In our case, every individual is coded as a vector of floating point numbers and each element is forced to be within the desired range. With crossover operator this can be easily done with the proper initial random generation. Each chromosome represents a VMEC input parameter and an individual is, in fact, a configuration for the device (a single configuration which will be evaluated). The first execution of the genetic algorithm generates a random population of 1,000 individuals where the initial values of every parameter are into some predefined values for each of them.

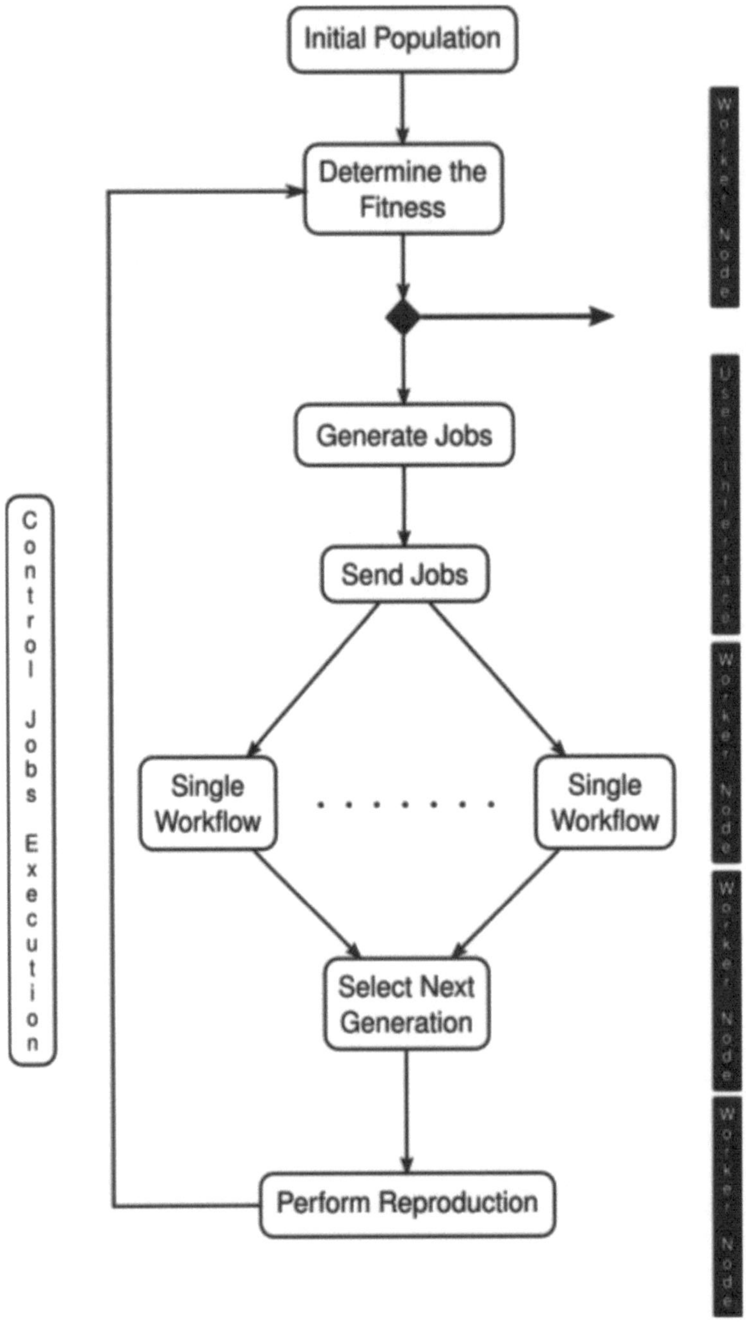


Fig. 4. Overview of a GA on the grid.

Once the equilibrium for the configurations has been obtained, the algorithm selects the different individuals of the population by pairs, using a tournament selection method, and performs a crossover replacing the chromosomes of the worst element, i.e., the one with higher value for the fitness function, and inserting the new element instead of the selected one.

The second technique is the Mutation-based GA, which uses the sample standard deviation of each chromosome in the entire population to perform the mutation. This function assures some level of convergence in the values of chromosomes, even though this is only noticed after a long number of generations, as well as a large diversity of the population. Each selected chromosome is added or subtracted with a value between 0 and the standard deviation for that value not including these extreme values. The mutation using the standard deviation value could be used too, but with that approach the dispersion of the population would become higher. Figure 4 shows a GA running in the grid.
A third algorithm has been tested: the Scatter Search (SS) one. It is a metaheuristic process that has been applied to many different optimisation areas with optimal results. SS works over a set of solutions, combining them to get new ones that improve the original set. But, as main difference with other evolutionary methods, such as GA, SS is not based on large random populations but in strategic selections among small populations: while GAs usually work with populations of hundreds or thousands of individuals, SS uses a small set of different solutions. An overview of this algorithm is shown in Figure 5. Like for GAs, in this case all the control over the execution of the fitness functions, in fact, all the logic needed to carry out this algorithm, is executed in the User Interface, while the fitness function, which is the time demanding process, is executed in the different Worker Nodes of the grid infrastructure.

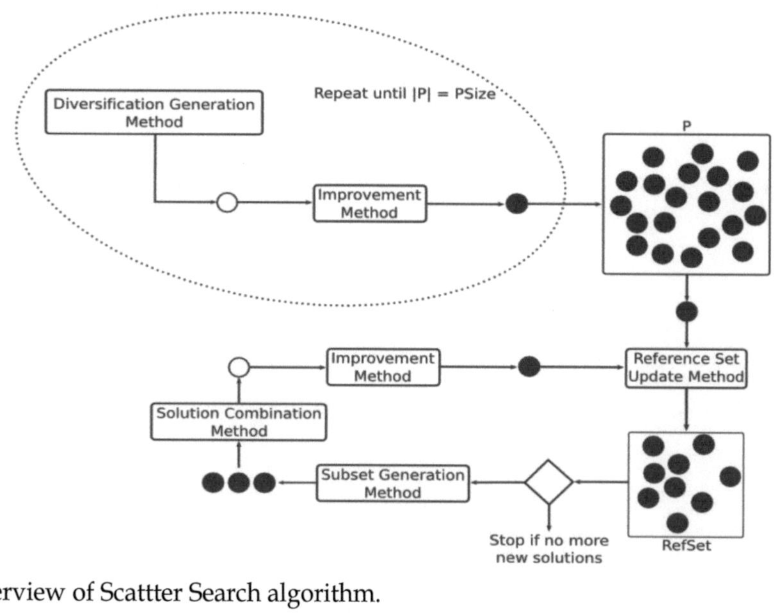


Fig. 5. Overview of Scattter Search algorithm.

The next step will be to include more target functions that can take into account different optimization criteria and not only one, as has been performed in this work. The main advantage of porting this application to the grid is the capability of exploring a wide extension of the parameter space, which happens to be huge for this problem. The usual optimization applications has the disadvantage of exploring a limited zone of the parameter space, so a local optimum is reached, while the parameter exploration performed here allows one to explore a wider parameter range and, probably, to find different locally optimal configurations.

## 5. Porting of a PIC code for plasma-wall interaction: BIT1

BIT1 is a particle in cell application. PIC simulations are used practically in all branches of laboratory and astrophysical plasma physics. These applications are highly time consuming because of the large number of simulation particles ($10^5$-$10^{10}$) and the phase space grid cells ($10^2$-$10^7$), which could be needed in the simulation. BIT1 consist of two different parts:

- Traditional PIC module: solver of the Maxwell equations.
- Monte Carlo code simulating collisional plasmas.

The PIC simulation is based on a simple idea: it simulates the motion of each plasma particle and calculates all macro-quantities from the position and velocity of these particles. During a PIC simulation the trajectory of all particles is followed, which requires the solution of the equations of motion for each of them. But the plasma-surface interaction processes cannot be attributed to a classical PIC method, so here is where we need a Monte Carlo code.
This code is important to simulate the interaction of the plasma with some critical points of fusion devices, specially the divertor at the bottom of a vacuum vessel of a fusion reactor: its function is to protect the walls from the strong plasma fluxes and to exhaust the escaping power. Almost all the nonlinear Coulomb collision operators used in PIC codes are based on the binary collision model, where each particle inside a cell is collided with one particle from the same cell.
We have successfully ported to the grid the serial version of this application. Some problems were found during this process:

- The use of X11 libraries.
- The makefile was not working in grid environments.
- Some bugs appeared during our tests.

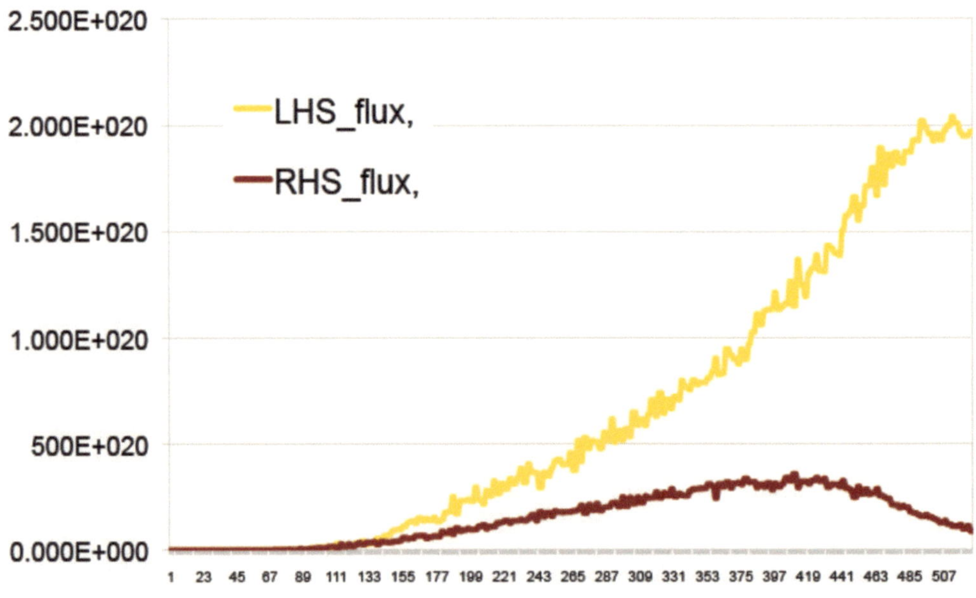


Fig. 6. Time evolution of inwards (LHS) and outwards (RHS) particle fluxes (in arbitrary units) as functions of time, estimated on the grid.

Working together with the code author we have successfully fixed all these bugs, which represents a complete success in the achievements of our work. After fixing these problems, a python script interacting with the grid environment was developed. Thanks to this, users do not have to interact with the grid, take care of proxy problems or job management, since this script performs all these tasks without human supervision.
In order to obtain relevant physical results we decided to carry out a parameter scan of the input file. Several different parameters can be explored like scrape-off layer width or the impurity species that are under consideration. In our case, we have different scrape-off layers and impurity concentrations. 64 jobs were executed with the following computational results:

| | |
|---|---|
| Average CPU Time per Job | 156:23:00 |
| Cumulative CPU Time | 10010:32:53 |

The code provides the time evolution of several quantities, estimated in the inner and outer walls. For example, in Figure 6, we show particle fluxes in a grid simulation. The use of the grid for this application allows to explore a huge number of input parameters, which will provide an extensive study of the plasma-wall interaction depending of those parameters.

## 6. Complex workflows in fusion

Fusion modelling is characterised by the wide range of applications that work on different fields of physics, which makes that one can have serial, parallel and shared memory applications. This applications work on different plasma regions and use different physical models, so it is not easy at all to include all of them in a single code. Moreover, a large range of time and space scales makes very difficult to include all of them in a single application. In order to simulate complex phenomena that interact one another it is mandatory to communicate applications and to build complex workflows. These ones can be cyclic, linear or more complex and can include applications that run on different infrastructures. In fact, fusion research needs the plug of grid applications with HPC ones. Ideally, both types of large scale computing platforms must be available in order that the suitable architecture can be used for the application to run since both parallel and serial applications are needed in fusion, as has been discussed above. Moreover, the future numerical fusion reactor will need the data interchange between both type of codes. So it is necessary to develop experiences in this direction. Here we show several examples of workflows that have been built up to date.

### 6.1 FAFNER-ISDEP

This is an example of basic binary workflow. As it has been described above, FAFNER estimates the birth point of fast ions in the 5D phase space (3D in real space plus 2D in velocity space). These birth points can be taken as starting positions for running ISDEP and this exactly what we have done. In this way it is possible to study the confinement properties of fast ions in arbitrary geometries. Specifically, the hit points of these fast ions have been studied, which allows one to estaimate the heat losses on the stellaator vacuum vessel and hence determine if there exist hot points on the vessel. Figure 3 shows the distribution of hit points on the vacuum vessel of the TJ-II stellarator. FAFNER can run both on an HPC with its version that uses MPI or on the grid, while ISDEP is a grid code.

### 6.2 ASTRA-MaRaTra

A very fruitful and flexible way to build workflows is to take the transport equations of the plasma. For instance, the heat transport equation is given by:

$$\frac{3}{2}n\frac{\partial T}{\partial t}+\nabla\cdot(n\chi\nabla T)=P_{in}-P_{loss}$$

Here $n$ and $T$ are the plasma density and temperature, $P_{in}$ and $P_{loss}$ are the power input and losses respectively and $\chi$ is the heat diffusivity. This equation could be integrated symbolically, giving the temperature evolution, in this way:

$$\Delta T=\frac{2n}{3}\left[P_{in}-P_{loss}-\nabla\cdot(n\chi\nabla T)\right]\Delta t$$

The right hand side of this equation is can be given by function as complex as ne could imagine that need to be estimated numerically on HPC or on the grid. For instance, this evolution equation can be solved by the transport code ASTRA (Authomatic System for Transport Analysis), where a complex heat diffusivity that must be estimated on an HPC using MPI has been introduced. As a case example we estimate the input power $P_{in}$ coming from a microwave beam and given by MaRaTra code that runs on the grid. The physical problem is that the results of MaRaTra, which are an input for ASTRA, strongly depend on the plasma parameters that are estimated by ASTRA. So this code calls MaRaTra when the plasma parameters are changed. An example of the plasma evolution estimated using this workflow can be seen in Figure 7. The results produced by this workflw are physically relevant and have published in [17].

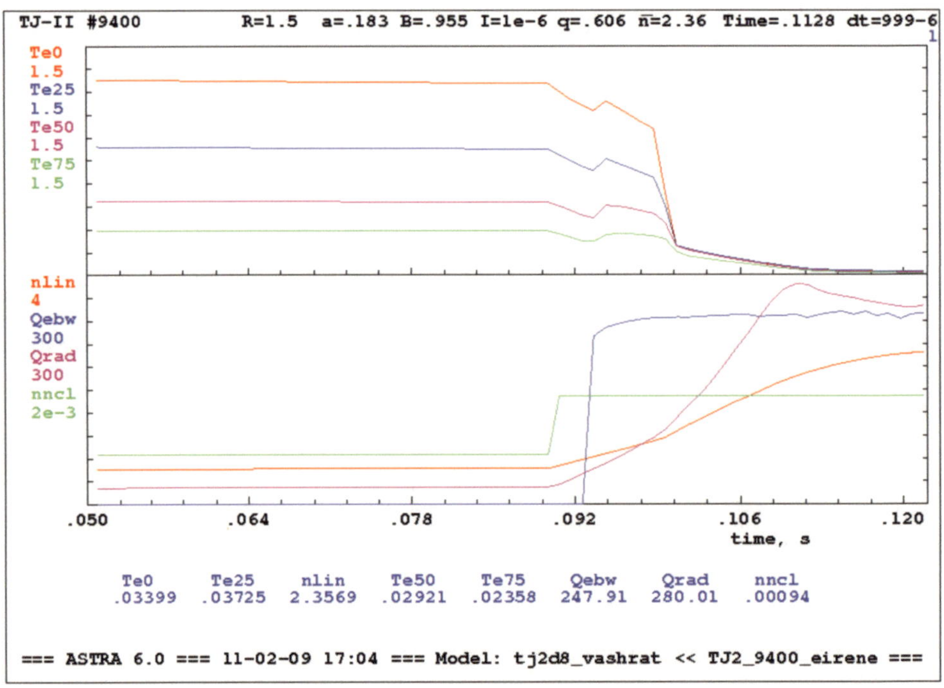


Fig. 7. Evolution of plasma parameters estimated by ASTRA, linked to MaRaTra.

## 7. Conclusions

An increasing number of fusion applications has been ported to the grid, showing the utility of such computing paradigm for fusion research. The range of problems solved and the techniques used have been increased from the first use of the grid for fusion. Nowadays, we are running Monte Carlo codes, parameter scan problems, ray tracing codes, genetic algorithms, etc. Besides the large variety of grid applications, it is remarkable the wide range of problems solved using the grid. The fusion research involves a large variety of physics problems that go from the Magnetohydrodynamics to the kinetic theory, including plasma heating by NBI or microwaves. Grid computing is present in almost all of them. Moreover, the present work shows the capability of grid techniques for helping to reach the full simulation of the numerical reactor, helping to the traditional HPC applications. Finally, complex workflows have been developed beyond the simple applications in order to simulate more complex phenomena in fusion devices. These workflows allow one to connect codes that run on different platforms (grid and HPCs) and that deal with different physical models and scales.

## 8. References

[1] K. Ikeda et al. Nuclear Fusion 47 (2007). Special Issue.
[2] http://www.ipp.mpg.de/ippcms/eng/pr/forschung/w7x/index.html
[3] F. Castejón et al. Proc. of the 2005 EGEE Conference. 2005, Pisa (Italy)
[4] EUFORIA: http://www.euforia-project.eu/
[5] F. Castejón. Summary of Fusion Session. Proc. of the 4th EGEE/OGF User Forum. 2009, Catania (Italy)
[6] F. Castejón, L. A. Fenández, J. Guasp, V. Martín-Mayor, A. Tarancón, and J. L. Velasco. Plasma Physics and Controlled Fusion 49 (2007) 753
[7] S.P. Hirshman and J. C. Winston. Physics of Fluids 26 (1983) 3553
[8] F. Castejón, Á. Cappa, M. Tereshchenko, and Á Fernández. Nuclear Fusion 48 (20089 075011
[9] J. Guasp and M.Liniers: "The Complex FAFNER/EIRENE at Ciemat: Scripts and file structure". Reports Ciemat. October 2008, Madrid, Spain.
[10] EIRENE: http://www.eirene.de/
[11] F. Castejón, A. Gómez-Iglesias, D. Tshkakaya, and A. Soba. Proc. of the 4th EGEE/OGF User Forum. 2009, Catania (Italy)
[12] F. Castejón, J. M. Reynolds, J. M. Fontdecaba, R. Balbín, J. Guasp, D. López-Bruna, I. Campos, L. A. Fernández, D. Fernández-Fraile, V. Martín-Mayor, and A. Tarancón. Fusion Science and Technology 50 (2006) 412.
[13] F. Castejón, A. López-Fraguas, A. Tarancón, and J. L. Velasco. Plasma and Fusion Research 3 (2008) S1009.
[14] J.L. Velasco, F. Castejón, L.A. Fernández,V. Martin-Mayor, A. Tarancón and T. Estrada. Nucl. Fusion 48 (2008) 065008.
[15] E. Huedo, R.S. Montero and I.M. Llorente. Journal Scalable Computing - Practice and Experience 6 (2005) 1 Editorial Nova Science. ISSN 1895-1767

[16] J. L. Vázquez-Poletti, E. Huedo, R. S. Montero and I. M. Llorente. "A Comparison Between two Grid Scheduling Philosophies: EGEE WMS and GridWay" Multiagent and Grid Systems 3 (2007) 429
[17] Á. Cappa, D. López-Bruna, F. Castejón, et al."Calculated evolution of the Electron Bernstein Wave heating deposition profile under NBI conditions in TJ-II plasmas". Contribution to Plasma Physics, in press.

# A Grid Enabled Framework for Ubiquitous Healthcare Service Provisioning

Oludayo, O., Olugbara[1], Sunday, O. Ojo[2], and Mathew, O. Adigun[3]
[1]*Durban, University of Technology*
[2]*Tshwane Univerity of Technology*
[3]*University of Zululand*
*South Africa*

## 1. Introduction

The trend in modern healthcare is towards making quality services ubiquitous so as to improve accessibility and to reduce costs of services. The aspiration of government around the world is to improve the wellbeing of citizens and to deliver quality services that can add value to the people. Healthcare is one of those important services that can significantly improve the wellbeing of citizens and add value to people's quality of life because metaphorically, health is wealth. Moreover, healthcare represents a huge portion of Gross Domestic Products (GDP) and it sustains a strong public interest across the world. But, the conventional healthcare system is generally being confronted with the problems of low quality of services, lack of easy accessibility to service varieties and high costs of services.

The advancement in healthcare technology and the constantly changing nature of healthcare environment have brought about high costs of treatments. Many hospitals across the world cannot afford to pay for high costs of sophisticated healthcare equipment to provide cost-effective services. Those few special hospitals that are able to afford the costs of expensive healthcare equipment are charging patients high service fees to breakeven. These healthcare equipment are available in specialized hospitals having highly skilled experts to utilize them successfully. This implies that people who are living in rural areas need to travel long distances to access quality healthcare services at expensive costs.

Moreover, disabled people and nomadic individuals living in rural seclusion find it difficult and expensive traveling long distances to access quality healthcare services. These challenges are particularly conspicuous in developing countries and rural world, making the realization of the health related Millennium Development Goals (MDG) a mirage. The general challenges facing the rural world are intermittent power, intermittent connectivity, long travel distances, variable population density, limited education, underemployment, limited disposable income and lack of secure storage (Parikh & Lazowska, 2006).

Even in the developed world where there are claims of highly skilled expertise and accessibility to sophisticated healthcare resources, there is still the problem of aging population in this part of the world. The aging population quandary has led to more disabilities and is continually pulling renowned experts out of active services. This has serious ramifications on the social expenses incurred on healthcare. There is also evidence that low quality of service provisioning caused by variation and dichotomy in healthcare services and misuse of healthcare resources is also a challenge in many parts of the world. A comprehensive discussion on the general challenges facing the healthcare sector has been given (Sneha & Varshney, 2006).

The process of healthcare management is indisputably a life-critical one that demands for the involvement of human beings to manage the health of others. Patients' health data are usually kept and managed securely within an hospital environment. Anywhere a patient goes, the history of his/her treatments is supposed to follow, but this is currently not the case around the world. Each time a patient visits a new hospital there would be demand for history of treatments from the patient. Consequently, patient mobility is not supported by the conventional healthcare system. This process definitely requires transformation in order to accurately diagnose a patient, because it is practically impossible for patients to correctly remember all the history of their treatments for accurate diagnosis to take place.

The non-standardization of diagnosis and treatment often expressed by the slogan different hospital, different treatment is another important issue in healthcare management. Moreover, the direct involvement of human beings in the main activities of healthcare implies high probability for making mistakes as a result of possible incorrect prescriptions of medications that can be made for patients and this can lead to lives being lost. An important question to ask is to what extent can healthcare practitioners avoid mistakes? It is difficult to completely avoid human mistakes, but mistakes can be considerably minimized by using automated procedures, tools and systems to support our daily activities and to transform the conventional ways that we do things. Automated systems have the capability to correct a user in the process of making mistakes.

The conventional healthcare system therefore, strives to overcome the difficulties inherent in the management of patient data, standardization of diverse data formats to support interoperability, acquisition of data from remote patients, efficient extraction and analysis of relevant content knowledge, federation of disparate healthcare databases as well as privacy and confidentiality of healthcare information. As such, many private and public hospitals are still in the practice of using conventional healthcare system to facilitate the process of diagnosis, treatment and prescription. This process is mainly manual, labor intensive, prone to mistakes and involves much paper work and the use of standalone systems for productivity enhancement. This approach gives variation and disparity in healthcare services and makes standardization and interoperability of healthcare infrastructure extremely difficult.

Today, the healthcare challenge facing many developing countries, including South Africa is how to extend quality and affordable healthcare services to a large number of people, especially those in the rural areas. This challenge suggests the necessity for ubiquitous healthcare service provisioning system and attests to the relevance of this study to our immediate society. The remainder of this chapter is succinctly outlined as follows: Section 2 presents our contributions. Section 3 discusses the state of the art in telemedicine technology. Section 4 discusses the state of the art in grid computing in healthcare. Section 5 presents our grid enabled framework for ubiquitous healthcare service provisioning. Section 6 presents an evaluation of our framework based on ubiquitous evaluation areas. Section 7 gives conclusion of the chapter and discusses our future work.

## 2. Contributions

This chapter describes our current effort to design and evaluate a grid enabled framework for ubiquitous healthcare service provisioning. The limitations of conventional healthcare system are low quality of service provisioning, lack of easy accessibility to service varieties and high costs of services. But, the emergence of technologies such as telemedicine, wireless body area network and wireless utility grid computing provides a unique opportunity to overcome the limitations of conventional healthcare system. These technologies can enable improved quality of healthcare by eliminating variation and dichotomy in healthcare services and misuse of healthcare resources. Moreover, they can provide easy accessibility to service varieties by allowing distributed healthcare resources to be massively reused to provide cost-effective services without individuals physically moving to the locations of those resources. In addition, they can reduce costs of healthcare services by allowing individuals to access ubiquitous services to support their healthcare.

Exploiting these novel technologies, our contribution is threefold. First we examine the roles of emerging technologies in enabling ubiquitous healthcare service provisioning. Second we illustrate how these technologies can be integrated to realize a grid enabled framework for ubiquitous healthcare service provisioning. Third we provide an evaluation of our framework based on ubiquitous computing evaluation areas. Moreover, our framework was compared with some three other existing ubiquitous healthcare frameworks and it promises to address the challenges of healthcare system better than those that it compares with by taking advantages of grid computing and mobile computing technologies. In future, we plan to deploy our framework and to test its efficacy for enabling ubiquitous rural healthcare service provisioning.

## 3. Telemedicine technology – state of the art

The significant roles of telemedicine technology in enabling high quality, cost-effective and easy accessibility to healthcare services are enormous. Telemedicine is the science and art of the maintenance of health, prevention, alleviation, rehabilitation and cure of diseases in patients using Information and Communication Technologies (ICT) (Van Beijnum et al., 2009). The main objective of telemedicine is to improve quality of healthcare and to minimize costs of healthcare services by making communication of crucial information between healthcare practitioners easy.

Telemedicine facilities include virtual reality, virtual community, mobile virtual community, mobile dynamic virtual community and wireless body area network and it potentially

a. Provides a means to effectively share knowledge and to overcome several challenges caused by geographical locations, scarcity of qualified healthcare practitioners and inadequate transportation systems to rural areas.
b. Brings healthcare services more closely to the people, improves quality and accessibility to healthcare services and minimizes number of case referrals.
c. Saves patients the inconvenience, stress and cost of travelling long distances to specialist centers for treatment because diagnosis and treatment can be provided at a distance.
d. Bridges the gap between highly curative healthcare services often concentrated in urban areas and pitiable healthcare services sometimes found in rural areas.

### 3.1 Virtual Reality

Virtual Reality (VR) as a telemedicine facility has attracted much research interest in healthcare. VR is a simulation of a real or an imagined environment that can be visually experienced in 3-dimensions and that may provide an interactive visual experience in real-time motion with sound and tactile feedback (Roy, 2003). The main characteristic of VR technology is the full immersion of human sensory-motor channels into a vivid and global communication experience (Riva & Gamberrini, 2000; Roy, 2003). These authors asserted that VR based healthcare systems provide the following three important aspects to offer new possibilities for assessment and treatment of diseases. It allows for

a. Direct manipulation interfaces to allow content manipulation through pointing devices such as mouse and joystick. VR systems allow the manipulation of multiple sensory representations of entire environment by natural actions and gestures.
b. Effective control method to monitor, capture and process all properties of body actions or signals. These actions are then translated into other actions that have more effect on the world being controlled.
c. Capability to display feedbacks in multiple modalities. The feedbacks are then translated into alternative senses for users with sensory impairments.

VR based remote environments and related technologies provide improved healthcare services and savings in material resources (Moline, 1997). VR technologies have been applied to different healthcare applications including the augmented surgery and surgical training that are critically dependent on eye-hand coordination (Riva & Gamberini, 2000) and the treatment of phobias (Roy, 2003). But, they are still faced with the problems of high costs of Reduced Instructions Set Computer (RISC) platforms upon which they are based, lack of reference standards and non-interoperability of the systems (Riva & Gamberini, 2000). Moreover, VR worlds are generally believed to be visually unconvincing and full of encumbrances.

### 3.2 Virtual Community

Virtual Community (VC) based solutions to healthcare system allow for the building of shared communities, networks and organizations contexts of understanding and knowledge where the real-world knowledge affects the virtual interaction that modifies real-world therapies (Scarlet et al., 2007). A VC is a group of people who gather because of a common interest such as healthcare service provisioning and whose members interact independent of time and space using ICT as a platform (Leimeister et al., 2002). Scarlet et al. (2007) proposed a VC home rehabilitation approach as a realistic solution to the Romanian healthcare system. This allows for the possible rehabilitation of patients that are geographically dispersed and to access a distributed virtual platform that is able to provide communication and shared knowledge with healthcare practitioners (doctors, nurses and therapists), social workers and those involved in the rehabilitation process.

There are different criteria proposed in the literature for characterizing VC and examples include (Porter, 2004; Van Beijnum, 2009):

a. Purpose for the community to exist and shared common interests among community members.
b. Structural property of the community where the interaction happens, whether the community members interact in a physical location or the interaction is mediated by technologies whilst in different geographical locations.
c. Interaction platform or modality among the community members that is supported. This can be synchronous, asynchronous or hybrid of both interaction platforms.
d. VC defined three options of population, which are VC as computer supported social networks, VC as small groups and VC as networks.

e. VC provides a profit model to know whether the community is revenue generating or non-revenue generating.

But, the challenges in VC research have been identified to include the need to (Abuelmaatti & Rezgui, 2008):

a. Clarify and define the nature of virtual business modes that take place amongst communities.
b. Specify the technological, regulatory and socio-organizational environment to support communities effectively.
c. Discover the factors that facilitate virtual business modes adoption and use across communities.

### 3.3 Mobile Virtual Community

The wide proliferation of mobile wireless consumer devices, simply called mobile devices and the advancement in wireless positioning technologies for location based services have led to the emergence of Mobile Virtual Community (MVC) (El Morr & Kawash 2007; van Beijnum et al., 2009; van't Klooster et al, 2010). A MVC can be considered as a natural evolution of a VC to which mobile services are added. A MVC facilitates real-time social connection and social interaction amongst community members anywhere anytime.

The important properties of a MVC that differentiate it from a VC are discussed as follows (Van Beijnum et al., 2009). First, MVC can make use of mobile service platform such as Short Message Service (SMS), mobile messaging and mobile Voice over Internet Protocol (VoIP) to support effective communication. Second, MVC offers enhanced mobile services that provide users with the ability to interact within the community anytime anywhere. Third, MVC results in entirely different usage patterns as it focuses on an individual user rather than around a specific interest. Apart from the fact that a MVC is a VC with extra mobility support, MVC can generally be characterized as follows (Rheingold, 2003):

a. VC, internet resources and their software agents are instantly available in MVC irrespective of their locations.
b. MVC is used to coordinate actions of groups of people in diverse geographic spaces.
c. MVC provides gaming environments and can start with young people as means for entertainment and light social interaction and then diffuse into other institution.

There are different dimensions to viewing mobility issues in VC, but mobility is generally associated with the use of mobile devices to facilitate effective information communication and interaction. The following four basic modes of mobility were defined (Schulzrinne & Wedlund, 2000; Van Beijnum et al., 2009):

a. Terminal mobility relates to the mobility of a device and it allows an end-device to be connected to the communication network while being on the move. Terminal mobility support will cause network connections to remain whenever there is a change between access points.
b. Session mobility allows a user changing from using one terminal to another to maintain the ongoing media session. This mobility is achieved by Session Initiation Protocol (SIP) to enable the transfer of application sessions between different devices without interruption.
c. Personal mobility allows a user having multiple terminals to be addressed by one and the same logical address. This form of mobility supports the user to change its device on-the-fly and the state is transferred from one device to the other, thereby allowing seamless terminal changes.

d. Service mobility is the capability of using services in the case of moving or changing devices and network service providers. This form of mobility includes any relevant personal service configuration setting or preferences.

A MVC is a useful facility for providing interaction between patients, healthcare practitioners and hospitals. Patients need to share experiences and testimonies with one another for emotional support. They also participate in self-help group activities to obtain information and to establish interactions to assist in the prevention and treatment of diseases. But, according to El Morr & Kawash (2007), little research has been conducted to understand how network providers can turn MVC services into profit making venture and to discover requirements and acceptance trends of users. Moreover, MVC is not likely to support strong community cohesion as community memberships can be short lived and communities can suffer from weak membership commitments. This is because a common interest does not necessarily lead to membership loyalty and durable cooperation.

### 3.4 Mobile Dynamic Virtual Community

A Mobile Dynamic Virtual Community (MDVC) is a VC whose members are able to change locations while the provided services remain available (Waldburger & Stiller, 2005). MDVC extends VC with respect to dynamicity and mobility and service provisioning is concerned with the entity providing services. Akogrimo support for DMVC completely differentiates it from many other existing grid based solutions. The driving force behind the Akogrimo project is to merge large scale properties of telecommunication platforms and their support for multimedia applications with the cross-organization collaboration concepts of service-oriented Grids into a coherent and integrated service platform (Jähnert, et al., 2010).

A MDVC is characterized by a strong dynamic element with respect to its organizational composition and business processes. The dynamicity and mobility characterization of MDVC is explained as follows (Waldburger & Stiller, 2005):

a. Dynamicity, as members can freely join or leave the community and there is the need to manage entity that arises during the active existence of members in the community.
b. Mobility, if a Dynamic Virtual Community (DVC) allows at least for a subset of its members to change locations and still being able to profit or to provide services while moving, the DVC is called a MDVC.

### 3.5 Wireless Body Area Network

The Wireless Body Area Network (WBAN) (Van Dam, et al., 2001; Latre, et al., 2010) is an emerging wireless sensor networks telemedicine facility that uses intranet, internet or satellite communication for remote patient vital signs monitoring. WBAN technology allows for the automatic real-time acquisition of vital signs to provide flexibility and to support patient mobility. The technology is used in surgical and intensive care units of modern hospitals, at homes and in emergency situations to rescue patients who need urgent help. WBAN uses wearable sensor devices and actuators, mobile devices and wireless network devices to manage physical health conditions of patients. The health conditions are usually indicated through some physiological signals such as body temperature, body weight, waistline, blood pressure (BP), pulse rate (PR), oxygen saturation (SpO2), blood sugar electrocardiogram (ECG), electroencephalograph (EEG) and electromyography (EMG) without any particular emphasis on geographical locations of patients.

The sensors and actuator devices, simply called motes can remotely collect many vital signs for diagnosing patients' health conditions and providing efficient and cost-effective treatment in real-time. A critical component of WBAN is a device Network Connector (NC) or hub that is capable of processing, displaying and transmitting sensors information to a remote telemedicine system. Because sensors do not need to communicate with each other, they communicate with a central Personal Server (PS) through the NC. The PS either processes the information sensed from human body and displays the results through a multimodal interface or transmits the sensed information to a telemedicine system.

ZigBee and the Bluetooth standards are generally used for radio interface between motes and PS in WBAN systems. However, performance, reliability and security of WBAN based healthcare applications have been investigated (Ylisaukko-oja et al., 2004; Li et al., 2008; Chavez-Santiago et al., 2009; Nam, 2009; Peiravi & Farahi, 2010). Interestingly, the suitability of ZigBee and Bluetooth for healthcare applications has been questioned. ZigBee has high vulnerability to interference, Bluetooth has scalability problem and both ZigBee and Bluetooth support low data rate communication. They are therefore, not suitable for novel applications such as wireless medical imaging (Chavez-Santiago et al., 2009).

The Ultra WideBand (UWB) (Ryckaert et al., 2005) transmitter with low power consumption and low complexity was proposed to be used in the WBAN context. Chavez-Santiago et al. (2009) also proposed UWB for wireless interface between sensors and a PS because of the several advantages of the wireless technology. For examples, UWB signals do not cause significant interference to other systems operating in the vicinity. They do not constitute a threat to patient's security because they protect the transmission of patient's data by reducing the probability of detection. This therefore, rescinds the need for health data encryption that results in lower complexity of the electronics and smaller size of the devices. A novel Signal to Noise Ratio (SNR) estimator algorithm was designed for quality control in UWB communication (Barrera et al., 2010).

## 4. Grid Computing in healthcare – state of the art

El Morr & Kawash (2007) asserted that ubiquity of MVC is a reconciliation factor to keep virtual communities going smoothly. They justified this assertion that while a common interest can keep a member attached to the community, this can only occur for a rather transient period of time, but that community hopping can be a sustaining power for MVC. Ubiquity of MVC can be facilitated by emerging technologies such as mobile web services and mobile grid computing by allowing distributed resources and expertise to be massively shared. A Grid is able to effectively manage different kinds of hardware and software resources that are within its environment. It can integrate web services, distributed hospital information system, high performance computing, interoperable health records and Peer-to-Peer (P2P) system to provide electronic infrastructure. The real and specific problem that underlies grid concept is coordinated resource sharing and problem solving in dynamic, multi-institutional virtual communities (Foster et al., 2001).

Moreover, as demonstrated by Shaikh, et al. (2009) web services or more generally, Service Oriented Architecture (SOA) is known to play a significant role in telemedicine systems for solving interoperability problem. This then allows diverse telemedicine systems to effectively talk to each other. Grids are classified according to the functionalities they offered and the applications they supported. Commonly used grid taxonomy include computational grid, data grid, service grid, interaction grid, knowledge grid, utility grid, science grid, bio grid, sensor grid, cluster grid, Healthgrid, campus grid, Tera grid and commodity grid. However, the following checklist has been proposed to determine the real meaning of a grid system (Foster, 2002): a grid is a system that

a. Coordinates resources that are not subject to a centralized control and it addresses the issues of security, policy, payment and membership that arise in this setting.
b. Uses general purpose protocols and interfaces that are standard and open to address issues such as authentication, authorization, resource discovery and access to resources.
c. Delivers nontrivial quality of service relating to response time, throughput, availability, security and co-allocation of multiple resources to meet complex user demands.

Examples of application demonstrations of the usefulness of grid computing to healthcare include Bioprofiling over the grid for healthcare in which BIOPATTERN grid was developed for Biopattern analysis and Bioprofiling to support individualization of healthcare (Sun et al., 2006). The BIOPATTERN grid was designed to facilitate secure and seamless sharing of geographically distributed Bioprofile databases and to support the analysis of Bioprofiles to overcome diseases such as brain and cancer. The distributed mammography data retrieval and processing (MammoGrid) (Amendolia et al., 2005), the eDiaMoND (Lioyd et al., 2005) and the multi-centre neuro-imaging (BIRN) (Grethe et al., 2005) are also examples of useful applications of grid computing to healthcare.
Additionally, the Intensive Care Grid (ICGrid) (Gjermundrod et al., 2007) is a novel system framework based on the Enabling Grids for E-sciencE (EGEE) to enable the seamless integration, correlation and retrieval of clinical interesting episodes across Intensive Care Unit (ICUs). The ICGrid allows doctors to utilize the EGEE grid infrastructure through simple intuitive user interfaces, while the infrastructure itself handles the complex task of information replication, fault tolerance and sharing (Gjermundrod et al., 2007). The CardioGrid (Risk et al., 2009) is a grid based framework for analyzing cardiological signals. This infrastructure allows a user to process on the grid, the electrocardiogram (ECG) signals obtained from a portable data acquisition device. The World-wide In Silico Docking On Malaria (WISDOM) is a European initiative to enable the in Silico drug discovery pipeline on a grid infrastructure. The WISDOM initiative demonstrated an efficient process of drug discovery by speeding up the entire process and reducing the cost to develop new drugs to treat diseases such as malaria (Jacq et al., 2006).

### 4.1 Grid computing technology

A grid is a flexible distributed information technology environment that enables multiple services to be created with a significant degree of independence from the specific attributes of underlying support infrastructure (Travostino et al., 2006). Grid computing is conventionally associated with high computational capability and ability to handle enormous amount of data to be processed (Foster & Kesselman, 1999; Berman et al., 2003). Grid provides a means for massively distributed parallel processing such as Search for Extra-Terrestrial Intelligence (SETI), Symmetric Cryptographic Cracking (SCC), Human Genome Project (HGP), MOlecular Visualization (MOV) and Multimedia Content Distribution (MCD). Grids are determined by the following three main characteristics: resources coordination, general purpose protocol and quality of service support (Foster, 2002). The pervasive nature of grid allows remote computing resources to be accessible from different platforms (desktops, laptops, PDAs, mobile phones) using the web browser. The Healthgrid community is focusing on the use of grid in healthcare management as a way to resolve the challenges of conventional healthcare system.

Grid middleware infrastructures such as Condor, Gridbus, Globus and gLite provide functionalities for security (authentication and authorization), resource management (resource allocation and job management), data management (grid file transfer protocol and replica management) and data service support such as Grid Service Architecture Data Access and Integration (OGSADAI). The Condor is an open-source grid middleware that allows users to reliably submit jobs to grids. The Gridbus aims to develop next-generation cluster and grid technologies that support utility-based service-oriented computing. The Globus is an open-source codebases and a set of protocols for implementing grid applications. The gLite is a lightweight middleware framework of EGEE for building grid applications.

### 4.2 Wireless Grid Computing

A wireless grid is a virtual network system that integrates different types of wireless devices, thereby extending grid computing capability to wireless devices such as sensors, actuators, mobile phones, laptops, special instruments and edge devices. Wireless Grid Computing (WGC) supports the sharing of grid resources amongst mobile and fixed wireless devices within a VC. The general characteristics of WGC are summarized as follows (Manvi & Birje, 2010): It

a. Does not provide centralized control of resources.
b. Consists of small and low powered devices.
c. Includes heterogeneous resources, applications and interfaces.
d. Allows sharing of new types of resources types like cameras, GPS trackers and sensors.
e. Is dynamic with unstable users and resources.
f. Provides geographically dispersed resources with different management policies.
g. Provides different security requirements and policies.

Wireless grids can be classified according to their relative accessibility and interaction modality supported. Four categories of wireless grids are (Li et al., 2009; Manvi & Birje, 2010):

a. Fixed wireless grids extend grid resources to wireless devices of varying sizes and capabilities where these devices are usually static. In this type of grids, wireless devices can act as real nodes for data processing and storage to take place.
b. Mobile wireless grids make grid services accessible through mobile devices such as smart phones and Personal Digital Assistants (PDA). This type of grids allows devices to connect to the internet, support P2P network connection, take advantage of the resources of wired grid networks and make their own resources available to the wired grids.
c. Mobile Ad Hoc grids consist of devices with a high degree of heterogeneity. These grids can be instantly constructed anytime, anywhere, especially for an emergency situation by integrating grid resource aggregation model with mobile ad hoc networks.
d. Sensor network grids are composed of tiny devices dedicated to a single purpose and they integrate detection, processing and communication capabilities into grids.

Due to mobility of wireless devices and inherent limitations of communications technology, a number of challenges have to be surmounted to build robust grid applications for resource constrained devices. This is because wireless devices were not viewed as having sufficient capability to be both clients and services (Chu & Humphrey, 2004). Some of the requirements and challenges of wireless grids have been discussed (Manvi & Birje, 2010). Among those research efforts that currently extended mobility into grids to address resource limitations and intermittent network connectivity problems associated with wireless devices are:

a. Mobile Open Grid Service Infrastructure (OGSI) dot net (OGSI.Net) (Chu & Humphrey, 2004) is an important step towards making mobile devices first-class entities in grids based on OGSI or Web Service Resources Framework (WSRF). OGSI extends the statelessness of web services to accommodate grid computing resources that are transient and stateful. WSRF captures the state requirement of web services, making it possible to use grid services as web services. Both OGSI and WSRF provide a unique support to host grid services on mobile devices, but WSRF seems more promising with the release of Globus toolkit 4 (Foster, 2006), which implemented WSRF.
b. Wireless Grid based Mobile Agent System (WGMAS) (Leu & Wang, 2006) is a grid service platform that integrates mobile agent technique and wireless environment with a grid system to provide a wireless access mobile agent system to users.

### 4.3 Utility Grid Computing

Grid computing was originally introduced as a means to solve high computationally intensive scientific problems. But, the influence of grid computing has speedily extended from scientific applications to more resourceful applications domains such as healthcare, business and commerce. Utility Grid Computing (UGC) extends the original grid computing to incorporate business model and it presents resource management as a crucial element of grid computing. The utility model of grid computing draws on an analogy to the commercial electrical power system for metered service provisioning.

The electrical power from any generating, transmitting and distributing stations can serve the purpose of any consumer without a geographical obstacle. Moreover, consumers of electrical power do not need to worry about the complicated intricacies of the electrical transformers and the peak load management that occurs through the power generation, transmission and distribution grids. This implies that accessing computer power from a computer grid would be as simple as accessing electrical power from an electrical grid and one would be able to request for computing services and get it on payment. The Harvard Presentation (HP) grid Utility Data Center (HP/UDC) that focused on the data center market and the International Business Machine (IBM) autonomic grid computing and E.Liza to build self-healing and self-organizing devices are two famous models of UGC.

### 4.4 Wireless Utility Grid Computing

Wireless devices are undoubtedly popular and generally accepted by everyone because of their impact, portability, low-cost and easy handling. The number of potential owners and users of wireless devices continue to amazingly increase on a daily basis, making these devices resourceful for boosting business opportunities. The amazing growth in the number of wireless device owners and users can be exploited to leverage numerous business opportunities, especially when wireless technology is fully integrated into grids. Wireless Utility Grid Computing (WUGC) extends the capability of UGC to support wireless technology. WUGC is rich in functionalities, can provide on demand access to appropriate services and can give high-bandwidth to a large constellation of distributed time-varying resources, thereby increasing the quality of service provisioning.

Integrating wireless devices into utility grids to form WUGC provides an opportunity for sustainable ubiquitous healthcare service provisioning by harnessing the potentials of diverse resources on the grid. This will also create enormous new business opportunities as WUGC promises to deliver high quality services at low costs to alleviate the suffering of common people and to make small businesses to flourish. WUGC will definitely create enormous potentials for emerging resources such as cameras, microphones, videos, sensors and positioning system to improve ubiquitous healthcare service provisioning.

### 4.5 Healthgrid and Grid Service discovery

Healthgrid is an emerging grid based technology that promises to resolve a number of complicated healthcare challenges by integrating healthcare information systems, practitioners and diverse resources into a common, usable, accessible and shareable platform. Healthgrid provides an environment where healthcare data are stored, processed and made available to end-users as on demand services. Several Healthgrid projects are currently being undertaken to facilitate health data systems interoperability and to support improved data management, diagnosis and treatment of diseases. Examples of such projects include DataGrid (Breton et al., 2003), e-Diamond (Brady et al., 2003), NeuroGrid (Geddes et al., 2005) and MEDIGrid (Boccia et al., 2005).

Grid service discovery is one of the most important functionalities expected from the Healthgrid and it generally represents an interesting problem in grid research. Grid service discovery is the task of matching a query for services described in terms of the required characteristics to a set of services that meet the expressed requirements (Kaur & Sengupta, 2007). Grid service discovery is a kind of Constraint Satisfiability Problem (CSP) (Yokoo et al., 1998), complicated by the dynamic changes in service information. The challenge is to devise highly distributed service discovery techniques that are fault tolerant and highly scalable (Kaur & Sengupta, 2007).

A Grid Service (GS) is a resource on the grid that is transparent to consumers and extends the stateless nature of a Web Service (WS) to deal with state and notification. A WS based grid extends the capabilities of WS by providing common and powerful mechanisms for service consumers to access all kinds of services. The Universal Description, Discovery and Integration (UDDI) plus rich query (Kaur & Sengupta, 2007) is a novel web-services based grid services discovery model. UDDI already contains basic entities such as businessEntity, businessService, tModel and bindingTemplate for efficient service discovery when a powerful query model is applied. In a recent development, Naseer & Stergioulas (2010) proposed a new novel WS based service discovery model for service discovery in Healthgrid based on WS and WS technologies to transform virtual healthcare into a reality.

## 5. Grid enabled healthcare service provisioning

The challenges facing the conventional healthcare system demand for improved infrastructure and novel methods for healthcare service provisioning. A Grid enabled Framework (gFrame) is proposed for ubiquitous healthcare service provisioning. The goal of gFrame is to integrate MDVC of healthcare service providers, individuals, personal space and smart space into Healthgrid for the purpose of enabling ubiquitous, quality and cost-effective healthcare service provisioning, thereby surmounting the challenges of the conventional healthcare system. In this context, services represent resources (experts, equipments and operations) that can be provided on the grid and consumed as web or grid services.

Zhang et al. (2004) defined a personal space as a space equipped with a network of WBAN and enriched with context information, ranging from static information (particulars, contact number, subscribed health insurance and health profile) to dynamic information (health status, location and socializing record). Similarly, they defined a smart space as a physical environment (house, hospital and car) of individuals, whereby the context information is made available through sensors and actuators techniques and information technologies. Context information range from low-level context, such as temperature, noise level and location of coordinates to high-level context, such as activity schedule, relationship between individuals and event profile.

The integration of a MDVC into grids generally offers an enticing surrogate for resource demanding applications by leveraging the power of several devices to collectively provide the Quality of Service (QoS) required by individual service consumers. Our own specific reason for considering the integration of a MDVC of healthcare into Healthgrid is to help individuals in the rural world to access quality healthcare services at reduced costs within and across boundaries without the individuals moving to the physical locations that those services are produced. To describe the gFrame architecture, it is important to first discuss the services that can be provided within a typical VC of healthcare and on the Healthgrid and the challenges of integrating mobile devices into grids for enabling ubiquitous healthcare service provisioning.

### 5.1 Virtual Community and Healthgrid services

The healthcare services to be provided within a VC and on the Healthgrid have been discussed (van Beijnum et al., 2009; Naseer & Stergioulas, 2010; van't Klooster et al., 2010) and these services were categorized into management-level and operational-level services (Naseer & Stergioulas, 2010). The management-level services are responsible for making resources available within the community.

The operational-level services are used for monitoring, diagnosing and treating patients for illness. These services implement all types of operations that are related to healthcare service provisioning including treatment, follow-up, consultation, dose computation, self-care, mobile-care, preventive-care, home-care, clinical annotation, drug prescription, group based analysis and diagnosis.

### 5.2 Integration challenges

The era of ubiquitous computing provides interaction convenience and mobility support as individuals can now access services on the move and on the bed through mobile devices that they carry about. While mobile computing community has succeeded in entering virtually all application domains to enrich human lives with increased personal and business productivity, it has not yet entered into the grid computing domain. The ongoing debate amongst members of the grid community is whether mobile devices should be considered as clients into the grid that is originally meant for high performance computing. This argument is anchored on the lucidity of considering resource-constrained devices on the grid, especially when only a small fraction of internet-connected desktop computers contribute to the grid (Phan et al., 2002).

However, the fact that mobile devices represent a large percentage of the world computing power is sufficient for it to be leveraged for finding more ways to harness the enormous potentials. But, the limiting force in leveraging the enormous potentials of mobile devices in a grid enabled environment include, slower processing power, unreliable low bandwidth wireless connectivity, and unreliable extended period of complete disconnection, heightened power-consumption sensitivity, small secondary storage and lack of adequate security mechanism. Moreover, while wired resourceful devices such as desktop computers are designed to function continuously over a long period of time, mobile devices have shorter battery lifespan and the battery cannot automatically self-charge when the devices are engaged.

Several researchers have proposed a proxy-based architecture to address the logjams of integrating mobile devices into grids. This architecture plays two significant roles in the integration of mobile devices into grids. First is to execute a request on behalf of mobile devices using appropriate grid middleware system. The proxy system sends the result back to the requester, thereby shielding the service requester from device heterogeneity. In this particular scenario, a mobile device is regarded as a pure service consumer, thereby leading to a Client and Server (CaS) kind of architecture. Second is to distribute a request to be naturally executed on a single mobile device amongst several computing devices. The proxy system waits for the results and sends them to the requester. The second scenario seems to be more promising as mobile devices serve as both service consumers and service providers, thereby leading to a Peer-to-Peer (P2P) kind of architecture. But the data partitioning to be solved in P2P architecture is a challenging task within the parallel computing community.

The proxy-based system provides an efficient way to integrate virtual communities into grids, instead of direct connectivity that does not solve many of the logjams of constrained devices. Table 1 shows some proxy-based architectures for integrating mobile devices into grids and the problems addressed.

### 5.3 Framework description

This section describes gFrame, which improves on our previous grid based Healthcare Service Broker (HSB) for remote vital signs management (Olugbara et al., 2007a, Olugbara et al., 2007b). This new framework extends HSB architecture to MDVC and it supports context awareness and personalized grid service discovery based on UDDI Technical Metadata (UDDI-$M^T$) (Miles et al., 2003). The UDDI-$M^T$ approach supports the storage of arbitrary metadata through a tunneling technique that associates the metadata store to the original UDDI directory. Service metadata such as reliability metrics and QoS data can originate from both service providers and service consumers. The metadata registry can be queried using Resource Description Query Language (RDQL), which is a graph-based query language that exploits the graph structure of Resource Description Framework (RDF).

The design objectives of our gFrame that eventually translate into system requirements are the following.

a. To construct a MDVC infrastructure to facilitate collaboration amongst healthcare service providers and service consumers for the purpose of ubiquitous healthcare service provisioning.
b. To make the infrastructural framework operate on multiple device platforms to obtain a platform independent system configuration.
c. To address the particular characteristics of mobile devices in the framework using grid computing technology.
d. To support personal health, spatial-temporal and technical context awareness to allow healthcare service provisioning to be inherently personalized and mobile.

e. To allow for the creation of local healthcare communities of patient categorise.
f. To allow patients to be grouped by their diseases to make easy for market volume estimation.

| Platform Description | Problems Addressed |
|---|---|
| Proxy-based clustered architecture (Phan et al., 2002) creates clusters of baseline units with each cluster centered on an interlocutor proxy, which represents minions to the grid. The interlocutor runs appropriate grid middleware to publish itself as a node that can contribute a certain amount of computational, networking and storage resources. | Device heterogeneity, low-bandwidth, high-latency connectivity and power consumption. |
| iMobile EE (Chen et al., 2003) is an enterprise mobile service platform that provides a scalable, secure and modular software platform, which makes enterprise services easily accessible to a growing list of mobile devices. | Security, scalability and availability. |
| Mobile OGSI.NET (Chu & Humphrey, 2004) promotes resource sharing and collaboration that improves the user experience. It extends an implementation of grid computing OGSI.NET to mobile devices by adhering to the OGSI specification to support the hosting of grid services on mobile devices. | Resource limitations and intermittent network connectivity. |
| Scalable inter-grid network adaptation layers (Hwang & Aravamudham, 2004) integrates mobile devices with grid platforms to conduct P2P operations through a proxy-based middleware architecture that executes jobs submitted to mobile devices. The proxy monitors other mobile nodes, providing measurements, reporting actual QoS delivery and enforcing the necessary resource reservations. | Network and QoS adaptation between wireless devices and network infrastructure. |
| Lightweight grid platform (Isaiadis & Getov, 2005) groups the same subnet mobile devices to create a virtual cluster to be presented to grid. The design uses a number of proxies that provide the interface point between the grid and the lightweight cluster of devices. | Service availability, failure recovery and performance enhancement. |
| Wireless grid-based mobile agent system (Leu & Wang, 2006) is a service platform that integrates agents, services, brokers and resources to realize a robust and reliable environment. It is a hard-wired grid integrated with wireless network and a SIP to establish a wireless grid environment for user to access grid resources through wired or wireless networks. | Communication failure, message chasing and maximizing resource utilization. |
| Mobile service platform (van Halteren & Pawar, 2006). is a middleware based on JINI surrogate architecture to extend SOA paradigm to mobile devices. It facilitates the development and deployment of services on the mobile device for clients to discover anywhere on the internet. | Nomadic service provisioning. |

Table 1. Proxy-based architectures integrating mobile devices into grids

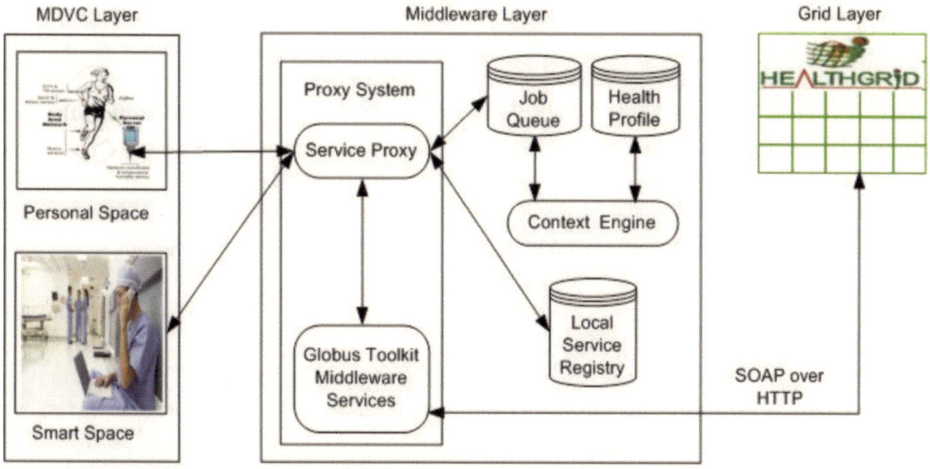


Fig. 1. The gFrame architecture

Figure 1 shows our gFrame architecture that features three main layers, MDVC, Middleware and Grid. The MDVC layer consists of personal space and smart space that interact with the middleware layer through wired/wireless communication network. The personal space provides access to motes that collect vital signs and environmental parameters in a Clinical Document Architecture (CDA) format. The smart space allows individual members of the MDVC to access community and Healthgrid services. The middleware layer integrates the MDVC to the Healthgrid through the Globus system using Simple Object Access Protocol (SOAP) over Hypertext Transfer Protocol (HTTP) as an ideal solution to access grid services. The Grid layer provides high quality services and supports the federation of diverse healthcare resources to be globally shared.

The middleware layer has proxy system, context engine, Local Service Registry (LSR) Job queue and Health profile database as components. The proxy system has a service proxy component that receives requests from the MDVC and it runs a Globus middleware to publish itself as a node that contributes to networking and service provisioning. The proxy system manages service requests from the MDVC using job queuing approach to achieve processing efficiency. Additionally, the proxy system is responsible for local and global service discovery within and outside the MDVC, respectively.

A local service discovery technique provides the opportunity for the global world to access local services that are provided within the MDVC. Similarly, the global service discovery enables the MDVC to benefit from some high-quality and cost-effective services that are offered outside the MDVC. The service proxy publishes certain frequently demanded grid services into the LSR to improve the efficacy of the service discovery algorithm. Whenever a particular service in the LSR is no longer visible or accessible the service proxy removes it from the LSR, thereby providing efficient service management functionality. The service proxy queues job and context requests into the job queue to be processed by the context engine and the service proxy is left with the tasks of service discovery and service rendition to the requester.

The context engine processes a context request and performs reasoning based on health and environment contexts associated with a request. The context engine is also responsible for generating patient-based recommendation services, determining when to generate specialist-based notification services about the current state of a client, managing patients and community-related profiles and generating adaptation services according to terminal context. In addition, the context engine acquires the context information from the job queue to produce a grid service based metadata request by performing an automatic service annotation in an appropriate format suitable for personalized service discovery. A Fuzzy logic system is proposed for the implementation of the context engine to be enriched with intelligence and explanation capabilities as well as ability to properly describe human reasoning. This enables the context engine to be able to provide an explanatory service for every decision taking on behalf of the service requester.

Our gFrame architecture integrates a MDVC of healthcare into the Healthgrid to potentially address the following research challenges.

a. Healthcare system challenges are addressed using an integrated MDVC and Healthgrid as a potential solution to provide ubiquitous, quality and cost-effective healthcare services.
b. Bandwidth availability and extended periods of disconnection are addressed, because grid applications naturally address these challenges and they do not depend on low latency in communication.
c. Device heterogeneity problem is potentially addressed using a proxy-based system to shield service requesters from the integration intricacies by making available the aggregated resources on demand.
d. Service discovery problem is simplified through personalized metadata, powerful query technique, web services and middleware technologies.
e. Power consumption problem is mitigated as much function will be performed by the proxies (service proxy and Globus system) on behalf of the service requesters.

## 6. Framework evaluation

This section considers evaluating gFrame based on Ubiquitous Evaluation Areas (UEA) (Scholtz & Cansalvo, 2004). The purpose is to obtain a usable implementation of the framework through cross comparison with some existing ubiquitous healthcare system frameworks. The need to consider evaluating a design framework is important for revealing direct impacts of a system and framework evaluation offers the following technology and business gains (Kobryn, & Sibbald, 2004; Scholtz & Cansalvo, 2004; Shirazi & Zahedian, 2009). To

a. Ensure conformance to architecture best practices and promote systems interoperability.
b. Help developers to become aware of strong and weak points of the system and ensure that the right business system is being developed.
c. Effectively reduce time, cost, energy and probability of system failure and to accelerate time to market.
d. Help stakeholders to get a uniform view of the system, support appropriate view of various stakeholders and to capture and protect intellectual property.
e. Provide a situation in which the system can be uniformly generated, developed and implemented by separating business logic from technical infrastructure.
f. Increase the knowledge of developers, generate better systems and reveal hidden properties of the systems through evaluation results.

g. Improve comparability across research efforts and give a clearer picture of the final system to implement.
h. Enable the development of a more comprehensive structure and avoid overlooking of the ambivalent areas of system requirements.
i. Reduce defeat density and volatility rate that can be naturally caused by requirements unpredictability and ambiguity in system requirements.

### 6.1 Evaluation metrics

There are different methods and techniques for evaluating framework of architectures and architectural framework evaluation was considered crucial in order to develop information systems (Shirazi & Zahedian, 2009). These authors developed a uniform method for evaluating the Department of Defense Architecture Framework (DoDAF) complaint products using a checklist created for the evaluation. However, the ubiquitous computing environment has more stringent and constrained usability requirements that make most of the evaluation techniques less effective. As a result, the UEA technique was specifically developed for evaluating ubiquitous computing application frameworks.

The UEA (Scholtz & Cansalvo, 2004) has a set of nine evaluation areas with thirty five associated metrics and several conceptual measures. A metric associates meaning to a value by applying human quantitative judgment. These observable values when associated with meanings are called conceptual measures. However, not all of these areas, metrics and conceptual measures are directly applicable to all situations. A user has to decide on which of these areas, metrics and conceptual measures are applicable to the situation being considered. In our particular situation, only four UEA and ten metrics are applicable and the areas are trust, adoption, impact and invisibility.

Trust is the belief that a system will use the personal data it collects from patients appropriately and in innocuous manner. Adoption refers to willingness to use a system and the rate of use. Impact is the utility that the system offers for users and the contributions it makes to someone's life. Invisibility concerns the integration of the system into user environment to support the individual users. Table 2 shows the selected UEA metrics,

| UEA | Metric | Code | Conceptual Measures |
|---|---|---|---|
| Trust | Awareness | (T1) | Ease of coordination with users in multi-user application. |
| | Privacy | (T2) | Availability of user's information to others. |
| | Control | (T3) | Ability of users to establish right over their data. |
| Adoption | Value | (A1) | Perceived costs and benefits of the system. |
| | Cost | (A2) | Ease of acquiring, setting up and maintaining the system. |
| | Availability | (A3) | System ability to attract large number of users. |
| Impact | Social Acceptance | (M1) | Needs on users outside of norms to accept the system. |
| | Environment Change | (M2) | Willingness to accommodate system in user's environment. |
| Invisibility | Intelligibility | (I1) | User understanding of the system explanation. |
| | Customization | (I2) | Ease to enter personalization information. |

Table 2. UEA based vehicle metrics for comparing system frameworks

which we called vehicle metrics, and their corresponding codes and conceptual measures. The vehicle metrics provide a means to describe some outcomes, which we called tenor metrics. These tenor metrics are the particular outcomes that we expect the framework to deliver and they form the basic metrics for the frameworks evaluation. For example, we want the frameworks to address the three challenges of conventional healthcare system.

The purpose of the evaluation is to compare our gFrame with some existing ubiquitous healthcare system frameworks to determine its strengths and weaknesses. In doing so, we need to map the vehicle metrics onto the tenor metrics, which from the challenges of healthcare system are access to services, quality services and cost reduction. Table 3 shows our tenor metrics and their corresponding codes and conceptual measures derived from the following important healthcare considerations.

a. How the framework can help to improve accessibility to healthcare services.
b. How the framework can help to improve the quality of healthcare service provisioning.
c. How the framework can help to reduce the cost of healthcare service provisioning.

| Consideration | Code | Conceptual Measures |
|---|---|---|
| Access to Services | A | Mobility support, community membership, quality of services. |
| Quality Services | Q | Personalized service, service discovery, security and trust. |
| Cost Reduction | C | Membership support, available aid and mobility support. |

Table 3. Tenor metrics derived from healthcare considerations

The access to healthcare services can be directly influenced by quality of services, mobility support, collaboration and information sharing amongst community members. The quality of services can be influenced by the functionalities delivered and performance requirements. These may include personalized service functionality, service discovery, security and trust requirements. The costs of healthcare services can be reduced when there are membership support, available aid and mobility support. Moreover, providing more efficient utilization of healthcare resources, reducing number of case referrals and frequency of hospital visits can contribute to reduced costs of healthcare services. Figure 2 shows the mapping of the vehicle metrics onto the tenor metrics by associating their corresponding conceptual measures, making the tenor metrics a concrete choice for the evaluation.

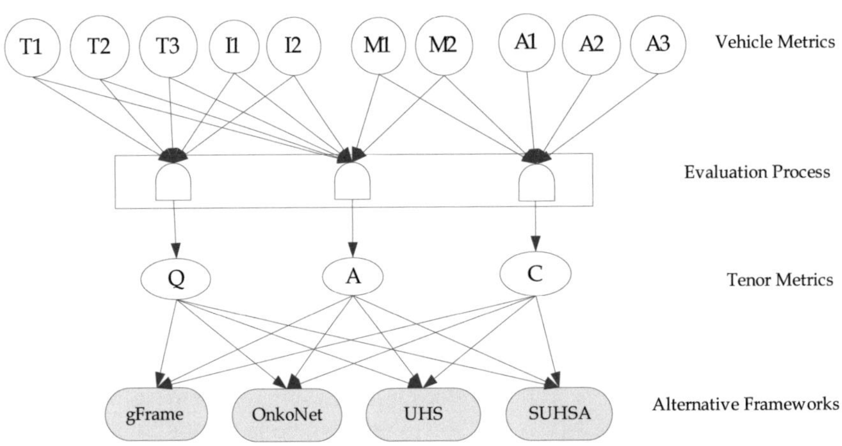


Fig. 2. Mapping of vehicle metrics onto tenor metrics for frameworks evaluation

The mapping of the vehicle metrics onto the tenor metrics is described as follows. Quality of service is measured in terms of five vehicle metrics, awareness, privacy, control, intelligibility and customization. These metrics can guarantee that services are of high quality when the infrastructure supporting healthcare services can enable secure and ubiquitous discovery of personalized services, thereby satisfying the quality requirement of the tenor metrics. Cost reduction is measured in terms of the vehicle metrics, value, cost and availability. Based on cost reduction tenor metrics, membership support, availability of aid and mobility support can guarantee reduced costs of healthcare services. Access to services is measured in terms of vehicle metrics, social acceptance and environmental change. According to the tenor metrics, mobility support, community membership commitment, low-costs of resources and quality of services can guarantee social acceptance and willingness of users to modify their environment to accommodate the system. But the quality of services might not be a good measure of cost reduction as quality services are expected to be more expensive. But access to services can guarantee possible cost reduction.

### 6.2 Frameworks comparison

To evaluate our gFrame for its effectiveness in addressing the challenges of the conventional healthcare system it is compared with three other frameworks based on the tenor metrics. These systems were carefully selected from the literature based on their promises to deliver ubiquitous healthcare service provisioning. The comparative study also enables us to establish the novelty and uniqueness of our framework for ubiquitous healthcare service provisioning. These frameworks are OnkoNet (Kirn, 2002), Ubiquitous Healthcare System (UHS) (Jung et al., 2008) and Secure Ubiquitous Healthcare System Architecture (SUHSA) (Nikolidakis et al., 2010).

The OnkoNet is a mobile agents-based architecture to address the problem of accessibility to healthcare services by individual consumers using mobile devices. The OnkoNet architecture supports knowledge intensive cooperation among humans and software agents to produce, deliver, control and consume healthcare services in virtual communities supporting the cooperation of actors involved in cancer diagnosis and therapy. The OnkoNet supports local and mobile access and achieves a much better integration of patients and healthcare practitioners. While the architecture promises to support community based healthcare management that can facilitate cost reduction, it does not integrate into grids to fully support accessibility and quality of service provisioning.

The UHS consisted of vital signs devices and environment sensor devices to acquire context information to monitor and manage health status of patients anytime anywhere. The framework targeted the development of four healthcare applications including self-diagnosis, remote monitoring, exercise management and emergency services. However, the framework is not based on virtual community and does not integrate into grids to fully provide quality and ubiquitous services at reduced costs.

The SUHSA was proposed to enable a real-time collection of healthcare data from body sensors. The collected data are converted to a CDA format, digitally signed, encrypted and securely transmitted over the Internet protocol Multimedia Subsystem (IMS) and Health Level 7 (HL7) messaging standards to a central hospital from where data can be accessed by doctors to assess the patient's health condition. The IMS provides internet services with QoS and integrates different services as well. While this architecture supports patient's mobility and security, it does not support grids and community based technologies for service provisioning.

Table 4 shows the summary of comparing four different ubiquitous healthcare service frameworks where the rating of 0 means a column framework does not support row metric, 1 means partial support and 2 means full support. The total evaluation score received by each framework based on ability to address the challenges of conventional healthcare system shows that gFrame seems to be more promising because of its vision to integrate MDVC into the Healthgrid for ubiquitous, quality and cost-effective healthcare service provisioning. It can also be observed that OnkoNet seems to address the cost reduction challenge and SUHSA addresses the quality service challenge of the conventional healthcare system. However, OnkoNet, SUHSA and UHS frameworks do not consider all the three challenges of conventional healthcare system in the way that gFrame does, therefore making our framework unique in addressing the important challenges of healthcare system.

| Metrics/Framework | gFrame | OnkoNet | UHS | SUHSA |
|---|---|---|---|---|
| **Quality Services** | 2 | 1 | 1 | 2 |
| **Access to Services** | 2 | 1 | 1 | 1 |
| **Cost Reduction** | 2 | 2 | 1 | 1 |
| **Total Score** | 6 | 4 | 3 | 4 |

Table 4. Frameworks comparison based on tenor metrics

## 7. Conclusion

This particular chapter discusses the roles of telemedicine, wireless body area network and wireless utility grid computing technologies to address the challenges of conventional healthcare system. We discuss the possible integration of these technologies to realize a framework for ubiquitous healthcare service provisioning. Moreover, our framework was compared with some three other ubiquitous healthcare frameworks and it promises to address the challenges of healthcare system by taking advantages of grid computing and mobile computing technologies. Our framework integrates MDVC of healthcare into the Healthgrid through a proxy based approach for performance benefits. The framework allows for remote vital signs acquisition and personalized grid service discovery through a metadata and Fuzzy logic based intelligent context engine.

Our current approach to address the challenges of the conventional healthcare system builds on innovative exploitation of the emerging technologies to realize a grid enabled framework for ubiquitous healthcare service provisioning. This framework provides a means to empower individuals in the rural world to have convenient access to quality healthcare services at reduced costs through mobile devices that they carry about without necessarily moving to the physical locations that those services are offered.

The development of a grid enabled framework integrating virtual communities of healthcare into grids is generally challenging, but it promises to yield enticing outcomes to enable ubiquitous healthcare service provisioning. In addition to addressing the challenges of healthcare system, our framework also addresses a number of research problems to support context awareness, mobility and personalized grid service discovery. The framework infrastructure is currently under development and we hope to deploy it in the future. It is also part of our future plan to consider evaluating the framework from a user perspective and to test its efficacy for enabling ubiquitous rural healthcare service provisioning.

## 8. References

Abuelmaatti, A. & Rezgui, Y. (2008). Virtual organizations in practice: a European perspective. *Proceedings of Americas Conference on Information Systems (AMCIS).*

Amendolia, S.R., Estrella, F., Frate, C.D., Galvey, J., Hassan, W., Hauer, T., Manset, D, McClatchey, R., Odeh, M., Rogulin, D., Solomonides, T. & Warren, R. (2005). Development of a Grid-based medical imaging application. *Proceedings of Healthgrid* 2005, 59-69.

Barrera, M., Betancu, L., Navarro, A., Cardona, N. & Rodrigo, V.M. (2010 ). SNR estimation for on body communications in MB OFDM ultra wide band communications. *Proceedings of the Fourth European Conference on Antennas and Propagation*. Barcelona, Spain. 1-5.

Berman, F., Fox, G. & Hey, T. (2003). The Grid: past, present, future: in grid computing: making the global infrastructure a reality. *John Wiley & Sons*, 9-50.

Boccia, V., Guarracino, M.R., D'Amore, L. & Laccetti, G. (2005). A grid-enabled PSE for medical imaging: experiences on MediGrid, *In Proceedings of 18th IEEE Symposium Comput-Based Med. Syst.* (CBMS), 529-536.

Brady, M., Gavagham, D., Simpson, A., Parada, M.M. & Highnam, R.(2003). eDiaMoND: a grid-enabled federated database of annotated mammograms. In Grid Computing: Making the Global Infrastructure a Reality, 3rd ed. *New York Wiley Series, 923-943.*

Breton, V., Medina, R. & Montagnat, J. (2003). DataGrid, prototype of a biomedical grid. *Methods Inf. Med. (MIM)*, 42, 143-148.

Chavez-Santiago, R., Khaleghi, A., Balasingham, J. & Ramstad, T.A. (2009). Architecture of an ultra wideband wireless body area network for medical applications. *Proceedings of 2nd IEEE Intl. Symp. On Applied Sciences in Biomedical and Communication Technology (ISABEL* 2009), Bratislava, Slovakia.

Chen, Y.F., Huang, H., Jana, R., Jim, T., Hiltunen, M., John, S., Jora, S., Muthumanickam, R & Wei, B. (2003). iMobile EE - an enterprise mobile service platform. *Wireless Networks, 9, 283-297.*

Chu, D.C. & Humphrey, M. (2004). Mobile OGSI.NET: grid computing on mobile devices. *5th IEEE/ACM International Workshop on Grid Computing*, 182-191.

El Morr, C. & Kawash, J. (2007). Mobile virtual communities research: a synthesis of current trends and a look at future perspectives. *International Journal of Web Based Communities*, 3(4), 386-403.

Foster, I. & Kesselmann, C. (1999). The grid: blueprint for a new computing infrastructure. *Morgan Kaufmann, San Francisco.*

Foster,I., Kesselman, C. & Tuecke,S. (2001). The anatomy of the grid: enabling scalable virtual organizations. *International Journal of Supercomputer Applications*, 15(3), 200-220.

Foster, I. (2002). What is the grid? A three checklist, *GridToday*, 1(6), 22-25.

Foster, I. (2006). Globus toolkit version 4: software for service-oriented systems. *Journal of Comput. Sci. & Technol.*, 21(4), 513-520.

Geddes, J., Lloyd, S., Simpson, A., Rossor, M., Fox, N., Hill, D., Hajnal, J.V., Lawrie, S., Mcintosh, A., Johnstone, E., Wardlaw, J., Perry, D., Procter, R., Bath, P. & Bullmore, E. (2005). NeuroGrid: using grid technology to advance neuroscience,. *In Proceedings of 18th IEEE Symposium Comput-Based Med. Syst.* (CBMS), 570-572.

Gjermundrod, H., Dikaiakos, M.D., Zeinalipour-Yazti, D., Panayi, G & Kyprianou, T. (2007). ICGrid: enabling intensive care medical research on the EGEE grid. In from Genes to Personalized HealthGrid: Grid Solutions for the Life Sciences. *Proceedings of Healthgrid*, 248-257.

Grethe, J.S., Baru, C., Gupta, A., James, M., Ludaescher, B., Martone, M.E., Papadopoulos, P.M., Peltier, S.T., Rajasekar, A. & Santini, S. (2005). Biomedical informatics research network: building a national collaboration to hasten the derivation of new understanding and treatment of disease. *Proceedings of Healthgrid*, 100-109.

Hwang, J. & Aravamudham, P. (2004). Middleware services for P2P computing in wireless grid networks. *Internet Computing*, 8(4), 40-46.

Isaiadis, S., & Getov, V. (2005). A lightweight platform for integration of mobile devices into pervasive grids. *In Proceedings of High Performance Computing and Communications, Sorrento, Italy*, 1058-1063.

Jacq, N., Salzemann, J., Legre, Y., Reichstadr, M., Jacq, F., Zimmermann, M., Maab, A., Srihar, K., Schnichtenberg, H., Hofmann, M. & Breton, V. (2006). Demonstration of in silico docking at a large scale on grid infrastructure. *Proceedings of HealthGrid Conference Studies in Health Technology and Informatics*, 120, 155-157.

Jähnert, J.,Mandic, P.,Cuevas, A.Wesner, S. Moreno, J.I., Villagra, V., Olmedo, V. & Stiller, B. (2010). A prototype and demonstrator of Akogrimo's architecture: an approach of merging grids, SOA and the mobile internet. *Computer Communications*, 33, 1304–1317.

Jung, J., Ha, K., Lee, J., Kim, Y. & Kim, D. (2008). Wireless body area network in a ubiquitous healthcare system for physiological signal monitoring and health consulting. *International Journal of Signal Processing, Image Processing and Pattern Recognition*, 1(1), 47-54.

Kaur, D. & Sengupta, J. (2007). Resource discovery in web-services based grids. *World Academy of Science, Engineering and Technology*, 31, 284-288.

Kim, S. (2002). Ubiquitous healthcare: the OnkoNet mobile agents architecture. *Proceeding Workshop on Mobile Computing in Medicine*, 105–118.

Kobryn, C. & Sibbald, C. (2004). Modeling DoDAF compliant architectures. A Telelogic White Paper.
*URL: www.uml-forum.com/docs/papers/White_Paper_Modeling_DoDAF_UML2.pdf.*

Latre, B., Braem, B., Moerman, I., Blondia, C. & Demeester, P. (2010 ). A survey on wireless body area networks. Wireless Networks Manuscript.
*URL: www.pats.ua.ac.be/content/publications/2010/bbraem10wbansurvey.pdf*

Leimeister, J.M., Daum, M. & Kremar, H. (2002). Mobile communication and computing in healthcare - designing and implementing mobile virtual communities for cancer patients. *In Proceedings of the Tokyo Mobile Business Roundtable*, Tokyo.

Leu, F. & Wang, T (2006). A wireless grid service platform using SIP and agents. *Proceedings of the Seventh ACIS International Conference on Software Engineering, Artificial Intelligence, Networking and Parallel/Distributed Computing.*

Li, G., Sun, H., Gao, H., Yu, H. & Cai, Y. (2009). A survey on wireless grids and clouds. *Eight International Conference on Grid and Cooperative Computing*. 261-267.

Li, H., Takahashi, T., Toyoda, M., Katayama, N., Mori, Y. & Kohno, R., (2008). An experimental system enabling WBAN data delivery via satellite communication links. *IEEE International Symposium on Wireless Communication Systems - ISWCS* '08, 354-358.

Lioyd, S., Jiritka, M., Simpson, A.C., Highnam, R.P., Gavaghan, D.J., Watson, D. &Brady, J.M. (2005). Digital mammography: a world without film? *Methods of Information in Medicine*, 44(2), 168-169.

Manvi, S.S. & Birje, M.N. (2010). A review on wireless grid computing. *International Journal of Computer and Electrical Engineering*. 2(3), 469-474.

Miles, S., Papay, J., Dialani, V., Luck, M., Decker, K., Payne, T. & Moreau, L. (2003). Personalised grid service discovery. *IEE Proceedings of Softw*, 150(4), 252-256.

Moline, J. (1997). Virtual reality in health care: a survey. In: Riva, G. ed. Virtual reality in neuro-psycho-physiology. *Amsterdam: IOS Press*, 3-34.

Nam, J. (2009). A trust framework of ubiquitous healthcare with advanced Petri net model. *Electronic Healthcare*, 1, 122-129.

Naseer, A. & Stergioulas, L.K. (2010). Web-services-based resource discovery model and service deployment on HealthGrids. *IEEE Transactions on Information Technology in Biomedicine*, 14(3), 838-845.

Nikolidakis, S.A., Georgakakis, E., Giotsas, V., Vergados, D.D. & Douligeris, C. (2010). Secure ubiquitous healthcare system based on IMS and the HL7 standards. *Proceedings of the 3rd International Conference on Pervasive Technologies Related to Assistive Environments, (PETRA'10)*, Samos Greece, 42.

Olugbara, O.O., Ojo, S.O. & Adigun, M.O. (2007a). Requirements Engineering Framework for Information Utility Infrastructure for Rural e-Healthcare Service Provisioning. *Information Resource Management Association (IRMA), Doctorate Symposium*, Vancour, Canada, 1644-1647.

Olugbara, O.O., Adigun, M.O., Ojo, S.O. & Mudali, P. (2007b). Utility Grid Computing and Body Area Network as Enabler for Ubiquitous Rural e-Healthcare Service Provisioning. *Proceedings. of IEEE 9th International Conference on e-Health Networking, Application and Services*, 19-22 June, 2007, Taipei, Taiwan. 202-207.

Parikh, T.S. & Lazowska, E.D. (2006). Designing an architecture for delivering mobile information services to rural developing world. *International World Wide Web Conference (IW3C2)*, 791-800.

Peiravi, A. & Farahi, M. (2010). Reliability of wireless body area networks used for ambulatory monitoring and healthcare. *Life Science Journal*, 7(2), 91-97.

Phan, T., Huang, L. & Dulan, C. (2002). Challenge: integrating mobile wireless devices into the computational grid. *MOBICOM'02*, Atlanta, Georgia, USA.

Porter, C.E. (2004). A typology of virtual communities a multi-disciplinary foundation for future research. *Journal of Computer-Mediated Communication*, 10(1).

Rheingold, H. (2003). Mobile virtual communities. TheFeature.com Archives. *URL: www.thefeaturearchives.com/topic/Culture/Mobile_Virtual_Communities.html.*

Riva, G & Gamberini, L. (2000). Virtual reality in telemedicine. *Telemedicine Journal and e-Health*, 6(3), 327-340.

Risk, M., Castrillo, F.P., Eijo, J.F.G., Ortega, C.S., Fernandez, M.B., Diaz, A.P., Solar, M.R. & Pollan, R.R. (2009). CardioGrid: a framework for the analysis of cardiological signals in grid computing. *Network Operations and Management Symposium (LANOMS, 2009)*, Punta del Else, 1-4.

Roy, S. (2003). State of the art of virtual reality therapy (VRT) in phobic disorders. *Psychology Journal*, 1(2), 176-183.

Ryckaert, J., Desset, C., Fort, A., Badaroslu, M., De Heyn, V., Wambacq, P., Van der Plas, G., Donnay, S., Van Poucke, B. & Cyselinckx, B (2005). Ultra-wide-band transmitter for low-power wireless body area networks: design and evaluation. *IEEE Transactions on Circuits and Systems*, 52(12), 2515-2525.

Scarlat, E. Maracine, V. & Nica, A. (2007). Knowledge management for virtual reality applications in home rehabilitation virtual network. *The Electronic Journal of Knowledge Management*, 5(4), 477-486.

Scholtz, J. & Cansolvo, S. (2004). Towards a framework for evaluating ubiquitous computing applications. *Pervasive Computing*, 82-88.

Schulzrinne, H. & Wedlund, E. (2000). Application layer mobility using SIP. *ACM SIGMOBILE Mobile Computing and Communication Review*, 4(3), 47-57.

Shaikh, A., Memon, N., Memon, M. & Misbahuddin, M. (2009). The role of service oriented architecture in telemedicine healthcare system. *IEEE International Conference on Complex, Intelligent and Software Intensive Systems*. 208-214.

Shirazi, H. & Zahedian, A. (2009). A uniform method for evaluating the products of DoDAF architecture framework.*MASAUM Journal of Computing*. 1(3), 392-397.

Sneha, S. & Varshney, U. (2006). Ubiquitous healthcare: a new frontier in e-health. *Proceedings of Americas Conference on Information Systems (AMCIS)*.

Sriama, S.N., Jarke, M. & Prinz, W. (2006), Mobile web service provisioning. *Proceedings of the Advanced International Conference on Telecommunicat.ons and International Conference on Internet and Web Applications and Services (ICIW'06)*. Guadeloupe, French Caribbean.

Sun, L., Hu, P., Goh, C., Hamadicharef, B., Ifeachor, E., Barbounakis, I., Zervakis, M., Nurminen, N., Varri, A., Fontanelli, R., Di Bona, S., Guerri, D., La Manna, S., Cerbioni, K., Palanca, E. & Starita, A. (2006). Bioprofiling over grid for eHealthcare. *Proceedings of Healthgrid*, Valencia Spain.

Travostino, F., Mambretti, J. & Edwards, G.K. (2006). Grids networks: enabling grids with advanced communication technology. *John Wiley.*

Van Beijnum, B.J.F., Pawar, P., Dulawan, C.B. & Hermens, H.H. (2009). Mobile virtual communities for telemedicine: research challenges and opportunities. *International Journal of Computer Science and Applications*, 6(2), 19-37.

Van Dam, K., Pitchers, S. & Barnard, M. (2001). Body area networks: towards a wearable futures. *In Proceedings of WWRF kick off meeting*, Munich Germany.

Van Halteren, A. & Pawar, P. (2006). Mobile service platform: a middleware for nomadic mobile service provisioning. *IEEE International conference on ireless and Mobile Computing, Networking and Communication,(WIMOB2006)*, 292-299.

Van't Klooster, J., Pawar, P., van Beijnum, B., Dulawan, C. & Hermens, H. (2010). Perspectives on the viable mobile virtual community for telemedicine. *Encyclopedia of E-Business Development and Management in the Global Economy*, 824-835.

Waldburger, M. and Stiller, B. (2005). Towards the mobile grid: service provisioning in a mobile dynamic virtual organization. *Technical Report, University of Zurich*, 7, 1-12.

Ylisaukko-oja, A., Vildjiounaite, E. & Mantyjarvi, J. (2004), Five-point acceleration sensing wireless body area network - design and practical experiences. *Eighth International Symposium on Wearable Computers. (ISWC2004)*, 1,184-185.

Yokoo, M., Durfee, E.H., Ishida, T. & Kuwabara, K. (1998). The distributed constraint satisfaction problem: formalization and algorithms. *IEEE Transactions on Knowledge and Data Engineering*, 10(5), 673-685.

Zhang, D., Yu, Z. & Chin, C. (2004). Context-aware infrastructure for personalized healthcare. *The International Workshop on Personalized Health*, Belfast, Northern Ireland.

# 13

# The Porting of Wargi-DSS to Grid Computing Environment for Drought Plans in Complex Water Systems

Andrea Sulis[1], Valeria Ardizzone[2], Emilio Giorgio[2] and Giovanni M. Sechi[1]
*[1]Hydraulic Sector, Department of Land Engineering, University of Cagliari*
*[2]National Institute of Nuclear Physics, Sezione di Catania*
*Italy*

## 1. Introduction

The increasing developments in computer technology have motivated the concurrent development of Decision Support Systems (DSSs) aimed at facilitating the planning and management of complex water systems (Assaf et al., 2008). Simulation and optimization models within DSSs provide the main tool for researchers and practitioners to analyze the behavior and performance of any proposed water resource system design or management policy alternative before it is implemented in real systems. Various strategies have been proposed to combine the adherence and flexibility of simulation models with the efficient exploration of mathematical optimization models (Loucks and van Beek, 2005).

AQUATOOL (Valencia Polytechnic University) (Andreu et al., 1996), MODSIM (Colorado State University) (Labadie et al., 2000), RIBASIM (DELTARES) (Delft Hydraulics, 2006), WARGI-SIM (University of Cagliari) (Sechi and Sulis, 2009a) and WEAP (Stockholm Environmental Institute) (SEI, 2005) are representative of DSSs used for preliminary analysis of alternative plans and policies. Those popular generic simulation models have been implemented world-wide in a large number of water systems and incorporate most of the desirable attributes of a simulation model. WARGI (WAter Resources Graphical Interface) is a generic DSS for planning and management complex water systems developed at the University of Cagliari (Italy). The DSS is specifically developed to meet the system management requirements to satisfy the growing demands in multi-reservoir systems under water scarcity conditions, as frequently, happen in the Mediterranean regions. Sechi and Sulis (2009a) have recently developed a full integration of the simulation module WARGI-SIM and the linear optimization module WARGI-OPT in the DSS. This mixed simulation-optimization approach was proposed with the aim of identifying and evaluating mitigation measures in a proactive approach that anticipates the trigger of these actions.

The processes that govern the behavior of multireservoir water systems are affected by uncertainty that increases with time and space investigation scales (Simonovic, 2000). Uncertainty is mainly associated with the value of hydrological exogenous inflows and users demand patterns. A common disadvantage of the traditional modeling approach is the large number of system simulations required to achieve acceptable levels of confidence treating data uncertainties in the model. In fact, the proactive approach to drought

mitigation must be based on a large number of hydrological scenarios that the water system might experience. In the case of computationally intensive software implementation, they can result extremely time and resources consuming and the applicability of these models is sometimes limited to relatively simple applications.
There's an upper limit to how fast a computer can complete an operation or how much information it can store. Most computers are upgradeable, which means it's possible to add more power or capacity to a single computer, but that's still just an incremental increase in performance. Grid computing is an innovative approach that leverages existing Information Technology (IT) infrastructure to optimize compute resources and manage data and computing workloads in a secure and collaborative environment: it links computer resources together in a way that lets someone use one computer to access and leverage the collected power of all the computers in the system. To the individual user, it is as if the user's computer has transformed into a supercomputer. Grid is not a new concept but one that has gained recent renewed interest and activity for Computing problems in several scientific and industrial fields. Grid involves processing large volumes of data and/or performing repetitive computations to the extent that the workload requirements exceed existing server platform capabilities. A grid is both hardware and software services, in the field of the advanced calculation and of the nets data transmissions to high speed network that allows to various geographic sites to share the own resources in dynamics and intelligent way and allowing the transparent, secure, controlled access by multiple users for public or private scientific and technologic research. Grids is built "on top of" hardware (like computers and networks), which forms the physical infrastructure of a grid. Networks link the different computers that form part of a grid, allowing them to be handled as one huge computer. Above the network layer lies the resource layer: actual grid resources, such as computers, storage systems, electronic data catalogues, sensors and telescopes that are connected to the network. The middleware layer provides the tools that enable the various elements (servers, storage, networks, etc.) to participate in a grid. Middleware is made up of many software programs, containing hundreds of thousands of lines of computer code. Together, this code automates all the "machine to machine" interactions that create a single, seamless computational grid. The highest layer of the grid architecture is the application layer, which includes applications in science, engineering, business, finance and more, as well as portals and development toolkits to support the applications. This is the layer that grid users "see" and interact with. A Virtual Organization (VO) represents a fundamental concept of Grid Computing technology: it is a group of grid users with similar interests and requirements who are able to work collaboratively with other members of the group and/or share resources (data, software, expertise, CPU, storage space, etc.) regardless of geographical location. A user will need to be a member of a VO before to be allowed to submit a request (properly called job) to the grid. Exceptionally, if an existing VO is not appropriate a new VO can be created.
An application that ordinarily runs on a stand-alone PC must be "gridified" before it can run on a grid. "Gridification" means adapting applications to include new layers of grid-enabled software. Once gridified, thousands of people will be able to use the same application and run it trouble-free on interoperable grids. Grid computing is the IT technology enabling worldwide scientific projects, such as the Large Hadron Collider (LHC) at CERN, and powering global efforts to combat climate change, discover new medicines, map the skies, reconstruct the sound of ancient instruments, covers some aspects of the preservation and the fruition of cultural heritages and so on. The Enabling Grids for E-sciencE (EGEE) project

(http://eu-egee.com/) began by working with two scientific groups, High Energy Physics (HEP) and Life Sciences, and has since grown to support formally astronomy, astrophysics, computational chemistry, earth sciences, fusion, and computer science. The full user community runs applications from research domains as diverse as multimedia, finance, archaeology, and civil protection (http://grid.ct.infn.it/egee_applications/).

The specific benefits that can be achieved from grid computing are dependent upon the grid-enabled applications and the degree of implementation. In general, grid computing can be a cost effective way to resolve IT issues in the areas of data, computing and collaboration, especially if they require enormous amounts of compute power, complex computer processing cycles or access to large data sources, because of its benefits include infrastructure optimization, more access to data and increased collaboration.

This paper describes a research project funded by the Italian Ministry of Education, University and Research (PON-CyberSar Project) and the Regione Autonoma della Sardegna (PO Sardegna FSE 2007-2013 - L.R. 7/2007) on the porting of the WARGI-DSS to the Italian National GRID. Specifically, this paper focuses on the possible use of the combined simulation and optimization approach in the WARGI-DSS within the GRID environment for the definition of drought mitigation measures based on a large number of possible future system evolutions. It is organized as follows. In Section 2, an overview of the development and features of WARGI-DSS is presented. Section 3 describes the implementation of the GRID approach to satisfy the requirements of massive simulation-optimization runs. Sections 4 and 5 show a practical application to a complex water system in the Mediterranean area, and conclusions and perspective of future works.

## 2. An overview of the WARGI-DSS

### 2.1 The WARGI-DSS structure

WARGI-DSS is a user-friendly tool specifically developed to help users understanding interrelationships between demands and resources for the management and planning of multi-reservoir water systems under water scarcity conditions, as frequently happen in the Mediterranean regions. The DSS makes it possible to take into account a large number of system components that typically characterize water resources models. The tool is flexible and generalized in the system configuration and data input, in the attribution of planning and operating policies and in processing output. Moreover, the software modularity allows easy coding changes and the addition of new objects and features in the system diagram.

The WARGI-DSS modeling capability includes several interrelated macro-modules implemented in C++ and Tcl/Tk (Figure 1), the main ones being: the Graphical User Interface (GUI) module, the System initialization and Data Input module (SDI), the SIMulation module (WARGI-SIM), the deterministic OPTimization module (WARGI-OPT), the QUALity optimization module (WARGI-QUAL), the SCENario optimization module (WARGI-SCEN), the Solver modules and the Result Evaluation and Output plotting module (REO).

As illustrated by Manca et al. (2004), in the GUI module there are procedures that create and set the various graphic objects of WARGI: the canvas, the palette, the menu bar and the relative drop down menus, the scroll bars and the state bar. The SDI module handles the values definition of the main parameters and the creation and possible modification of system elements. This module processes data coming from the GUI module, transfers data required by the simulation module WARGI-SIM and implements the optimization algorithm WARGI-OPT. The construction by means of independent modules also makes it possible to use the DSS either for system optimization alone or for simulation alone.

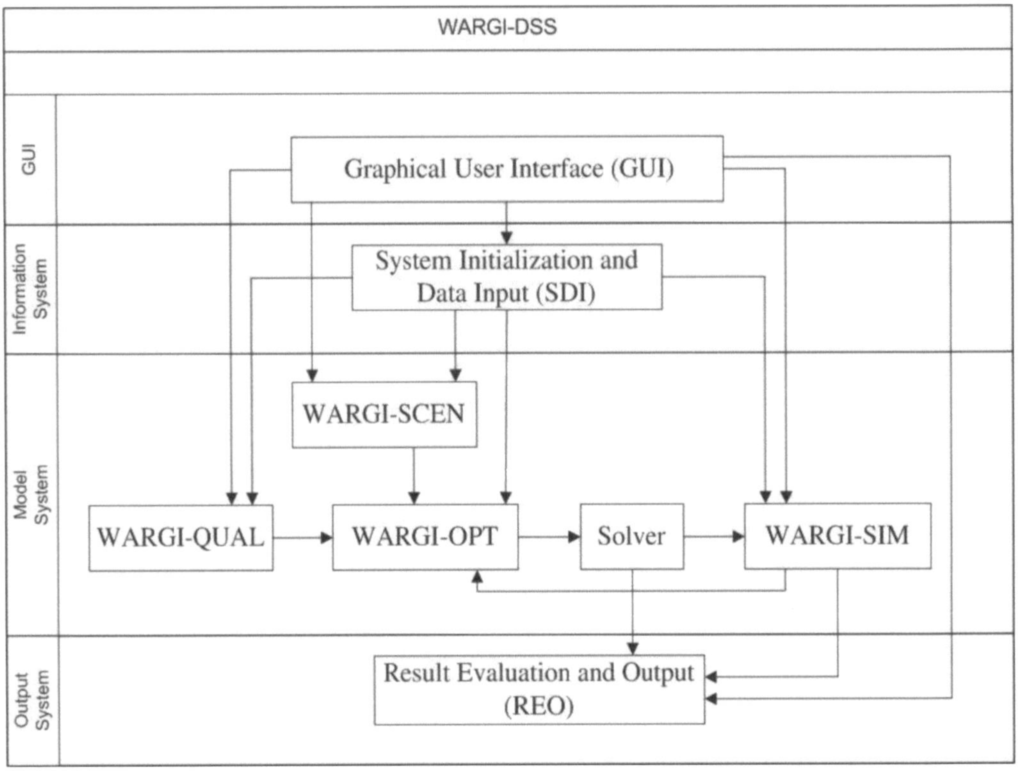


Fig. 1. General structure of WARGI-DSS.

When considering a single scenario in a deterministic analysis, WARGI-OPT models the problem by Linear Programming (LP) or Quadratic Programming (QP). The optimization model is supported by a multi-period dynamic graph (Sechi and Zuddas, 2007) and determines the construction of a file in the MPS (Mathematical Programming Standard) format to be submitted to a solver. The MPS is supported by efficient commercial and non-commercial mathematical programming computer codes. WARGI has been particularly tested using CPLEX (2006) and Lp_Solve (http://lpsolve.sourceforge.net/). Specific procedures in WARGI manage the dynamic link with the solver and allow to select the solving code.

If analysis with scenario optimization is required, WARGI-SCEN module passes to the WARGI-OPT module (Pallottino et al., 2005) parameters for model construction to consider different system evolutions. Moreover, water quality optimization considering synthetic quality indexes for water sources and demands is implemented in the WARGI-QUAL module (Sechi and Sulis, 2007b, 2009b).

WARGI-SIM does not require the input of specific operating rules (Loucks and Sigvaldason, 1982), but the definition of "preferences" and "priorities" by the user (Sechi and Sulis, 2009a). As usual, the preliminary requirement of WARGI-SIM is to represent in the model all the features the user thinks are important with respect to the objectives of the study. This enables WARGI-SIM to identify the technical and economic constraints of the system being modelled.

While the modular architecture allows the user to analyse multiple alternatives with the simulation or optimization alone, it is often advantageous to use both WARGI-SIM and WARGI-OPT. Sechi and Sulis (2009a) have recently proposed a combined optimization-simulation technique in WARGI-DSS. In the combined approach, WARGI-SIM processes the flows configuration provided by WARGI-OPT when foreseeing for many different hydrologic scenarios. The optimization results can be seen as a reference target for the simulation phase and WARGI-SIM can define drought mitigation measures that anticipate the occurrence of water scarcity. These measures are pre-emptive measures developed in a proactive approach to face drought events (Yevjevich et al., 1983; Rossi, 2000; Sechi and Sulis, 2007a).

This mixed optimization-simulation approach has to manage a large number of generated hydrologic scenarios and operating rules that might be tested in the simulation model and the GRID computing is very attractive to face this complex computation problem.

Previous papers have shown the wide applicability of GRIDs to solve large-scale computations and data-intensive computing problems in environmental systems. GRIDs appear to be promising in the optimization and simulation of complex systems but few applications have focused on the analysis of multi-reservoir systems (Sulis, 2009).

### 2.2 The data structure

WARGI-DSS represents a water resource system using a direct network (graph) that consists of nodes, both storage (water source) and non-storage (water demand, and hydropower, treatment, pumping plants), and arcs (pipeline, canals or natural rivers, and special arcs) (Figure 2). Nodes and arcs represent these physical and hydrologic features, but also symbolize artificial elements for modeling events (i.e. water scarcity conditions). These artificial elements are added automatically by WARGI-DSS. Each graphic element of the graph is denominated GOB (Graphical OBject) and is identified by both the type of GOB and the "identifying value" called Tk-id. Each element is inserted in a list of active GOBs.

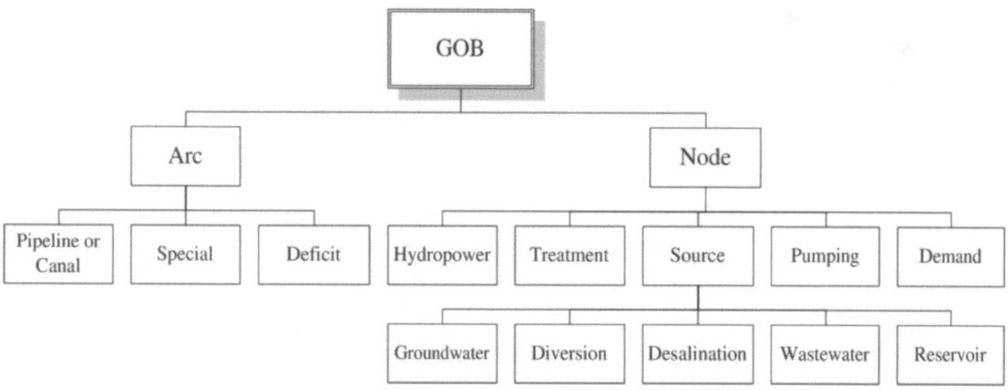


Fig. 2. GOB types.

A hash table contains the information associated to the GOB. The hash table is represented as a structure C of Tcl_HashTable type. The hash table associated to a GOB is generated as the GOB is created. The WARGI-DSS modules use scripts and procedures written in TCL/TK or C++ to communicate with hash tables getting or storing GOB data. Scripts and procedures are provided for the research and modification of old entries and the creation of new entries.

WARGI uses keys of the char* type to quickly localize its entry in the hash table. Such a key is associated to a value which is a pointer to the initial position of the hash table containing the information on the GOB attributes. The GOB attributes can be of a scalar, cyclic or vector

type and are stored inside the structure defined in C++, initialized by the information contained in the TCL variables. The TCL variables of a GOB contain the values inserted directly by the user with the graphic interface or through linked data files.
The access to the hash table is through the TCL library procedure, written inside the procedures C++; these allow the possibility of accessing information on the attributes of the GOB directly by the execution of script TCL, or directly through the calling of function C or C++. The communication between variables TCL and C/C++ is guaranteed by the mechanism called "variable linking" which allows the value of the TCL variables to be associated to the C/C++ variables and vice versa. Such a mechanism allows different variables to share the same values.
In the graph of the water system the correspondence node-arcs is represented by a matrix of adjacency. Every node maintains a memory of a dynamic list which points at the first outgoing arc and a dynamic list which points at the first incoming arc. Such a list is up-dated every time a new arc is created or destroyed.
The information on the global variables (year-length simulation and optimization horizons, number of periods per year, optimization-simulation linking period) is stored in the TCL and C/C++ global variables. Such variables and the GOB attributes set up the case to be resolved. Decision variables are TCL and C/C++ local variables. These variables are an array of a number of dimensions based on the temporal scale chosen by the user.
The information of the optimization model can be saved in a file with idr extension. When the idr file is opened, all the GOBs are created and all the GOBs attributes in the data structure are uploaded. In such a case, the graph is showed in the main window of the graphical user interface (Figure 3). The TCL/TK interpreter and library procedures manage the data regarding the graphic layout of elements such as line, color, masks, graphs and zoom effects.

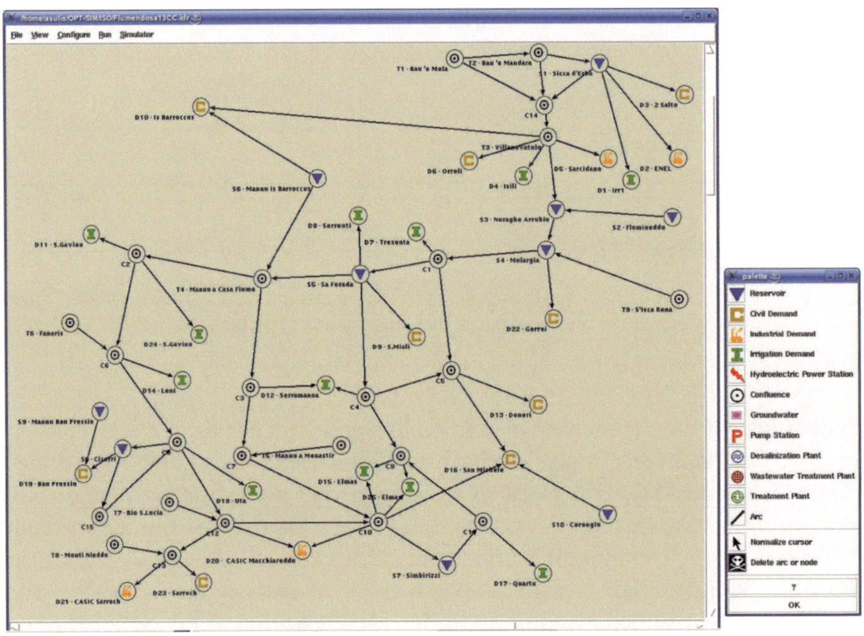


Fig. 3. Main windows in the GUI.

## 2.3 The graphical interface

WARGI-DSS employs an interactive graphical user interface that permits easy data entry and display, and control of model operations. A specific procedure creates and sets the graphic object of the GUI: the canvas, the palette, the menu bar and the relative drop down menus, the scroll and the state bars. The canvas allows user to create, locate and connect the components of the water system as shown in Figure 3. The core of the canvas is the graph of nodes and arcs (GOBs). The graph reflects the spatial relationships between the elements of the water system. A GIS layer can be added to provide clarity and impact. A central feature is the "drug-and-drop" that allows user to easy create and link GOBs. Each GOB must be associated with a hash table consisting of as many fields as the number of attribute in the GOB. The user can activate the GOB, open a window associated with that GOB and populate the hash table with the attributes of the GOB. The window of the reservoir GOB is shown in Figure 4 and the corresponding hash table must contain numerical information on the physical, hydrologic and management attributes of the reservoir. These attributes can be mandatory or optional; the latter may be included to further describe the reservoir.

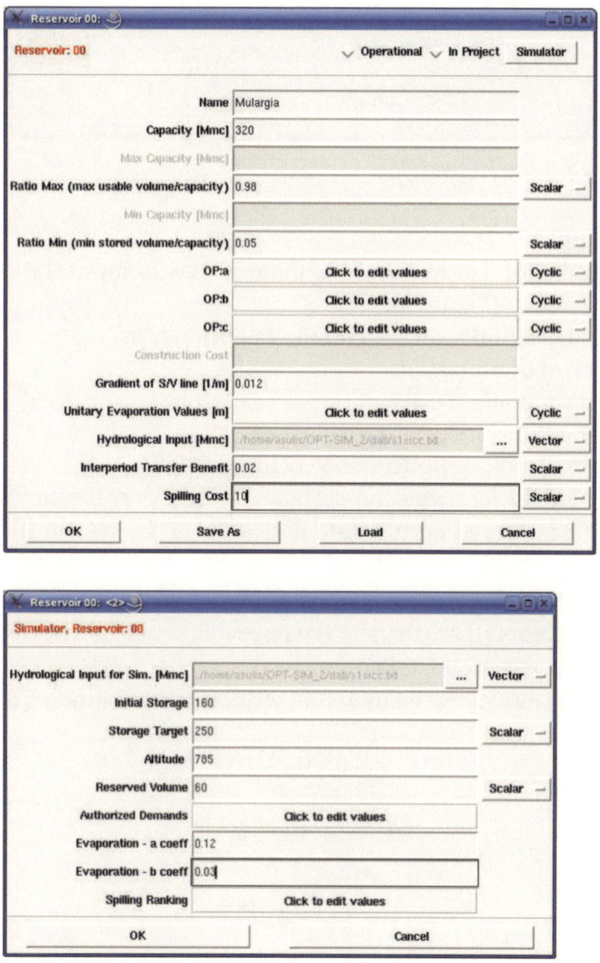


Fig. 4. Reservoir window in the GUI.

The menu bar provides access to the most important features of the DSS. The right-button mouse click on links opens the File (structure of the files), View (options to graphics), Configure (time settings and choice of optimization solver), Run (solver launch) and Simulation (simulation alone or mixed simulation-optimization) pull-down menus. Under the Configure menu, the Time menu allows the user to set the global variables (Figure 5) and the Solver menu to choose the solver. The Run and Simulation menus allow to use the DSS for system optimization alone (WARGI-OPT) or for simulation (WARGI-SIM), respectively.

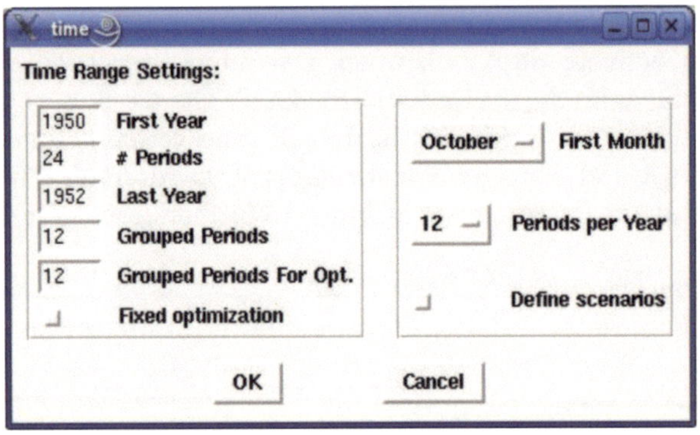


Fig. 5. Time window setting in the GUI.

### 2.4 The methodology

To perform the analysis of a water system, the user has to input the values of the global variables in the Time Menu (Figure 5):

T: time horizon of simulation for overall system analysis;
Δ: time horizon of optimization;
t=1,T: time step of simulation;
∂=1, Δ: time step of optimization;
$\tau = \tau_1, \tau_n$: period of simulation-optimization synchronization.

The WARGI-OPT module forecasts the system evolution on the time horizon Δ at each synchronization period $\tau_i$ based on the state indicators of the system [I] and a user-selected future hydrological synthetic scenario [$b_g$] (Figure 6). The state indicators [I] are used to trigger reactive measures; they are decision variables of the source GOBs. In multi-reservoir systems, the state indicators [I] are usually the reservoir storages. The hydrological scenarios [$b_g$] are attributes of the reservoir GOBs.

The linear optimization model can be therefore written in the following form:

$$\min_{t=(\tau,\tau+\Delta)} \quad (c_\gamma Y + c_i x_i + c_j x_j) \tag{1}$$

$$\text{s.t.} \qquad A[x] = b_g \tag{2}$$

$$F(Y,x) \geq 0 \tag{3}$$

$$l \leq x \leq u \tag{4}$$

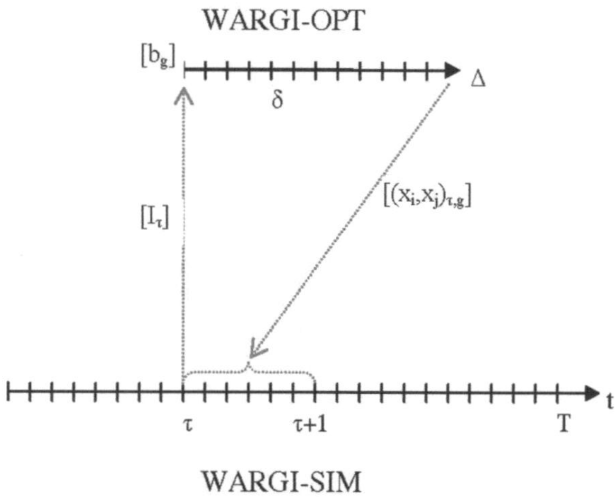


Fig. 6. Link between WARGI-OPT and WARGI-SIM (adapted from Sechi and Sulis, 2009a).

The GOBs attributes $[c_Y]$ are costs related to the decision variables of GOBs in project [Y], $[c_i]$ represents operative, maintenance, and replace costs (OMR) or user-defined costs of arc GOBs, and $[c_j]$ represents deficit costs based on priority ranking of demand GOBs. The decision variables $[x_i, x_j]$ are the subsets of the variables $[x]$ related to flows of pipeline or canal GOBs and to deficit of special arc GOBs, respectively. The GOBs attributes l and u are the lower and upper bounds on decision variables $[x_i, x_j]$.
In the WARGI-SIM module, preferences and priorities $[v]$ are attributes of sources and demands GOBs, respectively. Decision variables $[x_i, x_j]$, and preferences and priorities $[v]$ defines proactive mitigation measures $[z_\tau]$ that are attributes of sources and demands GOBs:

$$z_\tau = f_1\left(\left[x_i, x_j\right], v\right)_\tau \qquad \tau = \tau_1, \tau_n \tag{5}$$

The decision variables of water allocation $[X_t]$ in the system are the solution of a minimum cost flow problem between source and demand GOBs. These preemptive measures $[z_\tau]$ can modify the water allocations $[X_t]$ from those previously defined using the attributes of allocation rules [r] of arc GOBs and user-defined preferences and priorities $[v]$. Consequently, during the subsequent periods until $\tau_{i+1}$:

$$X_t = f_2\left(z_\tau, v, r\right) \qquad t = (\tau_i, \tau_{i+1}) \tag{6}$$

In the case of water scarcities more severe than those forecasted by WARGI-OPT, the preemptive measures $[z_\tau]$ do not make it possible to overcome the water scarcity, and WARGI-SIM introduces further restriction measures $[s_t]$ in a reactive approach. $[s_t]$ are attributes of source GOBs. These reactive actions are defined following the state indicators of the system $[I_t]$, the user-defined preferences and priorities $[v]$, and the pre-defined water allocations $[X_t]$:

$$s_t = f_3(I_t, X_t, v) \qquad t = (\tau_i, \tau_{i+1}) \tag{7}$$

The goal of this mixed optimization-simulation approach is to define the best combination of drought mitigation measures that minimizes the economic impact of drought in the water supply system. The economic response function R is the sum of the costs associated with the construction of new works in the system ([$C_Y$]), OMR costs ([$C_{OMR}$]), and costs related to mitigation measures ([$C_{PD}$] and [$C_{NPD}$]):

$$R = C_Y Y + \sum_{\tau_i} C_{PD} z_\tau + \sum_{t=1}^{T} C_{NPD} s_t + \sum_{t=1}^{T} \min\left(C_{OMR} X_t\right) \tag{8}$$

[$CP_D$] and [$C_{NPD}$] are associated with the drought mitigation measures in the proactive and reactive approaches, respectively. [$CP_D$] and [$C_{NPD}$] include the OMR costs for drought measures, agency income lost from reduced water sales, and reduced consumer surplus due to these measures.

## 3. The porting of WARGI-DSS to GRID computing

Uncertainty due to inherent randomness of hydrological events cannot be eliminated. Some of this uncertainty can be incorporated into models. Stochastic models have been applied to numerous water resources planning and management problems. Clearly if the system being analysed is very complex, the stochastic models are not robust enough to be applied to describe all complexities in the real world problem. An alternative approach is to solve a set of deterministic optimization models for each fixed interval over which the uncertain values can be discretized. A simulation phase is then performed to refine the optimization results (Loucks and van Beek, 2005) and to obtain a management policy for the system. In Sechi and Sulis (2009a) the proposed mixed optimization-simulation approach includes the hydrological uncertainty issue considering a large number n of synthetic hydrological series ($b_g$ in (2)). The model (1-8) was solved n-times considering one hydrological series at once to provide n sets of drought mitigation measures. The main disadvantages of that approach were:

1. Each set of drought mitigation measures was strictly related to the selected hydrological series. An ex-post sensitivity analysis was then carried out to estimate the economic impact of hydrological uncertainty on water system management;
2. The approach becomes rapidly time-consuming as the number of hydrological series increases.

In the proposed GRID approach (Figure 7), WARGI-SIM considers together n-sets of decision variables [$x_i$, $x_j$] (5) from the solution of n linear optimization models in the GRID environment. A weight is assigned to each set of decision variables [$x_i$, $x_j$]. A unique set of drought mitigation measures [$z_\tau$] on the number n of synthetic hydrological series [$b_g$] is then tested over the time horizon between the two synchronization periods $\tau_i$ and $\tau_{i+1}$.
Each model (1-4) is solved by the linear programming solver LpSolve downloaded on the Computing Elements that satisfy the job requirements. As expected, the user can get a significant reduction of computational time saving by applying the proposed GRID approach instead of the traditional local approach. Sulis (2009) discussed this computational advantage for the Implicit Stochastic Optimization (ISO) where the simulation and optimization models, not fully integrated, were used to define multireservoir operating rules, basically the optimum storage trajectories.
This article presents the porting of a DSS under which the simulation and optimization models have been implemented and fully integrated with the specific aim of defining drought mitigation measures. Details of the porting to the GRID environment of this integrated approach are presented in this section.

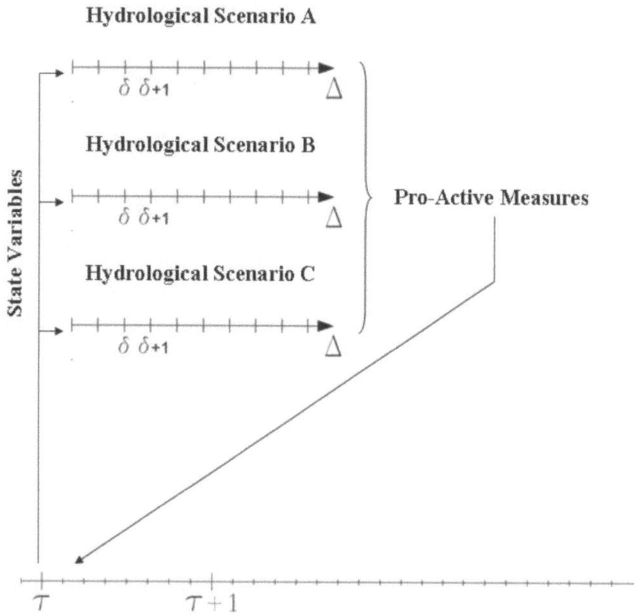


Fig. 7. Link between WARGI-OPT and WARGI-SIM in the proposed GRID environment.

### 3.1 Porting of the mixed optimization-simulation approach in WARGI-DSS

The middleware chosen for the implementation of the optimization-simulation approach is gLite. gLite is a full featured grid middleware stack, that provides to the user capabilities for interactions with grid elements at any level of complexity. In fact with gLite users can exploit directly resources, at low level, or let the so called central services the task of selecting, among those available, the most appropriate resource for the execution of the computational task. Clearly this second option is the most powerful, because it really enables the user to access the whole set of resources available.

In grid terminology, a computational task is defined as a job. In gLite, the WMS (Workload Management System) is the component deputy to accept users' job request, and dispatch them to the most appropriate resource. Users formalize the request through a declarative language, the JDL (Job Description Language), which allows them to specify job characteristics (as the executable name, additional files for the job execution, further requirements about resources, the output files to be retrieved...). The request for the job execution is the provision to the WMS of the file containing the job description; as outcome of the request, a job identifier is returned. This job identifier is eventually used for monitoring purposes, and finally for the job output retrieve, by the user.

Using the gLite middleware, a request for a job execution can trigger more than one computational task. Job of this type are called compound jobs, because they are actually made of sub-jobs, that can be still monitored and managed as if they were a single one, through a single job identifier. The advantage of this approach is that in case of big input files, they are transferred once to the resource, providing so an optimization of the bandwidth usage. Further, relationship among the sub-jobs can be expressed, allowing so the implementation of job workflows. For the WARGI-DSS porting, a simple compound job has been used, without relationship among the sub-jobs. This type of compound job is called

job collection, as they express a set of computational tasks having some common input. In this case, the job forming the collection have the common part made by the solver, while the sub-jobs differs each other for the different instance of the optimization to be solved.
There are two types of tools directly provided by gLite for the interaction with services: the Command Line Interface and the Application Programming Interface. The first one is a classic set of executables, in Unix style, invoked from the shell, while the second is a set of libraries, generally in C/C++ or Java. In the first case, users generally adapts their own applications such to make system calls invoking the CLI executable. Further, the output given from the CLI to the shell has to be parsed and adapted again for the application. While this approach is simple, and yet very powerful, allowing any kind of interactions, has the limit of the considerable computational overhead taken by the command line calls made from inside the application. For this reason, the approach with API is sometimes preferable, because it carries better performances and a cleaner design of the application interacting with the grid environment. Using the API approach, the users recompile their own application including the API libraries. Further interactions with grid services are then made using only structures and functions provided from the API, which is clearly cheaper, in computational terms, than invoking CLI through a system call. Further, there is no need of parsing executable outputs, because when services are invoked through API functions, their output are still API objects that can be easily dealt inside the native application. So, paying the price of a longer develop time, because application source code needs to be adapted, API's provide better performances, and a cleaner design of the grid application. The effort needed for the inclusion of API libraries is reduced by the choice of the embedding of only the needed functions, rather than the whole set of gLite API. For the WARGI-DSS porting, have been so exploited API functions for Job Submission, Job Status Control, and Job Output retrieve.
The Job Submission function, takes as input a Security Context, i.e. the location of user credential, the URL of the WMS service and the JDL which describes the submitting job. So, if they don't exist or they are unknown, all these parameters have to be generated before the execution of an instance of the application, but then can be then reused for further instances. If Submission is successful, the WMS register the job to the LB and gives back its job identifier, which is a string to be used for further queries about the job status. The Logging and Bookkeeping service (LB) is a central registry, where are logged all the steps of the job life cycle, for instance when it has been assigned to a resource, or when it's being executed or if some errors happens. LB so can be queried at any time in order to discover the job status and whether errors happened. Once the job collection is done, the resources where the jobs have been executed copy back the job outputs to the WMS; resources also register the Done status for the job. When performing the next query, the application will find the Done status, and, by means of Job Output retrieval, proceed to the download of the Output Sandbox, which contains the solutions as computed from the solver.

## 4. The application to Flumendosa-Campidano water system: results and discussion

The Flumendosa-Campidano water system (Figure 8) is located in the South Sardinia, Italy. The hydrologic regime is characterized by significant variation in both monthly and annual flows. The system is composed by 10 reservoirs that are expected to regulate the unstable streamflows and to assure sustainable supplies to nine urban, two industrial and eleven irrigation demands. Data of monthly streamflows into the reservoirs and at the diversion sections in the streams were provided by the Sardinia water authority (SISS, 1994) over a period 54 years in length. The urban, industrial and irrigation demands were also obtained from the authority and the average values per year are equal to 116, 19 and 224 millions of cubic meter, respectively. Table 1 shows the main statistical properties of the available hydrological series at the sites of interest.

| Site | Min ($10^6$ $m^3/yr$) | Max ($10^6$ $m^3/yr$) | Mean ($10^6$ $m^3/yr$) | Standard Deviation ($10^6$ $m^3/yr$) |
|---|---|---|---|---|
| Sicca d'Erba | 2.28 | 89.91 | 19.41 | 16.26 |
| Flumineddu | 4.32 | 177.86 | 46.19 | 37.18 |
| Nuraghe Arrubiu | 3.42 | 100.84 | 31.01 | 21.32 |
| Mulargia | 1.68 | 53.61 | 15.73 | 11.86 |
| Sa Forada | 0.00 | 0.26 | 0.08 | 0.07 |
| Is Barroccus | 1.11 | 32.74 | 12.28 | 8.85 |
| Simbirizzi | 21.7 | 22.79 | 22.06 | 0.25 |
| Cixerri | 2.59 | 102.03 | 32.88 | 23.58 |
| Bau Pressiu | 0.03 | 11.33 | 2.96 | 2.75 |
| Corongiu | 0.42 | 15.01 | 4.29 | 3.16 |
| Bau Mela | 5.84 | 92.33 | 24.84 | 17.22 |
| Mau Mandara | 1.24 | 26.23 | 5.68 | 4.44 |
| Flumendosa | 15.6 | 217.74 | 94.12 | 49.54 |
| Casa Fiume | 0.95 | 83.50 | 23.34 | 19.51 |
| Mannu Monastir | 1.72 | 74.75 | 24.06 | 19.08 |
| Fanaris | 0.52 | 20.42 | 5.90 | 4.25 |
| Santa Lucia | 0.40 | 15.89 | 5.47 | 3.61 |
| Monti Nieddu | 1.79 | 54.57 | 16.51 | 12.85 |
| S'Isca Rena | 4.24 | 141.60 | 51.70 | 36.39 |
| System | 134.80 | 1032.7 | 438.5 | 239.35 |

Table 1. Main statistics of inflows to reservoirs and diversion points in Flumendosa-Campidano water system.

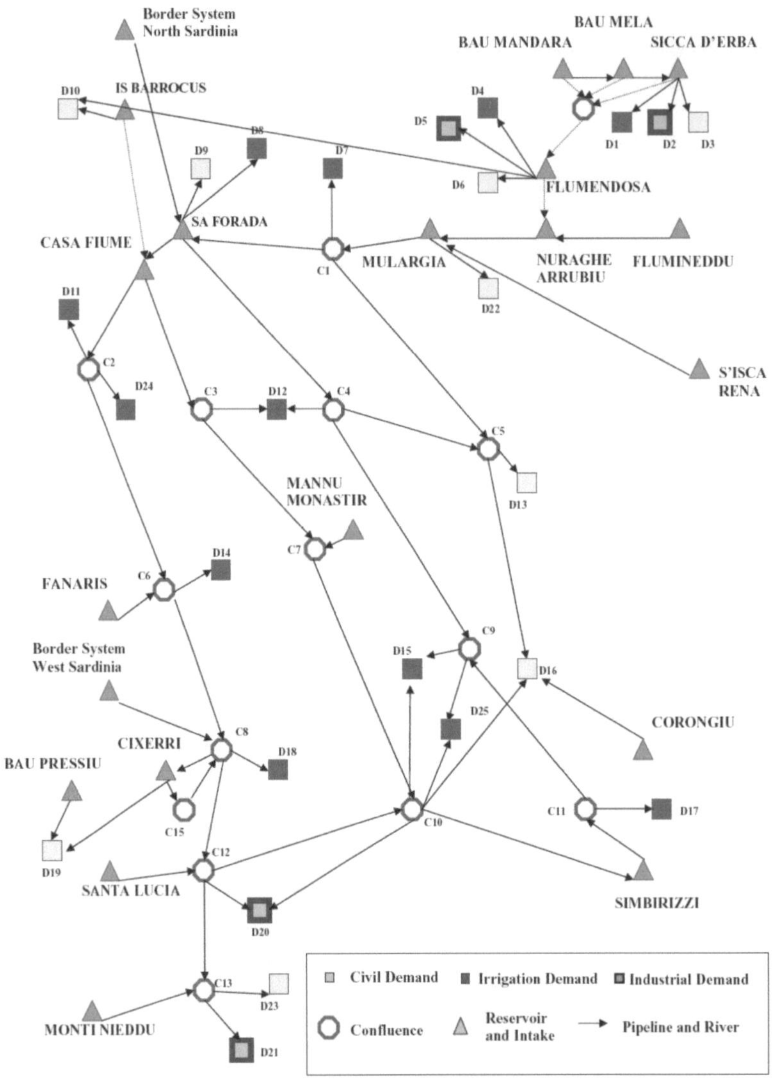


Fig. 8. Network representation of Flumendosa-Campidano water system.

| Measure | [z] | [s] |
|---|---|---|
| Supply Increase | Increase of available resources | Use of additional sources |
| Demand Reduction | Pricing and Use Reallocation | Restrictions and Rationing |
| Impact Minimization | Plans, Warning Systems and Education Activities | Temporary Resource Reallocation |

Table 2. General classification of drought mitigation measures currently applied or planned.

The increase in demand (particularly urban and agriculture) and the intense water scarcity events verified in recent years, require the water authority to revive drought mitigation plans to guarantee fulfilment of high priority demands during drought conditions. The success of these plans hinges on increasing the water system reliability, which is subject to hydrologic uncertainty probably related with long-term climate changes.

Table 2 shows proactive and reactive measures currently applied and planned in the Flumendosa-Campidano water system. The WARGI DSS has been applied to the system to provide the water authority of the Flumendosa-Campidano with a first estimate of the relationship between hydrologic uncertain data and drought mitigation measures.

The water authority often need to identify the sensitivity of the system economic performance associated with changes in hydrology and to quantify the consequences of alternative hydrological assumptions about the future. Consequently, the analysis of the system should be done with a wider range than, as usual, the only "best guessing" hydrological series or the "worst-case" sets. In Sechi and Sulis (2009a), the 2 years hydrological series were counted and selected in descending order of total flow from the historical records until 7 hydrological series were reached. They applied 7-times the mixed optimization-simulation approach obtaining 7 sets of drought mitigation measures at each synchronization period $\tau_i$. Each set contained both proactive and reactive measures: the proactive measures were selected based on the results of LpSolve under the selected hydrological series, 2 year length, whereas the proactive measures [z] were tested and reactive measures [s] eventually were implemented by WARGI-SIM under the historical record between the synchronization periods $\tau_i$ and $\tau_{i+1}$. Each set of drought mitigation measures was strictly related to the selected hydrological series. The best set, that is the set that minimizes the response function R (8) over the period of 54 years, was found through an ex-post sensitivity analysis. Figure 9 summarizes the results of this ex-post economic analysis showing the values of response function R of the Flumendosa-Campidano system for each of the seven selected hydrological series. Results showed that the "best guessing" produces a potential expensive mitigation plan, whereas, the "worst-case" set is very conservative. In particular, when the hydrological series are correctly assumed, R equals 1.3 million Euros per year with significant economic savings in respect to series with the lowest (too much pessimistic) or highest (too much optimistic) values foreseen for future hydrology (1.89 and 1.57 million Euros per year, respectively).

In the GRID approach those 7 linear programming models related to the selected hydrological series 2 year length, are solved at each synchronization period $\tau_i$ by LpSolve running in different Computing Elements. Results are weighted using the information provided by the Flumendosa-Campidano water authority, a weight representing the "importance" assigned by the authority to the running model. A unique set of proactive measures $[z_\tau]$ based on these weighted results is then tested and a unique set of reactive measures is implemented by WARGI-SIM until the next synchronization period $\tau_{i+1}$. Over the 54 time period of Flumendosa-Campidano system analysis, the value of the economic function R equals 1.39 million Euros per year. While the GRID approach provides a set of drought mitigation measures a little more expensive (+6.9%) than the best set in Sechi and Sulis (2009a), the presented approach does not need of an ex-post sensitivity analysis, quite subjective, and more important, it attempts to face the uncertainty issue by taking into account all different system evolutions corresponding to the selected hydrological series.

In the local approach of Sechi and Sulis (2009a), the software ran on an Intel Pentium with Single CPU clocked at 1.60 GHz having 1GB RAM. As shown in Figure 10, the computation time in the local approach vastly increased and the software simulated the system in about 21 min when the seven selected hydrological series were considered in the optimization phase. At that time of the presented research, there were 10 Intel Pentium Dual CPU running Scientific Linux SLC in the GRID authorized for a given job. The total Grid computation time is defined by the Grid latency (the time needed to submit a complete set of jobs, and collect a complete set of results), the waiting time in case a job is delayed in the Grid queues and the running time on the nodes. Figure 10 shows that the total GRID computation time at different hydrological series remains approximately stable (~ 8 min). The GRID approach seems promising for more than 2 hydrological series and the benefit improved as the number of hydrological series increases. The total computation time was reduced more than 60% in the case of seven hydrological series.

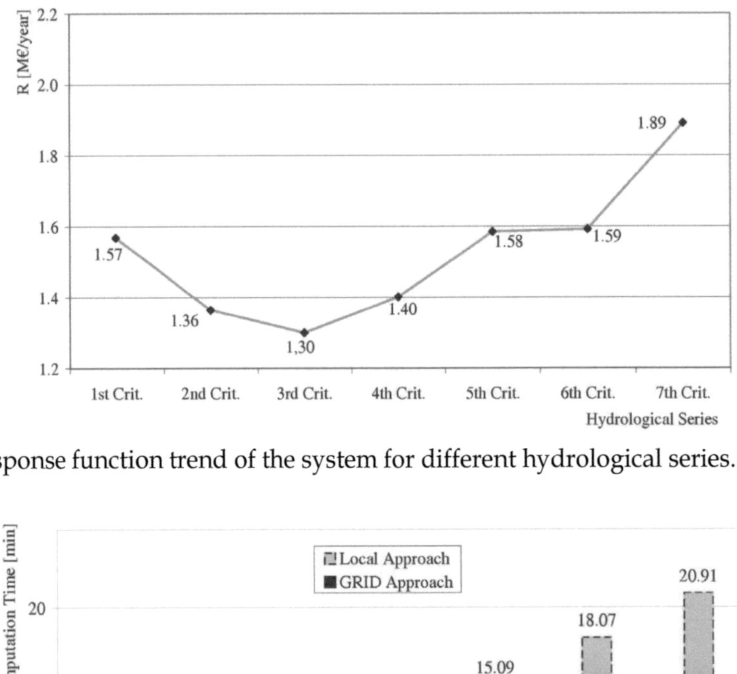


Fig. 9. Response function trend of the system for different hydrological series.

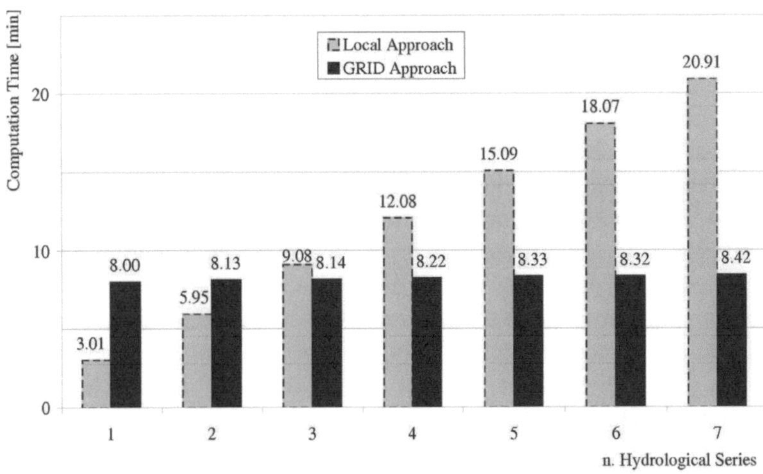


Fig. 10. Response function trend of the system for different hydrological series.

## 5. Final considerations on time-saving in a different GRID environment

In a more realistic GRID environment, where resources are shared with other VOs, their status is not known in advance as in the presented application, and there may be many factors that could affect the significant time saving of applying the proposed approach in a GRID environment. If we keep constant the number of operation totally executed by a collection, the global computation time decreases proportionally with the number of jobs executed in parallel in the GRID nodes (until a certain threshold is passed, as we will see). In addition, jobs could run simultaneously on nodes in the GRID with different hardware configurations, if jobs have no data or logic dependency. As the number of jobs increases, the heterogeneity of resources makes the jobs' running time different. Finally the latency time in a generic GRID environment would increase proportionally to the number of jobs to be submitted to the nodes. So it is rather expected that, as long as more jobs are added to the collection, the global execution time will be higher. However, this is not necessarily true, because the added jobs could be assigned to quick resources, thus not raising the global execution time.

The global computation time ($T_C$) for a collection of n jobs can be estimated as the sum of job latency times plus the time requested for the slowest job to be executed (in the meanwhile we expect other jobs to be done):

$$T_c = \sum_i T_{l,i} + max\left(T_{e,i}\right) \quad i = 1,n \tag{9}$$

The above expression suggests that the addition of a small number of jobs to the collection, might not increase significantly (or could not increase at all) the global running time. Let's try to estimate, in average, how many jobs (each of them representing an hydrological series) is convenient to add, before the performance will certainly decrease, and will no longer convenient to push further with parallelism.

To begin, we have to consider that for each job that is added to the collection, a small increase in latency time should be accounted. The latency time has been in fact defined before as the time needed to submit a collection, plus the time needed to collect its outputs. The times needed for the job submission and matchmaking don't need to be accounted, because in the job collection implementation, there is always one submission and one matchmaking, independently from the number of jobs actually forming the collection. The submission and matchmaking times can be so considered constant. The augment led by the addition of a job to the collection is given only by the increased time for the retrieve of this job's output. It is worth noting also that the "weight" of submission, matchmaking and job output retrieve is much minor respect to the execution time; it can be considered relevant only when dealing with a very large number of jobs (more than 200). So it's better to focus on the time that each job spends on resources. This quantity can be computed as the time that each job waits in the resource queue, plus its real running time. As said before, the addition of a single job to the collection, not necessarily increases the global execution time. However, the higher is the number of added jobs, the bigger is the probability that one of them is assigned to a slow resource. We can define slow resources those Computing Elements either non efficient (long running time), or busy, where jobs there scheduled have to wait a long time before they are actually ran (long queuing time). Is reasonable to expect that, as long as we add jobs to the collection, the 'quality' of them, either in terms of performance or busyness won't be improving. Although this is not always true, because for instance 'good' resources could have been released in the meanwhile by other jobs, we say that in general as long as we add job to the collection, its global execution time will be growing. Since it's not known the number of resources in advance, and their availability status, a rule of thumb is that collection size should not exceed half of the free CPUs available, at the submission, for the testbed. Otherwise, it's likely that one or more of the collection jobs will be assigned to a slow resource, degrading the global execution time. A ringing bell could be the fact that waiting time in the Computing Element queue has exceeded the running time, and this is indeed easy to spot, as we approximately know in advance how much time our jobs should be running.

## 6. Conclusions

Results demonstrate that GRID computing is a promising approach for scaled-up simulation analysis of complex water system with high uncertainty on hydrological series. However in the authors' view, there are still some hindrances for an extensive use in the water system field. A larger number of hydrological series used in the optimization phase to account for all the relevant statistics of drought events and different weights for the correspondent LP models should be of interest. Future research in the area of GRID approach for this combined optimization-simulation model also include its application in a more realistic GRID environment to estimate how many hydrological series is convenient to add before the performance of the GRID approach will certainly decrease.

## 7. Acknowledgements

The Authors gratefully acknowledge the support received from the Italian Ministry of Education, University and Research through grant under the PON-CyberSar Project (National Operation Programme Scientific Research, Technological Development, Higher Training - Activity 11.2: High Performance in Data Process and Simulation) and the Regione Autonoma della Sardegna that supports the final part of this research under the PO Sardegna FSE 2007-2013 (L.R.7/2007 - Promozione della Ricerca Scientifica e dell'Innovazione Tecnologica in Sardegna).

## 8. References

Andreu, J.; Capilla, J. & Sanchìs, E. (1996). AQUATOOL, a generalised decision-support system for water-resources planning and operational management. *Journal of Hydrology*, 177, 3-4, 269-291.

Assaf, H.; van Beek, E.; Borden, C.; Gijsbers, P.; Jolma, A.; Kaden, S.; Kaltofen M.; Labadie, J.W.; Loucks, D.P.; Quinn, N.W.T.; Sieber, J.; Sulis, A.; Werik, W.J. & Wood, D.M. (2008). Generic simulation models for facilitating stakeholder involvement in water resources planning and management. A comparison, evaluation, and identification of future needs, In: *Environmental Modelling, Software and Decision Support (3): The State of the Art and New Perspective*, Jakeman, Voinov, Rizzoli & Chen (Ed.), 229-246, Elsevier.

CPLEX Optimization, Inc. (2006). *Using the CPLEX Callable Library and CPLEX Mixed Integer Library*. Incline Village, Nevada.

Delft Hydraulics (2006). River Basin Planning and Management Simulation Program. *Proceedings of the iEMSs Third Biennial Meeting: "Summit on Environmental Modelling and Software*", Voinov, Jakeman & Rizzoli (Ed.), International Environmental Modelling and Software Society, Burlington, Vermont.

Hashimoto, T.; Stedinger, J.R. & Loucks, D.P. (1982). Reliability, Resiliency and Vulnerability Criteria for Water Resource System Performance Evaluation. *Water Resources Research*, 18, 1, 14-20.

Labadie, J.W.; Baldo, M.L. & Larson, R. (2000). *MODSIM: Decision Support System for River Basin Management: Documentation and User Manual*, Colorado State University and U.S. Bureau of Reclamation, Ft Collins, Colorado.

Loucks, D. P. & Sigvaldason, O.T. (1982). Multiple-reservoirs Operation in North America. In: *The Operation of Multiple Reservoir Systems - IIASA Collaborative Proceedings Series CP-82-S3*, Kaczmarek & Kindler (Ed.), 1-104, Institute for Applied Systems Analysis, Laxenburg, Austria.

Loucks, D.P. & van Beek, E. (2005). *Water Resources Systems Planning and Management: An Introduction to Methods, Models and Applications*. UNESCO Press, Paris.

Manca, A.; Sechi, G.M.; Sulis, A. & Zuddas, P. (2004). Complex water resources system optimization tool aided by graphical interface. In: *Proceedings of 6th International Conference on Hydroinformatics*. LLiong Phoon & Babovic (Ed.), 1059-1066, World Scientific Publishing Company, Singapore.

Mishra, S. (2009). Uncertainty and sensitivity analysis techniques for hydrologic modeling. *Journal of HydroInformatics*, 11, 3-4, 282-296.

Pallottino, S.; Sechi, G.M. & Zuddas P. (2005). A DSS for water resources management under uncertainty by scenario analysis. *Environmental Modelling & Software*, 20, 8, 1031-1042.

Rossi, G. (2000). Drought mitigation measures: a comprehensive framework. In: *Drought and drought mitigation in Europe*, Vogt & Somma (Ed.), 233–246, Kluver.

Sechi, G.M. & Sulis, A. (2007a). Mixed simulation-optimization technique for complex water resources systems analysis under drought conditions, Chapter 11. In: *Methods and Tools for Drought Analysis and Management*, Rossi, Vega & Bonaccorso (Ed.), 217-237, Springer, Berlin.

Sechi, G.M. & Sulis, A. (2007b). Multi-reservoir system optimization using Chlorophyll-a trophic indexes. *Water Resources Management*, 21, 5, 849-860.

Sechi, G.M. & Sulis, A. (2009b). Dynamic attribution of water quality indexes in a multi-reservoir optimization model. *Desalination*, 237, 1, 99-107.

Sechi, G.M. & Sulis, A. (2009a). Water system management through a mixed optimization-simulation approach. *Journal of Water Resources Planning and Management*, 135, 3, 160-170.

Sechi, G. M. & Zuddas, P. (2007). Multiperiod hypergraph models for water systems sptimization. *Water Resources Management*, 22, 3, 307-320.

SEI Stockholm Environment Institute (2005). *WEAP: Water Evaluation and Planning System, User Guide*, Somerville, Massachussets.

Simonovic, S.P. (2000). Tools for water management: A view of the future. *Water International*, 25, 1, 76-88.

Sulis, A. (2009). GRID computing approach for multireservoir operating rules with uncertainty. *Environmental Modelling & Software*, 24, 7, 859-864.

Yevjevich, V.; Hall, W. & Salas, J. (1983). *Coping with Drought*, Water Resources Publication, Littleton, Colorado.